CARS
NOW

CARS NOW

VOL.1

A GUIDE TO THE MOST NOTABLE CARS TODAY

EDITED BY INTER SECTION MAGAZINE

TASCHEN

PREFACE

by **DAN ROSS**, editor-in-chief
Intersection magazine

In the coming decade, if the fevered dreams of car executives come true, a billion new automobiles will join our roads.

A few of them, statistically speaking, will belong to you. What you choose to drive will determine all sorts of things: what proportion of those billion cars has an electric engine, a hybrid, a frugal diesel, or a fuel-efficient stop-start system. And therefore what amount of energy will avoid being lit, savored and exhaled into the atmosphere by those billion shiny machines.

Your choice determines if that magic billion number gets hit (to be multiplied by Dollars, Pounds, Euros, Yen and Yuan into trillions). Each vote tallies towards the rise and fall of corporate empires, and dictates the fluid architecture of our streets.

But rather than being a rational exercise in statistics and facts, it will likely come down to how you feel. Does your car make you feel accomplished, individual, smart and stylish? Does it adequately reflect your position and life-stage? Does it offer confidence to face the onrush of the world, or comfort you with its supple leather seats? Does it feel like a good fit, your relationship with this automated servant, mobile abode and honking spokesperson? Does it feel like you?

This book presents the options available should you find yourself with the need or desire to purchase an automobile. We've looked at almost every brand on earth making cars today, and sifted from among those thousands of models the ones that, at the end of it all, simply catch our eye. The striking thing is that so few do. And of those that stand out, so many are obscure – limited edition sportscars, niche environmental experiments – that we wonder, of the billion cars to come, how many should we really welcome onto our roads?

The perfect car would be fast, safe, comfortable, clean, spacious, stylish, affordable and unique. The Tesla S is a compelling answer – a seven-seat electric sportscar from the California start-up that has sidelines in spacecraft and solar panels. The Ferrari FF unticks many of those boxes, yet we want it more. It's furiously fast and excessively priced, but could almost be a daily ride. Closer to the bottom line, Nissan keeps producing quirky cars that fill niches you never knew existed. Sadly its electric Leaf is as bland as a Prius, if not as ugly as a Chevy Volt. Renault's Twizy – a bugged-out e-kart for cities – is a jolt to the senses but could yet become the Smart car of today. On the fringes, Morgan offers three-wheelers, Venturi builds Antarctic-ready EVs and Local Motors gets its online community to collaborate on limited editions like its stunningly adrenal debut, the Rally Fighter.

Mainstream manufacturers die, are reborn, merge and change continents, yet their cars seem always to revert to the mean. But from the least promising corners, boldness can emerge. Kia discovered it had a little Soul and Toyota birthed the iQ, so intelligently designed it was adopted by Aston Martin. Flick through this book and we hope you'll find more signs of talent amongst the rank and file.

Design has never been more important. As cars increasingly work just as well as one another, it's the key determinant of identity and desire. But after a decade or two of retro toys and flame-surfaced exuberance, design is having to reach deeper. BMW is introducing a new range of cars built from the ground up using new technologies from their materials and construction processes to their software and lifecycle. It's one of the first brands to engage directly with the new reality that the way we move needs to get up to digital speed.

Because into the industrial/consumer mix a virus is spreading. GPS, once sealed in the dashboard is now among us in iPhones and Androids. Zipcar has shown that rather than sitting unused for most of their lives, cars can be shared, with broader access at lower cost and without the administrative drag of owning a vehicle. Experiments initiated by the US military, now sponsored by Google question whether we should leave the driving to computers that hopefully won't crash as often. Our time, after all, is our greatest asset. And sitting in gridlock, belching out poison and handcuffed to a wheel, seems like a great business model to undo.

Who is going to do it? China has overtaken America as the largest car market. Emerging economies invite a land grab from established companies, but the direction is already starting to reverse. Volvo, once Swedish, then American, recently became Chinese. Jaguar, once British, then American, is now Indian. The car world is a mesh of poly-national parts, interlocking alliances, and shifting political tectonics. It binds together not just manufacturing, marketing and service sectors, but energy, infrastructure and finance. It's a puzzle to unpick, with the key yours to choose.

Intersection has spent the past decade championing far-sighted solutions and indulging in a little passion for the mythical past of free-fueled adventure. We love cars, partly for what they've been, partly for what they can become. In between is today's compromise. Do you need a car? If so, can it be part of the movement towards clean technology or on-demand ownership?

Ironically, as editors, we get to dodge the questions. We can be weekend racing drivers and then try an electric city car. Or borrow a luxury limo for a few days' frivolity then comfort ourselves we're down to earth by cycling to work or using an anonymous box on wheels to get from A to B when that basic function is really all we need.

It occurs to us that everyone would want the same option, given the choice – the omni-directional ease of a Swiss Army knife of mobility solutions within a set budget. And yes, in a hypothetical garage somewhere, outside the city limits where the roads are always clear, maybe we'd like to preserve a classic relic that tugs at us in weaker moments of irrational affection – for that ugly/beautiful French oddity, that kawaii-cute Japanese future box or an American muscle-flexing pick-up.

Because every period and place of the past is best signified by its cars. In tomorrow's interconnected globe, that will be replaced by something new. Read Intersection if you want to see it take shape, and check this book series each year to be updated on your choices. Cause and effect is the road, and you're in the driving seat. Safe travels.

VORWORT

von **DAN ROSS**, Chefredakteur des
Intersection Magazins

Sollten die kühnen Träume der Automobilmanager in Erfüllung gehen, werden in den nächsten zehn Jahren ca. eine Milliarde Fahrzeuge verkauft.

Statistisch gesehen werden Sie ein paar davon besitzen. Von Ihrer Kaufentscheidung wird dabei Einiges abhängen. So wird im Autohaus z. B. über den Anteil an Elektroautos, Hybridantrieben, einfachen Dieseln oder kraftstoffsparenden Start-Stopp-Systemen am weltweiten Automobilabsatz abgestimmt. Und damit auch über die Kraftstoffmenge, die von all den rollenden Maschinen gezündet und in die Atmosphäre ausgestoßen wird.

Von Ihrer Kaufentscheidung hängt auch ab, ob die riesige Milliardenzahl tatsächlich erreicht und mit Dollar, Euro, Pfund, Yen und Yuan zu unvorstellbaren Summen multipliziert wird. Sie als Verbraucher entscheiden über Aufstieg und Fall von Weltkonzernen und prägen die mobile Landschaft unserer Straßen.

Doch beim Kauf eines Autos spielen Statistik und Fakten eine eher untergeordnete Rolle – die Entscheidung ist letztendlich eine gefühlsmäßige. Was empfinden Sie, wenn Sie in Ihren Wagen steigen? Haben Sie das Gefühl, Ihre Ziele erreicht zu haben? In einem einzigartigen, schicken und eleganten Fahrzeug zu sitzen? Entspricht es Ihrer sozialen Stellung und Ihrem Lebensstil? Verleiht es Ihnen das Selbstbewusstsein, das in der erbarmungslosen Welt der Gegenwart so notwendig geworden ist? Bereitet Ihnen der Kontakt mit den geschmeidigen Ledersitzen Freude? Fühlen Sie sich wohl darin, in diesem Diener auf vier Rädern, in Ihrer mobilen Wohnung, bei Ihrem hupenden Gesprächspartner? Ist er der seelenverwandte Kamerad, der wirklich zu Ihnen passt?

Mit diesem Buch möchten wir all denjenigen eine Entscheidungshilfe an die Hand geben, die ein Automobil kaufen müssen bzw. möchten. Dafür haben wir uns nahezu alle Automobilhersteller dieser Welt genauer angesehen und eine Auswahl an Fahrzeugen zusammengestellt, die unsere Aufmerksamkeit erregt haben. Bemerkenswert ist jedoch, dass nur wenige Modelle unsere Seele berührt haben. Und dazu gehören einige Sonderlinge wie limitierte Sportwagenserien und umwelttechnische Experimente. Vor diesem Hintergrund stellt sich dringend die Frage, ob all diese neuen Fahrzeuge überhaupt eine Bereicherung für unsere Straßen sein werden.

Ein perfektes Auto stellen wir uns folgendermaßen vor: schnell, sicher, bequem, sauber, geräumig, elegant, erschwinglich und einzigartig. Der Model S des kalifornischen Start-up-Unternehmens Tesla erfüllt einige dieser Voraussetzungen: ein siebensitziger Elektrosportwagen mit Raumfahrttechnik und Solarpaneelen. Dagegen fällt der Ferrari FF bei einigen der obigen Kriterien durch – und trotzdem haben wir uns in ihn verliebt. Er fährt schneller, als das Herz ertragen kann und kostet ein Vermögen, aber langweilig wird es einem darin vermutlich nie. Auf einem preislichen Otto-Normalverbraucher-Niveau stellt Nissan seit Langem eigentümliche Autos für Marktnischen her, deren Existenz sonst niemandem aufgefallen war. Leider ist das Elektromodell Leaf langweilig wie ein Prius und obendrein hässlich wie ein Chevrolet Volt. Der Renault Twizy – ein futuristisch anmutender Zweisitzer – mag fürs Auge etwas gewöhnungsbedürftig sein, könnte sich aber als ernst zu nehmende Alternative für den Stadtverkehr erweisen. Am Rande des Mainstreams tauchen extravagante Erscheinungen auf wie die Dreirad-Modelle von Morgan, das Nutzfahrzeug für die Antarktis von Venturi und die mithilfe der Internetgemeinde entworfene Adrenalinspritze Rally Fighter von Local Motors.

Die etablierten Hersteller tendieren allen Veränderungsprozessen – Sanierungen, Restrukturierungen, Zusammenschlüsse, Werksverlagerungen – zum Trotz dazu, Durchschnittsautos nach einigermaßen bewährten Rezepten zu bauen. Mut zeigen ausgerechnet diejenigen, von denen es man am wenigsten erwarten würde. So entdeckte Kia neue, überraschende Rhythmen im Soul, während Toyota den iQ zur Welt brachte, ein so intelligentes Kind, dass Aston Martin es bald adoptierte. Wir hoffen, dass Sie beim Durchblättern noch weitere Talente entdecken.

Design ist heute wichtiger denn je. Da aus technischer Sicht die Unterschiede immer kleiner werden, müssen die Hersteller dazu übergehen, die eigene Identität über das Design zum Ausdruck zu bringen. Nach einem Jahrzehnt voller Retro-Modelle und Flame-Surfacing-Formen ist die Zeit für tiefer gehende Entwürfe reif. BMW arbeitet gerade an einer komplett neuen Fahrzeugreihe, die auf neuen Technologien basiert – von den verwendeten Materialien über die Fertigungsprozesse bis hin zu Software und Produktlebenszyklus. Die Münchner gehören zu den ersten Firmen, die sich ernsthaft auf das digitale Zeitalter einstellen.

Denn auf dem Automobilmarkt, wo Angebot und Nachfrage aufeinandertreffen, verbreitet sich ein Virus: die GPS-Technologie, die bisher nur am Armaturenbrett zu finden war, ist heute standardmäßig in jedem Smartphone und Tablet-Computer dabei. In immer mehr Städten beweisen Carsharing-Firmen, dass Autos gemeinschaftlich genutzt werden und damit u. a. Treibstoff-, Reinigungs- und Versicherungskosten gespart werden können. In Experimenten, die von der US-Armee angestoßen und nun von Google finanziert werden, wird untersucht, ob wir nicht den Computern das Fahren überlassen sollten, weil sie möglicherweise weniger Unfälle bauen würden. Wie die berühmte Volksweisheit besagt: Zeit ist Geld. Dass im Stau am Steuer gefesselt zu sitzen und dabei Gift und Galle zu spucken nicht die produktivste Beschäftigung darstellt, dürfte den meisten Fahrern langsam aufgehen.

Wer wird also den Sprung wagen? China hat die USA als größter Automobilmarkt abgelöst. Im Prinzip bieten die Schwellenländer attraktive Reviere, in denen sich die etablierten Automobilhersteller tummeln könnten, doch die Zeiten ändern sich. Volvo, einst der Stolz Schwedens, wurde von Amerikanern aufgekauft und ist seit Neuestem chinesisches Eigentum. Der britische Autobauer Jaguar, auch zwischendrin in amerikanischen Händen, gehört heute einem indischen Konzern. Der Automobilmarkt setzt sich heute aus multinationalen Firmen zusammen, die vor einem ständig wechselnden politisch-wirtschaftlichen Hintergrund immer neue Bündnisse schmieden. Die Hauptakteure stammen dabei nicht allein aus der Fertigung bzw. aus der Marketing- und Dienstleistungsindustrie. Auch Energie-, Infrastruktur- und Finanzunternehmen spielen eine Rolle. Ein unübersichtliches Netz, das Sie durchschauen müssen, um Ihre Entscheidung zu treffen.

Seit zehn Jahren tritt das Magazin *Intersection* für weitsichtige Projekte in der Kraftfahrzeugindustrie ein und frönt seiner Leidenschaft für die Mythen der Automobilgeschichte. Wir lieben Autos – und dabei lieben wir sowohl ihre legendäre Vergangenheit als auch ihre vielversprechende Zukunft. Zwischen diesen beiden Polen liegt nur der Kompromisslösungen der Gegenwart. Brauchen Sie einen Wagen? Wenn ja, werden Sie auf der umweltfreundlichen Welle reiten oder wünschen Sie eine maßgeschneiderte Lösung?

Ironischerweise können wir als Herausgeber einer Automobilzeitschrift diesen Fragen aus dem Weg gehen. Wir haben nämlich die Gelegenheit, mal in die Haut eines Rennfahrers zu schlüpfen, mal in das neueste Elektroauto zu steigen. Oder wir gönnen uns ein paar Tage eine dekadente Stretch-Limo und erobern unsere Bodenständigkeit wieder, indem wir zur Arbeit radeln oder in einer anonymen Kiste, deren einziger Zweck die bloße Personen- und Warenbeförderung ist, von A nach B fahren.

Jeder, der es sich leisten könnte, würde sich für eine solche Alternative entscheiden – für eine Mobilitätslösung mit der Multifunktionalität eines Schweizermessers innerhalb eines gewissen Budgets. Und in einer Garage irgendwo außerhalb der Stadt, wo die Straßen wenig befahren sind, da würden wir etwas Kostbares aufbewahren, einen raren Wein, dessen Genuss wir uns ab und zu hingeben würden – eine hässlich-hübsche Rarität aus Frankreich, eine niedliche Zukunftsvision aus Japan oder eine muskelbepackte Pick-up-Fantasie aus den USA.

Autos symbolisieren wie kein anderer Gegenstand die Epochen und Orte unserer Vergangenheit. In der globalisierten Welt der Zukunft werden Fahrzeuge andere Funktionen erfüllen. Lesen Sie *Intersection* und die dazugehörige Buchreihe, wenn Sie über die Entwicklung der Autowelt auf dem Laufenden sein möchten und fundiertes Wissen für Ihre Kaufentscheidung benötigen. Die Straße ist Ursache und Wirkung zugleich, und Sie sitzen auf dem Fahrersitz. Gute Fahrt.

PRÉFACE

par **DAN ROSS**, rédacteur-à-grand
Intersection magazine

Au cours de la prochaine décennie, si les rêves enfiévrés des dirigeants du secteur de l'automobile deviennent réalité, un milliard de nouvelles voitures arriveront sur nos routes.

Statistiquement parlant, quelques-unes d'entre elles seront à vous. Ce que vous choisirez de conduire déterminera toutes sortes de choses : combien de ces voitures seront équipées d'un moteur électrique, d'un hybride, d'un diesel sobre, ou d'un système stop & start économique. Et donc la quantité d'énergie qui sera économisée au lieu d'être engloutie et recrachée dans l'atmosphère par ce milliard de machines rutilantes.

C'est aussi en fonction de votre choix que l'on atteindra ou pas ce chiffre magique du milliard (qui sera ensuite multiplié en trillions en dollars, livres sterling, euros, yens et yuans). Chaque vote influence la grandeur et la décadence d'empires entiers, et dicte la fluidité de l'architecture de nos rues.

Mais plutôt qu'un exercice rationnel de statistiques et de faits, ce sera sans doute une question de ressenti. Est-ce que votre voiture vous donne le sentiment d'être une personne accomplie, singulière, intelligente et élégante ? Est-elle une représentation adéquate de votre statut social et du chemin que vous avez parcouru dans la vie ? Vous donne-t-elle de l'assurance pour faire face à la ruée quotidienne, ou vous berce-t-elle dans ses sièges de cuir souple ? Comment vivez-vous votre relation avec cette servante automatisée, cette demeure mobile, ce porte-voix klaxonnant ? Vous ressemble-t-elle ?

Ce livre présente les options dont vous disposez si vous avez envie ou besoin d'acheter une voiture. Nous avons examiné presque toutes les marques qui fabriquent des voitures dans le monde aujourd'hui, et avons passé au crible des milliers de modèles pour ne retenir que ceux qui, en fin de compte, retiennent l'attention. Ce qui est frappant, c'est le petit nombre de voitures qui remplissent ce critère. Et parmi celles qui se démarquent du reste, beaucoup sont très spécialisées (voitures de sport en édition limitée, expériences environnementales). Tant et si bien que l'on peut se demander, sur le milliard de voitures qui vont arriver sur nos routes, combien y ont vraiment leur place ?

La voiture parfaite devrait être rapide, sûre, confortable, propre, spacieuse, élégante, bon marché et originale. La Tesla S est une solution très convaincante : une voiture de sport électrique à sept places, fabriquée par une jeune entreprise californienne qui a également des intérêts dans les engins spatiaux et les panneaux solaires. La Ferrari FF laisse à désirer sur de nombreux aspects, et pourtant elle est plus désirable. Elle est furieusement rapide et son prix est excessif, mais on pourrait presque la prendre tous les jours pour aller au travail. Plus bas dans la gamme, Nissan continue de produire des voitures pleines de personnalité, qui occupent des niches jusqu'alors insoupçonnées. Malheureusement, sa Leaf électrique est aussi insipide que la Prius, sans toutefois être aussi laide que la Chevrolet Volt. La Twizy de Renault (un kart électrique urbain aux allures d'insecte) est un vrai choc pour les sens, mais pourrait encore devenir la Smart d'aujourd'hui. À côté de cela, Morgan propose des voitures à trois roues, Venturi construit des véhicules électriques capables de rouler dans l'Antarctique, et Local Motors demande aux internautes de collaborer à des éditions limitées, comme le Rally Fighter, son premier véhicule bourré d'adrénaline.

Les grands fabricants meurent, renaissent, fusionnent et changent de continent, et pourtant leurs voitures semblent toujours revenir dans la moyenne. Mais l'audace peut surgir des recoins les plus inattendus. Kia s'est découvert une âme dans la petite Soul, et Toyota a mis au monde l'iQ, un concept si intelligent qu'il a été adopté par Aston Martin. Feuilletez ces pages et nous espérons que vous trouverez de nombreux autres signes de talent dans les rangs.

Le design n'a jamais eu autant d'importance qu'aujourd'hui. Les performances se ressemblant de plus en plus, c'est le facteur déterminant de l'identité et de l'attrait d'un modèle. Mais après une décennie ou deux de jouets rétro et de texturisation des carrosseries, le design doit aller plus loin. BMW présente une nouvelle gamme de voitures entièrement construites à l'aide de nouvelles technologies, depuis les matériaux et les processus d'assemblage jusqu'aux logiciels et à la gestion du cycle de vie. C'est l'une des premières marques à vraiment réaliser que nos moyens de transport doivent se mettre au diapason du numérique.

Car un virus se répand dans la sphère de l'industrie et de la consommation. Le GPS était autrefois intégré aux tableaux de bord, mais nous accompagne maintenant dans les iPhone et les Android. Zipcar a montré que, plutôt que de rester au garage le plus clair du temps, les voitures peuvent se partager entre conducteurs, pour élargir l'accès à l'automobile à un moindre coût, et éliminer les tracas administratifs qui vont de pair avec la propriété d'un véhicule. Des expériences lancées par l'armée américaine, et maintenant sponsorisées par Google, suggèrent que l'on devrait peut-être confier la conduite aux ordinateurs, qui avec un peu de chance provoqueraient moins d'accidents. Le temps est après tout notre bien le plus précieux, et nous pourrions bien nous passer de rester coincés dans les bouchons, menottés au volant, à rejeter du poison dans l'atmosphère.

Qui va changer tout ça ? Le marché chinois est maintenant le plus grand marché automobile du monde, devant les États-Unis. Les économies émergentes invitent les compagnies établies à se battre pour la conquête de nouveaux territoires, mais la tendance commence déjà à s'inverser. Volvo était une marque suédoise à l'origine, puis américaine, et est récemment devenue chinoise. Jaguar est née britannique, est devenue américaine, et est maintenant indienne. Le monde de l'automobile est un tissu d'acteurs polynésiens, d'alliances complexes et sa tectonique politique est volatile. Il rassemble non seulement les secteurs de la fabrication, du marketing et des services, mais aussi de l'énergie, des infrastructures et de la finance. C'est un véritable casse-tête, et c'est à vous de le résoudre.

Intersection a passé la dernière décennie à défendre des solutions d'avenir et à s'adonner à sa passion pour le passé mythique de l'aventure motorisée. Nous aimons les voitures en partie pour ce qu'elles ont été, et en partie pour ce qu'elles peuvent devenir. Entre les deux, il y a le compromis actuel. Avez-vous besoin d'une voiture ? Et dans ce cas, peut-elle s'inscrire dans le mouvement vers une technologie propre, ou vers la propriété à la demande ?

En tant que rédacteurs, nous avons le privilège paradoxal de pouvoir esquiver ces questions. Nous pouvons être coureurs sur circuit le week-end, puis tester une citadine électrique la semaine. Ou emprunter une limousine de luxe pour quelques jours de frivolité, puis nous rassurer sur notre pragmatisme en allant au bureau en vélo, ou en utilisant une petite boîte sur roues anonyme pour aller du point A au point B lorsque nous n'avons pas besoin de plus.

Nous supposons que tout le monde voudrait pouvoir faire ce genre de choix – l'aisance tous azimuts d'un couteau suisse de solutions de mobilité, dans les limites d'un certain budget. Et effectivement, dans un garage hypothétique quelque part au-delà des limites de la ville, là où les routes sont toujours libres, nous aimerions peut-être préserver une relique classique qui taquine notre fibre sentimentale, une bizarrerie française laide et belle à la fois, une japonaise carrée futuriste et complètement kawaii, ou un pick-up américain plein de muscles.

Parce que les voitures sont les meilleures représentations de chaque époque et chaque lieu. Sur la planète interconnectée de demain, tout sera différent. Lisez *Intersection* si vous voulez voir ce que cela donnera, et consultez cette série de livres chaque année pour vous tenir au courant des choix qui vous sont offerts. La route est la cause et l'effet, et vous êtes dans le siège du conducteur. Bonne route.

GLOBAL CAR SALES

Badge size reflects each brand's 2010 car sales

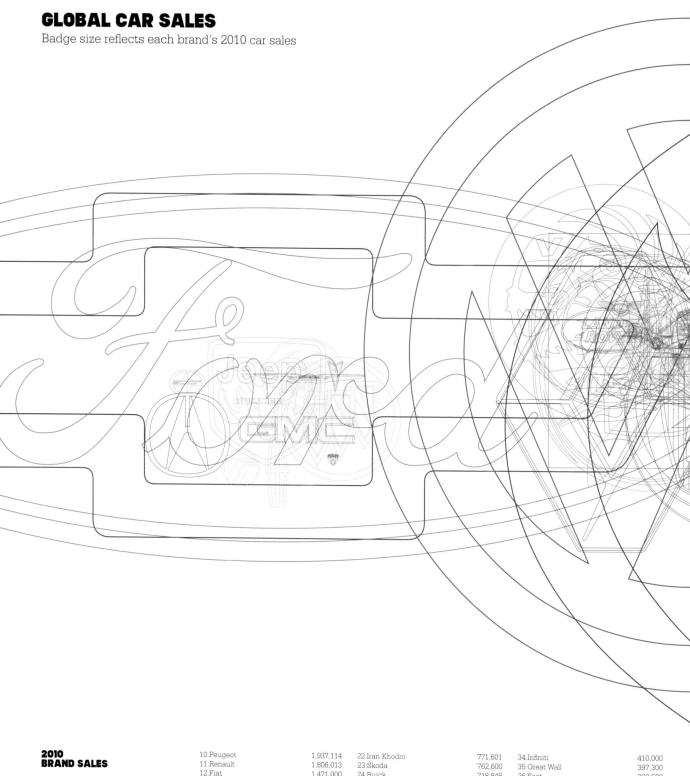

2010
BRAND SALES

1.Toyota	7,117,900	10.Peugeot	1,937,114	22.Iran Khodro	771,601	34.Infiniti	410,000
2.Ford	5,134,099	11.Renault	1,806,013	23.Skoda	762,600	35.Great Wall	397,300
3.Volkswagen	4,500,000	12.Fiat	1,471,000	24.Buick	718,848	36.Seat	339,500
4.Chevrolet	4,271,189	13.Citroen	1,285,152	25.Chana	710,000	37.Dacia	325,346
5.Nissan	4,080,588	14.BMW	1,224,280	26.Chery	700,000	38.Volvo	323,525
6.Honda	3,643,000	15.Opel/Vauxhall	1,206,620	27.Subaru	649,954	39.Jeep	291,138
7.Hyundai	3,431,138	16.Mercedez-Benz	1,167,700	28.Dodge	596,627	40.Mini	234,175
8.Kia	2,130,000	17.Wuling	1,149,060	29.Lada	569,324	41.Tata	230,715
9.Suzuki	1,940,000	18.Audi	1,092,400	30.BYD Auto	519,806	42.Chrysler	197,446
		19.Mitsubishi	1,019,142	31.GMC	446,547	43.Land Rover	181,395
		20.Mazda	921,763	32.Geely	415,286	44.Cadillac	180,724
		21.Daihatsu	783,000	33.Lexus	410,100	45.Samsung	161,917

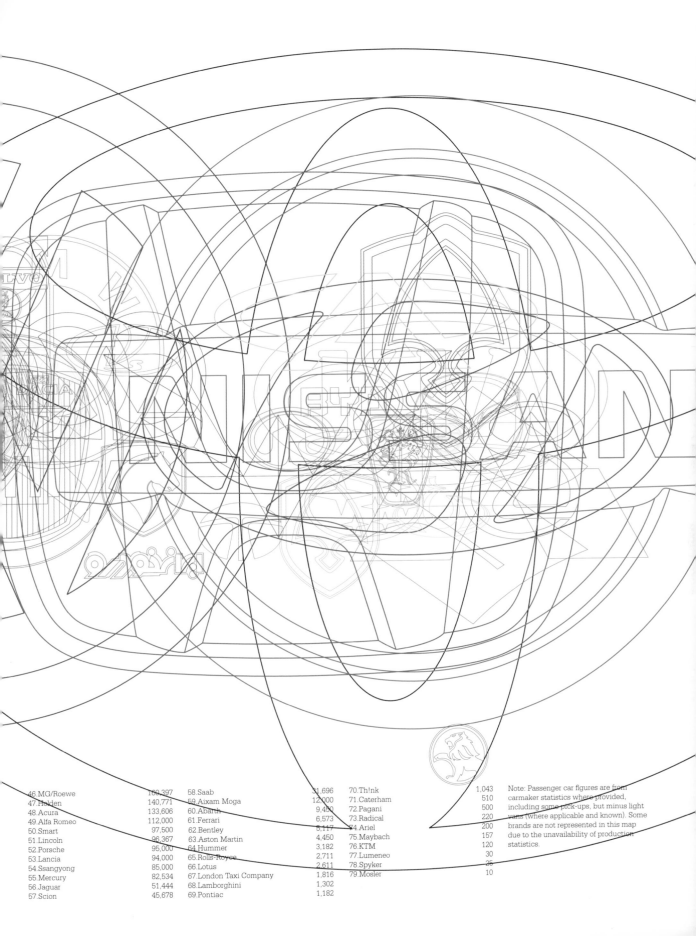

Note: Passenger car figures are from carmaker statistics where provided, including some pick-ups, but minus light vans (where applicable and known). Some brands are not represented in this map due to the unavailability of production statistics.

WORLDWIDE CAR PRODUCTION FLUCTUATION
Comparing 2008-2009

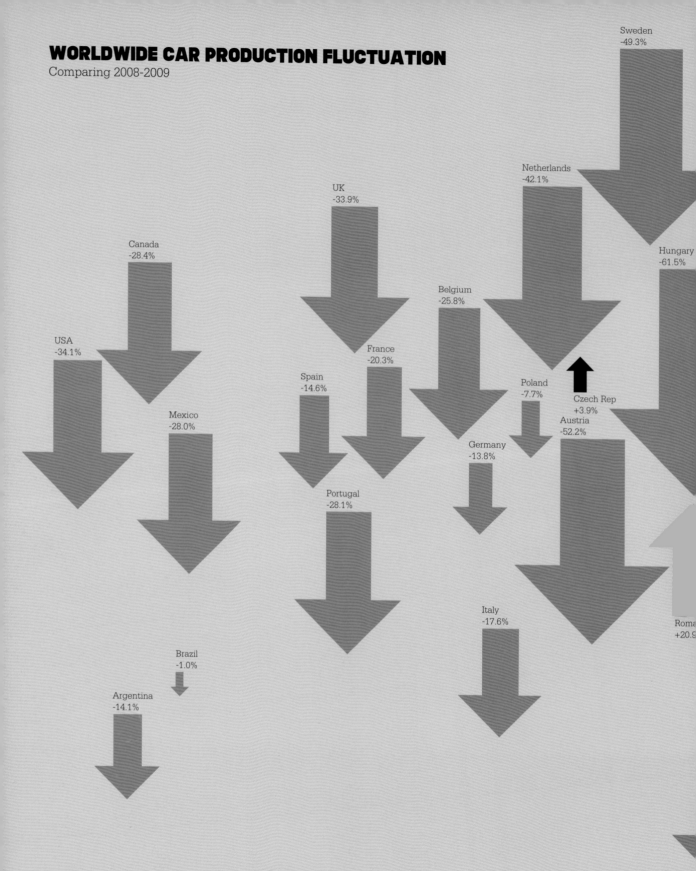

Sweden
-49.3%

Netherlands
-42.1%

UK
-33.9%

Hungary
-61.5%

Canada
-28.4%

Belgium
-25.8%

USA
-34.1%

France
-20.3%

Poland
-7.7%

Czech Rep
+3.9%

Austria
-52.2%

Mexico
-28.0%

Spain
-14.6%

Germany
-13.8%

Portugal
-28.1%

Italy
-17.6%

Roma
+20.9

Brazil
-1.0%

Argentina
-14.1%

Source:
OICA

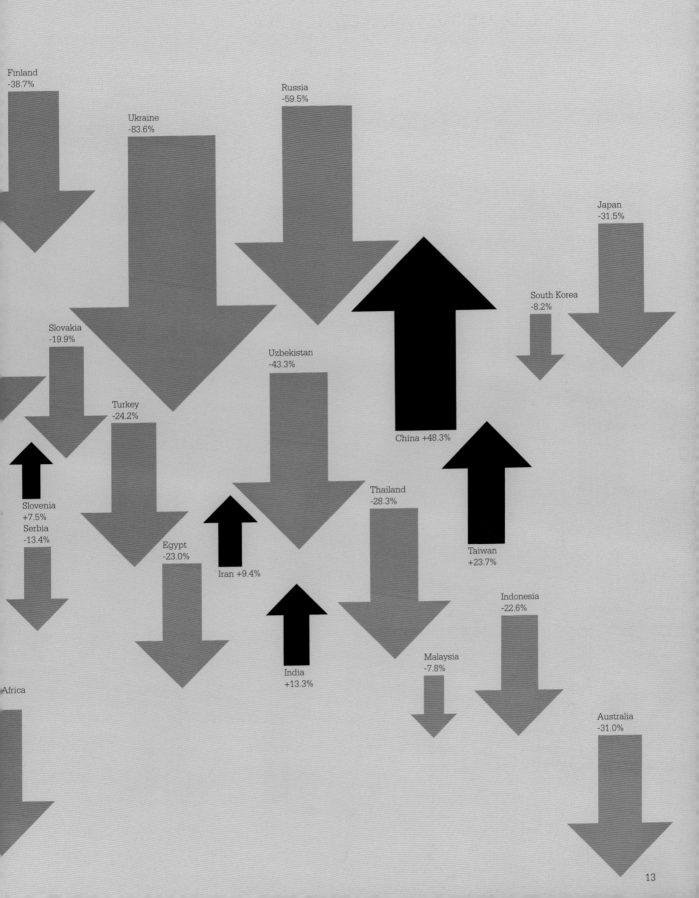

Finland
-38.7%

Ukraine
-83.6%

Russia
-59.5%

Japan
-31.5%

South Korea
-8.2%

Slovakia
-19.9%

Uzbekistan
-43.3%

Turkey
-24.2%

China +48.3%

Slovenia
+7.5%
Serbia
-13.4%

Thailand
-28.3%

Egypt
-23.0%

Iran +9.4%

Taiwan
+23.7%

Indonesia
-22.6%

India
+13.3%

Malaysia
-7.8%

Africa

Australia
-31.0%

13

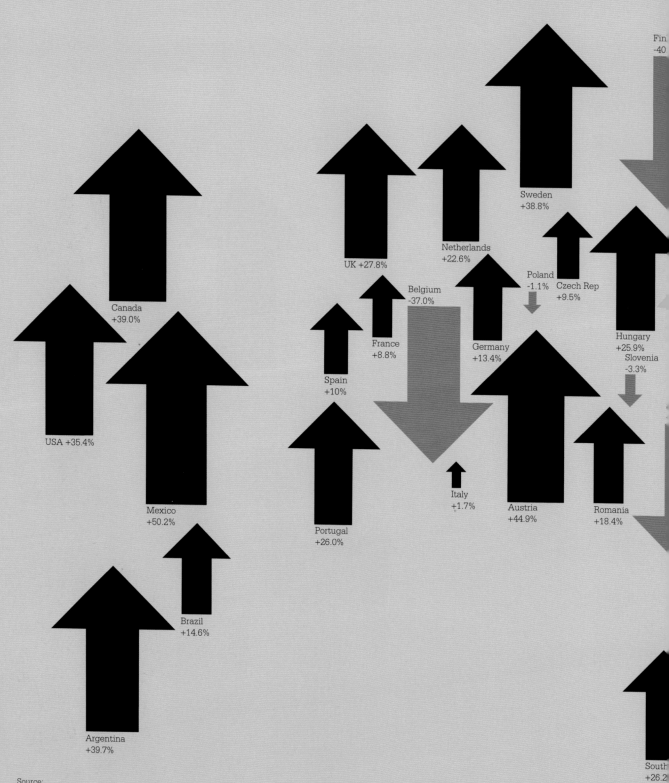

WORLDWIDE CAR PRODUCTION FLUCTUATION
Comparing 2009-2010

Fin
-40

Sweden
+38.8%

Netherlands
+22.6%

UK +27.8%

Belgium
-37.0%

Poland
-1.1%

Czech Rep
+9.5%

Canada
+39.0%

France
+8.8%

Germany
+13.4%

Hungary
+25.9%

Slovenia
-3.3%

Spain
+10%

USA +35.4%

Mexico
+50.2%

Portugal
+26.0%

Italy
+1.7%

Austria
+44.9%

Romania
+18.4%

Brazil
+14.6%

Argentina
+39.7%

South
+26.2

Source:
OICA

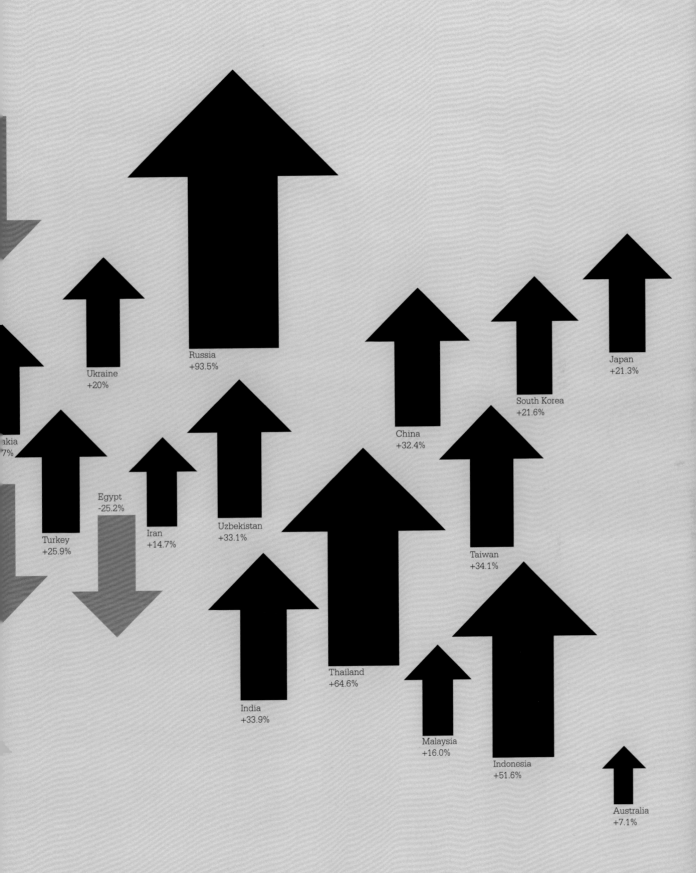

Russia
+93.5%

Ukraine
+20%

...akia
...7%

Japan
+21.3%

South Korea
+21.6%

China
+32.4%

Egypt
-25.2%

Turkey
+25.9%

Iran
+14.7%

Uzbekistan
+33.1%

Taiwan
+34.1%

Thailand
+64.6%

India
+33.9%

Malaysia
+16.0%

Indonesia
+51.6%

Australia
+7.1%

WORLDWIDE SPEED LIMITS

Miles of highway vs top speed

68
6

80
1

70 12
75 42
8
68 16
75 60

Digits: Top speed limit to be found anywhere in the country (not everywhere, so don't get too speedy without checking the local signs!)

Size of circle: Numbers of Miles of highways per country

●------------20,000 Miles

●------100,000 Miles

Note:
The biggest circles have been reduced to fit the page, the smallest circles have been enhanced to be visible. Disproportions are too great otherwise.

Sources:
Nation master, Wikipedia, countless embassies

68 18
56 110
50 111
62 82
50 37
56 67
62 76
34 41
50 144
62 66
50 103
50 158
50 105
154
45 158
80 156
75 4
62 56
75 88 **37** 121
75 52 **80** 21

CA
A
NO

RS
OW
A–Z

INFOGRAPHIC KEY

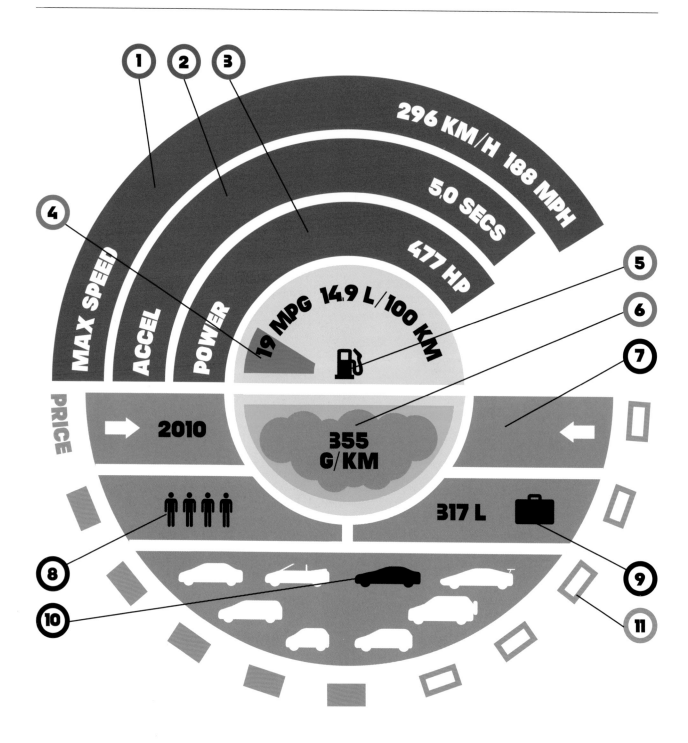

296 KM/H 188 MPH

5.0 SECS

477 HP

19 MPG 14.9 L/100 KM

355 G/KM

MAX SPEED

ACCEL

POWER

PRICE

2010

317 L

SAMPLE CAR: **ASTON MARTIN RAPIDE**

1	**MAXIMUM SPEED** Measured in km/h and mph.	**HÖCHSTGESCHWINDIGKEIT** Gemessen in km/h und mph.	**VITESSE MAXIMALE** Mesurée en km/h et mph.
2	**ACCELERATION** The car's 0-100 km/h and 0-60mph time, measured in seconds.	**BESCHLEUNIGUNG** Beschleunigungszeit von 0 auf 100 km/h und von 0 auf 60 mph in Sekunden.	**ACCÉLÉRATION** Le 0 à 100 km/h et 0 à 60 mph de la voiture, mesuré en secondes.
3	**POWER** Measured in horsepower.	**LEISTUNG** Gemessen in Pferdestärke.	**PUISSANCE** Mesurée en chevaux.
4	**FUEL EFFICIENCY** Measured in miles per (British) gallon and liters per 100 km (unless otherwise stated).	**KRAFTSTOFFVERBRAUCH** Gemessen in Miles per Gallon (britisch) und Liter pro 100 km (falls nicht anders angegeben).	**CONSOMMATION** Mesurée en miles par gallon et en litres aux 100 km (sauf indication du contraire).

5 — **FUEL TYPE** — Indicates what type of fuel the car runs on:

- Petrol or diesel
- Electric
- Hybrid

KRAFTSTOFFTYP — Gibt an, mit welchem Kraftstoff das Auto betrieben wird:

- Benzin oder Diesel
- Elektroantrieb
- Hybridantrieb

TYPE DE CARBURANT — Indique le type de carburant utilisé par la voiture:

- Essence ou diesel
- Électrique
- Hybride

6	**CO2 EMISSIONS** Measured in grams per km.	**CO2 AUSSTOSS** Gemessen in Gramm pro km.	**EMISSIONS DE CO2** Mesurées en grammes par km.
7	**PRODUCTION** Shows the year the model was introduced and when it is expected to end, if known.	**PRODUKTION** Markteinführung (Jahr) des Modells und ggf. voraussichtliches Produktionsende.	**PRODUCTION** Indique l'année de lancement du modèle et l'année de son retrait si cette information est disponible.
8	**SEATS** How many people can sit in the car.	**SITZE** Anzahl der Sitze im Auto.	**PLACES** Indique combien de personnes peuvent monter dans la voiture.
9	**LUGGAGE** How many pieces of luggage can fit in the car (and max. luggage space in liters)	**KOFFERRAUM** Anzahl der Gepäckstücke (und maximales Kofferraumvolumen in Litern).	**COFFRE** Indique la quantité de bagages que la voiture peut accueillir (et l'espace en litres).

10 — **BODY STYLES** — Which body styles the car is available in:

- City car
- Hatchback
- Sedan/Limousine
- Convertible
- Coupe/Sports Car
- Estate
- SUV
- Supercar

KAROSSERIE — Verfügbare Karosserieversionen:

- Kleinwagen/Kleinstwagen
- Fließheck
- Limousine
- Cabrio
- Coupé/Sportwagen
- Kombi
- SUV
- Supersportwagen

TYPES DE CARROSSERIE — Indique les carrosseries disponibles :

- Citadine
- Compacte
- Berline
- Décapotable
- Coupé/voiture de sport
- Break
- SUV
- Supercar

11 — **PRICE** — Each bar = $30,000 until 10th bar which = $300,000+.

PREIS — Pro Balken = 30.000 USD (20.800 EUR), ab 10 Balken = über 300.000 USD.

PRIX — Chaque barre équivaut à 30 000 $ (20.800 EUR). Dix barres = + de 300 000 $.

ABARTH

FOUNDED: **1949**
HEADQUARTERS: **TURIN, ITALY**
2010 PRODUCTION: **9450**

LOGO HISTORY:

Historically linked to Fiat since the 1950s, although independent for its formative years, Carlo Abarth's early business involved building cars for racing. Collaborations with Porsche and Simca cemented its reputation, and in the 60s Abarth began producing tuning kits for go-fast fans, establishing a consumer brand. The firm was snapped up by Fiat in 1971 to provide a racing team, but the name was allowed to fade into the background until, in the 80s, it existed merely as a performance option on some Fiat models. Abarth was therefore largely forgotten until its recent relaunch as a standalone performance brand within the Fiat Group. The cars launched since the re-emergence in 2007 – heavily badged with the brand's scorpion logo – don't attempt to disguise their Fiat roots, sharing their donor model's names. But bespoke standalone models are on the horizon, and no-one can mistake an Abarth for a regular Fiat once behind the wheel.

Zu den ersten unternehmerischen Aktivitäten von Carlo Abarth – der seit den 1950er Jahren mit Fiat verbunden war, in seinen Lehrjahren jedoch unabhängig blieb – gehörte der Bau von Rennfahrzeugen. Ansehen verschaffte sich Abarth durch die Zusammenarbeit mit Firmen wie Porsche und Simca. In den 60ern begann er, Tuning-Kits für Geschwindigkeitsliebhaber herzustellen, und etablierte damit seine Marke. 1971 wurde die Firma von Fiat aufgekauft, um einen Rennstall auf die Beine zu stellen. Doch der Markenname geriet immer mehr in den Hintergrund, bis er in den 80er Jahren nur noch für die Bezeichnung von besonders leistungsstarken Fiat-Modellen verwendet wurde. Erst nach einer kürzlich erfolgten Wiedereinführung als eigenständige Marke innerhalb der Fiat-Gruppe trat der Name Abarth wieder in den Vordergrund. Die seit dem Comeback von 2007 eingeführten Modelle – mit dem berühmten Abarth-Skorpion an sichtbarer Stelle – tragen den Namen ihrer Fiat-Basisfahrzeuge und legen damit ihre Wurzeln offen. Maßgeschneiderte eigenständige Modelle sind jedoch geplant. Und außerdem: Hinter dem Steuer kann kein Abarth mit einem gewöhnlichen Fiat verwechselt werden.

Liée à Fiat depuis les années 1950, mais indépendante pendant ses premières années, l'entreprise de Carlo Abarth était à l'origine consacrée à la construction de voitures de course. Ses collaborations avec Porsche et Simca ont cimenté sa réputation et, dans les années 1960, Abarth a commencé à produire des kits de transformation pour les amateurs de vitesse, ce qui lui a donné un statut de marque grand public. Fiat s'est emparée de l'entreprise en 1971 pour en faire une équipe de course. Le nom d'Abarth a commencé à glisser dans l'ombre jusqu'à ce que, dans les années 1980, elle ne soit plus qu'une indication de performance sur certains modèles de Fiat. Abarth était donc pratiquement tombée dans l'oubli lorsqu'elle a été relancée sous forme de marque autonome de véhicules performants au sein du groupe Fiat. Les voitures produites depuis cette réémergence en 2007 – garnies d'un badge bien visible portant un scorpion, logo de la marque – ne tentent pas de dissimuler leurs racines chez Fiat, et partagent les noms de modèle de leur protecteur. Mais des modèles indépendants se profilent à l'horizon et, une fois derrière le volant, nul ne peut confondre une Abarth et une Fiat normale.

PUNTO EVO
Rival: Renault Clio
RenaultSport 200 Cup

Fun, but only when you flick the sport switch.
Mach Spaß, aber nur im Sportmodus.
Amusante, mais seulement en mode sport.

500
Rival: Mini Cooper S

Ditto above, but in a more iconic design.
Wie der Punto Evo, nur schnittiger.
Idem, mais avec un design plus typé.

Fiat Group heir Lapo Elkann sitting atop his matte olive Abarth 500

AC

FOUNDED: **1901**
HEADQUARTERS: **HEYDA**, **GERMANY**

Its history might stretch back over 100 years, but for the vast majority of that time it seems to have been building the same car – or at least variations on a theme. Originally based on an AC Ace, with a huge American V8 engine slotted inside, the Cobra is one of the most enduring – and copied – shapes in the world. It remains in production today, with tiny numbers built in Germany. Always Ford-powered previously, the current model features that other massive power quick fix – a 6.2-liter V8 from Corvette. Just don't call it a Cobra.

Obwohl die britische Automarke auf eine über hundertjährige Firmengeschichte zurückblicken kann, erweckt sie den Eindruck, immer wieder dasselbe Fahrzeug bauen zu wollen – oder Variationen ein und derselben Grundidee. Der ursprünglich auf einem AC Ace basierende Cobra – in dem ein leistungsstarker amerikanischer V8-Motor steckt – wartet mit einer Karosserie auf, die zu einem echten Klassiker geworden ist und unzählige Male nachgeahmt wurde. Noch heute wird das Modell in kleinen Stückzahlen in Deutschland hergestellt. Die traditionell von Ford gelieferte Antriebstechnik wurde in aktuellen Modellen durch massive 6,2-Liter-V8-Motoren von Corvette ersetzt. Nur ist er dann kein Cobra mehr.

Son histoire remonte à plus d'un siècle, mais il semble que l'écrasante majorité de ces années aient été employées à construire toujours la même voiture, ou du moins des variations sur un même thème. Initialement basée sur une AC Ace, avec un énorme moteur V8 américain sous le capot, la Cobra a l'une des lignes les plus impérissables – et les plus copiées – au monde. Elle est toujours produite actuellement, au compte-goutte en Allemagne. C'est Ford qui avait toujours fourni le moteur, mais le modèle actuel est équipé d'une autre solution miracle : un V8 6,2 litres de Corvette. Mais ce n'est plus une Cobra.

MKVI

Rival: Any number of copies

Light and very fast, same old.
Leicht und schnell, wie man ihn kennt.
Légère et très rapide, comme l'ancienne.

ACURA

FOUNDED: **1986**

HEADQUARTERS: **TORRANCE, USA**

2010 PRODUCTION: **133,606**

LOGO HISTORY:

Acura is Honda's luxury nameplate – as Lexus is to Toyota and Infiniti to Nissan. Unlike those Japanese rivals, Acura was the first to sell in the US but has yet to venture far beyond those shores, additionally selling only in Canada, Mexico, Hong Kong and China. In the 80s Acuras were essentially tweaked top-end Hondas like the Legend, Integra and even NSX supercar. An unremarkable 90s was followed by better new product in the 00s culminating in the smart 2010 ZDX SUV coupe with neat hidden rear door handles and notable as the first Acura designed in its US studio. A sign of better things to come, the brand may finally have something to offer the rest of the world.

Acura ist Hondas Luxusmarke – ganz so wie Lexus für Toyota und Infiniti für Nissan. Den Konkurrenten aus Japan kam Acura in den USA zuvor, doch außerhalb der Vereinigten Staaten ist der Luxusableger nur noch in Kanada, Mexiko, Hong Kong und China präsent. In den 1980ern bestand die Fahrzeugpalette hauptsächlich aus aufgewerteten Honda-Modellen wie dem Legend, dem Integra und dem NSX-Sportwagen. Nach den unauffälligen 90ern wurden seit der Jahrtausendwende wieder beachtliche Modelle entworfen, so z. B. der ZDX – ein SUV-Coupé, dessen hintere Türgriffe im Fensterrahmen untergebracht sind und der das erste im US-Studio entworfene Modell darstellt. Es wäre zu begrüßen, wenn der gelungene ZDX sich als Wendepunkt für die Marke erweisen würde.

Acura est la marque de luxe de Honda, comme Lexus pour Toyota et Infiniti pour Nissan. Contrairement à ces rivales japonaises, Acura a été la première à vendre aux États-Unis, mais ne s'est pas encore aventurée bien loin de ce territoire : seulement au Canada, au Mexique, à Hong Kong et en Chine. Dans les années 1980, les Acura étaient essentiellement des Honda haut de gamme comme la Legend, l'Integra et même la supercar NSX. Les années 1990 se sont écoulées sans rien de remarquable, puis les années 2000 ont vu l'arrivée de nouveaux modèles améliorés, avec comme point fort l'élégant coupé SUV ZDX en 2010 et ses poignées arrière dissimulées. C'est la première Acura conçue dans le studio américain de la marque. Elle annonce une tendance ascendante. Cette marque a peut-être enfin quelque chose d'intéressant à offrir.

ZDX
Rival: Infiniti FX

Svelte US-designed and built SUV Coupe.
In den USA produziertes SUV-Coupé.
Coupé SUV svelte de facture américaine.

RDX
Rival: BMW X3

Compact crossover with high-tech AWD.
Kompakter SUV, High-Tech-Allradantrieb.
Crossover compact 4x4 high-tech.

MDX
Rival: BMW X5

Bigger, taller more SUV-like 7-seater.
Größer, höher, mehr SUV, 7-Sitzer.
Plus grande, plus haute, plus SUV, 7 places.

TSX
Rival: BMW 3

Bland compact sports sedan, better wagon.
Sanftere Sportlimousine, besserer Kombi.
Berline compacte, le break est plus abouti.

TL
Rival: Lexus ES

More stylish super-handling AWD large sedan.
Große wendige Allrad-Limousine.
Grande berline élégante, 4x4 high-tech.

RL
Rival: BMW 5 Series

Dull mid-sized high-tech AWD sedan.
Mittelgroße Limousine, High-Tech-Allrad.
Berline moyenne insipide, 4x4 high-tech.

ACURA ZDX

We thought Acura made watches. Unless you're from the US you might not know the brand. It isn't sold in most of the world. Even if you're as American as a Hummer you still might not have noticed Acura exists. The vaguely upmarket, somewhat futuristic looking generic Asian cars simply didn't register for most. Until this car. Its shape is lithe, full of elegantly resolved angles and rewarding details. The interior is spacious, minimalist and conspiratorial. It has the feel of a secret discovery. You can't place it, but not in the old bland Acura way. You can't place it because it's genuinely new.

Eigentlich hatten wir Acura immer für eine Uhrenmarke gehalten. Bekannt ist der Luxusableger von Honda nur in den USA. Sonst wird die Marke in nur wenigen Ländern vertrieben. Selbst viele Amerikaner kennen Acura nicht. Die exklusiv-futuristisch anmutenden Wagen waren einfach nie aufgefallen. Bis dieses Modell kam: geschmeidige Formen, elegante Winkel, überraschende Details, ein minimalistisch-verschwörerischer Innenraum. Wer hier einsteigt, hat das Gefühl, in geheimnisvolles Gefilde vorzudringen. Die Einordnung fällt schwer, weil es sich um etwas wirklich Neues handelt.

Nous pensions qu'Acura faisait des montres. Il se peut que vous ne connaissiez pas cette marque qui n'est vendue que dans une poignée de pays, dont les États-Unis. Ses voitures asiatiques génériques, vaguement haut de gamme et futuristes n'ont tout simplement pas marqué les esprits. Jusqu'à cette voiture. Sa ligne souple aux angles élégamment résolus est agrémentée de détails valorisants. L'intérieur spacieux et minimaliste invite à la conspiration. Il a le parfum des découvertes secrètes. Vous n'arrivez pas à la situer, pas parce qu'elle est trop neutre, mais parce que c'est une vraie nouveauté.

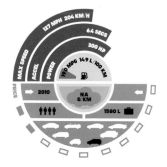

SECRET DETAIL

The center console subtly de-illuminates, while hidden rear door handles continue the stealth theme.

Die Beleuchtung der Mittelkonsole dimmt langsam herunter. Die hinteren Türgriffe sind im Fensterrahmen verborgen.

L'éclairage de la console centrale s'éteint graduellement, tandis que les poignées cachées des portes arrière complètent le thème de l'invisibilité.

AIXAM-MEGA

FOUNDED: **1983**
HEADQUARTERS: **AIX-LES-BAINS, FRANCE**
2010 PRODUCTION: **12,000**

LOGO HISTORY:

If ever you've found yourself in rural France you'll no doubt have encountered several of Aixam's quadracycles putt-putting leisurely along. Their popularity in their native land – as well as Italy, Portugal and Slovenia – is due partly to the fact they can be driven (often precariously) without a license but mainly because of their outstanding fuel economy thanks to tiny diesel engines and lightweight construction. 'Mega' branded versions pack electric power and are used in an all-electric Tropee Andros ice-racing series. This racing pedigree (of sorts) and impressively competent design mean Aixam-Mega's range belies its humble mechanics.

Wer sich gerne in den ländlicheren Gegenden Frankreichs aufhält, dürfte hin und wieder einem gemütlich vor sich hin tuckernden Aixam-Leichtkraftfahrzeug begegnet sein. Ihre Beliebtheit im Herkunftsland – sowie in Italien, Portugal und Slowenien – verdanken die Kleinwagen u. a. der Tatsache, dass sie ohne Führerschein gefahren werden können. Hauptsächlich werden sie aber für ihr verbrauchsarmes Design mit kleinen Dieselantrieben und ultraleichten Karosserien geschätzt. Unter dem Namen „Mega" werden Elektrofahrzeuge verkauft, die in der Eisrennserie „Trophée Andros" zum Einsatz kommen. Das beeindruckende Design des Aixam-Mega-Rennwagens wiegt ihre bescheidene Mechanik auf.

Si vous vous êtes promené dans la campagne française, vous y avez sans doute rencontré plusieurs voiturettes d'Aixam allant leur petit bonhomme de chemin. Leur popularité dans leur pays d'origine, ainsi qu'en Italie, au Portugal et en Slovénie, est due en partie au fait qu'on peut les conduire (souvent avec inconscience) sans permis, et surtout à leur remarquable économie de carburant grâce à un moteur diesel minuscule et une construction légère. Les versions estampillées « Mega » sont dotées d'un moteur électrique et participent à la série électrique de course sur glace du Trophée Andros. Ce pedigree de course (si l'on peut dire) et un design remarquablement compétent font que la gamme Aixam-Mega dépasse sa mécanique modeste.

CITY
Rival: Smart ForTwo

Teeny 2-seater, a firm favourite of French farmers.
Kleiner 2-Sitzer, bei französischen Bauern beliebt.
Petite 2 places favorite des fermiers français.

CROSSLINE
Rival: Tamiya Sand Scorcher

As above but with dubious SUV add-ons.
Wie oben, nur mit dubiosen SUV-Ansprüchen.
Idem, avec des ajouts douteux de style SUV.

SCOUTY R
Rival: Maxed-out Piaggio Ape

Convertible pickup/Hot Wheels mash-up.
Cabrio Pickup, großgewachsener Hot Wheels.
Mélange de pick-up décapotable et de jouet.

GTO
Rival: 1976 DeTomaso Mini

Faux racing body mods fool nobody.
Lediglich eine Rennwagen-Imitation.
Piètre imitation de voiture de course.

ALFA ROMEO

FOUNDED: **1910**
HEADQUARTERS: **TURIN, ITALY**
2010 PRODUCTION: **112,000**

LOGO HISTORY:

Italy's most stylish, and underappreciated, marque has a storied past which owners Fiat Group seem finally poised to turn into a bright future. With a sporting heritage founded on winning the first two F1s in the early 50s, and stablemates Ferrari, Maserati and Abarth, the recent 8C supercar served as a reminder that Alfa Romeo is more than a pretty face. But it's better known for offering stunning, unmistakable road cars, from icons like the 1966 Duetto Spider Dustin Hoffman drove in *The Graduate* to the more recent 2005 Brera coupe. Coupled with stylish interiors as cosseting and luxurious as anything on the market, Alfa's design has long helped mask weaknesses in reliability. Sales are essentially Europe-only for now, but Alfa plans to return to the US and elsewhere soon. With improved quality, an expanded range, and gorgeous genes, the brand may finally be poised to exploit its enviable niche of affordable exclusivity. As Ford's chief creative officer J Mays puts it: "Alfa Romeo makes the most beautiful cars in the world, period."

Keine italienische Marke versprüht mehr Eleganz – und keine wird stärker unterschätzt. Doch die Eigentümerin – die Fiat-Gruppe – scheint entschlossen, an einer besseren Zukunft zu arbeiten. Wie Ferrari, Maserati und Abarth hat auch Alfa Romeo eine große Rennsport-Tradition, die mit dem Sieg der zwei ersten Formel-1-Saisons begründet wurde. Der neue 8C beweist, dass Alfa Romeo mehr als nur ein schönes Auto ist. Doch zu Weltruhm haben es die Turiner durch unverwechselbares Design gebracht – so z. B. der Duetto Spider von 1966, den Dustin Hoffman in der „Reifeprüfung" fuhr, oder der Brera Coupé von 2005. Zusammen mit der elegant-luxuriösen Innenausstattung erhält man die Formel zur Kaschierung der mangelnden Zuverlässigkeit. Verkauft wird Alfa hauptsächlich in Europa, Amerika und weitere Märkte sind angepeilt. Mehr Qualität, mehr Auswahl, gesunde Gene – mit dieser Zaubermischung plant man, die Nische der erschwinglichen Exklusivität zu erobern. Wie Fords Kreativchef J Mays einmal sagte: „Alfa Romeo baut die schönsten Autos der Welt. Punkt."

La marque la plus chic et la plus sous-estimée d'Italie a un passé légendaire, que son propriétaire Fiat semble enfin prêt à exploiter. Avec un héritage sportif fondé sur ses victoires dans la F1 des années 1950 aux côtés de Ferrari, Maserati et Abarth, la récente supercar 8C a rappelé à tous qu'Alfa Romeo allie le fond et la forme. Mais elle est mieux connue pour ses superbes routières, depuis des icônes telles que la Duetto Spider 1966 que Dustin Hoffman conduisait dans *Le Lauréat* jusqu'au coupé Brera de 2005. Allié à des intérieurs raffinés, des plus confortables et luxueux du marché, le design d'Alfa a longtemps contribué à masquer une fiabilité défaillante. Les ventes sont essentiellement limitées à l'Europe, mais Alfa prévoit de retourner aux États-Unis et ailleurs prochainement. Avec une qualité améliorée, une gamme étendue et des gènes magnifiques, la marque pourrait enfin exploiter sa niche enviable d'exclusivité abordable. Comme l'a dit J Mays, directeur de la création de Ford : « Alfa Romeo fabrique les plus belles voitures au monde, point. »

MITO
Rival: Audi A1

Alfa's alternative supermini experiment.
Alfas alternatives Kleinwagen-Experiment.
Alfa tente la citadine polyvalente.

GIULIETTA
Rival: VW Golf

Ads by Uma Thurman, engines by Fiat.
Werbung mit Uma Thurman, Motor von Fiat.
Uma Thurman pour la pub, moteurs de Fiat.

159
Rival: BMW 3

Ageing, unconvincing. Giulia soon to replace.
Schlecht gealtert, bald von Giulia ersetzt.
Vieillissante. Bientôt remplacée par la Giulia.

BRERA | SPIDER
Rival: Audi TT

Beautiful concept. New one 2013.
Einfach wunderschön, neue Version ab 2013.
Magnifique concept. Une nouvelle en 2013.

TZ3 STRADALE
Rival: Dodge Viper

1 of 9 racecar for the road by Zagato.
1 der 9 Zagato-Rennwagen für die Straße.
9 engins de course pour la route, par Zagato.

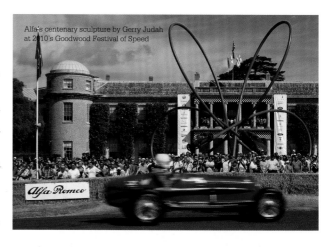

Alfa's centenary sculpture by Gerry Judah at 2010's Goodwood Festival of Speed

ALFA ROMEO MITO QUADRIFOGLIO VERDE

MiTo Quadrifoglio Verde

The "Milan-Torino" Mito is the latest to use 'Cloverleaf' the name to signify joyous performance in a pretty package. Based on the same underpinnings as the Fiat Grande Punto, the Mito has a more muscular and refined shape, best set off by a muted color scheme. Matte gray is our recommendation.

Der Alfa Romeo MiTo („Milan-Torino") ist das vorläufig letzte Modell mit dem Kleeblatt, das für atemberaubende Leistung und wahre Schönheit steht. Der Fiat Grande Punto spendete die Plattform für den muskulösen und formschönen MiTo. Für die Kurven des Schönlings steht eine breite Farbpalette zur Auswahl. Wir empfehlen einen matten Grauton.

La Mito « Milano-Torino » est la dernière en date à utiliser le nom « Quadrifoglio » (trèfle à quatre feuilles), synonyme de performance et style jubilatoires. La Mito partage les mêmes bases que la Fiat Grande Punto, mais avec une forme plus musculeuse et raffinée, mise en valeur par des couleurs neutres. Nous recommandons le gris mat.

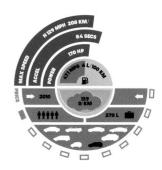

SECRET DETAIL

Four-leafed clovers have appeared on hot Alfas since Udo Sivocci found one beside the Targa Florio track in 1923 before winning.

Vierblättrige Kleeblätter sind beliebte Motive für Alfa Romeos, seit Udo Sivocci 1923 eins vor seinem Sieg bei der Targa Florio fand.

Des trèfles à quatre feuilles ont commencé à apparaître sur les Alfa de course lorsqu'Udo Sivocci en a trouvé un en 1923 sur le bord du circuit Targa Florio avant de remporter la compétition.

APTERA

LOGO HISTORY:

California start-up brings aero styling to the road with composite construction and electric power, years ahead of BMW's adoption of the same strategy for their forthcoming 'i' range. Still in its infancy, there's been much talk about Aptera's silent plug-in cars, but actual production models have yet to materialise, and the brand is in danger of stalling before it delivers a car. The usual delays, financial issues and management changes mean the Aptera is now running about two years behind schedule. The three-seat, electric-powered '2e' original was set to be joined by a larger model and a hybrid, but all efforts are now concentrated on the 2e. One for California dreamers with patience, the firm is still taking reservations on production cars – whenever they might arrive.

Vom Flugzeugbau inspiriert entwirft das kalifornische Start-up ein leichtes Elektrofahrzeug, das dem vergleichbaren i-Konzept von BMW um Jahre voraus ist. Obwohl das Projekt noch in den Kinderschuhen steckt, wurde über die leisen Aptera-Elektroantriebe schon viel gesprochen. Serienmodelle lassen jedoch auf sich warten, und es stellt sich die Frage, ob überhaupt jemals ein Aptera vom Band rollen wird. Die üblichen Entwicklungsverzögerungen, finanzielle Probleme und Änderungen im Management haben dazu geführt, dass die Kalifornier dem Zeitplan zwei Jahre hinterherhinken. Dem ursprünglichen Aptera 2e – ein 3-Sitzer mit Elektroantrieb – sollte ein größeres Hybridmodell folgen, doch zurzeit gelten alle Anstrengungen dem 2e. Die Visionäre aus dem sonnigen Bundesstaat sammeln fleißig Bestellungen für die Serienproduktion – wann auch immer diese beginnen wird.

Cette jeune entreprise californienne a amené l'esthétique aéronautique sur la route avec une construction composite et une propulsion électrique, des années avant que BMW adopte la même stratégie pour sa prochaine gamme « i ». Aptera est encore très jeune, et ses voitures silencieuses rechargeables ont déjà beaucoup fait parler, mais la production ne s'est pas encore concrétisée, et la marque court le risque de caler avant même de livrer son premier modèle. Les contretemps habituels, problèmes financiers et changements de direction, ont causé un retard de deux ans par rapport au programme prévu. Le modèle original « 2e » électrique à trois places était censé être rejoint par un autre modèle plus grand et par un hybride, mais aujourd'hui tous les efforts sont concentrés sur le 2e. Que les enthousiastes se rassurent et prennent leur mal en patience, Aptera accepte toujours les réservations – la date de production est cependant inconnue.

2E

Rival: Reva G-Wiz

Alluring concept yet to prove itself in production.
Ausgeklügeltes Konzept, Realisierbarkeit noch nicht bewiesen.
Un concept séduisant qui doit faire ses preuves en production.

ARASH

FOUNDED: **1999**

HEADQUARTERS: **CAMBRIDGE, ENGLAND**

LOGO HISTORY:

Founder Arash Farboud has been at the independent sportscar business for awhile, first in the very late 1990s using his surname for the Farboud GT and then in the early 00s the Farboud GTS, before a legal wrangle meant he had to switch to his first name for future projects. The GTS is now licensed and sold by another tiny UK exotic sportscar maker Ginetta as the F400 but Arash's latest project is in another league altogether, with a General Motors-sourced 550hp 7-liter V8 and aiming to be a Le Mans car for the road.

Der Gründer Arash Farboud ist in der alternativen Sportwagenszene seit einigen Jahren bekannt. In den späten 1990ern lieh er dem Farboud GT seinen Nachnamen, nach der Jahrtausendwende entwarf er den Farboud GTS. Aber nach einem Rechtsstreit musste er für seine Projekte auf seinen Vornamen ausweichen. Die Lizenz zum Bau des GTS wurde von einem anderen britischen Sportwagen-Exoten namens Ginetta erworben, der das Fahrzeug unter dem Namen F400 vertreibt. Inzwischen spielt Arash aber in einer ganz anderen Liga: Sein neues Design ist ein straßentauglicher Le Mans-Flitzer mit einem 7-Liter-V8-Antrieb von General Motors und 550 PS.

Le fondateur Arash Farboud n'est pas un nouveau venu dans le domaine des voitures de sport indépendantes. Il a utilisé son nom de famille à la fin des années 1990 pour la Farboud GT, puis au début des années 2000 pour la Farboud GTS, avant qu'une querelle juridique l'oblige à utiliser son prénom pour les projets suivants. C'est un autre petit constructeur britannique, Ginetta, qui détient aujourd'hui la licence de la GTS et la commercialise sous le nom de F400, mais les derniers projets d'Arash sont dans une tout autre catégorie, avec un moteur V8 7 litres de 550 chevaux de General Motors pour mettre sur la route une vraie voiture de course.

AF10

Rival: A Le Mans racecar

Lightweight supercar start-up.
Ultraleichter Supersportwagen.
Nouvelle supercar légère.

Arash founder Arash Farboud

ARASH AF10

The AF10 uses a GM-sourced 550hp 7-liter V8 with a carbon fibre monocoque and a narrow cabin like an aircraft jet. As owner Arash Farboud says: "The AF10 is basically a Le Mans car for the road and it's pretty extreme even for the road."

Die selbsttragende Kohlefaser-Karosserie und das Flugzeugcockpit des AF10 werden von einem 550 PS starken, 7-Liter-V8-Motor von GM angetrieben. Wie der Firmengründer Arash Farboud selbst sagt: „Der AF10 ist im Grunde ein Le Mans-Rennauto für die Straße, aber die Straße ist nicht genug für ihn".

L' AF10 est équipée d'un V8 de 7 litres et 550 chevaux de GM, d'une monocoque en fibre de carbone et d'une cabine étroite, comme celle d'un jet. D'après le propriétaire Arash Farboud : « L'AF10 est en fait une voiture faite pour Le Mans mais aussi pour la route, et elle est assez extrême, même pour la route. »

AF10

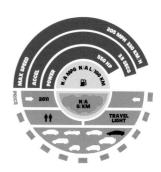

SECRET DETAIL

There's no electronic stability on this 550hp car, as Farboud explains: "We decided to make a car that you control rather than one that controls you."

Wie Farboud betont, verfügt der 550 PS starke Flitzer über keine elektronische Steuerung: „Wir wollten, dass der Fahrer den Wagen fährt, und nicht umgekehrt".

Il n'y a pas de stabilisateur électronique sur cette supercar de 550 chevaux, comme l'explique Farboud : « Nous avons décidé de faire une voiture que le conducteur contrôle, au lieu que ce soit elle qui contrôle le conducteur. »

ARIEL

GB

FOUNDED: **1999**

HEADQUARTERS: **CREWKERNE, ENGLAND**

2010 PRODUCTION: < **200**

LOGO HISTORY:

ARIEL

The Ariel brand name was resurrected from a long defunct Birmingham, UK-based company which once manufactured the iconic Victorian-era Penny Farthing bicycle. Its current bearer is somewhat faster. Exo-skeletal, stripped out and lightweight, Ariel's Atom is for many the ultimate trackday sportscar. The 'basic' car's blistering 3.4-second 0-62mph time is only beaten by the Bugatti Veyron, which costs around 30 times as much. Not much good for doing anything else, like carrying shopping or even a medium-sized bag, this is a pure thrillseeker's weekend toy, that can proudly park in much more extravagant company should it make its way down to Monaco for Grand Prix weekend. Worryingly, even faster variants are in the pipeline.

Der Markenname Ariel gehörte ursprünglich einem britischen Fahrrad-Hersteller aus Birmingham, der die berühmten Penny Farthing-Modelle aus der viktorianischen Zeit baute. Heute werden unter diesem Namen etwas schnellere Fahrzeuge verkauft. Der Ariel Atom, ein leichtgewichtiges Sportgerät mit Gitterrohrrahmen, ist für viele das ultimative Fahrzeug für die Rennstrecke. Schon in der Grundversion geht es von 0 auf 100 in 3,4 Sekunden. Da kann nur der Bugatti Veyron mithalten – nur kostet er ca. das 30-fache. Um den Wocheneinkauf zu erledigen, ist der Kleinwagen nicht geeignet – nicht einmal ein mittelgroßer Koffer findet darin Platz. Beim Atom handelt es sich um ein Spielzeug für kundige Hände, das selbst in einem hochkarätigen Setting wie dem Großen Preis von Monaco gut aussehen würde. Vorsicht: Schnellere Varianten sind schon in Planung.

La marque Ariel a été ressuscitée à partir d'une entreprise britannique de Birmingham disparue depuis longtemps, qui fabriquait le légendaire grand-bi victorien, ancêtre de la bicyclette. Sa descendante actuelle a fait des progrès en matière de vitesse. L'Atom d'Ariel, dépouillée et très légère, est dotée d'un exosquelette, et beaucoup la considèrent comme la voiture idéale pour la course sur circuit. Ce modèle « de base » passe de 0 à 100 km/h en 3,4 secondes foudroyantes, et n'est battu que par la Bugatti Veyron, qui coûte à peu près 30 fois plus cher. Inutile d'essayer de s'en servir pour autre chose, comme transporter les courses ou même un sac de taille moyenne, c'est un jouet du dimanche pour les amateurs de frissons qui saura faire bonne figure en compagnie des plus grands noms si elle arrive à se frayer un chemin jusqu'au Grand Prix de Monaco. Perspective inquiétante, des variantes encore plus rapides sont en cours de réalisation.

ATOM

Rival: A rocket launcher

Light speed and skeletal style.
Leichtigkeit und Geschwindigkeit.
Vitesse vertigineuse et style squelettique.

ARTEGA

FOUNDED: **2006**
HEADQUARTERS: **DELBRUECK, GERMANY**

LOGO HISTORY:

Founded in 2006 and showing its GT at the Geneva Motor show in 2007, Artega looked like it had a genuine Porsche Cayman rival on its hands. VW V6 power, crisp well-proportioned lines penned by Henrik Fisker (behind the Aston DB9, before founding his eponymous brand), and a realistic sales price all meant Artega wasn't your typical upstart. Economics has played its cruel hand though, with the market stalling for new sports cars – or at least those from little known brands – however stylish and accomplished they may be. Bankrolled now by new Mexican backers, Artega is still around, but its moment may have passed.

Das 2006 gegründete Unternehmen stellte auf dem Genfer Autosalon 2007 den GT und damit ein Konkurrenzmodell für den Porsche Cayman vor. Ein VW-Sechszylinder im Heck, die wohlproportionierten Formen Henrik Fiskers (der Designer des Aston Martin DB9 und Namensgeber von Fisker Coachbuild) und der erschwinglich Preis sind die Hauptvorzüge des GT. Mit der Finanzkrise wurde das Geld für die Entwicklung neuer Sportwagen knapp, jedenfalls für kleine, unbekannte Marken, da könnte der Entwurf noch so ausgeklügelt sein. Eine Finanzspritze aus Mexiko hält Artega über Wasser, doch seine Glanzzeit hat das Unternehmen möglicherweise bereits hinter sich.

Artega est née en 2006 et a présenté sa GT au Salon international de l'automobile de Genève en 2007. Ce modèle semblait bien capable d'inquiéter la Porsche Cayman. Un moteur V6 VW, une ligne impeccable et parfaitement équilibrée tracée par Henrik Fisker (qui avait dessiné l'Aston Martin DB9 avant de créer sa marque éponyme) et un prix de vente réaliste faisaient d'Artega une nouvelle venue atypique. Mais l'économie lui a joué un tour cruel en mettant le marché au point mort pour les nouvelles voitures de sport – du moins pour les marques les moins connues, quels que soient leurs mérites esthétiques et techniques. Artega a trouvé de nouveaux financeurs mexicains et n'a pas dit son dernier mot, mais son heure est peut-être passée.

GT

Rival: Porsche Cayman

Individuality at a convincing price.
Nicht überteuerte Individualität.
L'individualité à un prix convaincant.

ASCARI

GB
FOUNDED: **1995**
HEADQUARTERS: **BANBURY, ENGLAND**

LOGO HISTORY:

Named after F1 legend Alberto Ascari it may be, but this low-volume UK brand's history book also contains Lee Noble's name. The acclaimed engineer was responsible for Ascari's BMW-engined 1998 Ecosse sports car. Dutch racer and oil technology patent-holding millionaire Klaas Zwart was so impressed he bought the company. The Ecosse was replaced in 2003 by the KZ1. Only 50 were due to be produced, although it's evolved into the more focused and pricier A10. The Ascari name is fittingly also tied to the Ascari Race Resort near Ronda, Spain – a private race track and resort for wealthy car enthusiasts.

Benannt wurde das Unternehmen zwar nach der Formel-1-Legende Alberto Ascari, doch ebenso präsent in den Geschichtsbüchern des britischen Autobauers ist der Name Lee Noble. Der renommierte Ingenieur verantwortete 1998 den von einem BMW-Motor betriebenen Ascari Escosse. Der niederländische Ölmillionär und Rennfahrer Klaas Zwart war davon so beeindruckt, dass er die Firma kaufte. Der Ecosse wurde 2003 vom KZ1 ersetzt. Nur 50 Exemplare wurden hergestellt, dann kam die Weiterentwicklung in Form des zielgerichteter geplanten und kostspieligeren A10. Der Name Ascari wird ebenfalls mit dem Ascari Race Resort in Verbindung gebracht – einer privaten Rennstrecke unweit der spanischen Stadt Ronda für wohlhabende Liebhaber der Geschwindigkeit.

Baptisée d'après Alberto Ascari, légende de la F1, cette marque britannique qui produit au compte-goutte est aussi associée au nom de Lee Noble. C'est cet ingénieur de grand renom qui est responsable de l'Ecosse, la voiture de sport d'Ascari, sortie en 1998 avec un moteur BMW. Le millionnaire néerlandais Klaas Zwart, coureur et propriétaire de brevets technologiques, en a été si impressionné qu'il a acheté l'entreprise. L'Ecosse a été remplacée par la KZ1 en 2003. La production devait se limiter à 50 unités, mais son évolution a donné l'A10, plus ciblée et plus chère. Le nom d'Ascari est également associé à l'Ascari Race Resort, près de Ronda en Espagne, un circuit privé au sein d'un complexe de loisirs pour les amateurs d'automobile fortunés.

A10
Rival: Ferrari 599

More focussed, and even pricier.
Zielgerichteter und noch teurer.
Plus ciblée, et encore plus chère.

ASTON MARTIN

FOUNDED: **1913**
HEADQUARTERS: **GAYDON, ENGLAND**
2010 PRODUCTION: **4450**

LOGO HISTORY:

That this iconic UK sportscar maker is just two years shy of its centenary is nothing short of a miracle given its chequered past. Its name derives from co-founder Lionel Martin and Aston Hill in Buckinghamshire where he raced. Early cars broke speed records and established its sporting reputation while post-WWII owner David Brown added beautiful exteriors on the 'DB' model range that found fame in James Bond movies. From an all-time low of 30 cars sold in 1982, Ford ownership from 1994 brought renewed sales success before selling to a consortium backed by Kuwaiti investors in 2007. Rumors at the time that luxury goods conglomerate LVMH was circling demonstrate the cache of the Aston Martin name. Led by Ulrich Bez, the marque now has its most relevant line-up ever, from city car Cygnet to supercar ONE-77. The place occupied by the 4-door Lagonda model produced in the 70s and 80s was filled again by the recent, welcome addition of the Rapide. Outsourced to a manufacturer in Austria, it perhaps provides the strongest indication that the brand is intent on expansion. Lagonda will soon return as a standalone sister-brand offering ultra high-end SUVs, whilst the company is rumored to be taking over production of Daimler's ailing Maybach line. All whilst helping design London's new Routemaster bus, suggesting the independent company is as nimble and dashing as its cars and drivers.

Dass der mythische Sportwagenhersteller aus Großbritannien in zwei Jahren sein hundertjähriges Jubiläum feiern wird, erscheint angesichts seiner bewegten Geschichte wie ein Wunder. Der Firmenname setzt sich aus dem Nachnamen des Mitgründers Lionel Martin und dem Berg Aston Hill zusammen, wo er an einem Rennen teilnahm. Die Geschwindigkeitsrekorde der ersten Autos gaben der Marke einen ausgezeichneten Ruf. Nach dem Zweiten Weltkrieg entwarf David Brown die eleganten Designs der DB-Reihe, bekannt aus den James Bond-Filmen. 1982 erreichte die Marke mit 30 verkauften Autos einen Tiefpunkt, der erst unter der Regie Ford (ab 1994) und später der kuwaitischen Investoren (ab 2007) überwunden wurde. Gerüchte über das Interesse des Luxus-Konzerns LVMH machen aber deutlich, dass Aston Martin an Renommee kaum eingebüßt hat. Unter Ulrich Bez reicht das Angebot vom Kleinwagen Cygnet bis hin zum Sportwagen ONE-77. Die Lücke des in den 70ern und 80ern gefertigten 4-Türers Lagonda füllt heute der Rapide. Das nach Österreich ausgegliederte Modell ist das deutlichste Zeichen der Expansionsbestrebungen der Briten. Der Lagonda feiert bald als eigenständige Schwestermarke für Luxus-SUVs seine Rückkehr. Außerdem wird über einen Kauf der maroden Maybach-Sparte von Daimler spekuliert. Die Beteiligung am Design der Londoner Routemaster-Busse rundet das Bild eines erholten und für die Zukunft gerüsteten Autobauers ab.

Ce légendaire constructeur britannique sera bientôt centenaire, un petit miracle étant donné son passé accidenté. Son nom lui vient de l'un de ses fondateurs, Lionel Martin, et d'Aston Hill, dans le Buckinghamshire, où Martin participait à des courses. Les premiers modèles ont battu des records de vitesse. Après la Deuxième Guerre mondiale, le nouveau propriétaire David Brown a créé les lignes fascinantes de la gamme « DB » devenue célèbre dans les films de James Bond. Les ventes ont touché le fond en 1982 avec 30 unités. Ford a repris la marque en 1994 et a regonflé ses ventes avant de la vendre à un consortium d'investisseurs koweitiens en 2007. Selon la rumeur, le groupe LVMH était aussi intéressé, preuve du prestige d'Aston Martin. Sous la direction d'Ulrich Bez, la marque propose aujourd'hui une offre plus attrayante que jamais, de la citadine Cygnet à la supercar ONE-77. La Lagonda 4 portes des années 1970 et 1980 est maintenant remplacée par la Rapide, arrivée à point nommé. Fabriquée par un sous-traitant autrichien, c'est peut-être la meilleure preuve des envies d'expansion de la marque. La Lagonda réapparaîtra bientôt en tant que sous-marque autonome proposant des SUV haut de gamme, et l'on murmure qu'Aston Martin reprendra la ligne Maybach de Daimler. En plus de tout cela, Aston travaille à la conception des nouveaux bus Routemaster de Londres, ce qui suggère que cette compagnie indépendante est tout aussi fringante que ses voitures et leurs conducteurs.

CYGNET Rival: 695 Tributo Ferrari		Designer-suited Toyota iQ city car. Kleinstwagen auf Toyota iQ-Basis. La citadine Toyota iQ en habits de gala.
VANTAGE Rival: Porsche 911		'Entry-level' V8 & V12; some entrance. V8 und V12 für Einsteiger. V8 et V12 « entrée de gamme ».
DB9 Rival: Bentley Continental GT		2+2 Coupe made Aston great again. 2+2-sitziges Coupé, ein wahrer Volltreffer. Ce coupé 2+2 a rendu sa grandeur à Aston.
VIRAGE Rival: Jag XKR		New 497hp V12 in between DB9 and DBS. V12-Motor (497 PS) zwischen DB9 und DBS. Nouveau V12 de 497 ch. entre DB9 et DBS.
DBS Rival: Ferrari 599 GTB		More aggressive V12 coupe. Sportliches V12-Coupé. Coupé V12 plus agressif.
RAPIDE Rival: Porsche Panamera		4-door, 4-seat successful stretch of DB9. 4-Türer, 4-Sitzer, Weiterentwicklung des DB9. DB9 allongée, 4 portes, 4 places.
ONE–77 Rival: Bugatti Veyron		One of 77, carbon-fiber ultra-priced supercar. 1 von 77, teurer Kohlefaser-Supersportwagen. 77 unités, supercar ultra chère en carbone.
V12 ZAGATO Rival: Ferrari 599XX		Limited edition Zagato-inspired road and race cars. Limitierte Zagato-inspirierte Straßen-/Rennautos. Voitures de course et de route, par Zagato.

DESIGNER Q+A

Marek Reichmann
Design director, Aston Martin

On duty:
Suit: Henry Poole & Sons – "They have 200 years of heritage and invented the tuxedo for a more relaxed fit for gentlemen."
Shoes: Camper (socks by Paul Smith)
Watch: Jaeger-LeCoultre DBS – "It's the one that opens the doors of your Aston via a built-in transponder."
Off-duty:
Clothes: Strellson trousers, Brioni striped collar polo shirt, tan leather red-soled Nike Cortez iD

What does your brand stand for?
Past: "Elegance."
Present: "Beauty."
Future: "Purity."

ASTON MARTIN RAPIDE

You could almost hear the groan let out by Porsche when the wraps came off the production Rapide in 2008. While the Panamera ably mutates the brand's DNA into a four-door form, the Rapide seems more like an inevitable evolution for Aston Martin, a reach not a stretch, reviving as it does the template of the original Lagonda. Sales have however been slow in a challenging economic climate, with a glut of rivals honing in on the same niche, making a Rapide all the more exclusive a choice.

Man glaubte, einen Porsche aufheulen zu hören, als 2008 der Rapide endlich enthüllt wurde. Wo der Panamera Porsches Identität in die Formen eines 4-Türers zwängt, wirkt der Rapide wie eine selbstverständliche Evolution bei Aston Martin, ein natürlicher Lagonda-Nachfolger. Im Zeichen der Wirtschaftskrise verkauft er sich jedoch nur schleppend. Dass andere Hersteller in dieselbe Nische vorgestoßen sind, macht den Rapide zu einer hochexklusiven Alternative.

Lorsque la Rapide a été dévoilée en 2008, on aurait presque pu entendre Porsche laisser échapper une plainte. La Panamera fait habilement muter l'ADN de la marque vers une forme à quatre portes, mais la Rapide ressemble plus à une évolution naturelle pour Aston Martin, et donne un second souffle à la Lagonda. Le climat économique a ralenti les ventes, et de nombreux concurrents se sont jetés sur la même niche de marché, ce qui fait de la Rapide un choix encore plus exclusif.

Rapide

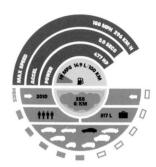

SECRET DETAIL

Aston's design team made this hard case concept luggage for the Rapide unveil at the 2009 Frankfurt motorshow. It never made production but with the Rapide Luxe edition you do get a soft leather set color-matched to your car's interior (see previous pages).

Das Design-Team von Aston entwarf diese Hartschalenkoffer für die Enthüllung des Rapide auf der IAA in Frankfurt 2009. Sie wurden nie produziert. Die Rapide Lux-Edition aus weichem Leder aber passt perfekt zum Innenleben Ihres Autos (s. o.).

L'équipe de design d'Aston a créé ce concept de bagages rigides pour la présentation de la Rapide au salon automobile de Francfort en 2008. Il n'est jamais arrivé jusqu'à la phase de production, mais la Rapide édition Luxe comprend un set de sacs en cuir souple assorti à la sellerie (voir les pages précédentes).

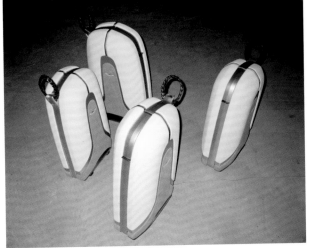

ASTON MARTIN CYGNET

Yachts carry tenders – small craft for ferrying people to and from land. Now Aston Martin has introduced the idea to supercar ownership. It's hugely controversial for the brand but oddly appealing too. And while a luxury city runabout has a certain logic, the rationale behind this oddity is more prosaic – the Cygnet conveniently lowers the manufacturer's average CO_2 emission figures, keeping its sportscars free to be as fierce as ever.

Jede Yacht führt sogenannte Beiboote mit – kleine Wasser-fahrzeuge zum Übersetzen der Passagiere. Nun hat Aston Martin dieses Prinzip auf den Supersportwagen angewendet. Eine kontroverse, aber reizvolle Maßnahme. Prinzipiell ist gegen einen luxuriösen Stadt-Kleinstwagen nichts einzuwenden. Entwickelt wurde der sparsame Cygnet jedoch aus einem anderen Grund: um den Flottenverbrauch von Aston Martin zu senken, damit die Stammklientel weiterhin mit furiosen Rennern fahren kann.

Les yachts ont des annexes – de petites embarcations qui assurent les trajets entre le yacht et le rivage. Et maintenant, Aston Martin reprend ce concept pour les supercars. C'est une démarche très discutable, mais aussi étrangement séduisante. Et bien qu'il y ait une certaine logique à proposer une petite citadine de luxe, la raison véritable est plus prosaïque : la Cygnet a l'avantage de faire baisser la moyenne des émissions de CO_2 du fabricant, ce qui lui permet de lâcher la bride à ses voitures de sport.

Cygnet

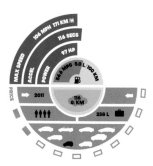

SECRET DETAIL

We admire the prototype's hexagonal seat theme, as seen in this limited edition by Colette, akin to sitting on the eye of a fly.

Besonders schön finden wir das hexagonale Muster der Sitzbezüge in der limitierten Sonderedition der Modefirma Colette, die an ein Fliegenauge erinnern.

Nous admirons le motif à hexagones de la sellerie dans cette édition limitée de Colette, qui donne l'impression de s'asseoir sur l'œil d'une mouche.

ASTON MARTIN DBS

The range-topping DB model can look a little exaggerated beside its elegant DB9 relative, and the addition of the nearly-as-fast Virage beneath it adds still more pressure on the model. James Bond doesn't drive one anymore but details such as the watch that opens its doors ensures it retains a frisson of danger.

Das leistungsgesteigerte DB-Modell wirkt neben seinem eleganten Verwandten, dem DB9, etwas übertrieben. Und auch der Virage, der fast so schnell wie sein großer Modellbruder ist, übt Druck auf den Supersportler aus. James Bond fährt zwar keinen Aston Martin mehr, ein Hauch seiner Filme ist jedoch in der Uhr zum Öffnen der Wagentüren erhalten geblieben.

Le modèle le plus haut de gamme des DB peut sembler un peu outrancier à côté de l'élégante DB9, et l'arrivée de la Virage, presque aussi rapide et juste en dessous dans la gamme, resserre encore l'étau. James Bond ne la conduit plus, mais des détails tels que la montre qui commande l'ouverture des portes lui confèrent une certaine aura de danger.

DBS Coupe (manual)

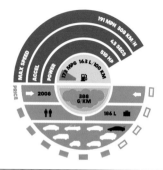

SECRET DETAIL

Specify the AMVOX2 DBS Transponder Jaeger LeCoultre watch and you'll never forget where you left your keys. Just be careful where you valet.

Bestellen Sie die Uhr Jaeger LeCoultre AMVOX2 DBS mit integriertem Transponder und vergessen Sie ruhig den Wagenschlüssel. Vorsicht aber, dass Sie nicht mit einem Geheimagenten verwechselt werden.

Prenez la montre AMVOX2 DBS Transponder de Jaeger-LeCoultre, et vous n'oublierez plus jamais où vous avez mis vos clés. Essayez juste de vous rappeler où la voiture est garée.

ASTON MARTIN VANTAGE

V8 Vantage S Cabriolet

The gateway drug to the addictive Aston Martin range is offered in V8, V12, Coupe and Volante (roadster) versions. All excite, but the V12 is especially bombastic, both in looks and performance. Achingly pretty, stupidly fast, when the bottom floor is a penthouse why go up?

Die Einstiegsdroge für das süchtig machende Angebot von Aston Martin ist in den Versionen V8, V12, Coupé und Volante (Roadster) zu haben. Alles aufregende Fahrzeuge, aber der V12 ist kaum zu toppen, weder im Aussehen noch in der Leistung. Blendend schön und wahnsinnig schnell – wieso sollte man höher ziehen, wenn das Erdgeschoss schon ein Penthouse ist?

Ce modèle, véritable produit d'appel menant à l'addiction à la gamme d'Aston Martin, est proposé en versions V8, V12, Coupé et Volante (roadster). Elles sont toutes irrésistibles, mais la V12 est particulièrement explosive, que ce soit en termes d'esthétique ou de performance. Belle à pleurer, rapide jusqu'à l'absurdité, lorsque le rez-de-chaussée est un palace avec terrasse et vue, pourquoi chercher à monter plus haut ?

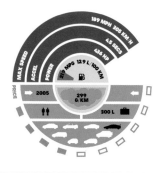

SECRET DETAIL

Order the carbon Kevlar composite seats on the and you'll save 17kg in weight. An expensive diet.

Wer die Schalensitze aus Carbon/Kevlar bestellt, spart 17 kg an Gewicht. Eine teure Diät allerdings.

Commandez les sièges en fibre de carbone et Kevlar pour lui faire perdre 17 kg. C'est un régime qui n'est pas donné.

ASTON MARTIN ONE-77

Maybe Design Director Marek Reichman got bored of working within the confines of the style established by previous Aston Martin design chiefs Ian Callum and Henrik Fisker. Or perhaps he just fancied having a go at building the most outrageous supercar in history. Either way, the world is a better place for the One-77.

Vielleicht hatte Designchef Marek Reichman keine Lust mehr, sich an den Vorgaben seiner Vorgänger bei Aston Martin Ian Callum und Henrik Fisker zu halten. Oder vielleicht wollte er wissen, wie es sich anfühlt, den unverschämtesten Supersportwagen aller Zeiten zu bauen. Wie auch immer, den One-77 werden wir lange in Erinnerung behalten.

Marek Reichman, le directeur du design d'Aston Martin, s'est peut-être lassé de travailler dans les limites du style établi par les directeurs du design qui l'ont précédé, Ian Callum et Henrik Fisker. Ou peut-être a-t-il juste eu envie d'essayer de faire la supercar la plus extravagante de l'histoire automobile. Quoi qu'il en soit, l'existence de la One-77 contribue à rendre ce monde meilleur.

One-77

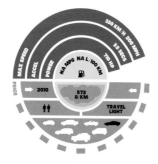

SECRET DETAIL

The full-width, double-horseshoe rear lamp belongs in the Guggenheim Museum; the wafer-thin filigrees of LED light it emits add a sense of delicacy to what is an otherwise very masculine design.

Die geschwungenen, als Band zusammengefassten Rückleuchten verdienen einen Ausstellungsplatz im Guggenheim. Die hauchdünnen LEDs sind der sanfte Kontrapunkt zum sonst maskulinen Design.

Les feux arrière en double fer à cheval sur toute la largeur de la voiture ont leur place au Guggenheim, et la finesse des motifs dessinés par les LED donne une touche de délicatesse à une ligne par ailleurs très masculine.

AUDI

FOUNDED: 1909
HEADQUARTERS: INGOLSTADT, GERMANY
2010 PRODUCTION: **1,092,400**

LOGO HISTORY:

Germany's fastest growing upscale brand has already overtaken Mercedes in sales and wants to become Europe's biggest selling premium brand by 2015. Its roots go back to the early 20th century and its logo born when it and three other German car brands merged to become Auto Union – thus the four rings in today's logo – but Audi as a sole brand remained a bit player until the 1980 Quattro coupe sprinted its way to critical, rally and sales success. The TT two-seater sportscar had a similar iconic effect in the late 90s and now in 2011 Audi has one of the biggest ranges of any premium player.

Die am schnellsten wachsende deutsche Edelmarke hat Mercedes bereits überholt und ist auf dem Weg, bis 2015 Europas größter Premiumhersteller zu werden. Die traditionsreiche Firma hat ihre Ursprünge im frühen 20. Jahrhundert. Die vier Ringe des Logos symbolisieren den Zusammenschluss von vier Unternehmen als Auto Union. Audi selbst spielte dabei nur eine Nebenrolle, bis ab 1980 das Sportcoupé Quattro seinen Siegeszug antrat. In den 90ern hatte der 2-Sitzer TT einen vergleichbaren Effekt. Zurzeit darf sich Audi mit einem der weltweit umfangreichsten Premiumpaletten brüsten.

La marque haut de gamme la plus dynamique d'Allemagne a déjà dépassé les ventes de Mercedes, et a l'ambition de devenir la première grande marque d'Europe en termes de ventes d'ici 2015. Ses racines remontent au début du XXᵉ siècle, et son logo est né de la fusion entre Audi et trois autres marques de voitures allemandes pour former Auto Union (c'est de là que viennent les quatre anneaux du logo actuel). Mais la marque Audi n'a vraiment pris le devant de la scène qu'en 1980, lorsque le coupé Quattro a pris la voie rapide vers le succès auprès des critiques, dans les rallyes et sur le marché. La sportive à deux places TT a eu un effet similaire à la fin des années 1990, et aujourd'hui, en 2011, Audi possède l'une des gammes les plus complètes de toutes les grandes marques.

A1
Rival: Mini Cooper

Credible posh new supermini.
Edler Kleinwagen.
Citadine polyvalente, chic et crédible.

A3 | S3 | CABRIO
Rival: VW Golf

Upscale Golf. S3 upscale Golf GTi.
Gehobener Golf, S3: gehobener Golf GTi.
Golf améliorée. Golf GTi pour la S3.

A4 | S4
Rival: BMW 3 Series

Classic sedan and wagon.
Klassische Limousinen und Kombis.
Berline et break classique.

A5 | S5 | CABRIO
Rival: BMW 3 Series
Coupe

Elegant 3-dr, 5-dr and drop-top.
Elegante 3- bzw. 5-Türer und Cabriolets.
Élégante en 3 portes, 5 portes et cabriolet.

A6 | S6
Rival: Merc E-Class

Classy large exec sedan and wagon.
Limousinen und Kombis, obere Mittelklasse.
Berline et break grand format très chic.

A7
Rival: Merc CLS

New large four-door coupe.
Neues 4-türiges Coupé.
Nouveau coupé 4 portes grand format.

A8
Rival: Jaguar XJ

Hi-tech, but dull, stretch version better.
Langweilige Oberklasse, die Langversion ist besser.
High-tech, insipide. Mieux en stretch.

Q3
Rival: Mini
Countryman

Q7 mini-me is best Audi SUV by far.
Kleine Q7-Version, mit Abstand Audis bester SUV.
Q7 en miniature, le meilleur SUV d'Audi.

TT
Rival: BMW Z4

Two generations, both icons.
Auch die 2. Generation ist ein Volltreffer.
Deux générations, deux légendes.

R8 | SPYDER
Rival: Porsche 911
Turbo

Audi's first supercar.
Audis erster Supersportwagen.
La première supercar d'Audi.

RS
Rival: Merc AMG

S = fast Audi, RS= really fast variants.
S = schnell, RS = rasant schnell.
S = Audi rapide, RS = Audi très rapide.

ALSO AVAILABLE
Q5, Q7

AUDI TT

This decisive, pretty coupe or roadster from Audi now comes in a multitude of options. To us it's the entry-level cars that make the most sense. They have all the beautiful detailing, and good looks of the faster, more expensive TT models with the surprising bonus that they are also sweeter to drive.

Der Schönling aus Ingolstadt, der als Coupé und Roadster zu haben ist, bietet jede Menge Optionen. Unserer Meinung nach handelt es sich dabei um ein höchstvernünftiges Einsteigermodell. Es wartet mit den schönen Details und dem hübschen Gesicht der schnelleren, teureren TT-Modellen auf, lässt sich aber überraschenderweise sanfter fahren.

Ce joli coupé ou roadster d'Audi est plein de caractère et est maintenant disponible dans une multitude de versions. Pour nous, ce sont les modèles d'entrée de gamme qui sont les plus intéressants. Ils ont les magnifiques détails et le style des modèles TT plus rapides et plus chers, avec un bonus surprenant : ils sont plus agréables à conduire.

2.0TFSI Sport

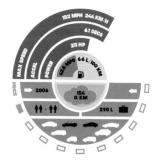

SECRET DETAIL

The beautifully finished aluminium trim in the TT's cabin is provided by Danish audio (and aluminium) specialists Bang & Olufsen.

Das elegante Alu-Interieur des TT ist dem Hi-Fi- und Aluminium-Spezialisten Bang & Olufsen zu verdanken.

Les superbes finitions en aluminium dans l'habitacle de la TT sont l'œuvre des spécialistes danois de l'audio (et de l'aluminium), Bang & Olufsen.

AUDI Q3

If you don't need the seven seats and acres of added length of the Q7, the shorter but still spacious five-seat Q3 crossover makes a lot more sense – the two-wheel drive two-liter diesel version delivers 54 mpg and fits down most streets.

Wenn Sie die sieben Sitzen und die sieben Kilometer Länge des Q7 nicht benötigen, ist der kürzere, aber immer noch geräumige Q3 eine vernünftigere Alternative. Die Version mit Zweiradantrieb und Zweilitermotor verbraucht 5,2 Liter auf 100 km und eignet sich für nahezu jede Straße.

Si vous n'avez pas besoin des sept places et de la surface supplémentaire de la Q7, le crossover Q3 à cinq places, plus court mais tout de même spacieux, sera un excellent choix. La version diesel 2,0 litres à deux roues motrices consomme 5,2 l/100 km/h et se faufile dans la plupart des rues.

Q3 2.0TDI 2WD manual
* Estimated CO2 emissions

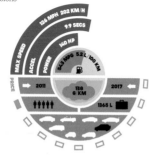

DESIGNER Q+A

Wolfgang Egger
Head of design, Audi Group

On duty:
Suit: Zegna
Shoes: Gravati (Milan)
Watch: Chronoswiss Lunar

Off-duty:
Clothes: Boss Jeans – "Only normal, I don't care, I'm not a label guy."

What does your brand stand for?
Past: "Sporty, pure and authentic – the 80s Quattro."
Present: "The same but more…"
Future: "We love the current brand values, so you cannot change them, so the same but even more."

AUDI S5 SPORTBACK

Our pick of the extensive, impressive A5 range is the S5 Sportback. Fluid, assertive looks, and rapid performance combine with four proper seats and a trunk big enough for an alternate form of transportation.

Aus der umfassenden, beeindruckenden A5-Reihe überzeugt uns am meisten der S5 Sportback. Mit seinen selbstbewussten Formen, seiner Geschwindigkeit, seinen bequemen vier Sitzen und dem großen Kofferraum ist der S5 Sportback ein kompletter Sportler.

Dans la vaste et impressionnante gamme A5, nous avons choisi la S5 Sportback. Elle allie la rapidité à une ligne fluide et affirmée, et elle dispose de quatre vraies places et d'un coffre suffisamment spacieux pour accueillir un mode de transport alternatif.

S5 Sportback

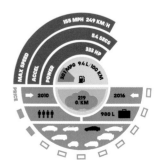

SECRET DETAIL

The S5 Sportback will take a full size bicycle through its hatch without detaching the wheel. Try that in a BMW 3 Series coupe.

Durch das Heck des S5 Sportback passt ein Fahrrad samt Lenkrad. Davon kann ein BMW 3er Coupé nur träumen.

Vous pouvez faire tenir un vélo dans le coffre la S5 Sportback sans démonter la roue. Essayez donc avec un coupé BMW Série 3.

AUDI R8 V10 SPYDER

Awesome first entrance by Audi into supercar territory and more than a match for the Porsche 911 Turbo and Lamborghini Gallardo in coupe and drop-top Spyder versions. We're waiting for the all-electric e-Tron version due late 2012.

Mit dem phänomenalen Supersportwagen-Erstling von Audi bekommen der Porsche 911 und der Lamborghini Gallardo einen ernstzunehmenden Gegner, der als Coupé und Spyder angeboten wird. Eine Elektroversion, der R8 e-Tron, lässt 2012 die Hüllen fallen. Wir warten schon gespannt darauf.

Audi fait une entrée remarquée sur le terrain des supercars et propose une rivale dangereuse pour la Porsche 911 Turbo et la Lamborghini Gallardo en version coupé et Spyder décapotable. Nous attendons la version e-Tron entièrement électrique, prévue pour fin 2012.

R8 V10 Spyder manual

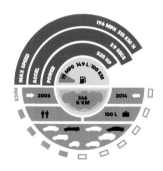

SECRET DETAIL

Metal-gaited manual gearbox with knurled shifter, takes a bit of getting used to but is a beautiful detail. Less money than auto too.

Für die manuelle Schaltung steht ein zunächst gewöhnungsbedürftiger, geriffelter Metall-Schalthebel, auf den man danach jedoch nicht mehr verzichten möchte. Ist auch billiger als das automatisierte Getriebe.

Il faut un temps d'adaptation à la boîte de vitesses manuelle, mais la grille en métal et le levier strié sont de superbes ornements. Et c'est moins cher que l'automatique.

BAC

FOUNDED: **2009**
HEADQUARTERS: **CHESHIRE, UK**

LOGO HISTORY:

Brothers Neill and Ian Briggs set up Briggs Automotive Company (BAC) after years of working for top flight carmakers like Bentley, Mercedes and Porsche. Neill (41) is the engineering brain and Ian (44) the design specialist and alongside other key designers and engineers they have created one of the surprises of 2011. Launching the brand with a single car – appropriately called the Mono due to its single seat – it trumps so many similar track-focused cars through its beautiful design, attention to detail and fit and finish. Not just a racer, the brothers say the Mono's perfectly able on normal roads too. Orders can be placed now.

Die Brüder Neill und Ian Briggs gründeten zusammen das Unternehmen Briggs Automotive Company (BAC), nachdem sie mehrere Jahre für Edel-Autohersteller wie Bentley, Mercedes und Porsche gearbeitet hatten. Neill (41) ist für den technischen Bereich zuständig, während Ian (44) sich um das Design kümmert. Zusammen mit ihren Designern und Ingenieuren bei BAC haben sie für eine der größten Überraschungen des Jahres 2011 gesorgt: ihren ersten Marktauftritt mit nur einem Automodell. Der Einsitzer – passenderweise „Mono" getauft – schlägt mit seinem bildschönen Design, Liebe zum Detail und einem vollendeten Gesamtbild die meisten Supersportwagen seiner Klasse. Die Brüder betonen, dass der Rennwagen absolut straßentauglich ist. Der Mono kann ab sofort bestellt werden.

Les frères Neill et Ian Briggs ont créé Briggs Automotive Company (BAC) après avoir travaillé pendant des années pour des constructeurs automobiles de premier ordre tels que Bentley, Mercedes et Porsche. Neill (41 ans) est le cerveau technique et Ian (44 ans) est le spécialiste du design. Entourés d'autres designers et ingénieurs de talent, ils ont donné naissance à l'une des grandes surprises de 2011. Ils ont lancé la marque avec une voiture unique, appelée Mono parce qu'elle n'a qu'une place, qui surpasse de nombreuses voitures de course similaires grâce à ses lignes superbes, ainsi qu'à l'attention portée aux détails, à l'ergonomie et aux finitions. Elle n'est cependant pas limitée aux circuits, car les frères déclarent que la Mono est aussi parfaitement capable de circuler sur les routes. BAC accepte les commandes dès maintenant.

BAC MONO
Rival: Ariel Atom V8

Beautifully sculptured, beautifully fast.
Vollendetes Design, atemberaubende Schnelligkeit.
Magnifiquement sculptée, magnifiquement rapide.

BAC MONO

"This is not just a trackday thrasher," says Neill Briggs, the engineering half of BAC, "we've also made sure it works on the road. You could chuck your tent in the front and go off to Le Mans in it". With a 284hp engine, a slim-fast 540kg kerb weight and only one seat that would be a very rapid journey, alone.

„Den Mono haben wir nicht nur für die Rennstrecke gebaut", beteuert Neill Briggs, einer der BAC-Chefs. „Er soll auch straßentauglich sein. Rein mit dem Zelt und ab nach Le Mans." Mit 284 PS, 540 kg und nur einem Sitz eine sehr schnelle – und sehr einsame – Reise.

« Ce n'est pas juste une bête de compétition », avertit Neill Briggs, le cerveau technique de BAC, « nous avons fait en sorte qu'elle soit aussi adaptée à la route. Vous pourriez embarquer votre tente à l'avant et partir au Mans dans cette voiture. » Avec un moteur de 284 chevaux, un poids à vide de 540 kg et un seul siège, ce serait un trajet rapide, et solitaire.

Mono
* Estimated CO2 emissions and MPG

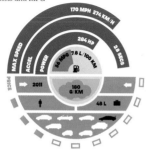

SECRET DETAIL

Each Mono customer can be fitted for his or her seat, pedal reach and preferred driving position along with specifically tailored gear ratio sets to suit the track of your choice.

Von jedem Mono-Käufer wird Maß genommen, um Sitz, Pedale, Lenkradposition und Übersetzungsverhältnis auf den jeweiligen Fahrer abzustimmen und alles da zu haben, wo es sich am besten anfühlt.

La Mono peut être adaptée à chacun de ses acheteurs : siège, distance des pédales et position de conduite préférée, ainsi que différents rapports de transmission sur mesure pour s'adapter au circuit choisi.

BAOJUN

LOGO HISTORY:

Baojun is a brand new marque in the mushrooming Chinese market formed by SAIC-GM-Wuling (SGMW), one of China's biggest multi-national joint ventures and the first to top more than a million annual sales. Launched to tap into the fastest-growing mid-sized sedan segment, Baojun's first model, the 630 is designed to appeal to those looking for a Chinese car but with the level of design, reliability and fuel-efficiency of an import. A full range of models is set to appear under the new nameplate in the coming years.

Die nagelneue Marke Baojun wurde von SAIC-GM-Wuling (SGMW) gegründet, das mit über einer Million verkauften Fahrzeugen pro Jahr als eines der größten multinationalen Joint Ventures in China gilt. Das erste Baojun-Modell, der 630, wurde für das am schnellsten wachsende Segment der Mittelklasse-Limousinen gebaut. Der Wagen spricht alle diejenigen an, die ein chinesisches Auto fahren möchten, das jedoch in Sachen Design, Zuverlässigkeit und Kraftstoffverbrauch dem Standard eines Importproduktes entspricht. In den kommenden Jahren soll ein umfassendes Sortiment unter dem Namen Baojun auf den Markt kommen.

Baojun est une toute nouvelle marque sur le marché chinois en pleine expansion. Elle a été créée par SAIC-GM-Wuling (SGMW), l'une des plus grandes joint-ventures multinationales de Chine et la première à dépasser le million d'unités vendues par an. Le premier modèle de Baojun, la 630, exploite le segment des berlines de taille moyenne, qui connaît la croissance la plus rapide. Il a été conçu pour plaire à ceux qui veulent une voiture chinoise, mais avec les qualités de design, de fiabilité et d'économie de carburant d'une importation. Une gamme complète de modèles sera lancée sous cette nouvelle marque dans les prochaines années.

630

Rival: BYD F3

Inoffensive mid-sized sedan.
Klassische Mittelklasse-Limousine.
Berline inoffensive de taille moyenne.

BENTLEY

GB

FOUNDED: **1919**
HEADQUARTERS: **CREWE, ENGLAND**
2010 PRODUCTION: **5117**

LOGO HISTORY:

Saved from half a century of churning out rebadged Rolls-Royce gin palaces by the sprawling VW Group in 1998, the winged 'B' has never been in ruder health. Pioneering Bentley Boys established the British marque's sporting reputation in the 1920s by risking their aristocratic necks at the 24 Heures du Mans motor race where arch rival Ettore Bugatti christened them "the world's fastest lorries". Today's line-up is equally stout but huge power reserves more than compensate. Two-tier range caters for ballers (Continental GT) and old money (6¾-liter-powered Brooklands) alike.

Nach einem halben Jahrhundert unter dem Dach von Rolls-Royce wurde Bentley im Jahr 1998 von der VW-Gruppe übernommen. Der „Winged B" erfreut sich heute bester Gesundheit. Die „Bentley Boys" begründeten in den 1920er Jahren beim 24-Stunden-Rennen von Le Mans den legendären Ruf der britischen Marke. Der Rivale Ettore Bugatti taufte den Bentley scherzend den „schnellsten Lastwagen der Welt". Noch heute ist die Marke für ihre robusten und dennoch kraftvollen Fahrzeuge bekannt. Zielgruppe sind neureiche Emporkömmlinge (Continental GT) ebenso wie Mitglieder des alten Geldadels (6¾-Liter-Wagen Brooklands).

En 1998, le tentaculaire groupe VW a sauvé Bentley d'un demi-siècle passé à produire à la chaîne des Rolls-Royce rebadgées. Aujourd'hui, le « B » ailé n'a jamais été en meilleure santé. Les « Bentley Boys » ont bâti la renommée sportive de la marque britannique dans les années 1920 en risquant leurs vies aristocratiques aux 24 Heures du Mans, où leur grand rival Ettore Bugatti les a baptisés « les camions les plus rapides du monde ». La gamme actuelle est tout aussi imposante, mais cela est largement compensé par d'énormes réserves de puissance. Elle se décompose en deux segments qui s'adressent aux parvenus (Continental GT) et aux héritiers (la Brooklands et son moteur 6,75 litres).

CONTINENTAL GT
Rival: Mercedes CL

Freshly-tailored new-money tourer.
Junger Sporttourer für Neureiche.
Nouveau tourisme pour fortunes récentes.

FLYING SPUR
Rival: Rolls-Royce Ghost

Awkward-looking limo, ace interior.
Plumpe Figur, famose Innenausstattung.
Extérieur maladroit, intérieur magistral.

BROOKLANDS
Rival: Ferrari FF

Sublime land-yacht, epic power.
Erhabene, kraftvolle Landyacht.
Sublime yacht terrien, puissance épique.

AZURE
Rival: Riva Aquariva

As above with unlimited headroom.
Wie oben, aber als Cabrio.
Idem, avec hauteur sous plafond infinie.

MULSANNE
Rival: Rolls-Royce Phantom

184mph Blenheim Palace.
296 km/h schneller Blenheim Palace.
Un palais baroque qui roule à 296 km/h.

BENTLEY CONTINENTAL GT

Subtle but effective restyle brings Bentley's consummate grand touring car up to date. Effortlessly rapid, sumptuously appointed and hugely comfortable the Continental GT has no real direct rivals, its phenomenal breadth of ability covering all bases at a price point that many consider a bargain, if only they could afford it.

Mit einem subtilen aber effektiven Neuentwurf bringt Bentley seinen Gran Turismo auf Vordermann. Der Continental GT (leichtfüßig und schnell, aufwendig ausgestattet und sehr komfortabel) hat keinen direkten Rivalen, denn er kann auf jedem Gebiet mithalten. Und das zu einem Preis, den viele als Schnäppchen empfinden würden, wenn sie nur genug Geld hätten.

Le grand tourisme impeccable de Bentley est remis au goût du jour grâce à un nouveau look revu avec subtilité mais efficacité. Rapide sans effort, somptueusement aménagée et extrêmement confortable, la Continental GT n'a aucune vraie rivale directe, et le vaste éventail de ses talents satisfait tous les désirs pour un prix que beaucoup considéreraient comme avantageux, si seulement ils pouvaient se le permettre.

Continental GT

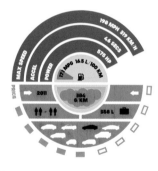

SECRET DETAIL

The GT's sharper detail lines are created by an innovative aerospace process called 'superforming' using high-pressure air and heat.

Die scharfen Bügelfalten des GT sind das Produkt eines innovativen Verfahrens aus der Raumfahrt namens „Superforming", bei dem Aluminium unter großer Hitze und Hochdruck geformt wird.

Les lignes de fuite plus acérées de la GT sont créées grâce à un procédé thermique issu de l'industrie aérospatiale appelé « superforming », qui emploie de l'air à haute pression.

BENTLEY MULSANNE

They say Rolls-Royce owners are driven, but Bentley owners like to drive. The Mulsanne delivers. Supremely comfortable, but surprisingly wieldy it's a gentlemanly thug in a smoker's jacket and running shoes. Hand crafted and beautifully old school the Mulsanne is a proper Bentley.

Es heißt, Rolls-Royce-Besitzer lassen sich gerne kutschieren, Bentley-Besitzer dagegen fahren lieber selbst. Der Mulsanne kommt seinen Kunden entgegen. Der hochkomfortable 2,6-Tonner lässt sich überraschend leicht handhaben und wirkt wie ein höflicher Gangster in Smoking und Laufschuhen. Tradition und Handarbeit – so lässt sich der Mulsanne beschreiben, ein richtiger Bentley also.

On dit que les propriétaires de Rolls-Royce aiment se faire conduire, et que les propriétaires de Bentley aiment conduire. La Mulsanne donne envie de conduire. Fabuleusement confortable mais étonnamment maniable, c'est un gentleman cambrioleur en veste de smoking et chaussures de sprint. La Mulsanne est une vraie Bentley, assemblée à la main et merveilleusement classique.

Mulsanne

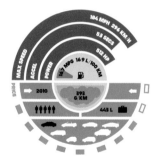

SECRET DETAIL

Bentley's 6.75-litre turbocharged V8 produces its massive torque of 1020Nm at just 1750rpm to enable its effortless performance.

Der 6,75-Turbo-Achtzylindermotor erzeugt ein Drehmoment von 1020 Nm bei nur 1750 U/min.

Le moteur V8 6,75 litres turbocompressé de Bentley atteint un couple formidable de 1 020 Nm à seulement 1 750 tours par minute, ce qui donne à ses performances une impression d'aisance parfaite.

BMW

FOUNDED: **1911**
HEADQUARTERS: **MUNICH, GERMANY**
2010 PRODUCTION: **1,224,280**

LOGO HISTORY:

Bayerische Motoren Werke started making aeroplanes – thus the graphic blue and white propeller in its logo – before switching to motorcycles in 1923 and cars in 1928. It produced the odd graceful sportscar in the 50s (507), but was a relatively small player until the iconic late-60s 2002 that led on to the brand-defining 3 Series. BMW's range expanded in the 1970s into bigger sedans, wagons and coupes, go-faster M models, with X-badged SUVs joining the fleet in the late 90s. 'Joy' might be its new and slightly odd tagline but its old one, 'The Ultimate Driving Machine' is still more apt. With a long-running program commissioning world-famous artists (Warhol, Calder, Koons) to create one-off art cars, and a Zaha Hadid-designed plant in Leipzig, BMW's avant garde credentials were crystallized by former design chief Chris Bangle, who engaged some whilst enraging others with his 'flame surface' styling and jutting trunks. The look ultimately came to define the past decade's automotive style, along with the retro-design trend launched by the New Beetle. Adrian van Hooydonk seemed to retrench in his first few years as design chief, restoring some sobriety to the lines. But the forthcoming 'i' range heralds the beginning of a new expressive language all his own.

Die Geschichte der Bayerischen Motoren Werke begann mit der Produktion von Flugzeugen – der blau-weiße Propeller im Logo erinnert noch heute daran –, bevor man im Jahr 1923 Motorräder und ab 1928 Autos herstellte. In den 1950er-Jahren brachte BMW den außergewöhnlich eleganten 507 auf den Markt. Für noch mehr Furore sorgte in den 60ern jedoch der legendäre 2002, mit dem der Grundstein für die berühmte 3er-Reihe gelegt wurde. In den 1970er Jahren konzentrierte sich BMW auf größere Limousinen, Kombis und Coupés. Ab den späten 1990ern schließlich kamen die schnellen M-Modelle und die Geländewagen der X-Reihe hinzu. „Freude ist BMW" mag zwar das neue Motto der Marke sein, der alte Grundsatz „Die ultimative Fahrmaschine" gilt jedoch noch immer. Mit einem Langzeitprogramm, in dessen Rahmen BMW weltberühmte Künstler wie Andy Warhol, Alexander Calder oder Jeff Koons Autos künstlerisch gestalten ließ, sowie mit dem von Zaha Hadid geplanten Werk in Leipzig setzte BMW avantgardistische Zeichen, während der frühere Leiter des Designteams von BMW Chris Bangle mit seinem „Flame-Surface-Design" und ausladenden Hecks kontrovers diskutiert wurde. Dieser Look dominierte zusammen mit der durch den VW New Beetle ausgelösten Retrowelle das Automobildesign des vergangenen Jahrzehnts. Der neue Chefdesigner Adrian van Hooydonk verfolgte diese Tendenz in seinen ersten Jahren bei BMW zunächst nicht weiter und sorgte für mehr Nüchternheit im Design. Die bald auf den Markt kommende i-Reihe steht indes für eine komplett neue und individuelle gestalterische Sprache.

Bayerische Motoren Werke a commencé par fabriquer des avions – c'est de là que vient l'hélice stylisée en bleu et blanc de son logo – avant de s'intéresser aux motos en 1923 puis aux voitures en 1928. L'entreprise a produit une voiture de sport élégante dans les années 1950 (507), mais est restée au second plan jusqu'à l'arrivée de la fameuse 2002 à la fin des années 1960. Elle annonçait la Série 3, qui a donné à la marque tout son charisme. La gamme de BMW s'est étendue dans les années 1970 pour proposer des berlines, des breaks et des coupés plus grands, des modèles M plus rapides, et des SUV badgés X ont rejoint la flotte à la fin des années 1990. « La joie » est peut-être son nouveau slogan, un peu étrange, mais l'ancien, « La machine à conduire », reste plus pertinent. BMW a la vieille habitude de demander à des artistes de renommée internationale (Warhol, Calder, Koons) de créer des art cars uniques, et Zaha Hadid a conçu l'usine de Leipzig. Mais la réputation avant-gardiste de la marque remonte à son ancien directeur du design Chris Bangle, qui a séduit certains et en a scandalisé d'autres avec son « flame surfacing » et ses coffres saillants. Ce look a fini par marquer le style automobile de la dernière décennie, tout comme la tendance rétro lancée par la New Beetle. Le successeur de Bangle, Adrian van Hooydonk, a semblé faire machine arrière lors de ses premières années, et a redonné une certaine sobriété aux lignes. Mais la prochaine gamme « i » annonce un tout nouveau langage visuel.

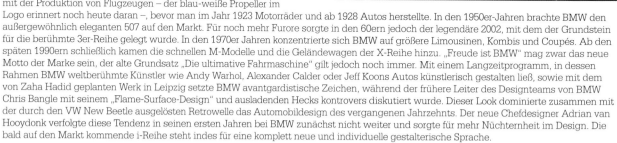

1 SERIES
Rival: Audi A3

Subtly designed hatch, cabrio & coupe.
Dezentes Heck, als Cabrio und Coupé.
Compacte, cabriolet et coupé, belle ligne.

3 SERIES
Rival: Audi A4

Benchmark mid-size sedan, wagon, coupe.
Mittelklasse-Limousine, als Kombi und Coupé.
Berline, break et coupé de référence.

5 SERIES
Rival: Merc E-class

New simpler design, same great drive.
Vereinfachtes Design, gleicher Drive.
Ligne plus simple, excellente conduite.

6 SERIES
Rival: Merc CLS

Another Bangle-banishing clean design.
Eins der Designs, das den Bangle verdrängt.
Un design épuré qui s'éloigne de Bangle.

7 SERIES
Rival: Merc S-class

Sober new limo design, same best drive.
Schlichteres Design, gleicher Drive.
Nouvelle limo sobre, conduite impeccable.

X1
Rival: Audi Q3

Smallest BMW SUV yet, surprisingly good.
Kleinster SUV von BMW, überraschend stark.
Le plus petit SUV de BMW, très bien.

X3
Rival: Audi Q5

Improved new version of mid-sized SUV.
Optimierte Version des Mittelklasse-SUV.
Nouvelle version améliorée de ce SUV.

X5
Rival: LR Discovery

Mk2 huge, assured and now with 7 seats.
Riesig, sicher, 7 Sitze.
Deuxième génération, énorme, avec 7 places.

X6
Rival: Range Sport

Striking, sporty crossover coupe.
Auffälliges, sportliches Crossover-Coupé.
Coupé crossover sportif à forte personnalité.

Z4
Rival: Merc SLK

Agile convertible hardtop.
Wendiger, vielseitiger Roadster mit Hardtop.
Cabriolet agile à toit rigide.

M
Rival: Merc E AMG

BMW's revered go-fast badge.
BMWs viel geliebter, flinker Klassiker.
L'excellent badge de BMW pour la vitesse.

BMW Z4

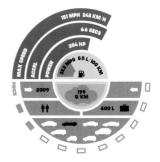

sDrive23i

BMW's roadster grew up in 2009, gaining a hardtop and softening its edges. It's best sampled as the sDrive23i – bigger engines under its long bonnet only underline it's no Porsche Boxster to drive – but it's wrapped up in a beautifully mature design.

Die neue Roadster-Generation von BMW kam 2009 mit einem Klappdach und sanfteren Linien auf den Markt. Wir haben den sDrive23i getestet – der größere Motor unter der langen Haube macht nur deutlich, dass man nicht in einem Porsche Boxster sitzt, dessen Technik in ein sehr ansprechendes Design gehüllt ist.

En 2009, le roadster de BMW s'est vu ajouter un toit rigide rétractable et des contours adoucis. La meilleure version est la sDrive23i. Sous son long capot, le moteur devenu plus puissant ne fait que souligner que sa conduite n'à rien à voir avec celle d'une Porsche Boxster, et sa ligne est d'une superbe maturité.

SECRET DETAIL

The 28i badge no longer signifies six-cylinders, a victim of engine downsizing it's now a four-cylinder turbo. Not that you'd notice.

Die Bezeichnung 28i bedeutet nicht mehr Sechszylinder. In Zeiten des Downsizing wurde daraus ein Vierzylinder-Turbo gemacht. Merkt man aber kaum.

Le badge 28i ne signifie plus six cylindres, la politique de réduction de la puissance des moteurs étant passée par là, c'est maintenant un turbo quatre cylindres. Mais vous ne vous en apercevrez même pas.

BMW X6

Genre bursting SUV-cum-four-door-coupe from BMW that answers questions nobody asked. Removing the utility from SUV, it's a fastback-shaped slice of Bavarian 'up yours' that's difficult to categorise, but then that's part of its appeal – especially in V8 guise.

Das unkonventionelle viertürige SUV-Coupé von BMW gibt Antworten auf Fragen, die niemand gestellt hat. Bezeichnend, dass BMW den X6 nicht SUV, sondern SAC (Sport Activity Coupé) nennt – schwer zu kategorisieren … Dieses Münchner Schrägheck hat aber das gewisse Etwas, vor allem die V8-Version.

Ce coupé sportif-tout terrain à quatre portes de BMW mélange les genres et répond à des questions que personne n'avait posées. C'est un SUV qui s'éloigne de l'utilitaire, un bras d'honneur bavarois à toit fastback qui ne rentre dans aucune case, mais c'est justement ce qui fait son charme, particulièrement dans sa version V8.

X6 xDrive50i

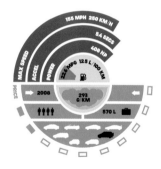

SECRET DETAIL

Some markets get the ActiveHybrid X6, the stealthy electric-only mode perfect for when you're out checking on your corners.

In manchen Ländern wird auch die Elektroversion ActiveHybrid X6 angeboten, ein bärenstarker Teilzeitstromer.

Certains marchés ont droit à l'ActiveHybrid X6, un mode entièrement électrique et très discret, parfait pour passer inaperçu en terrain ennemi.

BMW 1M COUPE

After X5 and X6 M aberrations this chunky little M coupe is something of a return to form. Straight six engine, sharper suspension and more muscle than Venice Beach's Gold's Gym. Brilliant. Shame it's a limited run model, then.

Nach den scheußlichen X5 und X6 M ist der bullige, kleine M eine Art Rückbesinnung auf formbewusstes Design. Reihensechszylinder-Motor, scharfe Aufhängung und mehr Muskelkraft als im Fitnessstudio vor den Sommerferien. Einfach klasse. Schade nur, dass es sich um eine Kleinserie handelt.

Après l'aberration du X5 et du X6 M, ce petit coupé M trapu est une sorte de retour aux sources. Six cylindres en ligne, une suspension pointue et plus de muscle que dans un club de gym de Venice Beach. Excellent. Dommage que ce soit une série limitée.

1M Coupe

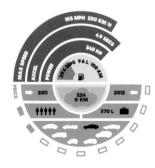

DESIGNER Q+A

Adrian van Hooydonk
Design director, BMW Group

On duty:
Suit: 'Hugo' by Hugo Boss – "It's a tighter cut and more modern."
Boots: Unknown, zip-up black leather
Watch: Heuer Calculator (vintage)

Off-duty:
Clothes: Levi's or G-Star jeans, shirt and jacket

Shoes: Converse Allstars, Onitsuka Tiger (Mini edition)

What does your brand stand for?
Past/Present/Future
"Lightness, sharpness and agility have always been expressed by BMW cars from the 328 and 3.0 CSi to today's latest concepts."

CARCHITECHTURE BMW WELT

Designed by Coop Himmelb(l)
au, 'BMW Welt' ('BMW World')
cost a reported 250m euros and
opened in 2007 with two aims.
Yes there is a museum alongside,
but this carchitecture acts more
as an 'experience centre' with a
delivery area where customers
can come to be wowed before
collecting their vehicle – courtesy
of a massive spiral ramp on which
the car arrives from a vortex-
like structured roof. The whole

building is incredibly complex,
and overtly so, physically mirroring
to some extent BMW's current
range of elaborately concave
and convex surfaced cars while
also suggestive of the brand's
technological expertise. It is
currently Munich's top tourist
attraction.

Die vom Architekturbüro Coop
Himmelb(l)au entworfene und
ca. 250 Millionen Euro teure
„BMW Welt" öffnete 2007
ihre Türen. Die Erlebnisstätte
beherbergt zwar auch ein
Museum, wird aber eher als
Auslieferungszentrum geschätzt,
wo die Kunden in einem
unvergleichbaren Schauplatz
ihre Autos abholen – und unter
der schwebenden Dachwolke
über einer spiralförmigen

Rampe hinausfahren können.
Die komplexe, futuristsiche
Gebäudearchitektur wirkt wie
eine Anspielung auf die aktuelle
BMW-Palette aus Fahrzeugen
mit aufwendig nach innen und
außen gewölbten Formen und
unterstreicht das technologische
Können der bayrischen Marke.
In München wollen die Touristen
nichts anderes besuchen.

« BMW Welt » (« Monde BMW ») a été dessiné par Coop Himmelb(l)au et aurait coûté 250 millions d'euros. L'édifice a ouvert ses portes en 2007 et sert deux objectifs. Oui, il y a bien un musée, mais cette œuvre de « c'architecture » est avant tout un « centre expérientiel » doté d'un espace de livraison où les clients peuvent venir s'émerveiller avant de récupérer leur voiture, qui arrive par une énorme rampe en spirale descendant d'une structure évoquant une tornade. Le bâtiment tout entier est incroyablement et ostensiblement complexe, c'est une sorte de représentation physique de la gamme actuelle de BMW et des surfaces concaves et convexes que l'on retrouve sur ses voitures, mais c'est aussi une allusion à l'expertise technologique de la marque. C'est actuellement la plus grande attraction touristique de Munich.

Part sculpture, part interior experiment, BMW, with Kvadrat fabrics and Flos lighting, commissioned *The Dwelling Lab* by Patricia Urquiola and Giulio Ridolfo for the 2010 Milan Design Week. Essentially an inside-out BMW 5 Series GT, a fully customized interior lurks behind the five exploded cones, to which are fixed the paraphernalia of these artists' car journeys.

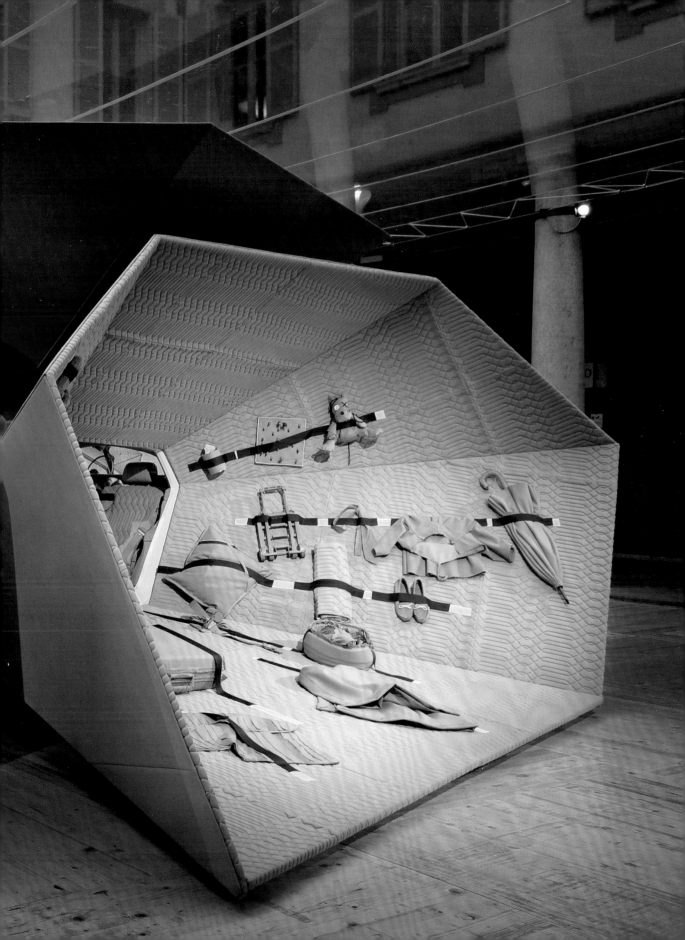

BOWLER

GB

FOUNDED: **1997**

HEADQUARTERS: **HAZELWOOD, ENGLAND**

2010 PRODUCTION: **< 20**

LOGO HISTORY:

RALLY
Rival: Nothing

All-terrain racer with Ferrari pace.
Geländewagen mit Ferraritempo.
Tout-terrain à l'âme de Ferrari.

EXR
Rival: Porsche
Cayenne Turbo

All-terrain racer for the road.
Straßentauglicher Geländerennwagen.
Tout-terrain de course pour la route.

This UK firm produces ridiculously rapid all-terrain vehicles. The first one was made in the mid-80s, but 1997 was when Bowler officially existed as an individual entity. Its success in rally-raid racing has been tremendous with its Tomcat, Wildcat and Nemesis models – all of which were based on Land Rover technology. Usually producing around 20 vehicles a year, 2011 is set aside for development of its new model, which, for the first time in the company's history, will be offered in both full race and 'road-going' form. There's little faster off-road and the new model promises to be equally fast on it. Bought by Coventry-based coachbuilders CPP in 2011, so expect bolder expansion plans for 2012.

Diese britische Marke, die mit ihrem unverwechselbaren, schnellen, auf dem Land Rover Defender basierenden Geländewagen Mitte der 1980er Jahre auf den Markt kam, wurde erst im Jahr 1999 offiziell gegründet. Der Erfolg im Bereich der Geländerennen begann mit dem Tomcat. Mit dem Wildcat – dem ersten Modell, das keine Abwandlung eines Land Rover darstellte – etablierte sich die Marke schließlich. Das Unternehmen, das normalerweise etwa 20 Wagen pro Jahr produziert, widmete sich 2010 komplett der Entwicklung des neuen Nemesis-Modells, das als SUV-Rennwagen sowie als straßentaugliches Auto angeboten wird. Bowler wurde von dem in Coventry ansässigen Karosseriebauer CPP aufgekauft, der zudem das Sportwagensegment von Spyker übernahm (somit kann sich Spyker auf seine Neuerwerbung Saab konzentrieren). Bowler wird unter dem neuen Besitzer voraussichtlich weiter wachsen.

Cette marque britannique a lancé ses premiers SUV de course au milieu des années 1980, mais l'entreprise Bowler Off Road est officiellement née en 1999. Son succès dans les courses tout-terrain a commencé avec le Tomcat, et s'est confirmé avec le Wildcat, sa première voiture enregistrée en tant que nouveau modèle, et non simple modification de Land Rover. L'entreprise produit environ 20 voitures par an, sauf en 2010, année consacrée au développement de son nouveau modèle, Nemesis, proposé en version de course et de route. Bowler est depuis peu la propriété de CPP, un carrossier de Coventry, qui a également repris l'unité supercar de Spyker (ce qui à permis à Spyker de se concentrer sur Saab, sa récente acquisition). La nouvelle direction donnera sûrement un coup de fouet à Bowler.

BRISTOL

FOUNDED: **1946**

HEADQUARTERS: **BRISTOL, ENGLAND**

2010 PRODUCTION: **< 25**

LOGO HISTORY:

Faced with excess staff at its plane production facility post-WWII Bristol set about building cars. It stuck largely to its aviation principles, using hand-formed aluminum and superior engineering to create its unique cars, and still does so today. Rescued from administration in 2011 by the Frazer-Nash Group its loyal customers are well-healed enthusiasts wanting something truly individual and discreet, the model range being sold through its single Kensington High Street showroom in London. Expensive and exclusive, Bristol has a 'contemporary' range but will also re-build your classic V8 Bristol into a Series 6, or upgrade any of its older models with more modern components and engines.

Aufgrund der schlechten Auftragslage nach dem Zweiten Weltkrieg begann der Flugzeughersteller Bristol mit der Produktion von Autos. Das Unternehmen hielt an den Prinzipien der Flugzeugproduktion fest und setzt bis heute zur Herstellung seiner einzigartigen Autos handgeformtes Aluminium sowie Spitzentechnik ein. Im April 2011 wurde Bristol von der Frazer-Nash Group aus der Insolvenzverwaltung gerettet. Die treuen Kunden der Marke, deren Autos ausschließlich im Autosalon auf der Kensington High Street in London verkauft werden, legen höchsten Wert auf individuelles und dezentes Design. Bristol bietet teure und exklusive Neuwagen an, tauscht aber für seine Kunden auch einen V8-Motor gegen einen Series-6-Motor aus oder rüstet ältere Modelle mit modernen Komponenten und Antrieben auf.

Pour occuper le personnel de son site de production aéronautique, désœuvré après la Deuxième Guerre mondiale, Bristol s'est mise à fabriquer des voitures. L'entreprise est en grande partie restée fidèle aux principes qu'elle avait appliqués dans l'aviation, avec de l'aluminium formé à la main et une technologie de pointe pour créer ses voitures uniques. Délivrés de l'Administration en 2011 par le groupe Frazer-Nash, ses clients fidèles sont des enthousiastes qui se sont parfaitement remis et recherchent l'individualité et la discrétion : la gamme n'est vendue que dans un seul showroom, sur Kensington High Street à Londres. Bristol fait dans le cher et l'exclusif. Outre sa gamme « contemporaine », Bristol propose également de transformer votre V8 classique en Série 6, ou de moderniser les composants et moteurs de n'importe lequel de ses anciens modèles.

FIGHTER
Rival: Merc SLS

Aerodynamic, gull-wing 200mph express.
Aerodynamisch, Flügeltüren, 320 km/h.
Aérodynamique, portes papillon, 320 km/h.

BLENHEIM
Rival: Jenson Interceptor R

Fat Capri looks with V8.
Schickes Cabrio mit V8-Motor.
Un air de grosse Capri avec un V8.

ROADSTER
Rival: Bentley GTC

Open-topped oddity.
Kurioses Cabrio.
Une bizarrerie à toit escamotable.

SERIES 6
Rival: Bentley S3 Continental

Elegant, modernised classic.
Elegante, moderne Klassik.
Un classique modernisé et élégant.

BUFORI

LOGO HISTORY:

Owned by three brothers – Anthony, George and Gerry Khouri – Bufori started as a project to build one 1930s American-inspired sports car for each of the Australian-Lebanese siblings. Its name stands for Beautiful, Unique, Fantastic, Original, Romantic and Irresistible and while some may disagree with the sentiment, the retro sports cars are certainly individual enough to appeal to the eccentric, in a similar vein to the British Morgan sports cars. Each car takes 3500 man-hours to hand build. Its most ambitious model, the Geneva, was unveiled at the 2010 motor show of the same name to raised eyebrows thanks to its extrovert retro styling and huge footprint.

Das von den drei Brüdern Anthony, George und Gerry Khouri geführte Unternehmen Bufori startete als Projekt zum Bau eines Sportwagens im Stil der 1930er Jahre für jeden der australisch-libanesischen Brüder. Sein Name setzt sich aus den Anfangsbuchstaben der Wörter „Beautiful, Unique, Fantastic, Original, Romantic, Irresistible" zusammen. Auch wenn sich hinsichtlich dieser Eigenschaften die Geister scheiden, ist klar, dass diese nostalgischen Sportwagen individuell genug sind, um – ähnlich wie der britische Hersteller Morgan – die Herzen von Exzentrikern zu erfreuen. Jedes Auto wird in 3500 Stunden Arbeitszeit von Hand gebaut. Das bisher anspruchsvollste Modell Geneva, das im Jahr 2010 auf dem Genfer Autosalon enthüllt wurde, sorgte mit seinem extrovertierten Retrostil und seiner schieren Größe für Furore.

Bufori est la propriété de trois frères austro-libanais : Anthony, George et Gerry Khouri. Leur projet initial était de construire pour chacun d'eux une voiture de sport inspirée des américaines des années 1930. Le nom Bufori est l'acronyme de Beautiful, Unique, Fantastic, Original, Romantic et Irresistible, et bien que certains puissent leur trouver d'autres qualificatifs, ces voitures de sport rétro sont sans aucun doute assez originales pour séduire les excentriques, à l'instar des Morgan britanniques. Chaque voiture est montée à la main, et nécessite 3 500 heures de main-d'œuvre. Le modèle le plus ambitieux, la Geneva, a été présenté lors du Salon international de l'automobile de Genève, et a étonné par son style rétro extraverti et sa surface au sol démesurée.

LA JOYA
Rival: Morgan Aeromax

Vintage-looking carbon-fibre coupe.
Nostalgischer Coupé mit Kohlefaser-Karosserie.
Coupé de style vintage en fibre de carbone.

GENEVA
Rival: Maybach 57

Gargantuan luxury limo.
Gigantische Luxuslimousine.
Gargantuesque limousine de luxe.

BUGATTI

LOGO HISTORY:

Despite history stretching back 100 years including glorious racers, beautiful touring cars and the epic Royale limousine – which long held the record for the most expensive car sold at auction – it's only in recent years Bugatti has been revived as a modern-day brand. VW CEO Ferdinand Piëch revived Bugatti, tasking it to create a car capable of previously unthinkable performance. Each 253mph, 987bhp 16-cylinder Veyron hand-built carbon fiber supercar costs over seven figures whatever your currency and yet VW allegedly makes a loss on every one. Special editions offering more performance at higher cost have been developed as the Veyron model ends, with a replacement some time away. Meanwhile, an imposing but elegant 4-door sedan was shown in concept form with the 1930's Type 57-referencing 'Galibier' name, and is shortly to enter production. A hybrid option is planned to allow silent, emissions-free driving within city limits, and Bugatti has ambitions to greatly expand sales. Whilst million euro high velocity hybrid limousines are not an obvious niche, Bugatti's position in the VW Group stable means it needs to sit some distance above Bentley, rarified air indeed

The Bugatti Super Sport one-of-30 limited edition watch by Parmigiani costs more than most supercars – except Bugatti ones

Trotz seiner hundertjährigen Geschichte mit ruhmreichen Rennwagen, wunderschönen Tourenwagen und der legendären Limousine Royale – die lange den Rekord als teuerstes auf einer Auktion verkauftes Auto hielt – erlebte Bugatti erst vor wenigen Jahren ein Revival. Es war der Vorstandsvorsitzende von VW Ferdinand Piëch, der die Marke neu belebte, indem er einen Wagen mit bis dahin unvorstellbarer Leistung entwickeln ließ. Der 16-Zylinder-Supersportwagen Veyron mit 407 km/h und 987 PS verfügt über eine handgebaute Kohlefaser-Karosserie. Trotz des (in jeder Währung) siebenstelligen Verkaufspreises macht VW mit dem Veyron jedoch keinen Gewinn. Sondermodelle mit mehr Leistung bei höheren Preisen werden den Veyron eines Tages ersetzen. Indes wurde eine imposante und dennoch elegante viertürige Limousine als Konzeptauto vorgestellt. Der Wagen, dessen historisches Vorbild der Bugatti 57 Atlantic ist, geht in Kürze in Produktion. Für ein leises und emissionsfreies Fahren in der Stadt ist zudem ein Hybridmodell in Planung. Die Marke hat den Anspruch, ihre Verkaufszahlen zu steigern. Obwohl Hochgeschwindigkeits-Hybridlimousinen in Wert von mehreren Millionen Euro eine harte Marktnische darstellen, muss die Elsässer Edelschmiede ihre Position in der VW-Gruppe sichern, indem sie sich eindeutig von der Marke Bentley absetzt.

Bien que son histoire remonte à un siècle, avec de merveilleuses voitures de course, de superbes voitures de tourisme et l'épique limousine Royale – qui a longtemps détenu le record du prix de vente aux enchères le plus élevé pour une voiture, cela ne fait que quelques années que la marque Bugatti est entrée dans le monde moderne. C'est le président-directeur général de VW, Ferdinand Piëch, qui a redonné vie à Bugatti en lui demandant une voiture capable de performances jusque-là inimaginables. Chaque Veyron est construite à la main en fibre de carbone, arrive à 407 km/h avec une puissance de 987 chevaux et 16 cylindres, et son prix s'écrit avec au moins sept chiffres dans n'importe quelle monnaie. Pourtant, VW dit perdre de l'argent sur chaque modèle vendu. Des éditions spéciales proposant encore plus de performance à un prix encore plus élevé ont été réalisées alors que le modèle Veyron arrive en fin de course, et sera bientôt remplacé. En attendant, le concept d'une berline quatre portes imposante, mais élégante a été présenté. Elle a été baptisée « Galibier » en référence à la Type 57 des années 1930, et sera bientôt mise en production. Une option hybride est prévue pour une conduite silencieuse et sans émissions en milieu urbain, et Bugatti a l'ambition de voir ses ventes croître substantiellement. La limousine hybride ultra-rapide à plus d'un million d'euros n'est pas une niche évidente, mais la position de Bugatti dans l'écurie VW l'oblige à se situer quelques crans au-dessus de Bentley, dans le monde à part de l'automobile d'élite.

BUGATTI VEYRON GRAND SPORT

Insane performance, but as easy to drive as an Audi TT, the Veyron Grand Sport is the ultimate open-topped car for the incomprehensibly wealthy. It steers beautifully and accelerates like nothing else, although when open it 'only' manages 223mph.

Ein Cabrio, das schneller als schnell ist und sich trotzdem so leicht wie ein Audi TT handhaben lässt – der Veyron Grand Sport ist der ultimative offene Sportwagen für die Superreichen. Das Fahren geht leicht von der Hand und die Beschleunigung ist mit der eines Flugzeugs vergleichbar. Mit offenem Dach schafft der Veyron für Frischluftfans allerdings „nur" 360 km/h.

Avec des performances démentes mais une conduite aussi souple que celle de l'Audi TT, la Veyron Grand Sport est le cabriolet suprême pour les gens dont le compte bancaire dépasse l'entendement. Elle se manœuvre au doigt et à l'œil et accélère comme aucune autre, mais n'atteint « que » 360 km/h lorsqu'elle est découverte.

16.4 Grand Sport

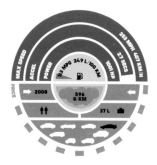

SECRET DETAIL

The get-me-home umbrella emergency roof only allows 99mph driving, so check the weather before leaving the proper one at home.

Der Grand Sport verfügt über ein mitführbares Stoff-Notverdeck, mit dem die Geschwindigkeit auf 159 km/h begrenzt ist.

La capote-parapluie d'urgence n'autorise que 159 km/h, alors vérifiez la météo avant de laisser le toit en dur à la maison.

BUICK

(USA)

FOUNDED: **1903**
HEADQUARTERS: **DETROIT**, USA
2010 PRODUCTION: **718,848**

LOGO HISTORY:

The oldest US car company was involved in setting up General Motors and – post GM's 2009 bankruptcy – still holds sway as an upmarket brand (pitched one notch down from Cadillac). Buick had become synonymous with old people until quite by surprise the marque became a massive hit in China, in large part due to memories of the old Chinese emperor having a fondness for rolling in Buicks back in the late 1920s and early 1930s. China is now Buick's biggest market and new designs (Enclave, LaCrosse), aimed primarily east and adapted to home tastes, have changed a brand that looked to be on death row to one with a rosier future.

Der älteste Autohersteller der USA baute General Motors mit auf und hält auch nach der Insolvenz von GM im Jahr 2009 seine Position im gehobenen Segment, unmittelbar nach Cadillac. Das verstaubte Image von Buick wurde aufpoliert, als die Marke überraschenderweise in China einen enormen Erfolg erlebte. Dieser beruhte in erster Linie auf der Erinnerung an den alten chinesischen Kaiser, der Ende der 1920er und Anfang der 1930er Jahre eine Vorliebe für Buicks entwickelte. China ist heute der größte Markt für den Autohersteller, und neue Modelle (Enclave, LaCrosse) werden eigens für den Fernen Osten entwickelt, wo eine Marke, die bereits tot schien, neu belebt wurde.

La doyenne des compagnies automobiles américaines a participé à la création de General Motors et (après la faillite de GM en 2009) est toujours en bonne place sur le marché des marques haut de gamme (un cran en dessous de Cadillac). Son image de marque poussiéreuse a pris un coup de jeune lorsqu'elle a rencontré un succès énorme et inattendu en Chine, dû en grande partie au souvenir de l'ancien empereur qui aimait rouler en Buick à la fin des années 1920 et au début des années 1930. La Chine est aujourd'hui le plus grand marché de Buick et ses nouveaux modèles (Enclave, LaCrosse), conçus pour l'Extrême-Orient et adaptés aux goûts locaux, ont transformé cette marque qui semblait condamnée, mais contemple à présent un avenir plus prometteur.

EXCELLE
Rival: BYD F3

Top-five best-seller in China.
Unter den Top 5 in China.
Dans le top cinq des ventes en Chine.

VERANO
Rival: Ford Focus

Chevy Cruze-based posh new 4dr.
Viertürer auf Chevy Cruze-Basis.
4 portes chic basée sur la Chevrolet Cruze.

REGAL
Rival: Toyota Avensis

Mid-sized Opel Insignia-based sedan.
Basiert auf der Limousine Opel Insignia.
Berline basée sur l'Opel Insignia.

LACROSSE
Rival: Nissan Teana

Stylish & curvy exec-sized sedan.
Schicke und kurvige Großlimousine.
Grande berline élégante et tout en courbes.

LUCERNE
Rival: Honda Legacy

Park Avenue-replacing sedan in US.
Neue Park-Avenue-Limousine für die USA.
Remplace la Park Avenue aux États-Unis.

ENCLAVE
Rival: Acura MDX

Big upmarket 7- to 8-st crossover SUV.
Großes SUV mit 7 bis 8 Sitzen.
SUV crossover de luxe de 7 à 8 places.

GL8
Rival: Chrysler Voyager

Recently re-designed large minivan.
Kürzlich neu aufgelegter großer Minivan.
Grand monospace récemment remodelé.

PARK AVENUE
Rival: An old barge

China-only old-school big sedan.
Klassische große Limousine für China.
Grande berline vendue en Chine.

BYD AUTO

FOUNDED: **2003**

HEADQUARTERS: **GUANGDONG, CHINA**

2010 PRODUCTION: **519,806**

LOGO HISTORY:

BYD – Build Your Dreams – has been doing just that since 2003 when the company was set up as an offshoot of the world's largest rechargeable battery maker. A shockingly naïve copy of BMW's propeller emblem signaled the firm's first public image but it quickly utilized its parent company's battery know-how to accelerate the development of a hybrid and electric car range (and change its logo). This caught the eye of Warren Buffet who bought a 10% stake in its parent company in late 2008 although in 2010 the firm's shares have plummeted due to lower than expected sales and prices have been slashed in 2011. Too soon to write off, BYD may yet prove a good bet for the world's most savvy investor.

BYD – Build Your Dreams – verwirklicht seit 2003 Autoträume. Das Unternehmen wurde als Ableger des weltgrößten Akku-Herstellers gegründet. Zunächst verwendete BYD eine schockierend naive Kopie des Propellerlogos von BMW, änderte dann aber Logo und Strategie und entwickelte aus dem Know-how seines Mutterunternehmens ein Sortiment an Hybrid- und Elektroautos. Damit wurde Warren Buffet auf die Marke aufmerksam und erwarb Ende 2008 10 % des Unternehmens. Allerdings stürzte der Aktienkurs 2010 aufgrund unerwartet niedriger Verkaufszahlen in den Keller. Im Jahr 2011 wurden die Verkaufspreise reduziert. Es besteht dennoch weiterhin die Chance, dass BYD doch ein weiterer Treffer des geschicktesten Investors der Welt wird.

BYD (Build Your Dreams – Construisez vos rêves) fait honneur à son nom depuis sa naissance en 2003. C'est une filiale du plus grand fabricant de batteries rechargeables au monde. La première version du logo était une copie terriblement naïve de l'emblème à hélice de BMW, mais BYD a vite exploité le savoir-faire de sa maison-mère pour accélérer le développement d'une gamme de voitures hybrides et électriques (et changer de logo). Cela a piqué l'intérêt de Warren Buffet, qui a acheté 10 % des parts de la maison-mère fin 2008. Mais en 2010 la valeur des actions s'est effondrée car les objectifs de vente n'ont pas été atteints, et il a fallu casser les prix en 2011. BYD n'a cependant pas encore dit son dernier mot, et pourrait se révéler être un pari gagnant pour l'investisseur le plus futé du monde.

F0
Rival: Toyota Aygo

So-similar city car to Toyota's Aygo.
Verblüffende Ähnlichkeit mit dem Toyota Aygo.
Citadine jumelle de l'Aygo de Toyota.

F3
Rival: Toyota Corolla

Top-selling car in China.
Eines der meistverkauften Autos in China.
L'une des plus vendues en Chine.

F3DM
Rival: Nissan Leaf

Plug-in hybrid version of F3.
Hybridversion des F3.
Version hybride rechargeable de la F3.

F6
Rival: Honda Accord

Higher spec family-sized sedan.
Hochwertige Familienlimousine.
Berline familiale de qualité supérieure.

G3
Rival: Buick Excelle

Another smart budget sedan.
Eine der preisgünstigeren Limousinen.
Une autre berline économique.

S8
Rival: Renault Megane CC

Coupe/cabrio with old Merc E lights.
Vorne wie ein alter Mercedes-E-Klasse.
Coupé/cabriolet avec des airs de Classe E.

E6
Rival: None

Full-electric 5st crossover/compact MPV on trial.
Kompaktes E-Auto mit 5 Sitzen (Probemodell).
Électrique compacte à 5 places (essai).

CADILLAC

FOUNDED: **1902**
HEADQUARTERS: **MICHIGAN, USA**
2010 PRODUCTION: **180,724**

LOGO HISTORY:

America's most luxurious brand can thank Frenchman Antoine de la Mothe Cadillac – the founder of Detroit – for its name. Founded in 1902 by Henry Leland he chose the Cadillac name for his new company and it quickly became known for precision engineering and quality. Sold to GM in 1909 it introduced the first mass production V8 in 1915, the post-WWII tailfin design craze and the 60s classic Eldorado. After a period of less-than-great cars the brand had a mini-revival in the 00s through the Escalade luxury SUV plus the highly credible CTS sedan and coupe. A shortage of new ideas making it to the dealership can be attributed to GM's tangle with bankruptcy, but with recent concepts like the Converj sports car convincingly leveraging the group's electric technology, decisive management willing to take risks on groundbreaking new product is what's needed now if the brand is to regain its status as an adjective of excellence. As one character on *The Wire* famously remarked, when an aging hardware salesman congratulated her on choosing 'the Cadillac of nail guns', "he meant Lexus but he ain't know it."

Die Nummer eins unter den amerikanischen Luxus-Automarken wurde im Jahr 1902 von Henry Leland gegründet. Namenspate der für beste Ingenieurskunst und hohe Qualitätsansprüche bekannte Firma ist Antoine de la Mothe, Sieur de Cadillac, Stadtgründer von Detroit. 1909 ging das Unternehmen an GM, im Jahr 1915 hatte der erste in Massenproduktion hergestellte V8 seinen Marktauftritt. Nach dem Zweiten Weltkrieg sorgten die aufsehenerregenden Heckflossen sowie der legendäre Eldorado der 1960er-Jahre für den unvergänglichen Ruhm von Cadillac. Nach einer längeren Durststrecke erlebte die Automarke in den Nullerjahren des neuen Jahrtausends mit seinem Luxus-SUV Escalade und mit dem zuverlässigen CTS (als Limousine und Coupé) ein Revival. In den letzten Jahren leidet Cadillac unter einem chronischen Ideenmangel, der sicherlich auch auf die Insolvenz von GM zurückzuführen ist. Mit jungen Konzepten wie dem Elektro-Sportwagen Converj und einem durchsetzungsfähigen Management mit Mut zu innovativen Produkten kann es der Hersteller letztendlich noch schaffen, seinen Status als Exzellenzmarke zurückzugewinnen. In einem in der englischsprachigen Welt berühmt gewordenen Zitat der amerikanischen Serie „The Wire" gratuliert ein ältlicher Verkäufer im Werkzeugladen einer Figur zur Wahl des „Cadillac unter den Nagelpistolen". Später erklärt sie ihrem Freund: „Der meinte eigentlich Lexus, aber er hat halt keine Ahnung."

La marque américaine la plus luxueuse peut remercier le Français Antoine de la Mothe Cadillac – le fondateur de Detroit – pour son nom. C'est Henry Leland qui choisit le nom de Cadillac lorsqu'il créa sa nouvelle entreprise en 1902. Elle devint vite connue pour la précision et la qualité de sa mécanique. Vendue à GM en 1909, elle est à l'origine de la première production en série d'un V8 en 1915, de l'engouement pour les ailerons après la Deuxième Guerre mondiale, et du grand classique des années 1960, l'Eldorado. Après avoir produit des voitures sans grand intérêt pendant une période, la marque a connu une petite renaissance dans les années 2000 grâce à son SUV de luxe Escalade et à la CTS, très crédible dans ses versions berline et coupé. Les difficultés financières de GM ont empêché la concrétisation de nombreuses nouvelles idées. Mais il faut que la direction sache prendre des décisions et des risques sur un nouveau produit révolutionnaire si la marque veut retrouver son statut d'excellence, par exemple avec la voiture de sport Converj, qui tire parti de la technologie électrique du groupe de façon très convaincante. Comme le fait remarquer l'un des personnages de la série *Sur écoute* lorsque, dans une quincaillerie, un vendeur vieillissant le félicite d'avoir choisi « La Cadillac des cloueurs pneumatiques », « Il voulait dire Lexus, mais il ne le savait pas. »

SRX
Rival: Lincoln MKT

MkII SUV bests MkI long/large wagon.
Schlägt seinen Vorgänger um Längen.
Le nouvel SUV surpasse l'ancien break.

CTS
Rival: BMW 5

Sharply styled sedan, wagon and coupe.
Limousine/Kombi/Coupé, scharfe Kanten.
Berline, break et coupé aux lignes acérées.

CTS-V COUPE
Rival: BMW M3

Angular good looks, V8 power. Nice.
Eckig und dennoch attraktiv, V8-Power.
Beauté angulaire, puissance du V8. Pas mal.

STS
Rival: Mercedes
E-Class

Big but old school sedan.
Große klassische Limousine.
Grande berline classique.

DTS
Rival: Lincoln
Towncar

Even bigger and older-school sedan.
Noch größere, noch klassischere Limousine.
Berline encore plus grande et plus classique.

ESCALADE
Rival: Lincoln
Navigator

Mega-brash & huge 7-seat SUV.
Auffälliger, riesiger SUV mit 7 Sitzen.
Énorme SUV à 7 places, ultra agressif.

ESCALADE EXT
Rival: Lincoln
Navigator L

Pick-up version of above.
Pick-up-Version des Escalade.
Version pick-up de l'Escalade.

CADILLAC CTS-V COUPE

If its Lockheed F-117 Nighthawk-inspired 'Art and Science' design language isn't enough to smash Cadillac's blue-rinsed Floridian image, its supercharged V8 will do the trick by painting a thick black number 11 along Highway 75 from Tampa to Miami.

Wenn die vom Lockheed F-117 Nighthawk inspirierte Designsprache „Art and Science" nicht ausreicht, um Cadillacs weichgespültes Florida-Image abzulegen: Hier ist die massige Urgewalt aus Michigan, um Ungläubige zu überzeugen.

Si son langage visuel « Art and Science » inspiré par le Lockheed F-117 Nighthawk ne suffit pas à faire voler en éclats l'image de marque pour retraités bling-bling dont souffre Cadillac, son V8 surcomprimé s'en chargera en révolutionnant la route partout où il passera.

CTS-V Coupe
* MPG based on US gallon

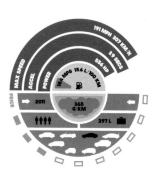

CATERHAM

FOUNDED: **1973**

HEADQUARTERS: **CATERHAM, ENGLAND**

2010 PRODUCTION: **510**

LOGO HISTORY:

Its core 7 model might be over 50 years old, but Caterham Cars is a phenomenal international success. The plucky firm bought the rights to Colin Chapman's Lotus 7 in 1973 and has been building them – or letting you build it yourself – ever since. The Caterham 7 has evolved to use more modern technology, but key to its appeal is its staggering performance and driving purity. The marginally wider-bodied SV recognized our fast-food lifestyles, but however much we increase in weight Caterham remains resolute in losing it. Superlight models are featherweights with heavyweight knockout punch, and all Caterhams are raced enthusiastically worldwide. Bought by Team Lotus in 2011.

Das berühmte Modell „7" von Caterham ist bereits über 50 Jahre alt, und dennoch gilt Caterham Cars immer noch als internationales Erfolgsphänomen: Das wagemutige Unternehmen kaufte im Jahr 1973 die Rechte des legendären Lotus 7 von Colin Chapman und baut ihn seitdem unter dem Namen „Caterham 7" unermüdlich weiter – oder lässt ihn vielmehr von seinen Kunden selbst zusammenbauen. Mittlerweile setzt Caterham zwar modernere Technologie ein, das Geheimnis des 7 liegt jedoch seit jeher in seiner erstaunlichen Leistung sowie in einer unschlagbar sauberen Fahrweise. Der leicht breitere SV ist ein Zugeständnis an unsere Fast-Food-Essgewohnheiten. Doch während wir ständig zunehmen, verliert der Caterham kontinuierlich an Gewicht. Die Superlight-Modelle sind Federgewichte, unter deren Haube die Kraft eines Schwergewichts steckt. Sämtliche Caterham-Modelle werden weltweit als Rennautos leidenschaftlich geliebt. Der Formel 1-Rennstall Team Lotus kaufte Caterham im Jahr 2011.

Son modèle phare, la Seven, a peut-être plus de 50 ans, mais Caterham Cars est un immense succès international. Cette entreprise dynamique a acheté les droits de la Lotus 7 de Colin Chapman en 1973 et la fabrique (ou donne à ses clients la possibilité de la construire eux-mêmes) depuis lors. La Caterham 7 a évolué avec la technologie, mais son pouvoir de séduction réside surtout dans sa performance stupéfiante et la pureté de sa conduite. Le châssis légèrement plus large de la SV tient compte de l'arrivée du fast-food dans nos vies, mais quel que soit notre tour de taille, Caterham a la ferme résolution de surveiller sa ligne. Ses modèles Superlight sont des poids plume dotés d'une puissance de poids lourd, et toutes les voitures Caterham font le bonheur des enthousiastes de la course dans le monde entier. Team Lotus a racheté Caterham en 2011.

CSR
Rival: Lotus Elise

Road and track with some comfort.
Straße und Rennstrecke, etwas Komfort.
Route et circuit avec un certain confort.

SUPERLIGHT
Rival: Westfield SE

Less weight, more speed.
Weniger Gewicht, mehr Geschwindigkeit.
Moins de poids, plus de vitesse.

ACADEMY
Rival: Renault Clio
Cup racer

Car & novice race model.
Für Motorsport-Einsteiger.
Voiture et modèle de course pour novices.

ROADSPORT
Rival: Tiger R6

Simple driving pleasure.
Schlichtes Fahrvergnügen.
Le simple plaisir de la conduite.

CLASSIC
Rival: Tiger Avon

Old-style appeal and inexpensive.
Günstiges Modell im alten Stil.
Séduction classique et abordable.

CATERHAM CSR 260

Super low, super light and super quick – its 3.1-second 0-60mph time bests all but the top supercars – this vehicle is one of Intersection's art director's favorites for endless drifting along wet roads. Just don't expect much comfort, adjustability or luggage space in the process.

Superniedrig, superleicht und superschnell – der Caterham CSR 260, mit dessen 3,1-Sekunden-Beschleunigung nur Supersportwagen mithalten können, gehört nach Meinung des Art Director unserer Zeitschrift zu den besten Autos, um endlos durch regennasse Straßen zu kurven. Allerdings sollte man nicht auch noch Komfort, Anpassbarkeit oder Stauraum erwarten.

Surbaissée, super légère et super rapide – son 0 à 100 km/h en 3,1 secondes bat presque toutes les supercars – cette voiture est l'une des favorites du directeur artistique d'*Intersection* pour rouler sans but sur les routes humides. Mais ne vous attendez pas à beaucoup de confort, d'adaptabilité ou d'espace pour vos bagages.

CSR 260
* Estimated CO2 emissions and MPG

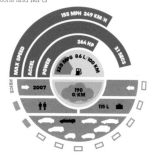

SECRET DETAIL

At 575kg this car is so light you can easily push it around with the engine off for 'low-emission parking'.

Mit seinen 575 kg ist diese rollende Zigarre so leicht, dass man sie mit der eigenen Muskelkraft emissionsfrei parken kann.

Avec ses 575 kg, cette voiture est si légère que vous n'aurez aucun mal à la manœuvrer avec le moteur éteint pour vous garer sans polluer.

CHANA

(CN)

FOUNDED: **1862**

HEADQUARTERS: **CHONGQING, CHINA**

2010 PRODUCTION: **710,000**

LOGO HISTORY:

Chana is the domestic brand of China's fourth biggest vehicle maker, the Chang'an Automobile Group that claims roots as far back as the 19th century as a weapons business. It boasted 2,378,800 vehicle sales in 2010, although as with many Chinese makers that figure includes a large chunk of foreign-badged vehicles made with joint venture partners like Ford, Suzuki and Peugeot/Citroen plus light commercial vehicles. Unusually, Chana also makes a lot of self-badged simple small cars too (700,000-plus) and even has its own Turin-based design centre complete with an Italian design director to up its future product game – witness the credible 2009 E301 concept for evidence.

Chana ist die Hausmarke des viertgrößten Autoherstellers von China, der ursprünglich im 18. Jahrhundert als Waffenproduzent gegründeten Chongqing Changan Automobile Company. Im Jahr 2010 verkaufte die Gruppe 2.378.800 Fahrzeuge. In dieser Zahl ist jedoch das Nutzfahrzeug-Segment sowie ein großer Anteil an Fahrzeugen internationaler Hersteller enthalten, die in Zusammenarbeit mit Joint Venture-Partnern wie Ford, Suzuki und Peugeot/Citroën hergestellt wurden. Chana stellt zudem zahlreiche schlichte Kleinwagen unter eigenem Namen her (über 700.000 Exemplare) und gründete zur Stärkung seiner Marktposition ein eigenes, in Turin ansässiges Design-Zentrum mit italienischem Designchef. Ergebnis hiervon ist das überzeugende Konzept des E301 aus dem Jahr 2009.

Chana est la marque nationale du quatrième constructeur de véhicules de Chine, le groupe Chang'an Automobile, dont les racines remontent au XIXᵉ siècle dans le secteur de l'armement. La marque a affiché des ventes de 2 378 800 véhicules en 2010, bien que ce chiffre comprenne, comme c'est souvent le cas chez les constructeurs chinois, une grande partie de véhicules étrangers rebadgés fabriqués en partenariat avec Ford, Suzuki et Peugeot/Citroën, ainsi que des véhicules commerciaux légers. Ce qui est moins ordinaire, c'est que Chana fabrique également beaucoup de petites voitures simples sous son propre badge (plus de 700 000) et possède même son propre centre de design à Turin, avec un directeur du design italien, afin d'améliorer ses produits dans le futur (la E301 de 2009, très crédible, confirme cette tendance).

BENNI Rival: Chery QQ3		No frills five-door city car. Schnörkelloses Stadtauto, 5-Türer. Citadine 5 portes sans fioritures.
ALSVIN Rival: Ford Focus sedan		No frills compact family five-door. Schlichtes, kompaktes Stadtauto, 5-Türer. Familiale compacte 5 portes sans fioritures.
CX20 Rival: Suzuki SX4		Slightly jacked-up supermini crossover. Leicht höhergelegter Minivan. Citadine crossover légèrement surélevée.
CX30 Rival: Ford Focus hatch		Bigger jacked-up 5dr hatchback. Größerer, höhergelegter 5-Türer mit Fließheck. Compacte surélevée plus grande à 5 portes.

2009 Chana E301 concept

CHERY

CN

FOUNDED: **1997**
HEADQUARTERS: **WUHU, CHINA**
2010 PRODUCTION: **700,000**

LOGO HISTORY:

This state-owned carmaker is the seventh biggest in China thanks in part to an increasing number of exports. Chery has hopped in and out of bed with its fair share of partners, including SAIC, GM, Volkswagen, Chrysler and Fiat, all ending acrimoniously. Its most bitter battle was fought out in the courtroom when GM Korea (née Daewoo) attempted to sue Chery over allegations of design duplication. The case was never proven. However, with Italian design house Pininfarina penning recent models and big investment in electric vehicle technology, Chery is transforming from copycat to major global player. It could do with inventing some model names of its own though…X1, A3?

Das Staatsunternehmen Chery ist vor allem aufgrund seiner hohen Exportzahlen der siebtgrößte Autohersteller in China. Die zahlreichen Kooperationen mit internationalen Autoherstellern wie SAIC, GM, Volkswagen, Chrysler und Fiat wurden stets im Unfrieden beendet. Der erbittertste Streit mit einem dieser Ex-Partner wurde im Gerichtssaal ausgetragen: GM Korea (ehemals Daewoo) verklagte Chery wegen angeblicher Produktpiraterie, der Fall wurde jedoch niemals vollständig aufgeklärt. Mittlerweile entwickelt sich Chery jedoch vom angeblichen Ideendieb zu einem größeren Global Player. Wirksame Strategien sind hierbei die Kooperation mit der italienischen Designfirma Pininfarina zur Entwicklung neuer Modelle sowie hohe Investitionen in die Elektroauto-Technologie. Wir empfehlen hierfür wärmstens die Erfindung eigener Modellnamen, wie wäre es mit X1 oder A3?

Ce constructeur de voitures contrôlé par l'État occupe la septième place en Chine, en partie grâce à la croissance de ses exportations. Chery a vécu plusieurs histoires tourmentées avec un certain nombre de partenaires, notamment SAIC, GM, Volkswagen, Chrysler et Fiat, qui se sont toutes terminées dans l'amertume. L'épisode le plus désagréable s'est réglé au tribunal lorsque GM Corée (anciennement Daewoo) a essayé de poursuivre Chery pour une affaire de design copié. Aucune preuve convaincante n'a pu être fournie. Mais avec la firme de design italienne Pininfarina, qui a dessiné certains de ses modèles récents, et un gros investissement dans la technologie automobile électrique, Chery ne se contente plus de copier, et devient un acteur majeur sur le marché international. Maintenant, il faudrait que le constructeur trouve des noms de modèles originaux… X1, A3 ?

QQ3
Rival: Haima M1

Daewoo Matiz clone, allegedly.
Angeblicher Daewoo Matiz-Klon.
Clone de la Daewoo Matiz, selon Daewoo.

QQME
Rival: VW Beetle

Odd symmetrical front, rear and doors.
Originell: Front, Heck und Türen.
Symétrie étrange avant, arrière, et portes.

M1
Rival: Chevrolet Spark

Cute supermini, electric option.
Süßer Kleinstwagen, auch als Elektroauto.
Mignonne citadine, option électrique.

A1
Rival: Ford Fiesta

Chery's compact global car.
Kompaktes Allround-Modell.
La compacte globale de Chery.

FULWIN2
Rival: Brilliance FRV

Reasonable compact sedan.
Praktische, kompakte Limousine.
Berline compacte raisonnable.

A3
Rival: Roewe 550

Pininfarina-designed mid-size hatch and sedan.
Limousine/Fließheck, Pininfarina-Design.
Berline et compacte par Pininfarina.

G6
Rival: Toyota Camry

Not-so fly like a G6.
Nicht ganz so schick wie ein G6.
Dull sedan.

X1
Rival: Brilliance A3

Distinctive mini-SUV.
Außergewöhnlicher Mini-Geländewagen.
Mini SUV original.

EASTAR CROSS
Rival: BYD E6

7-seat crossover.
Vielseitiger 7-Sitzer.
Crossover 7 places.

X5
Rival: Toyota Land Cruiser

Bold, full-size SUV.
Gewagter Geländewagen in Normalgröße.
Grand SUV audacieux.

CHEVROLET

FOUNDED: **1911**
HEADQUARTERS: **DETROIT**, USA
2010 PRODUCTION: **4,271,189**

LOGO HISTORY:

Unless you've lived in the US you might not be aware that Chevrolet is one of the very biggest car brands in the world and boasts selling one vehicle every 7.4 seconds. Born 100 years ago in Detroit, it was merged into General Motors in 1917 to take on local rival Ford as a low-cost, good value brand and that's pretty much what it's done ever since. Despite its everyman status it's produced some truly iconic cars in that time – many immortalized in popular music – from the classic Corvette, Suburban and Bel Air to the 2010 Camaro re-mix and genuinely innovative Volt range-extender electric sedan.

Wer nicht in den USA lebt, weiß vielleicht nicht, dass Chevrolet einer der größten Autohersteller der Welt ist, der alle 7,4 Sekunden ein Fahrzeug verkauft. Das vor 100 Jahren in Detroit gegründete Unternehmen ging 1917 in General Motors auf und nahm als günstige und dennoch hochwertige Marke den Kampf gegen Ford auf. Dieses Prinzip gilt noch heute. Trotz seines Durchschnitts-Images hat Chevrolet einige legendäre Autos geschaffen, die unter anderem in zahlreichen Popsongs verewigt wurden, darunter die Modelle Corvette, Suburban und Bel Air. Die Camaro-Neuauflage von 2010 und die wahrhaft innovative Elektro-Limousine Volt Range Extender sorgten in jüngster Zeit für Aufsehen.

Si vous n'avez jamais vécu aux États-Unis, vous ne savez peut-être pas que Chevrolet est l'une des plus grandes marques automobiles au monde, et vend un véhicule toutes les 7,4 secondes. Née à Detroit il y a 100 ans, elle a rejoint General Motors en 1917 pour contrer la concurrence locale de Ford en proposant des produits abordables et de qualité, et a continué dans cette veine depuis lors. Malgré son statut de marque pour Monsieur Tout-le-Monde, elle a produit des voitures réellement légendaires, dont beaucoup ont été immortalisées dans la musique populaire : des grands classiques que sont la Corvette, la Suburban et la Bel-Air jusqu'à la nouvelle Camaro 2010 et la Volt, une berline électrique qui vient ajouter un nouveau segment à la gamme.

SPARK
Rival: Hyundai i10

City car with smart styling.
Stadtauto mit smartem Design.
Citadine élégante.

SONIC
Rival: Ford Fiesta

Supermini with hidden rear door handles.
Kleinwagen, versteckte hintere Türgriffe.
Citadine avec poignées arrière cachées.

CRUZE
Rival: Ford Focus

Small and reasonable sedan.
Kleine praktische Limousine.
Petite berline raisonnable.

MALIBU
Rival: Honda Accord

Decent mid-size sedan.
Anständige Mittelklasse-Limousine.
Berline moyenne tout à fait honnête.

HHR
Rival: (Used) Chrysler PT Cruiser

Retro wagon/MPV thingy.
Retro-Kombi oder Minivan?
Un genre de monospace/break rétro.

IMPALA
Rival: Toyota Camry

Full-size sedan, shadow of former self.
Full-Size-Limousine in Neuauflage.
Grande berline qui a beaucoup baissé.

SUBURBAN
Rival: GMC Yukon

First launched 1935, now huge SUV.
1935 geboren, jetzt ein riesiger SUv.
Sortie en 1935, devenue un énorme SUV.

CAMARO
Rival: Dodge Challenger

Great 21st century muscle car.
Klein, stark, legendär und zukunftstauglich.
Excellente muscle car du XXIᵉ siècle.

CORVETTE
Rival: Merc SL

Formerly iconic sportscar has lost sparkle.
Ermattete Ex-Sportwagenlegende.
Voiture de sport anciennement culte.

SILVERADO
Rival: Ford F-150

Massive-selling massive pick-up.
Gut verkaufter Pick-up.
Énorme pick-up, énorme succès de vente.

VOLT
Rival: Nissan Leaf

Trailblazer of an electric auto future?
Der Wegbereiter des Elektroautos?
Une pionnière du futur électrique ?

ALSO AVAILABLE

Aveo, Agile, Captiva, Celta, Classic, Epica, Equinox, Prisma, Traverse, Tahoe, Orlando, Colorado, Avalanche.

CHEVROLET CAMARO

Retro may be passé to some but the Camaro transcends time with a heady mix of on-point styling, low price and a big old lump of Detroit iron under the hood. Ford Mustang and Dodge Challenger complete the reformed Pony Car club.

Auch wenn der Retrostil vielen schon unzeitgemäß erscheint, überzeugt der Camaro durch zeitloses Design, niedrigen Preis und einen ordentlichen Detroit-Block unter der Haube. Ford Mustang und Dodge Challenger runden die Neuauflage des Pony Car-Clubs ab.

Le rétro est peut-être passé de mode pour certains, mais la Camaro transcende les époques avec un mélange enivrant de style inspiré et de prix léger, et une bonne louche de métal de Detroit sous le capot. La Ford Mustang et la Dodge Challenger viennent compléter le club des pony cars, récemment reformé.

Camaro SS
* MPG based on US gallon

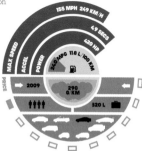

SECRET DETAIL

Console instrument pod lets you check vital stats while shifting between the six on the floor, just like the original.

Wie beim Original lassen sich wichtige Infos an den klassischen Rundinstrumenten ablesen, während man das 6-Gang-Getriebe manuell betätigt.

Sur la console, des indicateurs vous permettent de surveiller les statistiques vitales pendant que vous passez les six vitesses au plancher, comme sur le modèle original.

CHEVROLET VOLT

Hyper charged high-miler combines electric power with a range-extending petrol engine that generates charge when the batteries run flat. Bridges the gap between pure electric cars like the Nissan Leaf and more conventional hybrids. If only it didn't look like it does. The concept was passable, the production model is one to pass on. But the technology could easily be re-skinned and applied across the GM range. Books balanced, they may just go for it.

Der neue lektrische Chevy-Kompaktwagen hat einen Benzinmotor, der Strom liefert, wenn die Batterien leer sind: die ideale Ergänzung zu reinen Elektroautos wie dem Nissan Leaf und konventionelleren Hybriden. Schade nur, dass das Kind so hässlich ist (das Konzeptauto war noch ansehnlicher). Der innovativen Technologie könnte Chevrolet noch ein neues Gesicht verpassen, dann hat sich die Arbeit gelohnt.

Chargée à bloc avec un moteur à essence qui étend son autonomie en générant de l'électricité quand les batteries s'épuisent, elle comble le vide entre les électriques pures comme la Nissan Leaf et les hybrides plus classiques. Si seulement elle était jolie. Le concept était passable, mais le modèle de production ne donne pas envie. Cependant, la technologie pourrait adopter un extérieur différent et s'appliquer à toute la gamme de GM. Une fois les comptes assainis, pourquoi pas.

Volt
* MPG based on US gallon

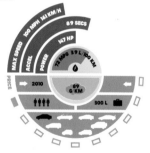

SECRET DETAIL

Smartphone app does sensible stuff like monitoring charging but also indulges any *Knight Rider* fantasies with remote engine start.

Mit der Smartphone-App können wichtige Aufgaben wie die Überwachung des Ladevorgangs erledigt werden – oder man kann sich für einen kurzen Augenblick wie *Knight Rider* fühlen.

L'app pour smartphone propose des fonctionnalités pratiques, comme le suivi du chargement des batteries, mais comblera également les fantasmes des fans de *K2000* avec le démarrage à distance.

CHRYSLER

(USA)

FOUNDED: **1925**

HEADQUARTERS: **MICHIGAN, USA**

2010 PRODUCTION: **197,446**

LOGO HISTORY:

Former Buick man Walter P Chrysler set up his own brand in 1925 and soon added other marques to the group – DeSoto, Plymouth, Dodge and later Jeep. The 1931 Custom Imperial was an early success – delivering prestige for less money than more exotic brands – and that's sort of where the brand has been positioned ever since. Other highlights include the 1946 'Woodie' Chrysler Town & Country and the 2005 300C – a true all-American sedan and Chrysler's last significant car. Chrysler has often failed financially, most recently with bankruptcy in 2009. This time Fiat came to the rescue but there are still tough times ahead…

Der ehemalige Buick-Mitarbeiter Walter P. Chrysler gründete im Jahr 1925 seine eigene Firma und holte kurze Zeit später mit DeSoto, Plymouth, Dodge und später Jeep weitere Marken mit ins Boot. Bereits im Jahr 1931 landete Chrysler mit dem Custom Imperial einen Verkaufsschlager. Das Geheimnis des Erfolgs liegt in der Herstellung von Prestigeautos, die gegenüber exotischen Marken unschlagbar günstig sind. Für diese Strategie steht das Unternehmen seit jeher. Weitere Highlights sind der aufgrund seines Holzaufbaus „Woody" genannte Chrysler Town & Country aus dem Jahr 1946 sowie der 300C von 2005, der als echte, durch und durch amerikanische Limousine und als letztes bedeutendes Auto von Chrysler gilt. Chrysler erlebte zahlreiche finanzielle Miseren, zuletzt mit der Insolvenz im Jahr 2009, bei der Fiat als Retter eingesprungen ist. Die Zeiten werden jedoch nicht besser …

Walter P. Chrysler a quitté Buick en 1925 pour créer sa propre marque, et n'a pas tardé à ajouter d'autres noms au groupe : DeSoto, Plymouth, Dodge, puis Jeep. La Custom Imperial de 1931 a été son premier grand succès. C'était un symbole de prestige, mais à un prix plus abordable que d'autres marques plus exotiques, et Chrysler a conservé ce positionnement depuis lors. On peut également citer la Town & Country de 1946 avec ses panneaux de bois, et la 300C en 2005, une vraie berline américaine, et le dernier modèle de Chrysler qui a compté. Chrysler a souvent eu des problèmes financiers, dont le plus récent a été la faillite en 2009. Fiat a volé à la rescousse, mais l'avenir est encore incertain…

200
Rival: Chevy Malibu

Emimen-backed ads. Anyone but in reality.
Legendärer Werbespot mit Eminem.
Eminem fait une apparition dans la pub.

200 CONVERTIBLE
Rival: Ford Mustang

Less lame Sebring replacer.
Schneller Sebring-Ersatz.
Remplaçante moins médiocre de la Sebring.

300
Rival: Dodge Charger

Lost swagger of previous model.
Misslungene zweite Generation.
Elle n'a plus la frime du modèle précédent.

TOWN AND COUNTRY
Rival: Dodge Caravan

Big very successful MPV.
Großer, äußerst erfolgreicher Minivan.
Grand monospace à succès.

GRAND VOYAGER
Rival: Ford Galaxy

7-seat Euro version of above.
Europäische Version mit 7 Sitzen.
Version européenne à 7 places.

CITROËN

FOUNDED: **1919**

HEADQUARTERS: **SEINE-SAINT-DENIS, FRANCE**

2010 PRODUCTION: **1,285,152**

LOGO HISTORY:

 CITROËN⌃

Despite being one of the most innovative brands in automotive history, a Citroen has always been a car for the people. Pivotal models include the 1934 Traction Avant (independent suspension, front-wheel drive and a 'monocoque' unified body and chassis), the 1948 2CV (a practical runabout produced for almost 40 years), the sublime 1955 DS (beautiful and technologically advanced with power-assisted steering, braking and gears) and the stunning if flawed 1968 SM (an oddball exotic alliance with Maserati). Acquired by Peugeot in 1974, some of its innovative flair seems to have dulled but the brand is still capable of flashes of that independent innovative spirit.

Trotz seiner Rolle als einer der innovativsten Autohersteller der Geschichte verkauft Citroën seine Autos zu realistischen Preisen. Zu den wichtigsten Modellen zählen der Traction Avant aus dem Jahr 1934 (mit innovativen Technologien wie Einzelradaufhängung, Vorderradantrieb und selbsttragender Karosserie), der 2CV von 1948 (die über 40 Jahre lang gebaute legendäre „Ente"), der erhabene DS von 1955 (wohlgeformt und technisch ausgereift, mit Servolenkung, Hochdruckservobremse und halb automatischem Getriebe) sowie der beeindruckende, jedoch leider kommerziell erfolglose SM von 1968 (der Exzentriker unter den Citroëns, das „M" steht für die Anlehnung an die Technik von Maserati). Das im Jahr 1974 von Peugeot gekaufte Unternehmen hat vielleicht einen Teil seines legendären Eigensinns eingebüßt, bisweilen blitzt der innovative Geist jedoch immer noch auf.

Bien que Citroën soit l'une des marques les plus innovantes de l'histoire de l'automobile, ses voitures ont toujours appartenu au peuple. Ses modèles phares comprennent la Traction Avant de 1934 (suspension indépendante, traction avant et un corps et châssis à structure monocoque), la 2CV de 1948 (une petite voiture pratique qui a été produite pendant presque 40 ans), la sublime DS de 1955 (superbe et à l'avant-garde de la technologie, avec direction, freinage et boîte de vitesses assistés) et la splendide mais imparfaite SM de 1968 (fruit excentrique d'une alliance exotique avec Maserati). Citroën a été achetée par Peugeot en 1974, et son sens de l'innovation semble s'être émoussé, mais la marque est toujours capable d'éclairs d'inventivité et d'indépendance.

C-ZERO
Rival: Mitsubishi iMiEV

Badge-engineered EV by Mitsubishi.
Technik: Mitsubishi iMiEV, Logo: Citroën.
Électrique développée avec Mitsubishi.

C1
Rival: Fiat 500

Practical and good value city car.
Praktischer, hochwertiger Kleinstwagen.
Pratique et bon rapport qualité-prix.

C3
Rival: Ford Fiesta

Pleasant supermini, now better quality.
Süßer Kleinwagen, jetzt in besserer Qualität.
Citadine agréable, qualité améliorée.

DS3
Rival: Mini

Not fully-convincing posh C3 with add-ons.
C3-Upgrade mit Add-ons, kleine Schwächen.
C3 snob, pas vraiment convaincante.

C3 PICASSO
Rival: Vauxhall Meriva

Great chunky little mini-MPV.
Bullig-frecher kleiner Minivan.
Excellent petit monospace trapu.

C4
Rival: Ford Focus

Higher quality but bland design and dull drive.
Gute Qualität, aber langweilig und plump.
Bonne qualité, ligne et conduite ternes.

C4 PICASSO
Rival: Ford C-Max

Stylish compact 5- or 7-seat MPV.
Modisch, kompakt, als 5- oder 7-Sitzer.
Monospace compact stylé à 5 ou 7 places.

C5
Rival: Ford Mondeo

Better, but no cigar, family sedan & wagon.
Ganz o.k., als Limousine oder Kombi.
Break et berline familiale.

C6
Rival: BMW 5

Amazing concept, large sedan reality, less so.
Famoses Konzept, enttäuschende Umsetzung.
Grande berline admirable, mal réalisée.

BERLINGO
Rival: Renault Kangoo

Cheap, cheerful van with windows.
Günstiger, verspielter Van mit Fenstern.
Camionnette bon marché et gaie.

C8
Rival: Ford Galaxy

Large 7-seat MPV with electric sliding doors.
Großer Minivan, elektrischen Türen, 7 Sitze.
Grand monospace avec portes électriques.

ALSO AVAILABLE

C-Crosser, Nemo, C2 VRC, C3 Aircross, C4 Grand Picasso, C-Elysee, C-Triomphe, Xsara Picasso.

CARCHITECHTURE CITROEN C42

It's not only luxury carmakers that have recently opened cathedrals to
their brands. Mainstream – but historically innovative – manufacturer
Citroen's 'concept store' opened in September 2007 at 42, Avenue
Champs-Elysees. The French manufacturer's main products are still
affordable everyday cars, but this store signaled their avant garde
ambitions. Architect Manuelle Gautrand's interior features seven rotating
platforms presenting selected cars from Citroen's history, covered by a
25-meter curved window façade featuring a repeated abstraction of the
brand's double chevron logo. Slim but tall, it's an unmistakable addition to
one of Paris' most prominent streets.

Es sind nicht nur die Luxushersteller, die Kathedralen zur Glorifizierung
ihrer Marken errichten können. Citroën, ein Mainstream-Autobauer
mit viel Innovationsgeist, eröffnete im September 2007 seinen an der
Avenue Champs-Elysees 42 liegenden internationalen Showroom. Nach
wie vor fertigen die Franzosen hauptsächlich erschwingliche Wagen
für den täglichen Gebrauch. Mit diesem modernen Ausstellungsort
spielen sie aber auf ihre avantgardistische Ader an. Im Innern der von
Manuelle Gautrand entworfenen Konstruktion stehen sieben rotierende
Plattformen mit historischen Modellen der Marke, die sich hinter der vom
Doppelwinkel inspirierten Glasfassade befinden. Die schlanke, hohe Figur
des Showrooms ist seit Fertigstellung des Baus ein weiterer Blickfang der
berühmtesten Pariser Promenade.

Les constructeurs automobiles de luxe ne sont pas les seuls à avoir
récemment ouvert de véritables cathédrales consacrées à leurs marques.
Citroën est une marque populaire – mais traditionnellement innovatrice
– qui a ouvert un « concept store » en septembre 2007 au 42, avenue
des Champs Élysées. Les modèles phares de ce fabricant français sont
toujours des voitures abordables pour la vie de tous les jours, mais ce
showroom marque ses ambitions d'avant-garde. À l'intérieur, l'architecte
Manuelle Gautrand a installé sept plateformes tournantes qui présentent
une sélection de modèles historiques de Citroën, et la façade vitrée
de 25 mètres est une interprétation abstraite des chevrons du logo.
Le bâtiment étroit mais haut se fait remarquer sur l'une des artères les
plus connues de Paris.

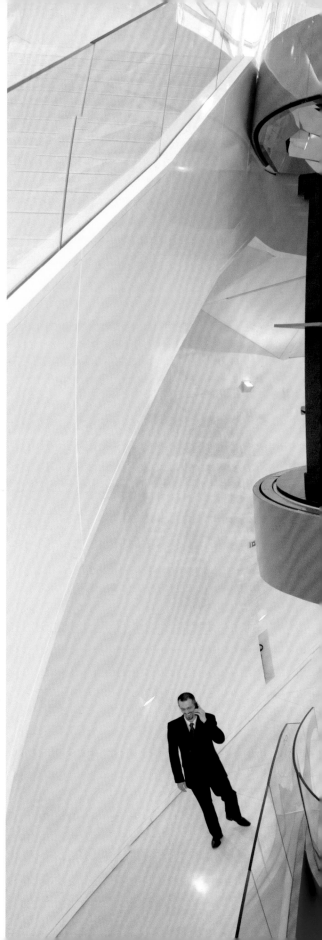

CITROEN DS3

If only we could overlook the fact its marketers have pillaged the original DS heritage, we'd be curious about this car's shark-fin styling and bijou shooting brake silhouette.

Könnten wir nur über die Schändung des Original-DS hinwegsehen, würden wir uns vielleicht mit diesem schmucken Shooting Brake im Stil einer Haifischflosse näher beschäftigen.

Si seulement on pouvait oublier que les experts du marketing ont saccagé l'héritage de la DS originale, on serait intrigué par cette voiture, avec son aileron de requin et sa silhouette de break de chasse précieux.

1.6 THP DSport

SECRET DETAIL

Dramatic window line cut disguises the fact its front end is shared with the taller and frumpier C3.

Die außergewöhnliche Linienführung der Fenster soll verbergen, dass der DS3 sich die Frontseite mit dem höheren und plumperen C3 teilt.

L'ampleur et le contraste de la ligne des fenêtres fait oublier que la DS3 a le même visage que la C3, plus haute et moins avenante.

The EVO concept by French designer
Ora-Ito for Citroen splices a footman-
powered 16th century carriage shape with
the fluid form of a futuristic spaceship.
The sculpture behind is by Oscar Niemeyer

DACIA

FOUNDED: **1966**

HEADQUARTERS: **MIOVENI, ROMANIA**

2010 PRODUCTION: **325,346**

LOGO HISTORY:

Budget car brand that started life building Renaults under licence in communist Romania. Early Dacia 1100 and 1300 models offered Romanians a previously unthinkable level of refinement and sophistication, creating huge waiting lists. The 80s and 90s were lean years with a lack of investment and an influx of imports as the Iron Curtain fell. Saviour came in 1999 when Renault bought the ailing marque. Four years later and the Logan models proved a massive hit. Dacias offer the sort of honest, utilitarian transport the European market has been crying out for. The smart new Duster crossover promises to galvanize recent success too.

Die Geschichte von Dacia begann mit dem Bau von Renault-Lizenzmodellen im kommunistischen Rumänien. Die frühen Modelle Dacia 1100 und 1300 standen für eine in Rumänien zuvor unvorstellbare Kultiviertheit und Eleganz, die zu ellenlangen Wartelisten führten. In den 80er und 90er Jahren durchlitt der rumänische Autobauer aufgrund steigender Importe sowie durch den Fall des Eisernen Vorhangs eine Flaute und wurde 1999 von Renault aufgekauft. Vier Jahre später landete Dacia mit dem Logan einen absoluten Verkaufsschlager. Die Marke bietet günstige, ehrliche und praktische Fahrzeuge an, die auf dem europäischen Markt gut ankommen. Auch das schicke neue Crossover-Modell Duster scheint an diesen Erfolg anzuknüpfen.

Dacia est une marque de voitures économiques qui a commencé son activité en fabriquant des Renault sous licence dans la Roumanie communiste. Les premiers modèles de Dacia, la 1100 et la 1300, ont offert aux Roumains un niveau de raffinement et de sophistication jusqu'alors inimaginable, et ont généré de longues listes d'attente. Les années 1980 et 1990 ont été maigres : l'argent faisait défaut, et la chute du Rideau de fer a entraîné un flot d'importations. Renault a sauvé la marque de ses difficultés en la rachetant en 1999. Quatre ans plus tard, les modèles Logan se sont révélés être un énorme succès. Les Dacia offrent un moyen de transport honnête et utilitaire dont le marché européen manquait cruellement. Le Duster, un nouveau crossover élégant, promet de rencontrer lui aussi un beau succès.

SANDERO
Rival: Kia Rio

Spacious, affordable supermini.
Geräumiger und preisgünstiger Kleinwagen.
Citadine polyvalente spacieuse et confortable.

LOGAN
Rival: Chevrolet Lacetti

Popular utilitarian sedan and estate.
Beliebt und praktisch, Limousine und Kombi.
Berline et break utilitaire populaire.

DUSTER
Rival: Nissan Qashquai

Honest, talented crossover.
Ehrlicher, talentierter Crossover.
Crossover honnête et talentueux.

DAIHATSU

J

FOUNDED: **1907**

HEADQUARTERS: **OSAKA, JAPAN**

2010 PRODUCTION: **783,000**

LOGO HISTORY:

Synonymous with tiny, Japanese tax-compliant Kei-cars, Daihatsu has earned a reputation for building quirky and characterful city cars, micro-SUVs and impossibly compact sports cars. As well as thriving in its native Japan, Daihatsu has also enjoyed periods of success overseas, particularly during the 1990s with models such as the Charade supermini and Cappuccino sports car. Toyota – a controlling stakeholder – also distributes cars to North America under its own name. Recently, unfavorable exchange rates and a raft of Korean competitors have decimated the brand's sales outside its domestic market, forcing a withdrawal from Europe.

Der Name Daihatsu ist Synonym für die in Japan steuerbegünstigten Kleinstwagen, die sogenannten Kei-Cars. Der Autohersteller ist für seine eigentümlich-individuellen Kleinwagen, Mikro-SUVs und extrem kompakten Sportwagen bekannt. Neben dem Erfolg in seinem Heimatland war Daihatsu in den 1990ern auch in Europa beliebt. Dafür sorgten Modelle wie der Kleinwagen Charade und der Sportwagen Cappuccino. Toyota, das die Aktienmehrheit von Daihatsu besitzt, verkauft zudem Autos unter eigenem Namen in den USA. In jüngster Zeit sind durch ungünstige Devisenkurse und die koreanische Konkurrenz die Absatzzahlen von Daihatsu außerhalb Japans so stark eingebrochen, dass das Unternehmen den Rückzug aus Europa antreten musste.

Synonyme de minuscules voitures Keijidosha fiscalement avantageuses, Daihatsu a la réputation de construire des citadines originales et pleines de personnalité, des micro-SUV et des voitures de sport incroyablement compactes. Cette marque prospère dans son pays natal, le Japon, mais a également connu des périodes de succès à l'étranger, surtout dans les années 1990 avec des modèles tels que la citadine polyvalente Charade et la sportive Capuccino. Toyota, actionnaire majoritaire, distribue également certains modèles de Daihatsu en Amérique du Nord sous sa propre marque. Récemment, des taux de change défavorables et l'abondance de concurrents coréens ont sérieusement entamé les ventes de la marque en dehors de son marché national, et l'ont forcée à quitter l'Europe.

MIRA
Rival: Suzuki Alto

Featherweight, spacious city car.
Federleichter geräumiger Kleinstwagen.
Citadine poids plume et spacieuse.

SIRION
Rival: Honda Jazz

Surprisingly good supermini.
Überraschend kompetenter Kleinwagen.
Excellente citadine polyvalente.

MATERIA
Rival: Nissan Cube

Manga-style boxy mini-MPV.
Kastiger Minivan im Manga-Stil.
Mini-monospace carré style.

TERIOS
Rival: Fiat Panda 4x4

Teeny soft-roader.
Jugendlicher Softroader.
Minuscule 4x4 urbain.

COPEN
Rival: Mazda MX-5

World's smallest sports car.
Das kleinste Sportauto der Welt.
La plus petite voiture de sport du monde.

DAIHATSU COPEN

Despite its embryonic Audi TT looks, the teeny Copen is a fully formed speedster. Built to comply with Japanese tax-break Kei car rules usually the reserve of upright boxes, the Copen harks back to simple British sports cars of the 1960s.

Trotz seiner Ähnlichkeit mit dem Audi TT ist das Teeny-Auto Copen ein ausgewachsener Speedster. Der in Japan als steuervergünstigtes Kei-Car zugelassene Copen steht ganz in der Tradition der einfachen britischen Sportwagen der 1960er Jahre.

Malgré ses airs d'embryon d'Audi TT, la minuscule Copen est un speedster parfaitement abouti. Conçue pour satisfaire aux normes des voitures Keijidosha, qui donnent droit à des avantages fiscaux au Japon et produisent habituellement des boîtes sur roues plus hautes que larges, la Copen opère un retour aux sportives britanniques simples des années 1960.

Copen

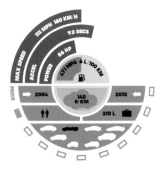

SECRET DETAIL

World's smallest folding hardtop roof transforms the Copen into a Lilliputian coupe. Aluminium construction keeps mass similarly miniscule.

Das weltweit kleinste abnehmbare Hardtop verwandelt den Copen in ein Mini-Coupé. Durch die leichte Alu-Konstruktion bleibt auch das Gewicht winzig klein.

Le plus petit toit rigide escamotable du monde transforme la Copen en coupé lilliputien. Grâce à l'emploi d'aluminium, le poids est également miniature.

DEVON

FOUNDED: **2008**
HEADQUARTERS: **CALIFORNIA**, USA

LOGO HISTORY:

Revealing its GTX at the 2009 Pebble Beach Concours d'Elegance underlined Devon founder Scott Devon's ambition for his new American supercar. Designed by Swede Daniel Paulin the GTX is described by the firm as 'classic yet futuristic'. Despite assurances that it'd go into production early in 2010 at a rate of 36 cars a year the initial momentum seems to have been lost. Power for the two cars comes from a 650bhp 8.4-liter V10 engine, which combined with the GTX's lightweight carbon fiber construction promises sensational performance. When that might be available remains anyone's guess. At $500,000 a time it'll be extremely rare too.

Auf dem Pebble Beach Concours d'Elegance 2009 bekräftigte Devon-Gründer Scott Devon mit der Präsentation des GTX sein Vorhaben, einen amerikanischen Supersportler herzustellen. Der von dem Schweden Daniel Paulin designte GTX ist nach eigenen Angaben „klassisch und dennoch futuristisch". Das Versprechen, den Wagen Anfang 2010 mit 36 Autos im Jahr in Produktion zu nehmen, scheint jedoch vergessen. Angetrieben werden die Fahrzeuge von einem 8,4-Liter-Zehnzylinder mit 650 PS, der in Kombination mit der ultraleichten Kohlefaser-Karosserie eine sensationelle Leistung verspricht. Wann die Autos vom Band rollen werden, steht noch in den Sternen. Der Preis von 500.000 USD (345.000 EUR) wird sicherlich die Exklusivität garantieren.

La présentation de la GTX au Concours d'Élégance de Pebble Beach en 2009 a révélé les ambitions que Scott Devon, le fondateur de Devon, nourrit pour sa nouvelle supercar américaine. Il qualifie son bolide, dessiné par le Suédois Daniel Paulin, de « classique mais futuriste ». La production était censée commencer début 2010 à un rythme de 36 unités par an, mais il semble que l'élan initial ait perdu de sa force. La puissance de la GTX vient d'un moteur V10 8,4 litres de 650 chevaux qui, combiné au châssis léger en fibre de carbone, promet des performances éblouissantes. Mais la date de mise sur le marché reste un mystère. À 500 000 dollars (345 000 euros) l'unité, ce sera une vraie rareté.

GTX

Rival: Ferrari GTO

Currently a pricey flight of fancy.
Zurzeit nur eine teure Fantasie.
Actuellement, rien de plus qu'un rêve très cher.

Devon also makes watches like this Tread 1 model, featuring patent-pending interwoven time belts

DODGE

FOUNDED: **1914**
HEADQUARTERS: **MICHIGAN, USA**
2010 PRODUCTION: **596,627**

LOGO HISTORY:

One of the oldest nameplates in the US and sister brand to Chrysler has some of the most evocative names in its line-up: Challenger, Charger and Ram all speak of the type of muscle-bound Marlboro-man image the US auto industry once thrived on. A period of producing outclassed products was partially responsible for the company coming perilously close to bankruptcy but under the stewardship of European giant Fiat, a big push for quality has improved its chances tenfold. It may well be down, but its vital signs are looking better.

Die Schwestermarke von Chrysler ist einer der ältesten US-Hersteller. Die Namen seiner Modelle sind in unserer Erinnerung mit altbekannten Bildern verknüpft: Challenger, Charger und Ram sind die Autos, die muskelbepackte Marlboro-Männer fuhren und das Bild der amerikanischen Automobilindustrie einst prägten. Dieses verstaubte Image brachte das Unternehmen an den Rand des Bankrotts. Unter der Führung des Giganten Fiat gelang jedoch der rettende Qualitätssprung. Auch wenn der einst kranke Mann noch nicht vollständig erholt ist, sind die Lebenszeichen unübersehbar.

L'une des marques américaines les plus anciennes, sœur de Chrysler, compte dans ses écuries quelques-uns des noms les plus évocateurs : la Challenger, la Charger et la Ram sont toutes associées à l'image du cow-boy Marlboro musclé qui a nourri l'âge d'or de l'industrie automobile américaine. Dodge a produit des modèles surclassés pendant une période, ce qui a contribué à lui faire frôler la faillite, mais depuis que le géant européen Fiat a repris les rênes et mise tout sur la qualité, l'avenir semble beaucoup plus prometteur. La marque est à terre, mais ses fonctions vitales remontent.

AVENGER
Rival: Chevrolet Malibu

Below-par mid-sized sedan.
Minderwertige Mittelklasse-Limousine.
Berline de taille moyenne décevante.

CALIBER
Rival: Nissan Rogue

Not so good compact crossover hatch.
Minderwertiger kompakter Crossover.
Crossover compact médiocre.

NITRO
Rival: Jeep Liberty

Four-wheeled Desperate Dan me-too 4x4.
Allradantrieb mit Viergangautomatik.
4x4 à gros bras, sans originalité.

CHALLENGER
Rival: Ford Mustang

Fantastic retro-styled 2dr US muscle car.
Gelungenes 2-türiges Retro-Muscle-Car.
Légendaire muscle car rétro à 2 portes.

CHARGER
Rival: Ford Taurus SHO

Family guy's 4dr muscle car.
4-türiges Muscle-Car für den Familienvater.
Muscle car à 4 portes pour père de famille.

JOURNEY
Rival: Chevrolet Equniox

High-riding 7st MPV/wagon, great cabin.
7 Sitze, Minivan oder Kombi.
Monospace/break 7 places, bonne cabine.

GRAND CARAVAN
Rival: Toyota Sienna

Full-sized 7st sliding-doored minivan.
Großer 7-Sitzer mit Schiebetüren, Minivan.
Monovolume 7 places, portes coulissantes.

DURANGO
Rival: Ford Explorer

Impressive big-boy 7st SUV/wagon.
Brillanter 7-Sitzer, als SUV oder Kombi.
Grand SUV/break imposant à 7 places.

RAM
Rival: Ford F-150

The iconic US pickup truck.
Der legendäre US-Pickup.
Le légendaire pick-up américain.

DODGE CHALLENGER

The best-designed US retro car – and the best Dodge – you can buy.
Referencing the first-generation 1970 model directly enough to evoke the
requisite nostalgia for its customers, the new model's chunkier stance,
chopped roof and bigger wheels avoid defiling the legend or merely
playing copycat. The lack of a drop-top has hit sales but who's counting?

Der beste US-Retrowagen – und der beste Dodge – überhaupt. Die
neue Generation weckt zwar die Nostalgiegefühle der Kundschaft durch
Anspielungen auf das Modell der 1970er. Eine größere Figur, ein neues
Dach und größere Reifen verhindern aber, dass die Legende verraten
wird. Ohne abnehmbares Dach verkauft er sich nur halb so gut, aber wen
kümmert das?

C'est la meilleure rétro américaine – et la meilleure Dodge. Les
références au modèle de 1970 sont assez directes pour susciter la nostalgie
requise, et l'allure ramassée, le toit découpé et les grandes roues évitent de
profaner la légende ou de tomber dans la copie. L'absence de décapotable
a fait du tort aux ventes, mais on ne va pas chipoter.

Dodge Challenger R/T 5.7 Hemi manual
* MPG based on US gallon

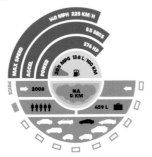

SECRET DETAIL

Designers placed the wing mirror well behind the A-pillar to make the
bonnet look longer – just like on the 1970 original.

Die Ingenieure haben den Außenspiegel weit hinter der A-Säule platziert,
um die Haube länger aussehen zu lassen – genau wie das Original von
1970.

Les designers ont placé le rétroviseur latéral loin derrière le pilier de la
porte avant pour que le capot semble plus long – exactement comme sur
le modèle original de 1970.

DONKERVOORT

FOUNDED: **1978**

HEADQUARTERS: **LELYSTAD, HOLLAND**

LOGO HISTORY:

Joop Donkervoort set up his car firm in the late 1970s building Lotus 7 replicas in Holland. Typical Donkervoorts are open-wheeled, low-slung lightweight machines with ample power to deliver shocking performance. The current range-topper, which like all Donkervoorts uses Audi power is the D8 GT, an odd gull-wing-doored lightweight coupe that looks like a Lotus 7 that's been designed for the pages of comic *2000 AD*. The D8 270 and D8 Wide Track are more conventionally styled but all these 7-style cars are perfect for non-conformists with a penchant for wild Dutch styling.

Joop Donkervoort baute sein Unternehmen in den 1970ern mit Nachahmungen des Lotus 7 auf. Typisch für den holländischen Autobauer sind niedrige, fliegengewichtige Fahrzeuge mit freistehenden Rädern und atemberaubender Leistung. Beim aktuellen Donkervoort D8 GT, der wie üblich mit einem Audi-Motor geliefert wird, handelt es sich um ein leichtes Sportcoupé mit Flügeltüren, das wie ein Lotus 7 in einem Science-Fiction-Comic aussieht. Der D8 270 und der D8 Wide Track wirken etwas konventioneller, doch alle diese Lotus-7-inspirierten Modelle sind wahre Schätze für rebellische Geister, die ein Faible für wildes Design aus Holland haben.

Joop Donkervoort a créé sa compagnie automobile à la fin des années 1970 en construisant des répliques de Lotus 7 en Hollande. En général, les Donkervoort ont des roues non carénées, et ce sont des machines légères et surbaissées qui ont largement assez de puissance pour offrir des performances hallucinantes. Le modèle haut de gamme actuel est motorisé par Audi, comme tous les autres modèles Donkervoort. Il s'agit de la D8 GT, un drôle de coupé léger à portes papillon. Elle ressemble à une Lotus 7 qui aurait été dessinée pour le magazine de BD *2000 AD*. La D8 270 et la D8 Wide Track ont une ligne plus conventionnelle, mais toutes ces héritières de la 7 sont parfaites pour les anticonformistes qui ont un penchant pour l'extravagance du design néerlandais.

D8 WIDE TRACK
Rival: Caterham Roadsport

'Basic' Donkervoort.
Donkervoorts Grundversion.
Donkervoort « de base ».

D8 270
Rival: Caterham CSV

270hp and a mild restyle.
270 PS starker Neuentwurf.
270 chevaux, et un look légèrement revu.

D8 GT
Rival: Morgan Aerosports

Oddball look, wild power.
Ein wilder Exzentriker.
Ligne excentrique, puissance ébouriffante.

ELFIN

LOGO HISTORY:

Founded in Australia in 1957 by former racer Garrie Cooper, Elfin has a long and successful history of producing competitive racecars. Like so many racecar firms road cars soon followed, with Elfin currently offering three. They're all as their Elfin name suggests – small – yet the MS8 Clubman and Streamliner come with big power. Big as in 5.7-liters of GM-sourced V8, that given the Elfin's tiny weight delivers quite silly pace. Little known outside its native Australia, Elfin remains a southern hemisphere special, but one nonetheless to be applauded.

Die 1957 in Australien vom ehemaligen Rennfahrer Garrie Cooper gegründete Marke hat als Hersteller von leistungsfähigen Rennautos eine lange, erfolgreiche Geschichte hinter sich. Wie viele Rennwagenhersteller nahm auch Elfin bald Straßenautos in die Produktion auf, derzeit sind drei Modelle im Angebot. Wie der Name Elfin (Elfe) bereits nahelegt, handelt es sich um kleine, vor allem aber – wie der MS8 Clubman und der Streamliner – beeindruckend starke Autos. Die V8-Motoren von GM mit 5,7 Litern Hubraum erreichen aufgrund des geringen Gewichts ein wahnsinniges Tempo. Der Ruhm der außerhalb von Australien eher unbekannten Marke beschränkt sich auf die Südhalbkugel, was ihre Leistung jedoch nicht weniger bewundernswert macht.

C'est l'ancien coureur automobile Garrie Cooper qui a créé Elfin en Australie en 1957. Cette marque a une longue trajectoire remplie de succès dans la production de voitures de course. Comme souvent dans ce domaine, les routières étaient la suite logique, et Elfin en propose actuellement trois. Elles sont toutes conformes à ce que le nom d'Elfin suggère (petites), mais la MS8 Clubman et la Streamliner ne manquent certainement pas de puissance. C'est grâce au moteur V8 de 5,7 litres fourni par GM qui, combiné à la légèreté des Elfin, développe une vitesse insensée. Elfin est peu connue en dehors de son Australie natale et reste une spécialité de l'hémisphère sud, mais n'en mérite pas moins d'être applaudie.

T5 CLUBMAN
Rival: Caterham 7

Small engine, big fun.
Kleiner Motor, riesiger Spaß.
Petit moteur, grand plaisir.

MS8 CLUBMAN
Rival: Lotus 2-Eleven

V8 in a tiny sportscar.
V8 in einem leichten Sportwagen.
Un V8 dans une minuscule voiture de sport.

MS8 STREAMLINER
Rival: Lotus 2-Eleven

As above, but prettier.
Wie oben, aber schöner.
Comme ci-dessus, mais plus belle.

FERRARI

FOUNDED: **1929**
HEADQUARTERS: **MARANELLO, ITALY**
2010 PRODUCTION: **6573**

LOGO HISTORY:

A racing team first and car manufacturer second, Ferrari's F1 involvement permeates the entire company – founder Enzo Ferrari reluctantly only built road cars to help fund his racing activities. The often controversial but hugely successful F1 team seemingly operates in a bubble – while its road cars are both hugely desirable and ridiculously capable. The company bankrolls itself, but Fiat holds the books. Its 458 Italia is incredible, the 599 and its hardcore GTO relative similarly so, while the 612 Scaglietti-replacing FF divides some with its looks to our eye it channels the expert taste of customers who have bespoke requests (and budgets to match) back into the bloodline. The softer California suits its name, while any number of limited edition day racers offer the ultimate rung on the ownership ladder for customers to climb. If the shameless merchandising does nothing for Ferrari's image, it is testament to the place this unique brand holds in the public imagination. With a sale or IPO mooted, pressure is mounting to increase sales, which are held far below demand to ensure long waiting lists. Still, with side-ventures like a Ferrari theme park in the UAE, there's clearly plenty of room – and various routes – for growth.

Der Name Ferrari geht auf das 1929 gegründete Rennteam zurück und wurde später auch für die Automarke verwendet. Die Formel 1 durchdringt die Geschichte der gesamten Firma, obwohl Gründer Enzo Ferrari zunächst – eher widerwillig – ausschließlich Straßenautos baute, um seine Rennwagen zu finanzieren. Das mitunter umstrittene, aber äußerst erfolgreiche F1-Team scheint abgeschottet von der Konzernumwelt zu arbeiten. Die Straßenmodelle sind extrem attraktiv und unglaublich leistungsstark. Ferrari steht finanziell auf eigenen Beinen, wird aber von Fiat kontrolliert. Nun die Modelle: Der 458 Italia, der 599 und das Hardcore-Sondermodell 599 GTO – einfach unbeschreiblich. Der FF – Nachfolger des 612 Scaglietti, mit neuartigem Aussehen etwas für den exklusiven Geschmack (und Geldbeutel). Der California – weiche, schmeichelnde Formen. Für die Kunden, denen es nicht teuer genug sein kann, sind mit den limitierten Auflagen nach oben hin nahezu keine Grenzen gesetzt. Mit seinem schamlosen Merchandising pflegt das Unternehmen sein Image. Gerüchte um einen Börsengang oder den Verkauf von Ferrari steigern die Nachfrage, das Angebot wird jedoch bewusst niedrig gehalten, um lange Wartelisten sicherzustellen. Mit Projekten wie dem Ferrari-Themenpark in den VAE hat das Unternehmen noch viel Spielraum, um das Wachstum zu steigern.

Ferrari est une écurie de course avant d'être un constructeur automobile, et la F1 imprègne toute la marque. Le fondateur Enzo Ferrari n'a fabriqué des routières que pour financer la compétition. L'équipe de F1 est sujette à controverse mais couronnée de succès, et fonctionne dans une bulle. Quant aux routières, elles sont extrêmement désirables et capables de performances démentes. L'entreprise se finance elle-même, mais c'est Fiat qui tient les comptes. La 458 Italia est incroyable, la 599 et sa version GTO déchaînée également, tandis que la FF, qui remplace la 612 Scaglietti et dont l'esthétique divise certains, satisfait les clients experts qui veulent du sur-mesure (et qui ont les moyens). La California, plus douce, porte bien son nom, et n'importe quelle édition limitée des voitures de course incarne le summum de ce qu'un amateur d'automobile peut aspirer à posséder. Le merchandising éhonté auquel Ferrari se livre n'apporte rien de bon à son image, mais témoigne de la place que cette marque tient dans l'imaginaire du public. Il serait question d'une vente ou d'une introduction en bourse, et la pression se fait sentir pour gonfler les ventes, qui sont maintenues en dessous de la demande pour créer des listes d'attente. Mais avec des projets parallèles tels que le parc à thème Ferrari aux Émirats arabes unis, les opportunités de croissance sont clairement là.

---

458 ITALIA
Rival: McLaren
MP4-12C

Sensational.
Einfach nur sensationell.
Sensationnelle.

599 GTO
Rival: Porsche 911
GT2 RS

Go-faster 599.
Noch schneller als der 599.
599 encore plus rapide.

CALIFORNIA
Rival: Merc SL

Less ferocious, still desirable.
Weniger wild, aber dennoch begehrenswert.
Moins féroce, mais toujours désirable.

FF
Rival: Porsche
Panamera Turbo

4x4 hatchback, works well.
Gut laufender 4x4 mit Fließheck.
Break 4x4 qui roule bien.

599
Rival: Lamborghini
V12

Ridiculously fast, yet useable.
Überirdisch schnell, trotzdem fahrbar.
Ridiculement rapide, mais maniable.

FERRARI FF

The FF's long-nosed shooting break profile is striking enough you'll forgive the unprecedented practicality of this Ferrari, with plenty of room for passengers and luggage. Just make sure all are firmly locked in place when you put your foot down.

Die langnasige Shooting Brake-Silhouette des FF ist so attraktiv, dass man getrost über die ungewohnte Zweckmäßigkeit des Maranello-Pferdes (jede Menge Raum für Passagiere und Koffer!) hinwegsehen kann. Aber Achtung: Vorm Losfahren auf jeden Fall überprüfen, dass alle und alles festgeschnallt sind.

Le profil de break de chasse à long nez de la FF est assez frappant pour qu'on puisse lui pardonner son pragmatisme, sans précédent chez Ferrari : elle offre un ample espace à ses passagers et à leurs bagages. Mais vérifiez bien que tout soit solidement attaché et rangé avant d'appuyer sur la pédale.

FF

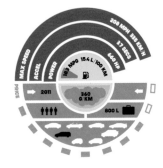

SECRET DETAIL

Unlike the 612 Scaglietti the FF has room for adults in the back, even tall ones.

Im Gegensatz zum 612 Scaglietti hat der FF hinten Platz für Erwachsene, selbst für große.

Contrairement à la 612 Scaglietti, la FF peut accommoder des adultes à l'arrière, même s'ils sont grands.

FERRARI 458 ITALIA

Enzo-fast yet very easy to drive – if you can work out all the steering wheel-mounted buttons that is. The 458 sounds magnificent, goes like hell and looks incredible, it is so sensational you wonder why Ferrari bothers to build anything else.

Schnell wie immer, aber dennoch handhabbar – wenn man mit den ganzen Knöpfen am Steuer zurechtkommt, versteht sich. Der 458 hört sich hammermäßig an, rast wie der Teufel und sieht umwerfend aus. Man fragt sich nur, warum Ferrari überhaupt andere Modelle baut.

Rapide comme la Enzo, mais très facile à conduire – enfin, si vous n'êtes pas déphasé par la multitude de boutons de commande installés sur le volant. La 458 produit un son magnifique, roule à un train d'enfer et en jette un maximum, elle est tellement sensationnelle qu'on se demande pourquoi Ferrari prend la peine de faire d'autres modèles.

458 Italia

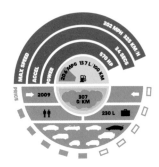

FERRARI WORLD, ABU DHABI

Ferrari-shaped rollercoaster carriages are just some of the attractions available in Abu Dhabi-based Ferrari World, reportedly the biggest (200,000 sq m) indoor amusement park in the world.

Die Achterbahn mit nachempfundenen Ferrari-Wagen ist nur eine der vielen Attraktionen von Ferrari World in Abu Dhabi, dem mit 200.000 Quadratmetern wohl größten Themenpark der Welt.

Les wagons de montagne russe en forme de Ferrari ne sont que l'une des nombreuses attractions que propose Ferrari World à Abu Dhabi. Il s'agirait du plus grand parc d'attractions couvert (200 000 m²) du monde.

FERRARI CALIFORNIA

California

Ferrari describes the California as its 'range-completing' model, a car that attracts new customers and allows its 458 Italia relative to be hardcore. It's a credible line, and the California impresses. A boulevardier with real ability, although its looks divide.

Ferrari selbst beschreibt den California als Modell zur Abrundung der Produktpalette. Mit dem Sportwagen soll Neukunden der Erwerb eines Ferraris schmackhaft gemacht werden, während sich an den 458 nur harte, vermögende Jungs herantrauen. Die Rechnung geht voll auf, müssen wir sagen. Ein echter Ferrari, auch wenn sich über sein Aussehen die Geister scheiden.

Ferrari décrit la California comme le modèle qui parachève sa gamme, une voiture qui attire de nouveaux clients et laisse toute latitude à la 458 Italia pour se déchaîner. C'est une ligne crédible, et la California cause vive impression. Elle parade sur les boulevards avec beaucoup de talent, même si son style divise les avis.

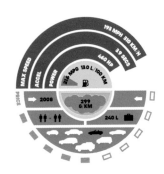

SECRET DETAIL

Renzo Piano's wind tunnel for Ferrari was apparently inspired by the idea of an engine component planted in a field, and like his Pompidou Centre, makes the building's function explicit in its form.

Für den Entwurf des Windkanals für Ferrari ließ sich Renzo Piano von der Idee eines auf einem Kornfeld liegenden Motorteils inspirieren. Wie bei seinem Centre Pompidou wird auch hier die Gebäudefunktion in der Form explizit gemacht.

Apparemment, pour la soufflerie que Renzo Piano a construite pour Ferrari, l'idée de départ était un composant de moteur planté dans un champ. À l'instar du Centre Pompidou, du même architecte, la forme du bâtiment rend sa fonction explicite.

FIAT

FOUNDED: **1899**
HEADQUARTERS: **TURIN, ITALY**
2010 PRODUCTION: **1,471,000**

LOGO HISTORY:

Fiat is an Italian industrial powerhouse. Recently teetering on financial disaster it's had an amazing turn-around – and has even bailed out beleaguered Chrysler in the US. Moves to re-badge vehicles and share platforms are pending, giving Fiat a long-needed US footing. Its cutesy, retro 500 has been a phenomenal success and Fiat's joint ventures in emerging markets – locating production facilities there and producing simple, inexpensive cars – have been astute. It remains a respected small car producer in Europe, but with Alfa Romeo, Lancia, Maserati, Ferrari and now Chrysler's brands within the group it is once again a global automotive force.

Das italienische Kraftpaket Fiat profitiert nach dem finanziellen Desaster der letzten Jahre von dem aktuellen Boom in der Autobranche – und hat sogar den angeschlagenen US-Autobauer Chrysler gerettet. Für Badge Engineering- und Platform Engineering-Projekte hat Fiat nun auch seine lang ersehnte Basis in den USA. Zu den weiteren Erfolgen zählen das niedliche Retromodell des 500, das zu einem phänomenalen Verkaufsschlager wurde, und die Joint Ventures in den Schwellenländern, die einfache und günstige Modelle produzieren. Fiat hat seine Position als kleiner, aber angesehener Autohersteller in Europa behauptet, ist aber mit Alfa Romeo, Lancia, Maserati, Ferrari und jetzt auch Chrysler wieder zu einer globalen Macht geworden.

Fiat est un moteur de l'industrie italienne. Le groupe a récemment frôlé le désastre financier, mais s'est récupéré avec brio, et a même secouru l'américain Chrysler qui était aux abois. Fiat travaille actuellement à des projets consistant à rebadger des véhicules et à partager des plateformes afin de construire sa présence aux États-Unis, une carence de longue date. La 500, mignonne petite voiture rétro, a été un succès phénoménal, et Fiat a formé des partenariats intelligents sur les marchés émergents en trouvant des installations de production locales et en fabriquant des voitures simples et abordables. C'est toujours un petit constructeur respecté en Europe, mais avec l'ajout d'Alfa Romeo, Lancia, Maserati, Ferrari et maintenant Chrysler, le groupe a retrouvé sa position de force mondiale dans le secteur de l'automobile.

500
Rival: Ford Ka

Small, cute, hugely popular.
Klein, süß, unheimlich beliebt.
Petite, mignonne, extrêmement populaire.

PALIO
Rival: GM Corsa

Rugged, simple, world car.
Robustes, schlichtes Weltauto.
Solide et simple, taillée pour l'international.

IDEA
Rival: GM Corsa

Monobox Brazilian.
Überarbeitetes Design, vorerst nur in Brasilien.
Brésilienne monocorps.

PANDA
Rival: Renault Twingo

Small but perfectly formed.
Klein, aber perfekt geformt.
Petite, mais proportions parfaites.

PUNTO | EVO
Rival: Ford Fiesta

Respectable, if ageing supermini.
Anständiger, aber ergrauter Kleinwagen.
Segment B respectable mais vieillissante.

BRAVO
Rival: Ford Focus

Sharply styled family hatchback.
Scharf gestyltes Familien-Auto mit Fließheck.
Compacte familiale au style aiguisé.

SEDICI
Rival: Suzuki SX-4

4x4 hatchback via Suzuki.
4x4 Fließheck, in Kooperation mit Suzuki.
4x4 compact via Suzuki.

QUBO
Rival: Citroen Berlingo

Small van with seats, neatly styled.
Kleiner, ordentlich gestylter Van.
Petit utilitaire bien dessiné.

DOBLO
Rival: Mudskipper

Larger van with seats, not neatly styled.
Etwas größerer, nicht ordentlich gestylter Van.
Utilitaire plus grand mais mal dessiné.

MULTIPLA
Rival: Vauxhall Zafira

Odd 3+3 MPV with clever interior.
Früher ungewöhnlicher, jetzt gewöhnlicher Minivan.
Monospace 3+3 avec un intérieur bien fait.

ULYSSE
Rival: Citroen C8

Bigger MPV, with an additional seat.
Größerer Minivan mit zusätzlichem Sitz.
Monospace plus grand, un siège en plus.

ALSO AVAILABLE

Chroma

166

FIAT 500

Another example of retro done right. The Fiat 500 is a global smash hit, now even starting to conquer the US. The appeal's not hard to deconstruct: a friendly and familiar front face in a world of aggressive automotive sneers, that suits all ages, genders and races, its small package and economical engines are the right for fit cities while customization possibilities and special editions keep it individual.

Noch ein Beispiel eines gelungenen Retrodesigns. Der Fiat 500 ist weltweit ein Blockbuster, der sogar den US-Markt erobert. Die Erfolgsgeschichte lässt sich einfach rekonstruieren: Die freundlich-vertraute Front wird angesichts der ganzen Aggronasen auf dem Markt von Kunden aller Couleur geliebt, die sparsame Motorisierung ist ideal für die Stadt, und schließlich lässt sich der kleine Italiener recht individuell gestalten.

Du rétro bien fait, qui séduit partout, même aux États-Unis. La raison est simple : visage amical et familier au milieu de voitures agressives, elle convient à tous et à toutes les bourses. Son format et son moteur sont parfaits pour la ville, tandis que les nombreuses possibilités de personnalisation préservent son individualité.

500 1.4 16v Sport

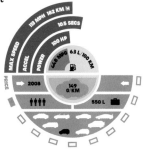

DESIGNER Q+ A

Roberto Giolito
Design director, Fiat

On duty:
Suit: Muji
Shoes: "Estate Agent shoes."
Watch: "My father's (RIP) 1939 custom-made Omega."

Off-duty:
Clothes: "T-shirts stolen from airport shops! And Havaiana flip-flops but not original ones now as I used to lose a lot so I have mismatched colours."

What does your brand stand for?
Past: "State of the art mechanics and anticipating trends."
Present: "Cars that people can afford to drive."
Future: "Total mobility."

FISKER

FOUNDED: **2007**

HEADQUARTERS: **CALIFORNIA, USA**

LOGO HISTORY:

Former Aston Martin design boss Henrik Fisker, with a CV containing the DB9, V8 Vantage as well as the Artega GT and BMW Z8 set up his namesake Automotive venture after dabbling first with Fisker Coachbuild. Unlike his Coachbuild creations Fisker Automotive doesn't use existing vehicles as its basis, indeed it's using groundbreaking technology to produce an electric vehicle with a gasoline engine range extender. It's named Karma, runs on battery power alone in Stealth mode, while its engine-assisted performance is dubbed Sport. In the latter the sensational-looking Karma can reach 62mph in just 5.9 seconds. Outsourced production should keep costs reasonable with models you can actually buy expected this year. Huge government support courtesy of the stimulus may have given Fisker the funds to test its hypothesis, but sales will determine the results of this exciting experiment.

Der Unternehmensgründer Henrik Fisker ist ehemaliger Designchef von Aston Martin und zeichnet unter anderem für den DB9, den V8 Vantage sowie den Artega GT und den BMW Z8 verantwortlich. Außerdem gründete er Fisker Coachbuild, das mittlerweile Teil vom Joint Venture Fisker Automotive ist. Anders als bei den Coachbuild-Kreationen verwendet Fisker Automotive keine bereits vorhandenen Modelle als Grundlage. Stattdessen wurde unter Einsatz innovativer Technologien eine Luxuslimousine mit Elektroantrieb und Range Extender entwickelt. Der Karma fährt im Sparmodus mit Batterie, während beim sogenannten Sportmodus der Motor anspringt. In letzterem erreicht der sensationell gut aussehende Flitzer 100 km/h in nur 5,9 Sekunden. Das Outsourcing-Modell soll noch 2011 zu einem vernünftigen Preis auf den Markt kommen. Mit finanzieller Unterstützung der US-Regierung konnte Fisker seinen Hybrid-Sportwagen zwar entwickeln, doch schließlich werden die Verkaufszahlen zeigen, ob das Experiment geglückt ist.

L'ancien chef du design d'Aston Martin, Henrik Fisker, dont le CV contient la DB9, la V8 Vantage ainsi que l'Artega GT et la BMW Z8, a créé son projet homonyme Fisker Automotive après avoir expérimenté avec Fisker Coachbuild. Contrairement aux créations de Coachbuild, Fisker Automotive ne se base pas sur des véhicules existants, et utilise d'ailleurs une technologie révolutionnaire pour produire un véhicule électrique dont les batteries pourront être relayées par un moteur à essence. Ce modèle baptisé Karma fonctionne uniquement sur batterie en mode « Stealth » (« furtif »), et le moteur à essence vient à la rescousse pour booster sa performance en mode « Sport ». La superbe Karma peut alors atteindre les 100 km/h en seulement 5,9 secondes. La sous-traitance de la production devrait assurer un prix raisonnable, et la mise sur le marché est prévue pour cette année. Les considérables aides gouvernementales reçues grâce au plan de relance ont peut-être donné à Fisker les moyens de tester son hypothèse, mais ce sont les ventes qui détermineront le résultat de cette expérience électrisante.

KARMA

Rival: Tesla Model S

Beautiful conscience-salving sedan.
Wunderschöne Sportlimousine für ein gutes Umweltgewissen.
Superbe berline sportive qui soulage les consciences.

FISKER KARMA

Former Aston Martin design boss' self-titled sports sedan blends land shark visuals with plug-in hybrid power. Choose fully-electric 'Stealth' mode for zero-emissions cruising or hit 'Sport' to feel the full-fat power. The next Hollywood must-have.

Das vom ehemaligen Aston Martin-Designchef als Sportlimousine bezeichnete Modell vereint das Aussehen eines Landhais mit Plug-in-Hybrid-Power. Wählen Sie die vollelektrische Version, um emissionsfrei zu fahren, oder die sportliche, wenn Sie die gewaltige Kraft des Hybriden spüren möchten. In Hollywood prügeln sich schon die Stars um ein Exemplar.

Cette berline qui porte le nom de l'ancien chef du design d'Aston Martin allie des airs de requin de terre et une motorisation hybride. Choisissez le mode « furtif » entièrement électrique pour rouler sans polluer, ou basculez en mode « sportif » pour sentir une puissance 100 % non allégée. C'est le prochain modèle que tout le monde voudra avoir à Hollywood.

Karma

Fisker founder Henrik Fisker

SECRET DETAIL

'Sunken Wood' interior trim is dredged from the depths of Lake Michigan, negating the need to fell or chemically patinate trees.

Das vom Grund des Lake Michigan geborgene Sunken Wood beweist, dass zur Verschönerung eines Luxuswagens keine Bäume gefällt werden müssen.

L'habillage intérieur « Sunken Wood » est fait en bois récupéré des profondeurs du lac Michigan, ce qui évite d'abattre des arbres ou de patiner le bois chimiquement.

FORD

(USA)

FOUNDED: **1903**
HEADQUARTERS: **DEARBORN, USA**
2010 PRODUCTION: **5,134,009**

LOGO HISTORY:

One of the US 'big three' carmakers, the Ford Group rode the recent financial turmoil better than most. It has offloaded many brands to do so – Land Rover, Jaguar, Aston Martin, Volvo and most of its interest in Mazda – but remains a huge worldwide firm. Its strength is in its product – Ford models typically define their mainstream segments – with US icons like the Mustang muscle car and F-150 pick-up and in Europe, the Fiesta, Mondeo and Focus family cars. While the company arguably sold its silver at the nadir of the market, and gave rivals in emerging markets a head start that may come back to haunt Ford, its focus on what the blue oval means and does has assured its future at a time when nothing could be taken for granted. Supported by interesting MPVs, SUVs and hybrids, GM's range pales in comparison. The only thing we miss is its design experiments, which once, going back to Marc Newson's 021C, offered the industry's strongest connection to contemporary culture. Where has that ambition gone?

Als einer von Amerikas „Big Three" hat die Ford Group die letzte Finanzkrise erstaunlich gut verkraftet. Zwar hat sie einige Marken wie Land Rover, Jaguar, Aston Martin, Volvo und den Großteil von Mazda abgestoßen, bleibt aber eine der größten Autoersteller der Welt. Die Stärke liegt im Produkt: In seiner Klasse sticht Ford stets hervor, ähnlich wie BMW im Premiumsektor. Absolute Spitze in allen Bereichen, ohne sich als Luxus- oder Sportwagen hervorzutun. Legendär sind in den USA das Mustang Muscle Car und der F-150 Pick-up, in Europa sind Fiesta, Mondeo und Focus bekannt. Obwohl man das Tafelsilber in der Krise verkauft und somit der Konkurrenz in den Schwellenländern einen Vorsprung ermöglicht hat, können wir uns weiterhin auf das blaue Oval verlassen. Gegenüber den spannenden Minivans, attraktiven SUVs, zuverlässigen Kleinwagen und einer wachsenden Zahl an Hybridautos scheint GM zu verblassen, und Chrysler kann Ford sowieso nicht das Wasser reichen. Wir vermissen jedoch die Designexperimente, die wie z. B. der 021c von Marc Newson bewiesen, dass man den Finger am Puls der Zeit hatte.

Le groupe Ford est l'un des trois plus grands constructeurs automobiles américains. Il a dû se débarrasser de beaucoup de ses marques pour surmonter la crise financière (Land Rover, Jaguar, Aston Martin, Volvo et la majorité de ses actions Mazda), mais reste une multinationale colossale. Ses produits sont sa force : les modèles Ford sont en général une référence dans leurs catégories, sans prétendre au tralala des voitures de luxe. Aux États-Unis, ses grands succès sont la Mustang pour les muscle cars et le F-150 pour les pick-ups, et en Europe ce sont la Fiesta, la Mondeo et la Focus. Le groupe a vendu ses actifs lorsque le marché était au plus bas, et a ainsi ouvert la porte à ses concurrents des marchés émergents, mais le fait de s'être recentré sur les valeurs de la marque a assuré son avenir. La gamme de GM est éclipsée par les monospaces irrésistibles de Ford, ses SUV séduisants et ses citadines bien pensées, ainsi que par son nombre croissant d'options hybrides. La seule chose qui nous manque chez Ford, ce sont ses expériences sur le design, qui, à l'époque de la 021C de Marc Newson, représentaient le lien le plus solide entre l'industrie automobile et la culture contemporaine. Où est passée cette ambition créatrice ?

FIESTA
Rival: VW Polo

Brilliant supermini, fun, capable.
Brillant, klein, mit Spaßfaktor.
Excellente sous-compacte fun et douée.

FOCUS
Rival: VW Golf

The hatchback benchmark.
Gut verkauftes Fließheck.
La référence de la compacte.

MONDEO
Rival: Vauxhall
Insignia

Fine family car, lacks prestige.
Gediegenes Familienauto, fehlendes Prestige.
Bonne familiale, mais manque de prestige.

C-MAX | GRAND
Rival: Renault Scenic

Compact MPV in two sizes.
Kompakter Minivan in 2 Größen.
Monospace compact en deux tailles.

S-MAX | GALAXY
Rival: VW Sharan

Larger 7st MPV in two styles.
Größer Minivan, 7 Sitze, 2 Varianten.
Grand monospace 7 places en deux styles.

EDGE
Rival: Nissan Murano

Decent mid-size US crossover.
Ordentlicher mittelgroßer SUV für die USA.
Honnête crossover américain.

MUSTANG
Rival: Chevy Camaro

Iconic muscle car with retro looks.
Legendäres Muscle Car im Retro-Look.
Muscle car légendaire au look rétro.

FLEX
Rival: Chevy Traverse

Big cool 6-seat box, useful inside.
Groß, cool, 6 Sitze, praktisches Innenleben.
Cube stylé à 6 places, intérieur pratique.

F-150
Rival: Chevy Silverado

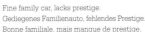

Huge-selling multi-variant pick-up.
Erfolgreicher Pick-up, zahlreiche Varianten.
Pick-up en multiples versions, gros succès.

ALSO AVAILABLE

Ka, Kuga, Escape, Explorer, Fusion, Taurus.

FORD FLEX

Limited EcoFlex

Mid-Century Modern crossover mixes supersized Mini Clubman profile with SUV size. If Mad Men's Don Draper drove a minivan it would be a Flex. There's enough room to accommodate his clients, kids and mistresses and fit his Eames desk in the trunk.

Der Lifestyle-Laster aus den USA hat das Profil eines Mini Clubman und die Größe eines SUV. Würde Don Draper, die Hauptfigur der Serie *Mad Men*, einen Minivan fahren, dann wäre er ein Flex. Darin könnte er seine Kunden, seine Kinder, seine Geliebten und sogar seinen Eames-Schreibtisch verstauen.

Ce crossover de milieu de siècle moderne plaque le profil d'une Mini Clubman sur un format de SUV. Si le Don Draper de *Mad Men* conduisait un monospace, ce serait un Flex. Il y a assez de place pour accueillir ses clients, ses enfants et ses maîtresses, et il peut même faire tenir son bureau Eames dans le coffre.

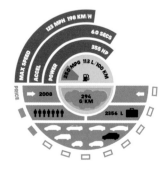

SECRET DETAIL

Horizontal body grooves evoke woody wagon panelling without resorting to felling giant oaks or fake veneer. Aftermarket kits are available if you must. But we prefer the original concept (right).

Im Innenraum sieht das Holzimitat täuschend echt aus – gut, dass keine Eichen dran glauben mussten. Ersatzteile sind bei Bedarf ausreichend vorhanden.

Les rainures horizontales le long de la caisse évoquent les panneaux de bois des breaks, sans recourir à l'abattage de grands chênes ou à un faux placage. Des kits sont disponibles si vous ne pouvez pas vous retenir.

GEELY

CN

FOUNDED: **1986**

HEADQUARTERS: **HANGZHOU, CHINA**

2010 PRODUCTION: **415,286**

LOGO HISTORY:

Despite only being approved by the state to produce cars in 2001, Geely is already firmly established in China's Top 10 automakers. Founded as a humble refrigerator manufacturer with borrowed family money in 1986, the Zhejiang Geely Holding Group bought legendary Swedish marque Volvo from Ford in 2010. Like other Chinese manufacturers Geely has been accused of taking some rather unsportsmanlike shortcuts to vehicle development by replicating others' products – it's impossible not to see strong hints of the Toyota Aygo in the LC city car for instance. But the model, also known as the Panda in its home market, has a different and appealing front face. Also like the others it's now able to stand on its own two feet. Let's see where it decides go.

Obwohl der Autobauer erst im Jahr 2001 die offizielle Lizenz erhielt, hat sich Geely in den Top 10 der chinesischen Automarken bereits etabliert. Die im Jahr 1986 mit von der Familie geliehenem Geld gegründete Firma stellte zunächst Kühlschränke her. 2010 kaufte die Zhejiang Geely Holding Group dem US-Riesen Ford die legendäre schwedische Marke Volvo ab. Wie auch andere chinesische Autohersteller wurde Geely bereits des Plagiats bezichtigt – und Hand aufs Herz: Die Ähnlichkeit des Kleinstwagens LC mit dem Toyota Aygo ist nun mal unbestreitbar. Doch genau wie die Branchenkollegen ist auch Geely fähig, auf eigenen Füßen zu stehen. Mal sehen, wo die Reise hingeht …

Bien que le gouvernement ne l'ait autorisé à produire des voitures qu'en 2001, Geely tient déjà une place solide parmi les dix premiers constructeurs automobiles de Chine. Humble fabricant de réfrigérateurs créé en 1986 avec de l'argent emprunté en famille, le groupe Zhejiang Geely a acheté à Ford la légendaire marque suédoise Volvo en 2010. À l'instar d'autres fabricants chinois, Geely a été accusé de prendre des raccourcis quelque peu déloyaux dans ses activités de développement et de copier d'autres produits – impossible de ne pas reconnaître certains traits caractéristiques de la Toyota Aygo dans sa citadine LC, par exemple. Mais, tout comme ses semblables, Geely est maintenant capable de voler de ses propres ailes. Voyons où la marque décidera d'aller.

FC
Rival: Chery Elara

Convincingly competent sedan.
Überzeugende Limousine.
Berline convaincante.

MK
Rival: Chery Fulwin2

Sharp-edged compact.
Scharfkantiger Kompaktwagen.
Compacte anguleuse.

CK
Rival: Chevrolet Spark

Below-par subcompact.
Unterdurchschnittlicher Kompaktwagen.
Sous-compacte décevante.

LC
Rival: Toyota Aygo

Strong whiff of Toyota Aygo.
Sieht aus wie der Toyota Aygo.
Un air de Toyota Aygo frappant.

MK2
Rival: Chery A1

Practical, high-riding hatch.
Praktisch, hochgelegt, mit Fließheck.
Compacte surélevée pratique.

GE
Rival: Audi A8

Rolls-Royce 'inspired' limo.
Von Rolls-Royce „inspirierte" Limousine.
Limousine « inspirée » par Rolls-Royce.

Geely LC/Panda

GINETTA

LOGO HISTORY:

Long established and well-respected builder of clubman racecars for use on road and track, Ginetta hasn't strayed far from its proven formula. That is to produce light, fast and simple cars that are enjoyable to drive and inexpensive to buy and run. Ginetta single-manufacturer championships provide a stepping-stone for many drivers in motorsport, with the G40 and G50/55 highly successful racing cars. The G40R is its biggest seller thanks to its relative low cost to performance ratio, though Ginetta also builds the F400, a 410hp mid-engined car that once wore a Farbio badge - now re-born as Arash.

Der alteingesessene und hoch angesehene Hersteller exklusiver Rennautos für Straße und Rennstrecke bleibt seiner Linie seit jeher treu. Die besteht darin, leichte, schnelle und schlichte Autos zu produzieren, die sich gut fahren lassen und erschwinglich in Kaufpreis und Unterhalt sind. Der Ginetta GT Supercup, auf dem ausschließlich identische Ginetta-Modelle ins Rennen gehen, stellt für viele Fahrer ein Trittbrett in den Motorsport dar – z. B. mit den höchst erfolgreichen Rennautos G40 oder G50/55. Der G40R verkauft sich wegen des guten Preis-Leistungs-Verhältnisses am besten. Von Ginetta stammt außerdem der F400 mit knapp 416 PS, der einmal Farbio GTS hieß und nun als Arash wiedergeboren wurde.

Constructeur de voitures de course clubman pour le circuit et la route établi et respecté de longue date, Ginetta ne s'est jamais beaucoup éloigné de sa formule gagnante. La marque produit des voitures légères, rapides et simples qui sont agréables à conduire et ne coûtent pas trop cher à l'achat et à l'usage. Les championnats de voitures Ginetta fournissent un tremplin à de nombreux coureurs automobiles ; la G40 et la G50/55 sont d'excellentes voitures de course. La G40R est le modèle qui se vent le mieux grâce à son prix relativement bas par rapport à sa performance, mais Ginetta construit également la F400, dotée d'un moteur de 410 chevaux en position centrale, et qui a porté un badge Farbio – aujourd'hui Arash.

G40 R
Rival: Lotus Exige

Simple, fun, fast and affordable.
Schlicht, schnell, günstig und mit viel Fahrspaß.
Simple, fun, rapide et abordable.

F400
Rival: Audi R8 V10

Ginetta's supercar.
Ginettas Supersportler.
La supercar de Ginetta.

GMC

FOUNDED: **1901**
HEADQUARTERS: **DETROIT, USA**
2010 PRODUCTION: **446,547**

LOGO HISTORY:

Another massive US nameplate, GMC sold almost half a million vehicles in 2010 and was, as recently as 2007, parent company GM's second-biggest selling division. Still a solid 5th in GM's rankings it got its name – General Motors Company – after GM merged two acquisitions from 1909 – the Rapid Motor Vehicle Company and Reliance Motor Car Company. GMC has always specialized in commercial vehicles, making military trucks, Greyhound buses and even a classic motorhome between 1973-78. It gains inclusion in this car book due to its current SUV and pick-up range that may expand if the recent promising compact 2010 Granite concept is developed. We hope it will be.

Als US-amerikanische Traditionsmarke verkaufte GMC im Jahr 2010 fast eine halbe Million Fahrzeuge – und 2007 war der Autohersteller der zweitstärkste Geschäftsbereich des Mutterunternehmens GM. Seinen Namen – General Motors Company – erhielt das derzeit fünftstärkste GM-Unternehmen, als GM im Jahr 1909 zwei neu erworbene Firmen vereinte: die Rapid Motor Vehicle Company und die Reliance Motor Car Company. GMC hat sich von Anfang an auf Nutzfahrzeuge spezialisiert, darunter Militär-Trucks, Greyhound-Busse und zwischen 1973 und 1978 sogar ein klassisches Wohnmobil. In dieses Buch aufgenommen wurde der Autohersteller aufgrund seines aktuellen SUV- und Pick-up-Sortiments. Dieses wird vielleicht sogar noch erweitert, wenn der vielversprechende Granite Concept aus dem Jahr 2010 in Serie geht. Wir hoffen darauf!

Voici un autre grand nom américain de l'automobile. GMC a vendu presque un demi-million de véhicules en 2010 et, en 2007, c'était la deuxième division de sa maison-mère GM en termes de ventes. Elle occupe aujourd'hui une bonne cinquième place. GMC (General Motors Company) tient son nom de la fusion de deux entreprises que GM a acquises en 1909 (Rapid Motor Vehicle Company et Reliance Motor Car Company). GMC a toujours été spécialisée dans les véhicules commerciaux : camions militaires, bus Greyhound et même un grand classique du camping-car entre 1973 et 1978. Si elle figure dans ce livre, c'est à cause de sa gamme actuelle de SUV et de pick-ups, qui pourrait s'élargir si le récent concept de 2010, la compacte Granite, est développé. Nous l'espérons.

TERRAIN
Rival: Chevy Equinox

Mid-size (in US terms) 5-st crossover.
SUV mit 5 Sitzen, in den USA Mitteklasse.
Crossover 5 places de taille moyenne.

ARCADIA
Rival: Chevy Traverse

Car-like but big 8-seat crossover.
Pkw-ähnlicher, aber riesiger SUV, 8 Sitze.
Crossover 8 places qui mélange les genres.

YUKON
Rival: Chevy Tahoe

Truck-like big SUV. Go Denali for posh.
Lkw-ähnlicher SUV, absolute Oberklasse.
Gros SUV. Version Denali pour faire chic.

CANYON
Rival: Chevy Colorado

Mid-size (in US terms) pick-up.
Pick-up, in den USA Mitteklasse.
Pick-up de taille moyenne.

SIERRA
Rival: Chevy Silverado

Full-size (i.e. massive) pick-up.
Ausgewachsener (d. h. riesiger) Pick-up.
Grand (c'est-à-dire énorme) pick-up.

GREAT WALL

FOUNDED: **1976**

HEADQUARTERS: **HEBEI, CHINA**

2010 PRODUCTION: **397,300**

LOGO HISTORY:

China's first public auto company since floating on the Hong Kong stock exchange in 2003 is appropriately named after the nation's Wonder of the World. However its products are unlikely to be added to that canon any time soon. Great Wall has gained an unenviable reputation for copying other manufacturers' designs, most notably its Peri city car, which Fiat attempted to prove was a facsimile of its Panda. However with ten new, hopefully original, models planned in the near future and an enviable history of exporting, being the first Chinese manufacturer to do so to the EU, it's one to watch.

Die nach einem der Sieben Weltwunder benannte Firma machte ihrem Namen alle Ehre und ging 2003 als erster Autohersteller Chinas an die Börse. Ihre Modelle jedoch sind einer solchen Würdigung derzeit noch nicht wert: Great Wall hat einen wenig beneidenswerten Ruf als Plagiator. Eine dieser Kopien ist der Kleinwagen Peri, dem Fiat eindeutig nachwies, ein Plagiat zu sein. Mit den zehn geplanten neuen (hoffentlich Original-)Modellen und einer brillanten Exportrate ist Great Wall der erste chinesischen Autohersteller, der in die EU exportiert – wir dürfen gespannt sein, wie es weitergeht!

C'est la première entreprise automobile publique de Chine depuis son entrée à la bourse de Hong Kong en 2003, et elle tient son nom de la Merveille du monde nationale. Ses voitures ne sont malheureusement pas des merveilles en termes de qualité, et rien ne permet de prévoir une amélioration prochaine. Great Wall s'est forgé la réputation peu enviable de copier les modèles des autres constructeurs, notamment pour sa citadine Peri. Fiat a tenté de prouver qu'il s'agissait d'un plagiat de la Panda. Mais Great Wall prévoit de lancer prochainement dix nouveaux modèles, que l'on espère originaux. Si l'on ajoute à cela le fait que Great Wall est le premier constructeur chinois à avoir exporté vers l'Europe, il semble que cette marque soit une concurrente sérieuse.

VOLEEX C10
Rival: Geely MK

Toyota Yaris clone, hideous grille.
Toyota Yaris-Klon, hässlicher Kühlergrill.
Une Toyota Yaris à calandre horrifique.

COOLBEAR
Rival: Nissan Cube

Scion xB-alike box.
Sieht aus wie der Scion xB.
Sosie de la Scion xB.

COWRY
Rival: Chery Estar Cross

Seven-seat minivan.
Minivan mit 7 Sitzen.
Monovolume à 7 places.

HAVAL M1
Rival: Chery X1

Fiat Panda 4x4.
Fiat Panda-Kopie, 4x4.
Alias Fiat Panda 4x4.

HAVAL H5
Rival: Chery X5

China's second-favourite SUV.
Der zweitbeliebteste SUV von China.
Le deuxième SUV préféré des Chinois.

WINGLE
Rival: Gonow Alter

Comedically-named pick up.
Pick up mit komischem Namen.
Pick-up au nom comique.

GUMPERT

(D)
FOUNDED: **2004**
HEADQUARTERS: **ALTENBURG, GERMANY**

LOGO HISTORY:

Form very much follows function with Gumpert's first car, the Apollo. It's insanely quick but many feel this pricey car has looks only a mother could love. Founded by Roland Gumpert the Apollo uses an Audi-sourced 650hp 4.2-liter twin-turbo V8 and the car is said to produce so much downforce it could drive on a tunnel roof at speed, though nobody's ever tried… The Apollo remains, and there's also a 'two-seater fast tourer' due soon, dubbed Tornante with styling taken care of by Touring Superleggera.

Bei dem ersten Gumpert-Modell Apollo steht die Funktion eindeutig an erster Stelle: Nach der Meinung zahlreicher Autoliebhaber hat der überirdisch schnelle und preisgünstige Flitzer ein Gesicht, das nur eine Mutter lieben kann. Der von Roland Gumpert entwickelte Apollo basiert auf einem 4,2-Liter-V8-Motor von Audi. Es wird gemunkelt, dass er so viel Abrieb erzeugt, dass er problemlos auch an der Decke fahren kann – aber niemand hat es bisher versucht … Der Apollo ist bald auch als zweisitziger, von Touring Superleggera gestalteter Fast Tourer unter dem Namen Tornante erhältlich.

Pour la première voiture de Gumpert, l'Apollo, la forme suit la fonction de très près. Elle est follement rapide, mais nombreux sont ceux qui pensent que cette voiture hors de prix est un vilain petit canard. Créée par Roland Gumpert, l'Apollo est dotée d'un moteur Audi V8 bi-turbo 4,2 litres de 650 chevaux, et il paraît que cette machine génère une déportance telle qu'à sa vitesse maximum elle pourrait rouler sur le plafond d'un tunnel, mais personne n'a jamais essayé… Une version « tourisme de vitesse à deux places » est prévue pour bientôt, baptisée Tornante et dessinée par Touring Superleggera.

APOLLO SPORT

Rival: SSC Ultimate Aero

Crazy pace, awful face.
Verrückte Geschwindigkeit, hässliche Formen.
Vitesse insensée, esthétique erronée.

HINDUSTAN

FOUNDED: **1942**

HEADQUARTERS: **WEST BENGAL, INDIA**

LOGO HISTORY:

Although it builds various Mitsubishis under license, it's Hindustan Motors' own car, the Ambassador that has become an Indian national icon. The fact its design dates back to the 1946 British Morris Oxford only adds to its post-colonial charm. Known as "the king of Indian roads", the Ambassador has been in constant production since 1957, with continual modification throughout its life by the factory and – more importantly – its owners. Taxis, flower-laden wedding cars, stretched limo-style people carriers, Presidential state cars – the venerable old Amby has truly mobilised a nation and will no doubt continue to do so for many more years.

Hindustan Motors produziert zwar mehrere Mitsubishi-Lizenzbauten, das eigene Modell Hindustan Ambassador jedoch ist in Indien zu einem nationalen Wahrzeichen geworden. Der koloniale Charme des Autos wird durch die Tatsache, dass das Modell auf den britischen Morris Oxford von 1946 zurückgeht, noch verstärkt. Der seit 1957 produzierte „King of Indian Roads" wurde seither vom Hersteller nur leicht modifiziert. Meist sind es jedoch die Besitzer selbst, die den Wagen nach ihrem eigenen Geschmack umgestalten: Egal ob als Taxi, blumengeschmückter Hochzeitswagen, Stretch-Limousine oder Präsidentenauto – der altehrwürdige Amby hat eine ganze Nation im wahrsten Sinne des Wortes mobilisiert und wird dies zweifellos in den nächsten Jahren weiterhin tun.

Hindustan Motors construit plusieurs modèles de Mitsubishi sous licence, mais c'est sa propre voiture, l'Ambassador, qui est devenue un emblème national de l'Inde. Le fait qu'elle soit basée sur la Morris Oxford britannique de 1946 ne fait qu'ajouter à son charme postcolonial. Baptisée « reine des routes indiennes », l'Ambassador n'a jamais cessé d'être produite depuis 1957, avec cependant de continuelles modifications du constructeur et, surtout, de ses propriétaires. Taxis, voitures de mariage chargées de fleurs, véhicules de transport public allongés comme des limousines, voitures présidentielles… la vénérable « Amby » a vraiment mobilisé une nation tout entière, et continuera certainement pendant de nombreuses années.

AMBASSADOR

Rival: Over-laden scooter

Relic of 1946 Britain still looks good.
Das britische Relikt aus dem Jahr 1946 sieht immer noch gut aus.
Relique de la Grande-Bretagne de 1946, encore très en forme.

HOLDEN

FOUNDED: **1856**

HEADQUARTERS: **PORT MELBOURNE, AUSTRALIA**

2010 PRODUCTION: **140,771**

LOGO HISTORY:

Antipodean arm of GM, best known for its muscle-bound, no bullshit, V8 sedans. Titanic battles with archrival Ford on the race track – most famously in the Bathurst 1000 – have split a nation's allegiance for generations. Those wanting a slice of the Mount Panorama circuit on the school run look no further than a Commodore by HSV (Holden Special Vehicles) which also offers a tweaked version of that most Australian of rides, the ute (short for 'utility' and usually involving a pick-up's open load bay). The lower end of the range consists of small, badge-engineered Chevrolets (née Daewoo) to satisfy demand for small, fuel-efficient transport.

Der Antipode von GM ist vor allem für seine muskelbepackten V8-Limousinen bekannt. Die legendären Schlachten beim Langstreckenrennen Bathurst 1000 mit dem Erzrivalen Ford haben die Nation über Generationen hinweg in zwei Lager gespalten. Diejenigen, die bei ihren alltäglichen Erledigungen einen Hauch vom Mount Panorama Circuit genießen möchten, sind mit einem Commodore von HSV (Holden Special Vehicles) gut bedient. Der Holden Ute (kurz für "Utility") ist die Pick-up-Nachfolgeversion des Commodore Utiliy. Die australische GM-Tochter bietet aber auch im unteren Preissegment mit kleinen Chevrolets (ehemals Daewoo) unter eigenem Namen wendige und sparsame Wagen an.

Filiale antipodale de GM, surtout connue pour ses berlines V8 musclées et sans chichis. Ses combats titanesques sur les circuits australiens (et surtout sur le Bathurst 1000) avec son ennemi juré Ford ont divisé tout le pays pendant des générations. Ceux qui veulent s'imaginer sur le circuit de Mount Panorama lorsqu'ils déposent leurs enfants à l'école n'ont pas à chercher plus loin que la Commodore HSV (Holden Special Vehicles), qui est aussi disponible dans une version modifiée d'une carrosserie typiquement australienne, la « ute » (pour « utility », généralement dotée d'une plateforme ouverte à l'arrière). À l'autre extrême de la gamme, on trouve de petites Chevrolets rebadgées (nées Daewoo) pour répondre à la demande en petits véhicules économes en carburant.

BARINA SPARK
Rival: Suzuki Alto

Quirky, upright city car.
Origineller, hochkantiger Kleinwagen.
Citadine verticale et pleine de personnalité.

BARINA
Rival: Mazda2

Below-par supermini, lacking finesse.
Minderwertiger Kleinwagen ohne Finesse.
Sous-compacte décevante, sans finesse.

CRUZE
Rival: Ford Focus

Decent global small sedan.
Anständige kleine Limousine.
Petite berline globale honnête.

EPICA
Rival: Toyota Camry

Bland, dependable family sedan.
Fade, aber zuverlässige Familienlimousine.
Berline familiale fiable et insipide.

COMMODORE
Rival: Ford Falcon

Family car by week, weekend racer.
Familienauto, das auch sportlich sein kann.
Famille la semaine, course le week-end.

SPORTWAGON
Rival: Ford FPV F6X

Chiselled estate version of the above.
Kantige Kombiversion des obigen Modells.
Version break effilée de la Commodore.

CAPTIVA
Rival: Nissan X-Trail

Efficient 5 and 7 seat SUV.
Effizienter SUV, als 5- und 7-Sitzer erhältlich.
Captiva – SUV efficace à 5 et 7 places.

UTE
Rival: Ford Falcon Ute

V8-powered backbone of Australia.
Starker Australier mit V8-Motor.
Épine dorsale de l'Australie, marche au V8.

HONDA

FOUNDED: **1948**
HEADQUARTERS: **TOKYO, JAPAN**
2010 PRODUCTION: **3,643,000**

LOGO HISTORY:

Founded by self-taught engineer, Soichiro Honda, Japan's second-biggest car manufacturer – and the world's largest producer of internal combustion engines – is built around its reputation for mechanical excellence and technical innovation. From pizza-delivery mopeds, through to the super-efficient HondaJet business plane, via the bread-and-butter Accord sedan, Honda has all bases covered. Its sporadic global design language spans thoroughly mundane to stargazing avant-garde. Going forward, its strategy includes a dedication to future mobility solutions, hybrid powertrains and the world's first Hydrogen-powered production car. All of which should ensure this idiosyncratic, fiercely independent global player remains so for the foreseeable future.

Der gute Ruf des zweitgrößten japanischen Autoherstellers basiert auf dessen mechanischer Exzellenz sowie auf technischer Innovation. Der größte Motorenhersteller der Welt wurde von dem Autodidakten Soichiro Honda gegründet. Honda deckt vom Pizzaservice-Moped über die Alltagslimousine Accord bis hin zum supereffizienten Geschäftsreiseflugzeug HondaJet eine Vielzahl von Segmenten ab, wobei die globale Designsprache von Zweckmäßigkeit bis Avantgardismus reicht. Die Strategie des Autoherstellers aus Ostasien umfasst zukunftsorientierte Mobilitätslösungen, Hybridantriebe sowie den weltweit ersten wasserstoffbetriebenen Serienwagen. Der eigenwillige Weltkonzern wird voraussichtlich auch in Zukunft seine hart verteidigte Unabhängigkeit behalten können.

Fondé par Soichiro Honda, un ingénieur autodidacte, le deuxième constructeur de voitures du Japon (et le plus grand fabricant de moteurs à combustion interne du monde) est bâti autour de sa réputation d'excellence mécanique et d'innovation technique. Depuis les mobylettes de livreur de pizza jusqu'au jet d'affaire HondaJet super-performant, en passant par l'Accord, grand classique des berlines, Honda touche à tout. Son langage visuel international et polymorphe englobe le pragmatisme le plus complet et l'avant-gardisme le plus visionnaire. Sa stratégie de développement comprend l'exploration des solutions d'avenir dans le transport et des groupes motopropulseurs hybrides, et la toute première voiture grand public propulsée à l'hydrogène. Tout cela devrait garantir à Honda sa place d'acteur mondial singulier et férocement indépendant pour un bout de temps.

FIT/JAZZ
Rival: Ford Fiesta

Ingeniously packaged spacious supermini.
Kompaktes Fließheck, Limousine und Kombi.
Sous-compacte spacieuse et habile.

CR-Z
Rival: Kia Forte Koup

Self-proclaimed 'world's-first hybrid sports car'.
„Erster Hybrid-Sportwagen der Welt".
« Première sportive hybride au monde ».

CIVIC
Rival: Ford Focus

Futuristic Euro spec, US spec for college kids.
Für europäische Verhältnisse futuristisch.
Futuriste dans sa version européenne.

INSIGHT
Rival: Toyota Pruis

Cheaper, simpler Prius clone, lacks sparkle.
Günstiger, glanzloser Prius-Klon.
Prius en moins cher et en plus simple.

FCX CLARITY
Rival: Silver bullet

Truly ground-breaking hydrogen fuel-cell.
Wasserstoffbetriebenes Brennstoffzellenauto.
Pile à hydrogène révolutionnaire.

ODYSSEY
Rival: Toyota Sienna

Minivan with lightening-bolt belt line.
Minivan mit blitzförmiger Gürtellinie.
Monovolume avec ceinture « éclair ».

ACCORD
Rival: Opel Insignia

Epitomizes smart, understated motoring.
Schicke, unauffällige Mittelklasse.
L'essence de l'élégance et de la sobriété.

CR-V
Rival: Nissan Qashqai

Car-like pseudo-SUV lacking versatility.
Wenig vielseitiger Pseudo-SUV.
Pseudo-SUV qui manque de polyvalence.

RIDGELINE
Rival: Dodge Dakota

Unibody midsize pick-up majors on refinement.
Mittelklasse-Pick-up, hoher Fahrkomfort.
Pick-up monocoque raffiné.

PILOT
Rival: Chevrolet Traverse

Boxy SUV ideal for hauling families in comfort.
Kastiger SUV, ideal für die ganze Familie.
SUV carré idéal pour transporter la famille.

ALSO AVAILABLE

Li Nian S1, StepWGN, Element, Life, Zest, Elysion, Freed, Legend, City, Vamios, Stream, Crosstour.

SADLY NOT AVAILABLE

S2000, NSX.

HONDA CR-Z HYBRID

CR-Z Hybrid

The production model may have lost some of its concept's design purity, but with sharp steering and a six-speed manual gearbox – a first for a hybrid – the CR-Z is the best small hybrid available to look at, drive and is good value. It's also weird enough that it's sure to become an under the radar classic long after the technology goes obsolete.

Das Serienmodell hat in Sachen Design zwar seine Reinheit eingebüßt, mit einem schnittigen Lenkrad und einem Sechsgang-Schaltgetriebe – das erste bei einem Hybrid – ist der CR-Z jedoch hinsichtlich Aussehen, Antrieb und Preis-Leistungs-Verhältnis der beste kleine Hybrid auf dem Markt. Verrückterweise ist jetzt schon sicher, dass er nach dem Zeitalter der Hybridtechnik ein stiller Klassiker wird.

Le modèle de production a peut-être perdu un peu de la pureté du concept d'origine, mais avec sa direction affutée et ses six vitesses (une première pour une hybride), la CR-Z est la petite hybride la plus jolie et la plus agréable à conduire du marché, et elle offre un bon rapport qualité-prix. Elle est également suffisamment étrange pour devenir un classique discret bien longtemps après que la technologie soit devenue obsolète.

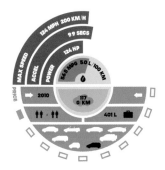

SECRET DETAIL

The US market only gets two seats plus an odd fold-down section and small compartment where the Euro and Japanese 'plus-two' rear seats go. That's a shame, because those rear seats can be useful.

Das Modell für den US-Markt hat nur zwei Sitze. Wo sich in Europa und Japan die zwei Rücksitze befinden, gibt es hier eine merkwürdige Umklapp-Konstruktion. Das ist ärgerlich, denn diese Sitze sind durchaus nützlich.

Le marché américain n'a droit qu'à deux places avant, complétées par un petit espace arrière pliable assez bizarre, alors que la version pour le Japon et l'Europe a deux vraies places à l'arrière. C'est dommage, les sièges arrière sont pourtant bien utiles.

HONDA FCX CLARITY

The FCX Clarity is the world's only hydrogen-powered fuel cell production car. It's spacious inside, has a 270-mile range, emits only water vapor from its tailpipe and can be refueled in minutes. The only problems are current cost – it's heavily subsidized for $600 per month and only made in small numbers – and a lack of hydrogen filling stations. Still, a genuinely groundbreaking, historically important car.

Mit dem FCX Clarity gelang Honda die weltweit erste Serienproduktion eines Brennstoffzellenautos. Es verfügt über ein geräumiges Innenleben und eine Reichweite von knapp 435 km. Aus dem Auspuff kommt wirklich nur Wasserdampf, und das Auftanken ist eine Sache von wenigen Minuten. Problematisch sind nur die Kosten – die Bezuschussung liegt bei 600 USD (420 EUR) pro Monat –, die kleine Auflage und die geringe Anzahl an Wasserstoff-Tankstellen. Trotzdem handelt es sich um ein innovatives und historisch wichtiges Auto.

La FCX Clarity est le seul modèle de production à pile à hydrogène combustible du monde. Elle a un intérieur spacieux, une autonomie de 434 kilomètres, son pot d'échappement ne rejette que de la vapeur d'eau, et elle peut être ravitaillée en quelques minutes. Les seuls problèmes sont son coût actuel (même subventionnée, elle coûte 600 $ (420 EUR) par mois, et n'est produite qu'en petit nombre) et le manque de stations d'hydrogène. C'est néanmoins une voiture révolutionnaire et historique.

FCX Clarity

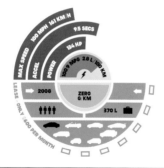

SECRET DETAIL

Under acceleration, its electric motor makes a sound akin to the not unpleasant muffled whistle of a dentist's drill.

Bei der Beschleunigung erzeugt der Elektromotor ein Geräusch, das wie ein gedämpfter Zahnarztbohrer klingt, aber dennoch nicht unangenehm ist.

À l'accélération, le moteur électrique produit un son qui ressemble au sifflement étouffé d'une roulette de dentiste, en moins désagréable.

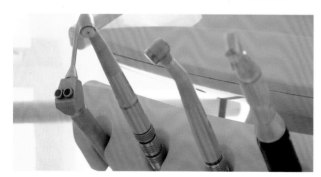

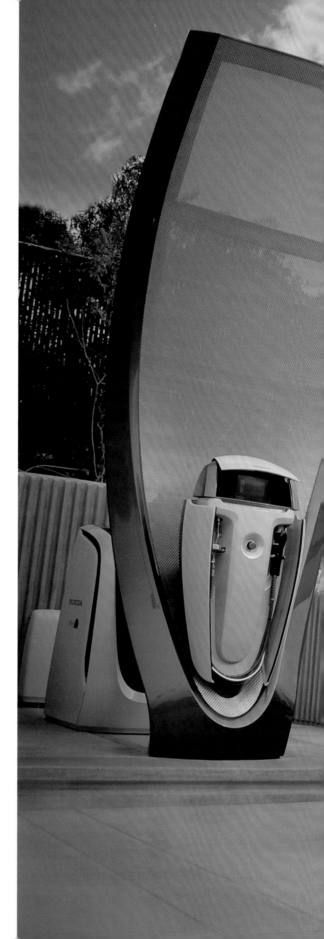

HUMMER

FOUNDED: **1992** DIED: **2010**
HEADQUARTERS: **DETROIT, USA**
2010 PRODUCTION: **3,182**

LOGO HISTORY:

HUMMER

What started off as an emblem of a nation's power and honor ended as a totem of all that was wrong with the world. The Humvee – or H1 as it was later badged – was developed to carry troops and supplies across the battlefields of the first Gulf War. Its size was dictated by a need to use the tracks left by tanks – no problem in the middle of the desert, less than handy in the local multi-storey. After buying the rights to the brand in 1998, General Motors developed smaller models which became instant targets for the anti-SUV movement. As the H numbers crept higher, Hummer moved closer to right-sized respectability but was culled before it could make good its past excesses. A missed opportunity to reinvent the brand with Governator-sourced environmental technology and less anti-aerodynamic lines perhaps, with Lamborghini proving that brutal design needn't be confined to right angles. Leaving a void that the more friendly Toyota FJ Cruiser has filled for many, the absence of Hummer opens up Jeep's future options. Ultimately, a brand of its time – one that most of us are grateful has passed.

Der einst für Macht und Autoliebe einer ganzen Nation stehende, benzindurstige Hummer ist zum Opfer der Wirtschaftskrise und steigender Spritpreise geworden. Ursprünglich für das amerikanische Militär entwickelt, erlangte der Humvee – später in H1 umbenannt – durch seine Medienpräsenz während des Ersten Golfkriegs Berühmtheit. Das Fahrzeug musste hierfür so groß sein, dass es in der Spur von Panzern fahren konnte – mitten in der Wüste kein Problem, inmitten enger Hochhausschluchten eher unpraktisch. Nachdem General Motors 1998 die Rechte an der Marke gekauft hatte, wurden kleinere Modelle entwickelt, die jedoch sofort zur Zielscheibe der Anti-SUV-Bewegung wurden. Mit den steigenden Zahlen hinter dem „H" stieg zwar auch der Respekt vor dem Kraftprotz, es blieb allerdings keine Zeit mehr, den schlechten Ruf vollständig loszuwerden: Trotz der Unterstützung von Gouverneur und Hummer-Liebhaber Schwarzenegger, umweltfreundlichen Technologien und einer aerodynamischeren Bauweise war es für eine Rettung der Marke bereits zu spät (Lamborghini hat die Kurve hingegen noch gekriegt). Die Lücke, die Hummer hinterlassen hat, füllt teilweise der familienfreundlichere Toyota FJ Cruiser und öffnet neue Perspektiven für den Jeep. Die Marke Hummer hatte ihre Zeit – und viele sind dankbar, dass diese vorüber ist.

Ce qui avait commencé par être l'emblème de la puissance et de l'honneur d'une nation a fini par se transformer en symbole de tout ce qui va mal dans le monde. Le Humvee (plus tard badgé H1) a été conçu pour transporter les troupes et le matériel à travers les champs de bataille de la première Guerre du Golfe. Sa taille répondait au besoin d'emprunter les traces laissées par les tanks. Aucun problème dans le désert, mais pas très pratique dans les virages des parkings couverts urbains. Après avoir acheté les droits de la marque en 1998, General Motors a développé des modèles plus petits qui sont immédiatement devenus la cible du mouvement anti-SUV. Au fil des modèles, Hummer s'est rapproché d'une taille plus respectable, mais a été supprimé avant de pouvoir faire amende honorable pour ses excès passés. C'est une opportunité manquée de réinventer la marque grâce à la technologie écologique impulsée par le Governator, peut-être aussi avec des lignes moins contraires à l'aérodynamique, Lamborghini ayant prouvé qu'une esthétique agressive n'est pas forcément condamnée aux angles droits. L'absence du Hummer a laissé un vide que la Toyota FJ Cruiser a rempli pour beaucoup, et ouvre de nouvelles options pour l'avenir de Jeep. C'est en fin de compte une marque qui était liée à son époque, et nous sommes pour la plupart bien contents qu'elle soit révolue.

H1
Rival: M1 Albrams

Civilianised troop carrier.
Zivilisierter Truppentransporter.
Transport de troupes version civile.

H2
Rival: Cadillac
Escalade

Big, stupid rapper's delight.
Großes dummes Rapper-Spielzeug.
Gros jouet stupide pour rappeurs.

H3
Rival: Range Rover
Sport

Failed attempt as acceptable face of excess.
Gescheiterter Versuch, den Ruf zu retten.
Toujours inacceptable. Essai raté.

HYUNDAI

FOUNDED: **1967**

HEADQUARTERS: **SEOUL, SOUTH KOREA**

2010 PRODUCTION: **3,431,138**

LOGO HISTORY:

Once the butt of many a Western car-snob's joke, Hyundai – and sister company Kia – is making sure that it has the last laugh in the global sales war. Currently ranked as the world's fifth-largest carmaker, it's eyeing up the Renault-Nissan Alliance for fourth place. Value for money has historically been the draw of Hyundai's unremarkable products but recent cars such as the drifters' new choice, the Genesis Coupe, gives it the sort of cars parked in its showrooms to reach its goal, especially if its design confidence continues to increase in direct correlation to its success.

Die einst von den westlichen Autosnobs verspottete Schwestermarke von Kia hat in Sachen weltweite Absatzzahlen mittlerweile gut lachen. Das derzeit als fünftgrößte Automarke der Welt gehandelte Unternehmen hat gute Chancen, den momentan von der Renault-Nissan-Allianz besetzten vierten Platz zu erobern. Das Preis-Leistungs-Verhältnis und unauffällige Produkte waren einst die typischen Merkmale von Hyundai, die neueren Autos jedoch – so z. B. der preisgünstige Flitzer Genesis Coupé – scheinen diesem Konzept nicht mehr zu entsprechen – und wenn der Mut zum Design mit dem Erfolg des Unternehmens wächst, können wir uns in Zukunft noch auf einige Schmuckstückchen freuen.

Hyundai (et sa filiale Kia) a été la victime des moqueries de nombreux snobs occidentaux de l'automobile, mais fait tout ce qu'il faut pour avoir le dernier mot dans la bataille mondiale des ventes. La marque coréenne est actuellement le cinquième constructeur de voitures dans le monde, et talonne l'alliance Renault-Nissan pour lui faucher la quatrième place. C'est le rapport qualité-prix qui a longtemps fait l'intérêt des produits assez quelconques de Hyundai, mais ses voitures les plus récentes, telles que la Genesis Coupé, la nouvelle favorite des amateurs de drift, lui donnent la présence requise dans les showrooms pour atteindre son objectif, surtout si son design continue de gagner en assurance proportionnellement à ses succès commerciaux.

I10
Rival: Fiat Panda

No-frills city car and all the better for it.
Schnörkelloses Stadtauto und mehr.
Citadine sans fioritures.

I20
Rival: Ford Fiesta

Supermini takes fight to chic Europeans.
Kleinwagen mit europäischer Eleganz.
Polyvalente à l'élégance européenne.

I30
Rival: Kia C'eed

Cut-price BMW 1 Series clone (from the rear).
Billiger, gewagter Klon der BMW 1er-Reihe.
BMW Série 1 (de l'arrière) à prix réduit.

ELANTRA
Rival: Chevrolet Cruze

Good-looking compact sedan.
Gut aussehende, kompakte Limousine.
Belle berline compacte.

SONATA
Rival: Toyota Camry

Swoopy family sedan, hideous Hybrid.
Familienlimousine, als Hybrid unbeliebt.
Berline curviligne, hideuse hybride.

GENESIS COUPE
Rival: Fod Mustang

Drifters' new favorite toy.
Neuer preisgünstiger Flitzer.
La nouvelle favorite des amateurs de drift.

VELOSTER
Rival: VW Scirocco

Asymmetric-doored curiosity coupe.
Seltsames Coupe, asymmetrische Türen.
Curieux coupé aux portes asymétriques.

EQUUS
Rival: Mercedes
S-class

Presidential-spec limo with hood ornament.
Edle Limousine, verspielte Motorhaube.
Limousine avec bouchon de radiateur.

TUCSON | IX35
Rival: Nissan
Qashqai

Bold, family-friendly crossover.
Selbstbewusstes familienfreundliches SUV.
Crossover audacieux et familial.

SANTA FE
Rival: Land Rover
Freelander

Convincing mid-sized SUV.
Überzeugender Mittelklasse-SUV.
SUV convaincant de taille moyenne.

H-1 | I800
Rival: VW Caravelle

Big van with windows and 8 seats.
Eiin Van mit 8 Sitzen, sonst nichts.
Grand van avec fenêtres et 8 places.

ALSO AVAILABLE

Getz, Accent, Azera, ix20, Veracruz.

IFR AUTOMOTIVE

(E)
FOUNDED: **2003**
HEADQUARTERS: **REUS, SPAIN**

LOGO HISTORY:

Luxury and open-wheeled Lotus 7 type cars might seem to mix like oil and water, but IFR Automotive is shaking up this unusual emulsion to produce the Aspid. It's as weird as it sounds, with scissor doors and butterfly roof access to its neatly appointed cabin. Its exterior looks like a cross between a Plymouth Prowler and a robotic grasshopper, and whether its design is successful is down to your individual taste. What's not in doubt is its performance, with the 400hp car able to reach 62mph in just 2.8 seconds. With a starting price north of $100,000 the Aspid range is not cheap compared to a Caterham though – making it an expensive plaything.

Luxuriöse Autos des Typs Lotus 7 und freistehende Räder scheinen sich zu beißen, doch IFR Automotive schafft mit dem Aspid eine reizvolle Mischung genau dieser Elemente. Das Ganze sieht dann mit Scherentüren, aufklappbarem Dach und aufgeräumtem Innenbereich so verrückt aus, wie es klingt. Von außen ist der Aspid eine gewöhnungsbedürftige Mischung aus Plymouth Prowler und einem Roboter-Grashüpfer – überzeugend jedoch ist seine Leistung: knapp 400 PS und 100 km/h in nur 2,8 Sekunden. Mit einem Grundpreis von 100.000 USD (70.000 EUR) ist das Modell im Vergleich zu einem Caterham aber ein eher teures Spielzeug.

Le luxe et les voitures de type Lotus 7 à roues non carénées ne font en général pas bon ménage, mais IFR Automotive les réconcilie dans son Aspid. Elle est évidemment fort étrange, avec ses portes-élytres et un accès papillon dans le toit vers la cabine bien aménagée. Elle ressemble à un croisement entre une Plymouth Prowler et une sauterelle robotisée, et chacun pourra décider de la réussite de cette esthétique selon ses goûts personnels. Ce qui ne fait aucun doute, c'est sa performance, car avec une puissance de 400 chevaux, cette voiture est capable d'atteindre les 100 km/h en seulement 2,8 secondes. Le premier prix étant supérieur à 100 000 $ (70 000 EUR), la gamme Aspid est cependant chère par rapport à une Caterham, ce qui en fait un jouet de luxe.

ASPID

Rival: Three fast Caterhams

Very light, fast and odd.
Sehr leicht, schnell und individuell.
Très légère, rapide et bizarre.

INFINITI

FOUNDED: **1989**
HEADQUARTERS: **TOKYO, JAPAN**
2010 PRODUCTION: **410,100**

LOGO HISTORY:

Nissan's luxury answer to Toyota's Lexus and Honda's Acura, this brand was initially only a US proposition (indeed the Japanese marque is still not sold in its country of origin). A dull and poorly-received set of sedans personified its 90s range but a rethink in the early 00s resulted in its first stand-out model, the 2003 FX mid-size crossover with pleasingly curvy coupe overtones, later seen on the (bigger) BMW X6. The long-awaited launch into Europe started in 2008 and tried to reposition the brand further upmarket promoting alternative luxury, boutique hotel-style showrooms and service levels plus diesels and hybrids joining its previously petrol-only range. More distinctive models are needed if it's to have the impact it's aspiring to.

Die luxuriöse Antwort von Nissan auf den Toyota Lexus und den Honda Acura: Verkaufsstart der Luxusmarke des japanischen Autoherstellers war in den USA, bis heute wird sie jedoch nicht in ihrem Heimatland verkauft. Glanzlose, schlecht verkaufte Limousinen prägten das erste Jahrzehnt, aber ein Umdenken in den frühen Nullerjahren mündete im ersten herausragenden Modell der Marke: dem 2003 FX, ein Mittelklasse-Crossover mit gefälligen kurvigen Coupé-Details, die dann später am (größeren) BMW X6 zu sehen waren. Der lang erwartete Markteintritt in Europa erfolgte im Jahr 2008, wobei versucht wurde, die Marke mit Luxus-Werbung, Verkaufsräumen im Boutique-Hotel-Stil, exklusivem Kundenservice und Hybridmodellen im Oberklasse-Segment anzusiedeln. Um dieses Ziel zu erreichen, braucht es jedoch extravagantere Modelle.

Cette marque est la réponse de Nissan sur le segment du luxe à la Lexus de Toyota et à l'Acura de Honda, et ne concernait à l'origine que les États-Unis (d'ailleurs cette japonaise n'est toujours pas vendue dans son pays d'origine). Dans les années 1990 sa gamme se composait d'une série de berlines insipides et critiquées, mais au début des années 2000 une remise en question a produit son premier modèle remarquable, la FX. Ce crossover de taille moyenne lancé en 2003 arborait des courbes agréables évoquant un coupé, que l'on a ensuite retrouvées sur la BMW X6 (plus grande). Le lancement européen longtemps attendu a commencé en 2008 et a tenté de repositionner la marque dans un segment supérieur proposant un luxe alternatif, avec des showrooms et un service reprenant les principes des hôtels-boutiques, ainsi que des versions diesel et hybrides qui se sont ajoutées à la motorisation jusqu'alors uniquement essence. Il faudra des modèles plus originaux si la marque veut avoir l'impact qu'elle désire.

G
Rival: BMW 3

Good sedan, coupe & cabrio, but better rivals.
Als Limousine, Coupé und Cabrio.
Bien, mais ses rivales sont meilleures.

M
Rival: BMW 5

Big, large quality sedan with hybrid option.
Große Qualitätslimousine mit Hybrid-Option.
Grande berline de qualité, option hybride.

EX
Rival: Audi Q5

Smaller crossover with luxury leanings.
Kleinerer Crossover mit Luxus-Ambitionen.
Petit crossover qui aime le luxe.

FX
Rival: RR Sport

Most distinctive Infiniti. Lairy large SUV.
Außergewöhnlicher, aggresiver Sport-SUV.
Le plus original : grand SUV tapageur.

QX56
Rival: Merc GL

Super ugly giant 5-dr SUV for the US.
Hässlicher, riesiger 5-türiger SUV (USA).
Énorme SUV 5 portes pour les États-Unis.

IRAN KHODRO

FOUNDED: **1962**
HEADQUARTERS: **TEHRAN, IRAN**
2010 PRODUCTION: **771,601**

LOGO HISTORY:

The Middle East's largest vehicle manufacturer initially built its business around manufacturing European and Asian cars under license, starting with the Paykan, based on the Hillman Hunter. Coalitions with Peugeot, Renault, Suzuki and Mercedes-Benz ensure the tradition continues. However Iran Khodro is also a manufacturer in its own right thanks to the locally developed Samand, Iran's national car. An updated version of the car is now also available with electric power with a 120-mile range. Strong industry relationships, expanding exports and growing local demand should ensure growth, provided political instability doesn't intervene.

Der größte Autohersteller des Mittleren Ostens hat ursprünglich europäische und asiatische Lizenzbauten produziert, das erste Modell war der auf dem Hillman Hunter basierende Paykan. Durch Abkommen mit Peugeot, Renault, Suzuki und Mercedes-Benz wurde diese Tradition zwar fortgesetzt, Iran Khodro tritt jedoch mit dem im Iran entwickelten Samand, der als Nationalauto des Landes gilt, auch als eigene Marke auf. Eine aktualisierte Version des Samand ist jetzt auch als Elektro-Modell mit einer Reichweite von 200 km verfügbar. Starke Beziehungen in der Branche, steigende Exportzahlen und eine wachsende lokale Nachfrage stellen das Wachstum des Autoherstellers in Zukunft sicher – solange keine politischen Unruhen dazwischenkommen.

Le plus grand fabricant de véhicules du Moyen-Orient a initialement bâti son activité autour de la production sous licence de voitures européennes et asiatiques, à commencer par la Paykan, basée sur la Hillman Hunter. Les alliances formées avec Peugeot, Renault, Suzuki et Mercedes-Benz veillent à la pérennité de cette tradition. Cependant Iran Khodro est aussi un véritable fabricant grâce à la Samand, la voiture nationale en Iran. Une version réactualisée de cette voiture est aujourd'hui disponible avec un moteur électrique d'une autonomie de 193 kilomètres. De solides relations dans le secteur automobile et la croissance des exportations et de la demande locale devraient garantir l'expansion de la marque, à condition que l'instabilité politique ne se mette pas en travers du chemin.

SAMAND
Rival: Dacia Logan

Warmed-over Peugeot 405.
Aufgewärmter Peugeot 405.
Version réchauffée de la Peugeot 405.

SOREN
Rival: Chevrolet Cruz

Warmed-over version of the above.
Noch einmal aufgewärmtes Modell des obigen.
Version réchauffée de la Samand.

JAGUAR

GB

FOUNDED: **1945**

HEADQUARTERS: **COVENTRY, ENGLAND**

2010 PRODUCTION: **51,444**

LOGO HISTORY:

This famous British marque traces its name back to the mid-1930s SS Jaguar model by SS Cars (SS standing for Swallow Sidecar after the firm's motorcycle sidecar roots). After WWII the 'SS' part was dropped due to unpleasant Nazi connotations and the model became a brand – Jaguar Cars. Success in 1950s racing led to road-going sports cars and sedans that majored on performance, streamlined beauty and good value. After a retro design period in the 90s and early 00s new owner Tata is getting the brand back on track, having inherited a revamped model range from Ford. If not quite up to its iconic 1960s E-type sportscar best, Jaguar's new/old mantra, to make "beautiful, fast cars" is looking good.

Namensgeber der berühmten britischen Marke war das 1930er-Modell „SS Jaguar" von SS Cars (SS steht hier für „Swallow Sidecar", was auf die ebenfalls von SS Cars produzierten Motorradseitenwagen zurückzuführen ist). Nach dem Zweiten Weltkrieg wurde das „SS" aus naheliegenden Gründen aus dem Namen entfernt, und das Modell wurde zur Marke: Jaguar Cars. Aufgrund des Erfolgs in den Rennen der 1950er wurden bald straßentaugliche Sportwagen und Limousinen auf den Markt gebracht, die durch Leistung, schnittige Schönheit und ein gutes Preis-Leistungs-Verhältnis überzeugten. Nach einer Retro-Design-Welle in den 90ern und frühen Nullerjahren übernahm der indische Autohersteller Tata Jaguar von Ford und führte ihn wieder zurück auf die Spur. Wenn die britische Luxusmarke auch nicht mehr ihren legendären Ruf des 1960er E-Type erreicht, bleibt der Grundsatz, schöne und schnelle Autos anzubieten, erhalten.

Le nom de cette célèbre marque britannique remonte aux années 1930, et vient du modèle SS Jaguar de SS Cars (SS signifie Swallow Sidecar, et vient des racines de l'entreprise dans la fabrication de side-cars). Après la Deuxième Guerre mondiale, le sigle « SS » a été abandonné en raison de sa désagréable connotation nazie, et le modèle est devenu une marque : Jaguar Cars. Les succès remportés sur les circuits dans les années 1950 ont mené à l'arrivée sur les routes de voitures de sport et de berlines particulièrement douées en termes de performance, de beauté aérodynamique et de rapport qualité-prix. Après une période de design rétro dans les années 1990 et au début des années 2000, le nouveau propriétaire Tata remet la marque sur les rails, Ford lui ayant légué une gamme de modèles revampés. Jaguar n'est pas revenue à sa forme olympique des années 1960 avec son emblématique voiture de sport Type E, mais son nouveau/vieux mantra, faire « des voitures belles et rapides », semble porter ses fruits.

XF | XFR
Rival: Merc CLS

4-dr coupe, ace interior, go-fast V8 XFR.
4-türiges Coupé, Luxus-Interieur, V8-Motor.
Coupé 4 portes, bel intérieur et moteur V8.

XK | XKR
Rival: Merc SL

Elegant large 2+2 coupe & cabrio.
Elegant, groß, 4 Türen, Coupe und Cabrio.
Grand coupé et cabriolet 2+2 élégant.

XJ
Rival: Merc S-Class

Dramatic flagship shaking up limo market.
Spektakuläre Spitzen-Limousine.
Spectaculaire vaisseau amiral.

Jaguar E-type's 50th anniversary sculpture by Gerry Judah at 2011's Goodwood Festival of Speed

JAGUAR XF

Not your traditional-looking Jaguar on the outside, yet nothing startling new either, the real standout is its interior. At start-up A/C vents rotate to open and a shifter knob rises out of the center console. A welcome return to the objective of delighting its drivers.

Von außen weder ein klassischer Jaguar noch ein überraschend neues Design – die Besonderheit ist das Innenleben. Beim Start schwenken die Lüftungsdüsen auf, und der Schalthebel fährt aus der Versenkung. Eine erfreuliche Rückbesinnung auf das Thema Fahrvergnügen.

De l'extérieur, cette voiture ne ressemble pas à une Jaguar traditionnelle, mais n'a pourtant rien de vraiment nouveau. C'est l'intérieur qu'il faut remarquer. Au démarrage, les bouches de l'air conditionné pivotent pour s'ouvrir et le levier de vitesse sort de la console centrale. C'est un retour bienvenu à l'envie de charmer les conducteurs.

XFR 5.0 V8 Supercharged

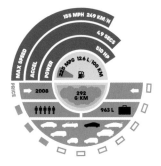

SECRET DETAIL

Recent facelift improves front headlights from one-time James Bond, Roger Moore's curiously raised eyebrows to big cat-serious.

Beim aktuellen Facelift blicken die Frontscheinwerfer nicht mehr neugierig-aufgerissen drein, sondern wirken jetzt ernster und raubkatzenhafter.

Un lifting récent a amélioré les phares avant, qui évoquaient des sourcils curieusement étonnés alors qu'ils prennent maintenant une expression grave de grand félin.

JAGUAR XJ

From old man to modern man in a single leap, the swooping roofline of the current aluminum-bodied XJ continues Jaguar's renaissance and banishes the previous retro-shaped namesake to history. The interior is also one of the best in the business offering a warm and luxurious antidote to the all-too-often cold Teutonic premium. A car British Prime Ministers can again be proud to be seen in.

Von der Vergangenheit in die Zukunft in einem Sprung: Die schwungvolle Dachlinie des aktuellen XJ mit Aluminiumkarosserie setzt die Jaguar-Revolution fort und verbannt den gealterten Namensvetter in die Vergangenheit. Das warme Interieur ist eines der hochwertigsten auf dem Markt – ein schöner Gegenpol zum häufig kühlen deutschen Luxus-Design. Hierin kann sich auch der britische Premierminister zeigen.

De la tradition à la modernité en un seul pas de géant, la ligne incurvée du toit de la dernière XJ en aluminium poursuit la renaissance de Jaguar et relègue l'ancienne forme rétro aux livres d'histoire. L'intérieur est également l'un des meilleurs du marché, c'est un antidote chaleureux et luxueux aux teutonnes haut de gamme trop souvent glaciales. Voici une voiture dans laquelle les premiers ministres britanniques pourront être fiers de rouler.

XJ 3.0L V6 Diesel

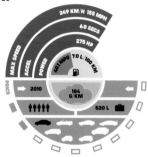

DESIGNER Q + A

Ian Callum
Design director, Jaguar

On duty:
Suit: Haryword bespoke
Shoes: Unknown
Watch: Kenneth Cole – "I buy watches because I like them not because of the name."
Off-duty:
Clothes: Levi's jeans – "they have to be 752s, they're exactly

the right shape," plus Church's Chelsea boots or Piloti car driving shoes

What does your brand stand for?
Past: "Adventurous turned conservative."
Present: "Adventurous again."
Future: "Very adventurous. The challenge is to keep the adventure going."

JEEP

FOUNDED: **1941**
HEADQUARTERS: **MICHIGAN, USA**
2010 PRODUCTION: **291,138**

LOGO HISTORY:

Synonymous with no-nonsense 4x4s, Jeep is one of the few car brands that needs little explanation. The brand's forebear was the WWII US Army Willys Jeep that led to the Jeep Wrangler – still the most iconic product within its range. A period in the doldrums offering poor quality vehicles with old and inefficient engines was part of the reason for the bankruptcy of parent company Chrysler Group in 2009. But now the business is back, as part of the Fiat Group and trying to instigate massive improvements in build and interior quality. The new Grand Cherokee SUV is a good example. Overall, faded glory, but some green shoots visible.

Jeep braucht als Inbegriff für geradlinigen Allradantrieb wenig Erklärung. Urahn der Marke war der im Zweiten Weltkrieg eingesetzte Army Willys der US-Armee, der durch den Jeep Wrangler ersetzt wurde. Letzterer gilt immer noch als größte Legende in seinem Segment. Eine längere Flaute und das Angebot qualitativ minderwertiger Fahrzeuge mit alten, ineffizienten Motoren war einer der Gründe für die Insolvenz des Mutterkonzerns Chrysler Group im Jahr 2009. Jetzt ist die Marke als Teil von Fiat zurück, wobei zum neuen Konzept massive Verbesserungen hinsichtlich Konstruktion und Innenleben gehören. Der neue Grand Cherokee SUV ist hier schon mal ein guter Anfang. Der alte Ruhm ist zwar verblasst, es sprießen jedoch schon wieder ein paar grüne Knospen.

Synonyme de 4x4 sans chichis, Jeep est l'une des rares marques de voitures qui se passent d'explications. L'ancêtre de la marque est la Jeep Willys de l'armée américaine à l'époque de la Deuxième Guerre mondiale, qui a donné naissance à la Jeep Wrangler, aujourd'hui encore le produit le plus emblématique de la marque. Une période d'apathie pendant laquelle les véhicules proposés étaient de qualité médiocre, avec de vieux moteurs peu performants, a contribué à la faillite de la société mère Chrysler en 2009. Mais l'activité a aujourd'hui repris sous la tutelle du groupe Fiat avec la volonté d'améliorer substantiellement la construction et l'aménagement intérieur. Le nouveau SUV Grand Cherokee en est un bon exemple. Dans l'ensemble, la splendeur est passée, mais de nouveaux bourgeons font leur apparition.

WRANGLER
Rival: LR Defender

Iconic basic 2/5-dr hard/soft-top.
Legendärer 2-/5-Türer, Hardtop oder Softtop.
Basique légendaire à 2/5 portes.

PATRIOT
Rival: Ford Edge

Chunkier 5dr crossover SUV.
Stämmiger Crossover-SUV mit 5 Türen.
SUV crossover imposant à 5 portes.

COMPASS
Rival: Nissan Rouge

2011 model looks less melted.
2011er-Modell mit klaren Formen.
Le modèle 2011 a moins l'air d'avoir fondu.

LIBERTY
Rival: Ford Edge

Formerly Cherokee, ageing and boxy.
Früher Cherokee, jetzt gealtert und kastig.
Ex-Cherokee, vieillissante et carrée.

GRAND CHEROKEE
Rival: VW Touareg

New quality large SUV.
Neues großes Qualitäts-SUV.
Nouveau grand SUV de qualité.

JEEP GRAND CHEROKEE

Generations deep as an auto legend it may be, but the last Grand Cherokee really disappointed. The 2011 model – arriving as parent group Chrysler emerged from bankruptcy – places it back on track from a design and quality perspective and is crucial to the brand's survival. Under Fiat's new ownership, a frugal diesel version is due in the US by 2013. We want them to bring back the Woodie next.

Der Grand Cherokee mag seit Generationen eine Legende sein – das letzte Modell war jedoch eine tiefe Enttäuschung. Das 2011er-Modell jedoch – das herauskam, als Chrysler vor dem Bankrott gerettet schien – hat wieder zu Design und Qualität zurückgefunden und soll nun das Überleben der Marke sichern. Unter der neuen Leitung von Fiat ist 2013 für die USA eine sparsame Dieselversion geplant. Wir wünschen uns als nächstes den Woodie zurück.

Le Grand Cherokee est peut-être une légende qui a marqué plusieurs générations, mais sa dernière version a vraiment déçu. Le modèle de 2011 – qui arrive alors que la maison mère Chrysler sort juste de la faillite – le remet sur le droit chemin en termes de design et de qualité, et c'est crucial pour la survie de la marque. Sous la nouvelle direction de Fiat, une version diesel frugale sortira aux États-Unis en 2013. Après cela, nous aimerions qu'ils ressuscitent la Woodie.

3.0L V6 CRD Limited

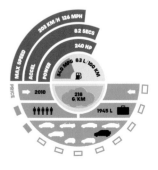

SECRET DETAIL

The Grand Cherokee's cabin represents a massive leap in quality.
Twiddle the knurled and rubberized air vent controls for evidence.

Die Fahrerkabine des Grand Cherokee hat sich in Sachen Qualität
erfreulich entwickelt. Spielen Sie zum Testen einfach mal an den
geriffelten und gummierten Lüftungsreglern herum.

La cabine du Grand Cherokee a fait d'énormes progrès en termes
de qualité. Manipulez les commandes striées et caoutchoutées des
bouches d'air pour vous en convaincre.

KIA

FOUNDED: **1944**
HEADQUARTERS: **SEOUL, SOUTH KOREA**
2010 PRODUCTION: **2,130,000**

LOGO HISTORY:

Former South Korean also-ran budget brand Kia is quietly storming up the sales charts worldwide with a line-up that – bar a few previous generation relics – is now made up of thoroughly well put together, reliable and competently styled mainstream vehicles. There's even the leftfield Soul for younger and more style-conscious drivers. And more's to come. Having hired superstar ex-Audi car designer Peter Schreyer in 2006 while sharing technology and economies of scale with sister brand Hyundai to become a top five global carmaker, expect Kia to launch some truly desirable, but still affordable cars very soon.

Die ehemalige Niedrigpreismarke Kia aus Südkorea erobert langsam, aber sicher die Verkaufscharts weltweit und wartet mit einem Sortiment auf, das – abgesehen von ein paar Überresten aus vorherigen Generationen – aus gut verarbeiteten, zuverlässigen und ansehnlichen Mainstream-Fahrzeugen besteht. Mit dem Soul hat Kia sogar ein richtig poppiges Modell herausgebracht, das ein jüngeres, stilbewusstes Publikum ansprechen soll. Und das ist noch nicht alles … Durch die Zusammenarbeit des Superstar-Designers Peter Schreyer (ehemals Audi) seit 2006 und mit der Entscheidung, Technologie und Massenproduktion mit der Schwestermarke Hyundai zu teilen, ist die Hyundai-Kia Automotive Group zum weltweit fünftgrößten Autohersteller aufgestiegen. Wir freuen uns auf weitere schöne Flitzer zu günstigen Preisen!

Cette marque économique sud-coréenne est longtemps restée à l'arrière-plan, mais prend discrètement d'assaut les classements des ventes dans le monde entier avec une gamme qui, à l'exception de quelques reliques des générations précédentes, se compose maintenant de véhicules remarquablement bien faits et fiables. Il y a même la surprenante Soul pour les jeunes conducteurs sensibles au style. Et d'autres surprises arriveront bientôt. Kia ayant embauché en 2006 la superstar des designers de voitures Peter Schreyer, qui a travaillé pour Audi, et partageant technologie et économies d'échelle avec sa maison-mère Hyundai pour prendre la cinquième place des plus grands constructeurs automobiles du monde, attendez-vous à voir la marque lancer très bientôt des voitures très séduisantes mais abordables.

PICANTO
Rival: Ford Ka

City car with new Kia style and quality.
Kleinstwagen mit Kia-Style und -Qualität.
Citadine avec la nouvelle qualité Kia.

RIO
Rival: Fiat 500

Brand new supermini for 2011.
Nagelneuer Kleinwagen von 2011.
Nouvelle citadine polyvalente pour 2011.

VENGA
Rival: Opel Meriva

High-roofed supermini with MPV feel.
Raumwunder mit hohem Dach.
Citadine polyvalente haute sous plafond.

CEE'D
Rival: Ford Focus

Decent 5dr hatch, 3dr Proceed & wagon.
Anständiger 5-Türer-Fließheck.
Compacte/Pro Cee'd 5/3 portes et break.

FORTE KOUP
Rival: Scion tC

Appealing small two-door coupe.
Ansprechendes kleines Coupé mit 2 Türen.
Petit coupé 2 portes séduisant.

SOUL
Rival: Nissan Cube

Kia's take on cool box car.
Cooler Kompaktwagen.
La voiture carrée et branchée selon Kia.

OPTIMA
Rival: Ford Mondeo

Smart new mid-size sedan.
Elegante neue Mittelklasse-Limousine.
Nouvelle berline élégante.

SEDONA
Rival: Ford S-Max

Cheap (and it shows) 7-seat large MPV.
Großer Minivan mit 7 Sitzen.
Grand monospace 7 places bon marché.

SPORTAGE
Rival: Nissan Rogue/
Qashqai

Genuinely good small crossover.
Wirklich gutes kleines Crossover-Modell.
Un petit crossover vraiment bien fait.

SORENTO
Rival: Hyundai
Santa Fe

Bigger crossover now seats 7.
Größerer Crossover, jetzt mit 7 Sitzen.
Un crossover plus grand avec 7 places.

CADENZA
Rival: Ford Taurus

New flagship sedan replaces Amanti.
Die neue Limousine ersetzt den Amanti.
Nouvelle berline, qui remplace l'Amanti.

ALSO AVAILABLE

Carens, Borrego, Forte.

KIA SOUL

Soul 1.6 CRDi 2

Although clearly influenced by Nissan's Cube and Scion's xB, Kia's Soul is still a decent boxcar and the first car from the South Korean brand that can be described as desirable rather than just good value. As a brand on a design and quality roll, it's just the start. We hope their recent Pop concept will follow.

Der Kia Soul ist zwar eindeutig vom Nissan Cube und vom Scion xB beeinflusst, stellt aber dennoch einen ordentlichen Kompaktwagen dar. Das erste Modell des südkoreanischen Autobauers steht für gute Wertarbeit und ein hervorragendes Design. Für eine Marke, die sich in Richtung Design und Qualität orientiert, ist das ein guter Anfang. Wir hoffen, das aktuelle Pop-Konzept geht in die gleiche Richtung.

Bien qu'elle soit clairement influencée par la Cube de Nissan et la xB de Scion, la Soul de Kia est une petite voiture carrée très honnête, et la première voiture de la marque sud-coréenne qui puisse être qualifiée de séduisante plutôt que simplement bon marché. Kia semble avoir le vent en poupe dans le domaine de la qualité et du design, et ce n'est qu'un début. Nous espérons que le récent concept de la Pop suivra le même chemin.

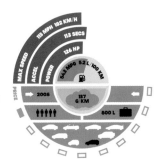

SECRET DETAIL

Open the Soul's glovebox and you'll be treated to a burst of red inside – a bit like an old jewellery box or a Paul Smith suit lining.

Das Handschuhfach des Soul ist knallrot wie ein antikes Schmuckkästchen oder das Futter eines Paul Smith-Anzugs.

Ouvrez la boîte à gants de la Soul pour révéler une explosion de rouge, comme une boîte à bijoux ancienne ou la doublure d'un costume Paul Smith.

KOENIGSEGG

FOUNDED: **1994**
HEADQUARTERS: **ÄNGELHOLM, SWEDEN**

LOGO HISTORY:

A young Swedish businessman with no automotive background made his dream of producing a supercar a reality – and amazingly it's not rubbish. On the contrary, the ultra niche maker – production of certain models can be counted in single figures – has broken numerous speed records and garnered critical acclaim. The CCX 'basic' model, at just shy of a million euros, has since spawned a more expensive special CCXR Edition model, but on the plus side it does 0-62mph in 3.1 seconds, with a 250mph top speed, and runs on ethanol for eco credentials. An even faster 910hp Agera model is due in 2011…drive where long racetracks and salt flats allow.

Ein junger schwedischer Geschäftsmann und kompletter Neuling in der Autobranche hat sich seinen Traum erfüllt, einen Supersportwagen herzustellen – und erstaunlicherweise ist dabei kein Schrott herausgekommen. Im Gegenteil: Der superspezielle Automacher – manche Modelle sind in nur einstelliger Auflage erschienen – hat zahlreiche Geschwindigkeitsrekorde gebrochen und viel Beifall von der Kritik erhalten. Das knapp über eine Million Euro teure CCX „Basic"- Modell, wurde nun durch ein noch teureres und noch spezielleres Modell der CCXR Edition ersetzt, das in 3,1 Sekunden auf 100 km/h kommt, eine Höchstgeschwindigkeit von ca. 400 km/h erreicht und mit umweltfreundlichem Ethanol betrieben werden kann. Mit dem Agera kommt 2011 ein noch schnelleres 910 PS-Modell auf den Markt, in dem man aber nur auf langen Rennstrecken und in Salzwüsten auf seine Kosten kommt.

Un jeune homme d'affaires suédois sans aucune expérience dans l'automobile a réalisé son rêve de produire une supercar, et, chose étonnante, elle n'est pas mal du tout. Au contraire, ce constructeur ultra spécialisé (la production de certains modèles est inférieure à 10 unités) a battu de nombreux records de vitesse et s'est attiré les faveurs de la critique. Le modèle CCX « de base », à tout juste moins d'un million d'euros, a donné naissance à une édition spéciale CCXR plus onéreuse, mais qui monte de 0 à 100 km/h en 3,1 secondes avec une vitesse maximale de 402 km/h, et roule à l'éthanol pour le côté écologique. Un modèle encore plus rapide est prévu pour 2011, l'Agera, avec 910 chevaux de puissance. À conduire sur de longs circuits ou sur des déserts de sel.

CCXR
Rival: Pagani Zonda

3.1-second to 62mph ultracar.
Ultra-Sportwagen: 100km/h in 3,1 Sekunden.
« Ultracar » qui passe de 0 à 100 en 3,1 sec.

AGERA
Rival: Space shuttle

New even faster, 910hp ultra-ultra supercar.
Neu und mit 910 PS sogar schneller.
Ultra-ultracar encore plus rapide, 910 ch.

Koenigsegg creator Christian von Koenigsegg

KOENIGSEGG AGERA

Agera R

Agera means 'to take action' in Swedish, which is what Koenigsegg apparently has done in replacing the CCX. Slipperier and even faster than its predecessor the Agera offers 940hp, and its R relative 1115hp. What's Swedish for 'slow down'?

Agera ist Schwedisch und bedeutet „agieren, handeln". Genau das hat Koenigsegg mit dem Nachfolgemodell des CCX getan. Der Agera ist schnittiger und schneller als sein Vorgänger und wartet mit 953 PS auf. Sein Bruder Agera R bietet gar 1.115 PS. Was heißt „Mach mal langsam!" auf Schwedisch?

Agera signifie « agir » en suédois, et il semble qu'en remplaçant la CCX, Koenigsegg ait effectivement décidé d'agir. Plus aérodynamique et encore plus rapide, l'Agera héberge 940 chevaux sous son capot, 1 115 pour sa cousine l'Agera R. Comment dit-on « ralentir » en suédois ?

SECRET DETAIL

The Agera can be fitted with a roofbox to carry your skis to the mountains at over 200mph. Will affect the aerodynamics a touch.

Der Agera kann mit einer Dachbox ausgestattet werden. So können Sie bei 320 km/h in die Berge zum Skilaufen fahren. Achtung: Die Aerodynamik wird durch die Box leicht beeinträchtigt.

Vous pouvez monter un coffre de toit sur votre Agera pour transporter vos skis jusqu'aux pistes à plus de 320 km/h. Mais l'aérodynamique ne sera plus exactement la même.

KTM

FOUNDED: **1934**
HEADQUARTERS: **METTIGHOFEN, AUSTRIA**
2010 PRODUCTION: **120**

LOGO HISTORY:

Cult off-road motorbike maker KTM – known to have a weakness for the color orange – took a shock turn into four-wheeled product back in 2007 when it launched the X-Bow at the Geneva motor show. The production model that followed in 2008 is a stripped-out, lightweight trackday special that uses an Audi-sourced 2.0-liter gasoline engine to achieve a very rapid 3.9-second 0-62mph time and a 137mph top speed. While featuring plenty of carbon fiber, a racing-style detachable steering wheel and lots of artfully bent metal it lacks a proper roof or much ground clearance so check the weather and your intended route carefully before setting off.

Der Offroad-Motorrad-Hersteller KTM – bekannt für seine Liebe zur Farbe Orange – verblüffte 2007 die Motorwelt beim Genfer Autosalon mit dem ersten Sportwagen der Firmengeschichte: dem X-Bow. Das leichte, puristische Serienmodell aus dem Jahr 2008 wird vom Zweiliter-Turbo-FSI befeuert und schafft es in beeindruckenden 3,9 Sekunden auf 100 km/h sowie auf eine Höchstgeschwindigkeit von 220 km/h. Viel Karbon, ein abnehmbares Lenkrad und schicke Metallstreben, aber kein Dach und wenig Bodenabstand: Also sind gutes Wetter und eine sorgfältige Routenplanung angesagt.

KTM, fabricant culte de motos tout-terrain (dont la faiblesse pour la couleur orange est bien connue) a pris un tournant radical vers la production de véhicules à quatre roues en 2007 avec le lancement de la X-Bow au Salon international de l'automobile de Genève. Le modèle de production qui a suivi en 2008 est une voiture de course sur circuit légère et dépouillée, équipée d'un moteur à essence Audi de 2,0 litres qui passe de 0 à 100 km/h en 3,9 secondes avec une vitesse de pointe de 220 km/h. Elle est constituée d'une abondance de fibre de carbone, et de métal aux formes ingénieuses, et dotée d'un volant de course amovible. Elle n'a pas de toit et sa garde au sol est minuscule, il faut donc bien étudier la météo et la route avant de partir.

X-BOW
Rival: Ariel Atom

Superbike with four wheels.
Superbike auf vier Rädern.
Supermoto à quatre roues.

KTM X-BOW

Gerald Kiska, the design brains behind the X-Bow described the car at its 2007 concept unveil as "a Lotus Super Seven for the 21st century". Not a bad description and one that's been enhanced since 2008 with more than 500 sales and now three versions, the Street, Clubsport and the new 300hp R model using Audi's S3 engine.

Der Designer des X-Bow, Gerald Kiska, beschrieb das Auto bei der Präsentation des Konzepts im Jahr 2007 als „Lotus Super Seven für das 21. Jahrhundert". Das ist keine schlechte Beschreibung für ein Auto, das seit 2008 über 500 Mal verkauft wurde und mittlerweile in drei Versionen erhältlich ist: als Street, als Clubsport und seit Neuestem als R mit 300 PS und Audi-S3-Motor.

Gerald Kiska, le cerveau du design qui se cache derrière la X-Bow, a décrit cette voiture comme la « Lotus Super Seven du XXIe siècle » lors de la présentation du concept en 2007. Ce n'est pas une mauvaise description, et elle a été confirmée depuis 2008 avec plus de 500 unités vendues et trois versions, la Street, la Clubsport et la nouvelle R 300 chevaux, équipée d'un moteur Audi S3.

X-Bow Street

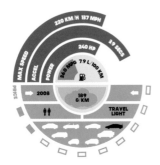

SECRET DETAIL

There is no real luggage space or windshield on the X-Bow but you can buy specially designed helmets to help with airflow and stray raindrops.

Der X-Bow hat weder Kofferraum noch Windschutzscheibe – aber es gibt speziell designte Helme zum Schutz vor Wind und Regen.

Il n'y a pas de place pour les valises dans la X-Bow, ni de pare-brise à proprement parler, mais vous pouvez acheter des casques conçus tout spécialement pour vous protéger du vent et des gouttes de pluie égarées.

LADA

FOUNDED: **1970**
HEADQUARTERS: **TOLYATTI, RUSSIA**
2010 PRODUCTION: **569,324**

LOGO HISTORY:

Russia's most well known global brand – sometimes for the wrong reasons – has provided budget, (helpfully) simple-to-fix, functional transport for 40 years. During the 1980s and 90s its no-fuss vehicles were sold in many countries worldwide (except notably the USA due no doubt to political animosity between the two superpowers) as utility vehicles for police forces, taxi firms and the military. As a trademark of Russian manufacturer AvtoVAZ which has been 25% owned by the massive Renault-Nissan Alliance since 2008, a new range of updated Lada vehicles with shared synergies from that tie-up are expected to refresh the hardline current line-up.

Die weltweit – zum Teil aus den falschen Gründen – bekannte russische Automarke bietet seit 40 Jahren preisgünstige, einfach zu reparierende, funktionale Fahrzeuge an. In den 80ern und 90ern wurden die schnörkellosen Ladas weltweit (außer – zweifellos aus politischen Gründen – in den USA) von Polizei, Taxiunternehmen und Militär gerne gekauft. Die Marke gehört zum russischen Autohersteller AvtoVAZ, an dem seit 2008 die riesige Renault-Nissan Allianz 25 % der Anteile hält. Aus dieser Zusammenarbeit heraus erwartet die Autowelt rundum aktualisierte Lada-Modelle.

La marque russe la plus connue dans le monde (parfois en mal) fournit depuis 40 ans des véhicules bon marché, faciles à réparer (heureusement) et fonctionnels. Dans les années 1980 et 1990, ses voitures sans fioritures se vendaient dans de nombreux pays du monde entier (sauf aux États-Unis, sans doute à cause de l'animosité politique entre les deux superpuissances) en tant que véhicules utilitaires pour la police, les compagnies de taxi et l'armée. Marque commerciale du fabricant russe AvtoVAZ, dont la puissante alliance Renault-Nissan détient 25 % du capital depuis 2008, Lada présentera bientôt une nouvelle gamme de véhicules réactualisés et influencés par la synergie résultant de ce lien, qui viendront rafraîchir son offre actuelle.

PRIORA
Rival: The bus

Budget 4dr/5dr/wagon/coupe.
Günstiger 4- bis 5-Türer, Kombi oder Coupé.
Break/coupé économique à 4/5 portes.

KALINA
Rival: Dacia Logan

Cheap supermini hatch & sedan.
Als Fließheck und Limousine zu haben, auch günstig.
Berline et compacte économique.

SAMARA
Rival: Skoda Favorit

Old-age cheap 3dr&5dr hatch + wagon.
Fließheck oder Kombi mit 3- oder 5-Türen.
Compacte + break 3/5 portes économique.

RIVA\CLASSIC
Rival: The train

1980s family sedan & wagon.
Familienlimousine oder Kombi aus den 80ern.
Berline familiale et break des années 1980.

NIVA
Rival: Daihatsu Fourtrak

Ancient, endearingly rugged 4x4.
Sympathisch-raubeiniger Allradantrieb.
Vieux 4x4 aux touchants airs de gros dur.

LAMBORGHINI

FOUNDED: **1963**

HEADQUARTERS: **SANT'AGATA BOLOGNESE, ITALY**

2010 PRODUCTION: **1302**

LOGO HISTORY:

Subtle, elegant, quiet, restrained… are not words ever associated with Lamborghini. The Italian 'supercar-only' brand with the raging bull logo lacks the racing pedigree of Ferrari or the beauty of Aston Martin but embraces its brashness by mixing the sex-meets-excess fashion sensibility of Versace with the design brutality of an AK47. Part of the VW Group since 1998, Lamborghini's models now work almost as well as they look, drive and sound. The range is about to get a refresh too: beyond the various smaller Gallardo variants, the Aventador LP700-4 is replacing the Murcielago and a four-door Estoque to take on Aston Rapide is back on the cards in a few years' time.

Dezent, elegant, ruhig, raffiniert … nicht immer stand Lamborghini für diese Eigenschaften. Der italienische Sportwagen-Hersteller mit dem Kampfstier im Firmenlogo kann zwar nicht mit einer Rennsport-Ahnentafel wie Ferrari oder der Schönheit von Aston Martin aufwarten, besitzt aber den Mumm, den sexy Luxus von Versace mit der Rohheit einer AK47 zu mixen. Die Modelle der seit 1998 zur VW-Gruppe gehörenden Marke arbeiten mittlerweile auch so gut, wie sie aussehen, fahren und sich anhören. Zudem ist geplant, das Sortiment ein wenig aufzufrischen: Neben den verschiedenen kleinen Gallardo-Varianten ersetzt der Aventador LP700-4 den Murcielago, und ein viertüriger Estoque als Konkurrent zum Aston Rapide soll in den nächsten Jahren herauskommen.

Subtilité, élégance, sérénité, sobriété… ne sont pas des mots qu'on associe à Lamborghini. La marque italienne arbore un taureau de combat sur son logo et fabrique exclusivement des supercars. Elle n'a pas le parcours brillant de Ferrari sur les circuits, ni la beauté d'Aston Martin, mais elle assume son caractère tapageur en alliant la sensibilité torride et excessive d'un Versace et la brutalité des lignes d'un AK-47. Lamborghini fait partie du groupe VW depuis 1998, et le fonctionnement de ses modèles est maintenant presque au niveau de leur esthétique, de leur conduite et du son qu'ils produisent. La gamme est sur le point d'être réactualisée : outre les différentes variantes de la petite Gallardo, l'Aventador LP700-4 remplace la Murcielago et une Estoque 4 portes est prévue dans quelques années pour concurrencer l'Aston Martin Rapide.

GALLARDO
Rival: Audi R8

Smaller V10 supercar coupe and cabrio.
Kleinerer V10-Sportler, Coupé und Cabrio.
Petite supercar, V10, coupé et cabriolet.

AVENTADOR
Rival: Ferrari 599 GTO

Big new 700hp V12 late 2011.
Groß, neu, 700 PS und V12-Motor, ab 2011.
Grande supercar, V12 de 700 ch. fin 2011.

LAMBORGHINI AVENTADOR LP700-4

Aventador LP700-4

Clean-sheet ground-up replacement flagship from Lamborghini dials up the usability without losing too much of the bonkers appeal. It's a sensational machine that's able to reach 217mph with ease. More hyper- than supercar, it looks like a relative bargain these days.

Als Nachfolger des Murcielago und völlig neues Lamborghini-Modell wartet der Aventator mit extremer Leistung und brachialem Sound auf. Ein sensationeller Kampfstier, der spielend leicht knapp 350 km/h erreicht. Eher ein Hyper- als ein Supersportwagen mit einem erstaunlichen Kaufpreis.

Le tout nouveau vaisseau amiral de Lamborghini gagne en maniabilité sans trop perdre de la folie pure qui fait la séduction de la marque. C'est une machine sensationnelle capable d'atteindre les 350 km/h sans sourciller. Hypercar plus que supercar, c'est en plus une bonne affaire si on la compare à ses rivales actuelles.

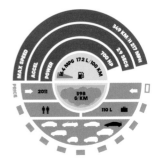

SECRET DETAIL

Buttons under technical-looking flaps tend to be associated with
villainous destruction in movies. This one just starts the car.

Ein digitales Cockpit und der unter einer roten Klappe verborgene Knopf
erinnern an Zerstörungsmaschinen aus Science-Fiction-Filmen. Keine
Angst: Das hier ist nur der Startknopf.

Dans les films, les boutons cachés sous des clapets high-tech sont
souvent associés à des actes de destruction infâme. Celui-ci ne fait que
démarrer la voiture.

LAMBORGHINI GALLARDO LP570-4 SUPERLEGGERA

The Gallardo gets better with maturity, shedding a few kilos here to create the most enjoyable model from the bullish bloodline. 200mph-plus ability and a noise to die for it's not without appeal, but newer rivals ace it.

Der Gallardo wird mit zunehmendem Alter immer besser: Dieser hier hat ein paar Kilo verloren und ist somit das schönste Mitglied seiner bulligen Familie. Mit über 320 km/h und einem wunderbaren Sound steht er ganz gut da – aber vielleicht ist das noch zu wenig für die junge Konkurrenz.

La Gallardo s'améliore avec l'âge. Elle a perdu quelques kilos pour devenir le meilleur modèle de cette lignée taurine. Elle dépasse les 320 km/h et produit un son enchanteur, mais ses nouvelles rivales sont très douées.

Gallardo LP570-4 Superleggera

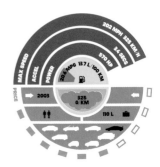

SECRET DETAIL

Forget trying to specify your Superleggera with leather inside, Alcantara is lighter, so Alcantara is all you can have.

Vergessen Sie die Leder-Innenausstattung – die Bezüge des Superleggera sind nur aus superleichtem Alcantara erhältlich.

N'essayez même pas de demander du cuir pour l'intérieur de votre Superleggera, l'alcantara est plus léger, c'est donc de l'alcantara que vous aurez.

LANCIA

(I)

FOUNDED: **1906**

HEADQUARTERS: **TURIN**, **ITALY**

2010 PRODUCTION: **94,000**

LOGO HISTORY:

Lancia is a massively important brand that unfortunately in its current state – with one exception – defines the phrase 'faded glory'. Its 100-plus years of history is full of pioneering innovation and beautiful cars including the elegant 60s Fulvias, rally-winning 70s Stratos to the brutally stylish 80s Delta HF Integrale. Its best recent effort is a stunning one-off homage to the original Stratos designed by Pininfarina for a private customer and potentially set for limited production. That aside, all there is to look forward to are a few tweaked Chryslers from parent firm Fiat's tie-up. Perhaps it'd be better to bow out gracefully?

Der Ruhm der für die Autowelt so wichtigen Marke Lancia ist – mit einer Ausnahme – leider verblasst. In über 100 Jahren Geschichte voller Innovationen und wunderschöner Autos glänzte Lancia unter anderem mit den eleganten Fulvia-Modellen aus den 60ern, den siegreichen Stratos aus den 70ern und dem robusten, aber stilvollen Delta HF Integrale aus den 80ern. Ein wirklicher Erfolg ist der für einen Privatkunden geschaffene New Stratos – eine Kreation der Designschmiede Pininfarina und eine wunderbare Hommage auf den alten Original-Stratos. Abgesehen davon gibt es außer ein paar Chrysler-Neuauflagen der mittlerweile zu Fiat gehörenden Automarke nichts Neues zu berichten. Vielleicht ist es manchmal besser, sich in Würde zu verabschieden …

Lancia est une marque extrêmement importante qui, malheureusement, illustre à la perfection l'expression « splendeur passée » (avec cependant une exception). Son histoire plus que centenaire est remplie d'innovations et de superbes voitures, notamment les élégantes Fulvia des années 1960, la Stratos victorieuse dans les rallyes des années 1970, ou encore la Delta HF Integrale des années 1980, à la beauté brutale. Son meilleur effort récent est un superbe hommage à la Stratos orginale, dessiné par Pininfarina pour un client privé, qui sera peut-être produit en série limitée. À part cela, il n'y a rien d'autre à attendre que quelques Chrysler modifiées issues du lien avec la maison-mère Fiat. Peut-être vaudrait-il mieux que la marque tire sa révérence avec dignité ?

YPSILON
Rival: VW Polo

Luxe-lite Fiat Punto-based supermini.
Schicker, Fiat Punto-basierter Kleinwagen.
Polyvalente chic basée sur la Fiat Punto.

MUSA
Rival: Opel Meriva

Small Fiat Idea-based high-roofed MPV.
Fiat Idea-Doppelgänger mit hohem Dach.
Petit monospace basé sur la Fiat Idea.

DELTA
Rival: VW Golf

Family hatch is pale shadow of 80s icon.
Blasser Schatten der 80er-Legende.
Compacte familiale, a beaucoup baissé.

THEMA
Rival: Peugeot 508

Large sedan based on Chrysler 300C.
Große, Chrysler 300C-basierte Limousine.
Grande berline basée sur la Chrysler 300C.

STRATOS
Rival: Ferrari F430

Ferrari-based limited edition supercar.
Ferrari-basierter Sportler in Kleinauflage.
Supercar en série limitée basée sur Ferrari.

LAND ROVER

FOUNDED: **1948**
HEADQUARTERS: **GAYDON, ENGLAND**
2010 PRODUCTION: **181,395**

LOGO HISTORY:

When your whole brand is associated with a shape – the SUV – and a powertrain – 4x4 – that are both increasingly socially divisive, it's a tricky marketing tightrope. But Land Rover's not any old SUV brand; it's the definitive SUV brand. With 60-plus years of experience providing the wheels for landowners, armies, explorers and more, the Land Rover brand has become renown for peerless go-anywhere ability while the Range Rover marque has added luxury and class. The plan is to differentiate these brands even further and with a new enthusiastic Indian owner, more frugal engines and striking compact models (Evoque), Land Rover is still a brand with a definite place in the world.

Wenn eine ganze Marke auf die zwei Faktoren „Form = SUV" und „Antrieb = 4x4" reduziert wird, die beide zudem noch zunehmend sozial geächtet sind, ergibt sich ein marketingtechnischer Drahtseilakt. Aber Land Rover ist eben nicht einfach ein alteingesessener Geländewagenhersteller, sondern *die* Geländewagen-Marke überhaupt. Seit über 60 Jahren stattet Land Rover Grundbesitzer, Armeen, Entdecker und andere Abenteuerhungrige mit Fahrzeugen aus und steht mittlerweile für zuverlässige Universal-Autos. Der Range Rover hat dem Ganzen etwas Luxus und Klasse hinzugefügt. Der Plan ist es, diese Marken noch weiter zu differenzieren, und mit dem neuen, enthusiastischen Eigentümer aus Indien, sparsameren Motoren sowie beeindruckend kompakten Modellen (Evoque) behauptet Land Rover immer noch seinen Platz in der Welt.

Lorsque votre marque est si profondément associée à une carrosserie (SUV) et une transmission (4x4) qui sont de plus en plus sujettes à controverse dans la société, le marketing devient un exercice de funambulisme. Mais Land Rover n'est pas qu'une marque de SUV parmi d'autres, c'est *la* marque de référence pour les SUV. En plus de 60 ans d'expérience dans la fabrication de véhicules pour les propriétaires terriens, les armées, les explorateurs et bien d'autres, la renommée de Land Rover s'est bâtie sur une capacité hors pair à se frayer un chemin partout, tandis que Range Rover lui a ajouté luxe et classe. La stratégie est de différencier ces deux marques encore plus et, avec un nouveau propriétaire indien enthousiaste, d'introduire des moteurs moins gourmands et des modèles compacts séduisants (Evoque). Land Rover a toujours une vraie place à tenir sur le marché mondial.

DEFENDER
Rival: Jeep Wrangler

Old, iconic, world's tallest gearstick.
Der größte Schaltknüppel der Welt – legendär.
Vieille légende à grand levier de vitesses.

FREELANDER 2|LR2
Rival: Audi Q5

Potted Land Rover for urbanites.
Abgespeckter Land Rover für Städter.
Succédané de Land Rover pour citadins.

DISCOVERY 4|LR4
Rival: Toyota Land Cruiser

Off-road 7-seat king.
Königlicher Offroad-7-Sitzer.
Roi du tout-terrain à 7 places.

EVOQUE
Rival: None yet -
Audi Q3 soon

Downsized, great design, sustainable luxe.
Nachhaltiger Edelwagen – klein und fein.
Plus petit, excellent design, luxe durable.

RANGE ROVER
Rival: Mercedes
GL-Class

Luxury SUV benchmark.
Luxus-SUV – Aushängeschild der Marke.
La référence des SUV de luxe.

RANGE ROVER SPORT
Rival: BMW X5

Brasher, lower Range Rover.
Frecherer, niedrigerer Range Rover.
Range Rover en plus agressif et plus bas.

60th anniversary sculpture by Gerry Judah at 2008's Goodwood Festival of Speed

LAND ROVER DEFENDER

Defender 90 Hard Top 3dr

Today's model can trace its genes back to the very first Land Rover. Indeed, the Defender's form-follows-function design defines many aspects of the rest of today's range – short overhangs and high sills for good off-road ability are just two examples. Despite its ancient underpinnings and a lack of refinement, still the most go-anywhere of the range, used by armies, farmers and the Queen of England.

Die Wurzeln des neuen Modells reichen zurück bis zum allerersten Land Rover. Der Ansatz des Defender – Funktion geht vor Design – prägt auch den Rest der Fahrzeugflotte. Die kurzen Überhänge und der hohe Einstieg des Geländeexperten sind nur zwei Beispiele. Trotz seiner uralten Ahnen und der fehlenden Raffinesse ist das superflexible Modell bei Armeen, Bauern und der Königin von England beliebt.

Ses gènes remontent jusqu'à la toute première Land Rover. La forme de la Defender suit la fonction, et son design définit de nombreux aspects du reste de la gamme actuelle : ses porte-à-faux courts et ses bas de caisse surélevés pour négocier les terrains accidentés n'en sont que deux exemples. Malgré l'ancienneté du principe et un certain manque de raffinement, c'est toujours le modèle le plus tout-terrain de la gamme, utilisé par les militaires, les fermiers et la reine d'Angleterre.

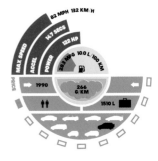

SECRET DETAIL

Has one of the biggest gear sticks in the car world, plus another stubby one right next to it for off-road low-ratio business.

Der wohl größte Schaltknüppel der Welt, plus ein kleiner Hebel daneben für die Geländeuntersetzung.

Elle possède l'un des plus grands leviers de vitesse existants, plus un petit juste à côté pour les terrains qui nécessitent des rapports de transmission plus faibles.

RANGE ROVER EVOQUE

Compact, wedgy and purposeful outside it's nonetheless spacious and luxurious on the inside, whether in three- or five-door versions. Range Rover's smallest production vehicle ever is also set to be its biggest seller. Perfect timing.

Sowohl der Drei- als auch der Fünftürer sind kompakt-zweckmäßig von außen und überzeugen durch ein geräumig-luxuriöses Innenleben. Das kleinste Serienfahrzeug von Land Rover ist gleichzeitig der größte Verkaufsschlager der Marke. Ein perfektes Timing …

Compacte, dynamique et déterminée à l'extérieur, elle n'en est pas moins spacieuse et luxueuse à l'intérieur, en version trois ou cinq portes. Le plus petit modèle de série de Range Rover sera sûrement celui qui se vendra le mieux. Juste à temps.

Evoque Coupe eD4 2WD
* Estimated CO2 emissions and MPG

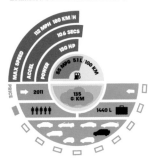

SECRET DETAIL

The transition from 2008 Land Rover LRX concept to 2011 Range Rover Evoque production car has mercifully left the original's design purity intact. See the LRX here for comparison.

Beim Übergang vom Land Rover LRX-Konzept von 2011 zum Range Rover Evoque-Serienmodell ist erstaunlich viel vom puristischen Originaldesign übriggeblieben.

La transition entre le concept de la Land Rover LRX 2008 et le modèle de production de la Range Rover Evoque 2011 n'a heureusement pas affecté la pureté du design d'origine. Voir la LRX ici pour comparer.

House-proud car designer Gerry McGovern invited us into his restored modernist home in the unsuspecting British countryside to shoot his stunning new creation, the Range Rover Evoque, on the eve of its debut. Parked precariously on a steep incline, like the building itself, the pair unsurprisingly go together like jam and bread.

In the manner of every shoot since time immemorial, we set up shop and within minutes the location has assumed the mingled atmosphere of a field command post, the backstage area of a gig, and a bus stop. Gerry works down the road at Land Rover's headquarters, but comes back to see how we were getting on and say hello. Stopping to talk to the photographer, models, assistants, and assorted staff from Land Rover, the design director scans each room vigilantly, clearly less concerned that we're making a mess or invading his privacy than that there might be an object out of place or needing a duster's attention.

He needn't have worried – the place is spotless, every object just so. A striking concrete and glass villa, sympathetically expanded along the horizon, filled with a curator's selection of iconic 20th Century furniture, it could pass for California in the '50s, if it weren't for the flatscreen TVs and drizzling rain outside. A nip and a tuck and it's a film set. But the place feels lived in and true, it's not a museum or a facade. And observing Douglas Coupland's theory that the garage is a house's subconscious, the area we've taken over has a bit more of a jumbled-up feel. DVDs that were never going to win an Oscar but would be good to put on over a delivered pizza, compete for shelf space with books that could've been gifts that it felt rude to throw out. Step through the door to the gym though, down a staircase and the cameras can start rolling.

Wearing a bespoke suit as always, Gerry leads me down through a tumbling set of crisp, bright spaces into his private lair

Der stolze Hausbesitzer und Autodesigner Gerry McGovern hat uns nach Großbritannien in sein restauriertes Haus auf dem Land eingeladen. Dort durften wir am Vorabend des Produktionsstarts seine beeindruckende Neukreation knipsen: den Range Rover Evoque. Gebäude und Wagen stehen waghalsig an einem steilen Hang – ein perfektes Bild.

Wie seit jeher bei Shootings üblich, verwandelt sich der Ort blitzschnell in eine Mischung aus Kommandoposten, Konzert-Backstage-Bereich und Bushaltestelle. Der Designchef von Land Rover arbeitet um die Ecke im Hauptsitz seines Arbeitgebers und schaut kurz vorbei, um nach dem Rechten zu sehen und uns zu begrüßen. Er unterhält sich mit Fotograf, Models, Assistenten und den Land Rover-Mitarbeitern und nimmt alles ganz genau unter die Lupe. Nicht weil er befürchtet, wir würden sein Haus durcheinanderbringen oder in seine Intimsphäre eindringen – er will nur nicht, dass ein Objekt deplaziert wirkt oder staubig aussieht.

Aber die Sorge ist unbegründet: Alles ist blitzblank, jedes Objekt am rechten Ort. Der beeindruckende Bau aus Beton und Glas erstreckt sich entlang dem Horizont und ist mit einer Sammlung der legendärsten Möbel des 20. Jahrhunderts ausgestattet. Man könnte sich wie in einer kalifornischen Villa der 50er Jahr fühlen – wären da nicht die Flachbildschirme und der Nieselregen. Nur ein paar Veränderungen, und es wäre eine perfekte Filmkulisse. Dennoch wirkt das Haus nicht künstlich oder museal, sondern belebt und einladend. Und wenn man an die Theorie von Douglas Coupland denkt, dass die Garage das Unterbewusstsein eines Hauses sei, sind wir hier in ein kleines Chaos geraten. DVDs, die weniger an die glamouröse Oscar-Verleihung als an einen Pizzaabend vor dem Fernsehen erinnern, und Bücher, die vermutlich Geschenke sind und aus Höflichkeit nicht weggeworfen wurden, drängen sich auf den Regalen. Wir durchqueren einen Fitnessraum, gehen die Treppe hinunter, und die Kameras legen los.

McGovern trägt wie immer einen Maßanzug und führt mich für das Gespräch durch eine

Gerry McGovern nous a invités chez lui dans la campagne anglaise pour photographier sa superbe création, la Range Rover Evoque, à la veille de son lancement.

Nous avons installé notre équipement et en quelques minutes le lieu s'est converti en poste de commandement de campagne. Gerry travaille non loin de là au siège de Land Rover, mais revient pour voir si tout va bien et dire bonjour. Il bavarde avec le photographe, les mannequins et les assistants. Il se préoccupe moins de nous voir envahir son intimité que de vérifier que tout est à sa place et que rien n'aurait besoin d'un coup de plumeau.

Son inquiétude est bien inutile : tout est impeccable. La magnifique villa en béton et en verre abrite une sélection experte de meubles du XXe siècle. Sans les écrans plats et la bruine insistante, on pourrait se croire dans la Californie des années 1950. Quelques petits ajustements, et l'on a un plateau de photographie. Mais l'endroit est habité, réel, ce n'est pas un musée ou une façade. Et conformément à la théorie de Douglas Coupland, selon laquelle le garage est l'inconscient d'une maison, l'espace que nous avons occupé donne une impression un peu plus confuse. Des DVD de films qui ne marqueront pas l'histoire du cinéma se disputent les étagères avec des livres qui ont sans doute été offerts. Mais passez la porte qui mène vers la salle de fitness, et les caméras peuvent commencer à filmer.

Vêtu d'un costume sur mesure, comme d'habitude, Gerry me conduit à travers plusieurs espaces immaculés qui descendent jusqu'à son antre privé, la seule pièce que l'on nous a demandé de ne pas déranger. Ce grand espace qui s'ouvre sur la pelouse fait penser à un club de gentlemen, un endroit où Dean Martin serait à son aise. Il faut prendre une minute pour absorber l'espace. On commence alors à en saisir l'intention : l'apaisement, la solidité. Un sentiment de mérite. C'est ici que Gerry vient méditer.

« J'ai acheté cette maison il y a quatre ans, et je l'ai pratiquement démolie », confie-t-il. Je le remercie de nous laisser l'utiliser pour

to talk. It's the one room we were asked not to disturb, and stepping through the solid door, the large room opening onto the descending lawn feels like a clubroom for the boys, somewhere Dean Martin would feel at home. Until he finds out there's no smoking or booze and that we're going to talk reverentially about design. It's a simulacrum of an era and a mood, but it has its own purpose. We sit on facing chairs, and it takes a minute to absorb the space. Then you feel its intention: calming, solid. Earned. It's where Gerry comes for his "meditation time".

"I bought this house four years ago, virtually knocked it down," he says. I thank him for letting us use it for the shoot. "I like to share it," he shrugs. Not far away is Skyward House, which is often used as a location – it was last seen in a Renault TV ad. "He worked for Norman Foster, had the same idea as me. He's a massive Range Rover fan. A modernist like I am. But he's minimalist, I'm more eclectic," he qualifies. "I am a design nut, others are car nuts. It gives me a sense of enjoyment – all the pieces I have in here talk to me." Joseph Albers prints hang on the walls, the Herman Miller chairs are originals not reproduction. "You can feel the difference, the originals are more comfortable." I sink back into the furniture a notch, and nod. Who doesn't prefer an original?

I AM A DESIGN NUT, OTHERS ARE CAR NUTS

Gerry was the first car designer I ever met. I interviewed him for the yet-to-launch Intersection almost ten years ago, when he was head of design at Lincoln. He'd famously ruffled feathers by drawing attention to the fact that Lincoln's average customer was aged almost 80 and therefore not likely to be around to buy the next model, so perhaps they should appeal to a younger clientele. The existing customers understandably didn't like that idea very much. But Ford's

Vielzahl frischer, heller Räume in sein privates Reich. Den Raum dürfen wir aber beim Shooting nicht betreten. Er ist riesig, bietet Ausblick auf eine Rasenfläche und wirkt wie ein Clubroom für Männer – Dean Martin lässt grüßen. Zigaretten oder Alkohol gibt es aber nicht, und wir werden vor allem über Design sprechen. Der Raum ist Abbild eines ganz bestimmten Zeitalters und seiner Stimmung, erfüllt aber einen eigenen Zweck. Wir setzen uns einander gegenüber auf Stühlen, und es dauert ein wenig, bis man sich eingefunden hat. Dann spürt man es: Ruhe, Beständigkeit. Hierher kommt McGovern, um zu „meditieren".

„Ich habe dieses Haus vor vier Jahren gekauft und praktisch komplett zerlegt." Ich danke ihm dafür, dass das Shooting hier stattfinden durfte. „Ich freue mich, wenn auch andere daran teilhaben dürfen", erwidert er. In der Nähe liegt das Skywood House von Graham Phillips, das häufig als Kulisse dient – zuletzt in einer TV-Werbung von Renault. „Graham Philipps arbeitete für Norman Foster, wir hatten ähnliche Vorstellungen. Er liebt Range Rover und ist ein Modernist wie ich. Aber er ist auch Minimalist, ich bin eklektischer. Ich liebe Design, andere lieben Autos. Es macht mich glücklich, die ganzen Gegenstände um mich zu haben – sie kommunizieren mit mir." Drucke von Joseph Albers hängen an den Wänden, die Herman Miller-Stühle sind Originale, keine Nachbildungen. „Man spürt wirklich einen Unterschied: Die Originale sind bequemer."

ICH LIEBE DESIGN, ANDERE LIEBEN AUTOS

McGovern ist der erste Autodesigner, den ich kennenlernte. Ich führte mit McGovern bereits vor zehn Jahren für die damals noch nicht herausgekommene „Intersection" ein Interview, als er noch Designchef bei Lincoln war. Er provozierte mit seinem Hinweis, dass der Durchschnittskunde von Lincoln 80 Jahre alt sei und das nächste Modell kaum kaufen würde. Also solle man sich eher nach einer jüngeren Klientel umsehen. Die damaligen Kunden reagierten verständlicherweise

la séance de photos. « J'aime la partager », répond-il avec un haussement d'épaules. Skyward House se trouve non loin. Elle sert souvent de décor pour des tournages, et est récemment apparue dans un spot télévisé pour Renault. « Il a travaillé pour Norman Foster, il a eu la même idée que moi. C'est un grand fan de Range Rover. C'est un moderniste, comme moi. Mais il est minimaliste, et je suis plutôt éclectique », précise-t-il. « Je suis un fou de design, d'autres sont fous de voitures. » Des reproductions de Josef Albers sont accrochées aux murs, et les fauteuils Herman Miller sont des originaux. « Les originaux sont plus confortables. » Je m'enfonce un peu plus dans mon siège, et je hoche la tête.

JE SUIS UN FOU DE DESIGN, D'AUTRES SONT FOUS DE VOITURES

Gerry a été le premier designer automobile que j'ai rencontré. Je l'ai interviewé il y a dix ans pour *Intersection* avant la première parution du magazine. Il était à la tête du design chez Lincoln. Il y avait froissé les sensibilités en faisant remarquer que le client moyen de Lincoln avait 80 ans et ne serait donc probablement plus là pour acheter le prochain modèle, et qu'il faudrait peut-être essayer d'attirer une clientèle plus jeune. Les clients n'ont pas beaucoup apprécié. Mais la direction de Ford a compris qu'il avait raison. Il était alors une étoile montante, mais était aussi connu pour sa franchise parfois brutale. J'ai pensé qu'il serait un bon guide pour commencer à explorer le monde de l'automobile. Il neigeait à Detroit. Gerry portait un costume sur mesure impeccable, une montre de frimeur et une cravate somptueuse. Il arborait un bronzage hollywoodien et avait l'air de sortir de chez le coiffeur. Il parlait, et parle toujours, avec un accent du centre de l'Angleterre, sans aucun complexe. C'est le genre d'accent dont la BBC a essayé de

management took the point. He'd acquired a reputation as a rising design star, ready to do some significant work; but also as someone who wasn't afraid to say what he thought. I figured he'd be a good place to start to get to know the car world. It was a snowy January in Detroit. Gerry wore an immaculately tailored suit, fuck-you watch, lavish tie, a Hollywood tan and looked like he had a hair stylist on standby backstage with an bag full of products. His accent was and is unapologetically Midlands English, the kind the BBC spent decades pretending doesn't exist, and then when forced to allow on air, set up elocution training to overwrite with their own tonal syntax. Against a show stand made out of cardboard and plastic, he looked like an authentic alien. The words came fast, and he was warm, funny, incisive and candid. His bravado gave me the opening phrase for my article. "Dressed to impress – ya basted!", he laughed when we saw each other next, in a bar in Geneva, at a designers' night party during the next car show on the international carousel I'd hopped on.

WHAT'S WRONG WITH DESIGN BEING THE ESSENCE OF A VEHICLE?

He'd been on the carousel for over 20 years at that point, with stints at Chrysler, Peugeot and Rover (before its inglorious end, it was still the owner of Land Rover and Mini). Lincoln should've been the perfect platform for his aesthetic. It was frustrating to watch as his beautifully executed proposals, riffing on Lincoln's relationship to mid-century modernism – the Case Study houses and Eames chairs – were allowed to die. McGovern saw the potential to build a new American vernacular for luxury, which would have appeal around the world, based on the foundation of this period, which it helped define. It wasn't to be. Someone in Ford's

verärgert. Aber das Management von Ford zog daraus Konsequenzen. McGovern hatte sich als vielversprechender Stardesigner bereits einen Namen gemacht. Er war jedoch auch für seine Unverblümtheit bekannt. Ich dachte mir damals, ein Gespräch mit ihm wäre ein guter Ausgangspunkt, um die Autowelt kennenzulernen. Es war ein verschneiter Januartag in Detroit. McGovern trug einen Maßanzug, eine Angeberuhr, eine auffällige Krawatte, war braun gebrannt und makellos frisiert. Er sprach ein selbstbewusstes Midlands-Englisch, den Dialekt, den die BBC jahrzehntelang ignorierte und dann – als seine Nutzung im Radio durchgesetzt wurde – den Sprechern abzutrainieren versuchte. Bei der Begrüßung stand er vor einem Präsentierständer aus Pappe und Kunststoff und sah einfach nur außergewöhnlich aus. Er sprach schnell, war freundlich, humorvoll, scharfsinnig und aufrichtig. Sein Auftreten gab den Ausschlag für den ersten Satz des Artikels. „Dressed to impress – das hast du gut getroffen!", lachte er, als ich ihn das nächste Mal in einer Bar in Genf traf. Ich hatte es mittlerweile geschafft, die internationale Autowelt zu betreten, und wir waren beide auf einer Designer-Party des Auto-Salons eingeladen.

WARUM DARF DAS DESIGN NICHT DER AUSGANGSPUNKT EINES FAHRZEUGS SEIN?

McGovern war damals schon seit über 20 Jahren dabei und hatte für Chrysler, Peugeot und Rover gearbeitet (kurz vor dem unrühmlichen Ende der Briten, als ihnen noch die Marken Land Rover und Mini gehörten). Lincoln schien perfekt für McGoverns Stil. Es war jedoch frustrierend, mit anzusehen, wie seine wunderschönen Vorschläge, die an Lincolns Modelle der Jahrhundertmitte erinnerten – die Haus-Studien und Eames-Stühle – einfach so untergingen. McGovern wollte eine neue amerikanische Luxussprache entwickeln, die zeitgenössisch und international sein sollte und daher weltweit

nier l'existence pendant des décennies. Sur fond d'un décor en carton et en plastique, il avait tout à fait l'air de descendre d'une soucoupe volante. Les mots coulaient à toute vitesse, et il était chaleureux, drôle, incisif et franc. Son caractère m'a inspiré la première phrase de mon article. « Dressed to impress – ya basted! » (« Habillé pour gagner – ouais mec ! »), a-t-il cité en riant lorsque nous nous sommes revus par la suite à Genève, à une soirée lors d'un salon automobile international.

POURQUOI LE DESIGN NE POURRAIT-IL PAS ÊTRE L'ESSENCE D'UNE VOITURE?

Cela faisait plus de vingt ans qu'il était sur ce circuit. Il avait travaillé chez Chrysler, Peugeot et Rover (avant sa fin peu glorieuse, lorsque le groupe possédait encore Land Rover et Mini). Lincoln aurait dû être une plateforme idéale pour l'expression de son esthétique. C'était frustrant de voir ses magnifiques propositions laissées sans suite. Elles surfaient sur la relation de Lincoln avec le modernisme du milieu de siècle (les Case Study Houses et les fauteuils Eames). McGovern comprenait le potentiel qu'il y avait à créer un nouveau langage américain du luxe qui séduirait le monde entier. Mais cela ne devait pas être. Les gens du service marketing de Ford doivent s'en mordre les doigts lorsqu'ils regardent *Mad Men*. L'acteur qui joue Roger Sterling apparaît dans les dernières publicités de Lincoln. Mais il est trop tard de dix ans, et la voiture qu'il aurait conduite n'a jamais vu le jour.

« Ils ont changé d'avis à cause de ce qui se passait. Firestone leur avait coûté cher, et le 11 septembre avait changé les priorités aux États-Unis. La direction de Ford a décidé que Lincoln ne devait pas devenir une marque de luxe mondiale. » Jac Nasser, le PDG qui avait créé le groupe Premier Automotive avec une écurie qui comprenait Jaguar, Land Rover, Aston Martin, Volvo et Lincoln, avait été

marketing department must watch Mad Men grinding their teeth. Lincoln's recent ads feature the actor who plays Roger Sterling, it's a decade late, and the car he would drive never got made.

"It was a consequence of business they changed their mind on what they wanted. Firestone cost them a lot of money, 9/11 changed priorities in America. Ford decided it didn't want Lincoln to be a global luxury brand, so they didn't implement the design strategy." Jac Nasser, the CEO who'd created the Premier Automotive Group, with the impressive stable of Jaguar, Land Rover, Aston Martin, Volvo and Lincoln assembled, was ousted, the group disbanded, and Lincoln returned to being best known as the car service workhorse that drops you off at JFK.

COMPANIES REFLECT THE PEOPLE RUNNING THEM.

McGovern was at Land Rover when the company was sold by Ford to Tata, the Indian conglomerate, along with Jaguar. "It's a breath of fresh air," he says. "There isn't the complexity of decision-making, so many people and levels. Tata has been incredibly supportive. Companies are a consequence of the people running them. Mr Tata trained as an architect in America, he knew Eames, Saarinen, the greats. So he's passionate about design, involved in the process, and puts importance on design in business – it's refreshing."

To Ford's credit, the Evoque production decision was made on its watch. And it's a startlingly faithful rendering of the concept version, the LRX, in a notoriously tricky transition where the eventual form gets dealt blows by budgetary reality, engineering limits, safety regulations and the general involvement of too many people: "I could probably count on one hand the number of cars that have been done well". Gerry refers to the '56 Continental as one of the few:

verstanden würde. Es kam nie dazu. Jemand in Fords Marketingabteilung sollte sich in der TV-Serie „Mad Men" einmal genauer ansehen, wie das Amerika der 50er/60er Jahre aussah. Im neuesten Spot wirbt „Roger Sterling" für Lincoln – leider ein Jahrzehnt zu spät –, aber das Auto, das *wirklich* zu seinem Stil passen würde, wurde nie gebaut.

„Es war eine Firmenentscheidung, die Strategie so plötzlich zu ändern. Mit Firestone haben sie viel Geld verloren, und der 11. September hat in Amerika alles verändert. Ford hat entschieden, Lincoln nicht zu einer globalen Luxusmarke zu machen. Daher kam meine Designstrategie nie zum Einsatz." CEO Jac Nasser hatte die Premier Automotive Group gegründet und somit Jaguar, Land Rover, Aston Martin, Volvo und Lincoln unter einem Dach vereint. Nach dem Rauswurf Nassers und der Auflösung der Gruppe wurde Lincoln wieder zum unspektakulären Arbeitspferd.

FIRMEN WERDEN IMMER VON DEN MANAGERN GEPRÄGT.

McGovern war schon bei Land Rover, als Ford die Marke an Tata verkaufte. „Hier bläst ein frischer Wind. Hier gibt es kein komplexes System aus Ebenen und Mitarbeitern. Tata hat uns sehr unterstützt. Eine Firma ist das, was die Menschen daraus machen. Ratan Tata hat Architektur studiert und kennt daher große Namen wie Eames oder Saarinen. Er liebt Design und legt auch in seinem Unternehmen Wert auf Ästhetik – für mich als Designer ist das ein Gewinn."

Man muss es Ford zugutehalten, dass sie sich für die Produktion des Evoque entschieden haben. Das Konzeptmodell LRX wurde detailgetreu umgesetzt. Die Umsetzung ist schwierig, die endgültige Form hängt von Budget, produktionstechnischen Grenzen, Sicherheitsvorschriften und zu vielen Menschen ab: „Wirklich gut gemachte Autos gibt es nur wenige." McGovern erwähnt den 1956 Continental als Beispiel: „Im Vordergrund stand die Eleganz, und es sollte das tiefliegendste Auto aller Zeiten werden.

évincé, le groupe démantelé, et la Lincoln est retournée à son statut de voiture de service, qui vous dépose à l'aéroport.

LES ENTREPRISES SONT UN REFLET DE LEURS DIRIGEANTS.

McGovern était chez Land Rover lorsque Ford a vendu la société à Tata, le conglomérat indien, en même temps que Jaguar. « C'est une bouffée d'air frais », déclare-t-il. « Les prises de décision ne sont plus aussi complexes qu'avant, le climat qui règne est incroyablement favorable. Les entreprises sont un reflet de leurs dirigeants. M. Tata a étudié l'architecture aux États-Unis, il a connu Eames, Saarinen, les grands maîtres. C'est un passionné du design, il participe au processus et accorde de l'importance au design dans les activités de son entreprise, c'est très rafraîchissant. »

Il faut reconnaître que la production de l'Evoque a été décidée sous la direction de Ford. Et le modèle de production est étonnamment fidèle au concept, la LRX, alors que l'on connaît bien les difficultés de la transition entre ces deux stades : les budgets, la technique, la sécurité et les avis contradictoires portent de rudes coups à l'idée initiale. « Je pourrais compter sur les doigts d'une main le nombre de voitures qui ont été faites correctement. » Gerry cite parmi elles la Continental de 1956 : « la priorité était l'élégance. Elle avait été conçue pour être le véhicule le plus surbaissé de l'histoire. La ceinture de caisse ne faisait que 47 centimètres de hauteur, ce qui est sacrément bas. Ils ont dit aux ingénieurs "DONNEZ-NOUS cette hauteur de ceinture et ce toit". C'est ce que nous avons fait ici : la ligne de ceinture qui monte, la ligne de toit qui descend, une robustesse générale. Ce qui est difficile, c'est d'adapter la technique à la forme. Mais cela fonctionne bien mieux que de faire le contraire. Pourquoi le design ne pourrait-il pas être l'essence d'une voiture ? Aujourd'hui, les designers ont

"the whole emphasis was elegance, it was designed to be the lowest slung vehicle ever. The critical height was the waistline – just 18 1/2 inches – which is bloody low. Their approach was to tell the engineers, 'GIVE ME that waist height, that roof'. That's what we've done here: the rising beltline, falling roof, an overall robustness. The challenge is to engineer to achieve that shape. It's a much better approach than starting from 'these are the engineering traits'. What's wrong with design being the essence of a vehicle? We designers sit as equal partners now to product development."

Aside from a few changes to the car's dimensions, the only one you'd notice is the loss of the concealed door handles. Concepts always acquire chunky, traditional handles when they become real cars due to cost, but apparently "Mr Tata is big on flush handles." So here it was a rare intrusion of function trumping form: "there were concerns about it freezing in markets where it gets really cold, like Russia."

LUXURY PRODUCTS ARE THINGS YOU DON'T NEED, YOU HAVE TO WANT THEM

If the new Range Rover looks a far cry from the archetypal Landie, an indestructible, go-anywhere box on wheels, it's an intentional distancing of the luxury model line. "Land Rovers look the way they do because of what they do. The Discovery 3 was too utilitarian for some markets," he says, but it had to look like a Land Rover, meaning "an emphasis on roots and overt functionality" more than what he calls 'jewel-like' looks. Whereas, "Range Rover will become a brand in itself", retaining the "integrity and capability" of the basic models, but with the freedom to focus on desirability. After the initial three-door model a five-door is on its way, and there's likely to be a convertible version. "They're

Als Richtwert galt die Gürtellinie, die mit 47 cm verdammt niedrig werden sollte. Man sagte den Ingenieuren, was sie zu tun hatten und nicht umgekehrt. Genau das haben wir hier auch gemacht: die ansteigende Gürtellinie, das abfallende Dach, die konsequente Robustheit. Die wahre Herausforderung ist es, die Vorgaben des Designers umzusetzen. Das ist doch viel besser als sich von vornherein von den technischen Grenzen einschränken zu lassen. Warum darf das Design nicht der Ausgangspunkt eines Fahrzeugs sein? Wir Designer sind zu gleichberechtigten Partnern der Produktentwickler geworden."

Bis auf ein paar kleine Abweichungen bei den Maßen ist die einzige sichtbare Änderung das Fehlen der verdeckten Türgriffe. Bei Konzeptautos, die in Produktion gehen, fallen die Griffe aus Kostengründen meist grob und eher traditionell aus, aber offensichtlich „legt auch Herr Tata Wert auf bündige Türgriffe." Doch hier musste man der Funktion den Vorrang vor der Form geben: „Wir hatten Bedenken, dass die Griffe bei großer Kälte – z. B. in Russland – einfrieren würden."

LUXUSGÜTER BRAUCHT MAN NICHT, MAN BEGEHRT SIE

Der neue Range Rover erinnert leicht an den archetypischen Landie – eine unzerstörbare Kiste auf vier Rädern – eine bewusste Abwendung von den Luxusmodellen der Marke. „Das Aussehen eines Land Rovers soll von seiner Nutzung bestimmt sein. Der Discovery 3 war für manche Märkte zu praktisch orientiert", aber er musste wie ein Land Rover aussehen, d. h. „die Betonung liegt bei den Wurzeln, bei der Nützlichkeit des Fahrzeugs", das nicht wirken soll wie ein „Schmuckstück". „Range Rover soll eine eigenständige Marke werden" und die „Zuverlässigkeit und Funktionalität" der Basismodelle behalten. Gleichzeitig sollen sie aber auch attraktiv sein. Nach dem 2-Türer ist auch ein 4-Türer geplant, und vielleicht kommt auch eine Cabrio-Version. „Die richtige Kombination macht es: eine gute

autant d'importance que les autres acteurs du développement des produits. »

À part quelques modifications dans les dimensions de la voiture, le seul changement que vous pourrez repérer est l'abandon des poignées de porte cachées. « Les concepts se voient toujours affubler de grosses poignées standard lorsqu'ils passent en production, pour des raisons de coûts, mais M. Tata a un faible pour les poignées plates. » Il s'est donc agi ici d'une rare intrusion de la fonction au détriment de la forme : « on a eu peur qu'elles gèlent dans les pays où il peut faire très froid, comme en Russie ».

VOUS N' AVEZ PAS BESOIN DES PRODUITS DE LUXE, IL FAUT QUE VOUS LES DÉSIRIEZ

La nouvelle Range Rover semble très différente de l'archétype de la « Landie », une boîte sur roues indestructible, et c'est bien l'intention de la ligne de luxe. « La forme des Land Rover découle de leur fonction. La Discovery 3 était trop utilitaire pour certains marchés », dit-il, mais il fallait qu'elle ressemble à une Land Rover, c'est-à-dire que « l'accent doit être mis sur les racines, une fonctionnalité visible » plutôt que ce qu'il appelle un style « précieux ». « Range Rover deviendra une marque autonome », qui conservera « l'intégrité et la capacité » des modèles de base, mais avec la liberté de s'orienter sur la séduction. Après le premier modèle deux portes, une quatre portes est prévue, et il y aura sans doute une version décapotable.

Beaucoup de gens se sont étonnés de la nomination de Victoria Beckham au poste de designer exécutif chez Range Rover, qui confirme d'ailleurs que la séduction prime sur la fonctionnalité. Il est difficile de cerner ce que les designers exécutifs font au juste, outre prêter leur influence à un projet. « Bien sûr il y a un côté relations publiques, mais ce n'est pas tout. Elle s'y connaît en luxe. Aucun

still linked. A well toned body in a tailored dinner jacket, instead of a tight T-shirt."

VICTORIA BECKHAM UNDERSTANDS LUXURY, BUT I'M THE BOSS, IT'S MY DESIGN INTEGRITY AT STAKE

Focusing on desirability over functionality, many were curious at footballer's wife Victoria Beckham becoming appointed an executive designer at Range Rover. A bit like executive producers in movies, it's hard to know exactly what they do except lend their influence to a project. "There's a PR side obviously, but it's more than that. She understands luxury. I don't have designers in my studio who've experienced her lifestyle. She's respectful of their level of training, craft and graft – she won't be designing Range Rovers. But she brings a point of view as a customer from our target audience. And she brings a fashion element." Describing the Evoque as "small but not feminine", the aim is nonetheless to attract more women to the brand, and an honest embrace of the fact that style attracts many to Range Rover, not function. "Off-road capability makes the brand irrelevant for some people. It's about versatility. You can park a Range Rover next to supercars. It's peerless."

Gerry McGovern's title, in common with many designers these days, is Chief Creative Officer, which he compares to the role of Jonathan Ive at Apple. Aside from cars, he casts his aesthetic eye over dealerships, brochures, show stands and advertising. Recalling a campaign that used a distinctly pre-modern palace as its backdrop, Gerry mocks the idea Range Rovers need to "be parked in front of Prince Charles's house. We need a more contemporary view of the world in our communications," he says, that nods to tradition but "isn't stifled by it."

"I inherited a rich heritage," he says. "When I arrived I assembled a design bible accumulating the cues, features, philosophy.

Figur und ein gut sitzender Maßanzug – und kein figurbetontes T-Shirt."

VICTORIA BECKHAM VERSTEHT ETWAS VON LUXUS, ABER DER CHEFDESIGNER BIN ICH

Attraktivität vor Funktionalität: Man fragte sich, was die Fußballerfrau Victoria Beckham als Executive Designer bei Range Rover sollte. Es ist wie beim Executive Producer in der Filmwelt: Man weiß nicht so genau, wofür er gut sein soll. „Klar war das auch Publicity, aber da steckte noch mehr dahinter. Sie versteht etwas von Luxus. Keiner meiner Designer hat so einen Lebensstil. Victoria hat großen Respekt vor den Kenntnissen und Leistungen der Designer und würde daher niemals einen Range Rover entwerfen. Aber sie kann sehr gut den Standpunkt unserer Zielgruppe einnehmen. Und sie versteht etwas von Mode." Der Evoque wird zwar als „klein, aber nicht feminin" beschrieben. Ziel ist es jedoch, die Marke für Frauen attraktiver zu machen. Dafür muss man einfach zugeben, dass sich viele Kunden vom Aussehen, und nicht von der Funktionalität, anziehen lassen. „Die Geländetauglichkeit ist vielen Käufern egal. Es geht eher um die Vielseitigkeit. Man kann problemlos einen Range Rover neben einem Supersportwagen parken. Er muss keinen Vergleich scheuen."

Gerry McGoverns Position trägt die moderne Bezeichnung „Chief Creative Officer". Er vergleicht seine Rolle mit der von Jonathan Ive bei Apple. Neben den Autos ist er auch für die Ästhetik von Autohäusern, Broschüren, Messeständen und Werbung zuständig. Wir erinnern uns an die Werbekampagne, in der ein vormoderner Palast als Hintergrund dient – McGovern macht sich damit über die überholte Vorstellung lustig, dass ein Range Rover „stets vor dem Schloss von Prinz Charles geparkt werden muss. Wir brauchen in unserer Kommunikation eine zeitgenössischere Sicht auf die Welt." Wir sollten die Tradition würdigen, „uns von ihr aber nicht die Luft nehmen lassen."

de mes designers n'a mené un train de vie comparable au sien. Elle ne va pas dessiner des Range Rover, mais elle apporte le point de vue de notre public cible. Sans oublier l'élément de la mode. » L'Evoque est décrite comme « petite, mais pas féminine ». Son but est néanmoins d'attirer davantage de femmes, et elle représente une prise de conscience honnête : c'est le style qui attire les clients de Range Rover, avant la fonction. « L'aspect tout terrain ne présente aucun intérêt pour certaines personnes. C'est la polyvalence qui compte. Vous pouvez garer une Range Rover à côté d'une supercar. »

VICTORIA BECKHAM COMPREND LE LUXE, MAIS C'EST MOI LE CHEF, C'EST L'INTÉGRITÉ DE MON DESIGN QUI EST EN JEU

Gerry McGovern est directeur général de la création. Il compare ce rôle à celui de Jonathan Ive chez Apple. Outre les voitures, il porte son regard d'esthète sur les concessionnaires, les brochures, les stands des salons et la publicité. Se remémorant une campagne qui utilisait comme décor un palais clairement prémoderne, Gerry raille l'idée selon laquelle les Range Rover devraient forcément « être garées devant la maison du prince Charles. Nous avons besoin d'une vision du monde plus moderne, qui respecte la tradition sans se laisser étouffer. »

« J'ai reçu un riche héritage », assure-t-il. « Lorsque je suis arrivé, j'ai confectionné une bible du design qui rassemblait toutes les influences et caractéristiques, toute la philosophie. Mais mon travail est de diriger, d'adapter une vision d'avenir. Notre évolution ne doit pas nous faire perdre de vue notre essence. Mais la technologie avance. Ce modèle est la Range Rover la plus légère de l'histoire ; elle utilise plus de matériaux durables, de polycomposites, de plastique recyclé. Nous travaillons beaucoup sur les

But my job is to direct, edit a vision for the future that will dictate our relevance. It's really important as we move on we don't lose the essence. But technology moves on. This is the lightest Range Rover ever; it uses more sustainable materials, polycomposites, and recycled plastic. We're doing lots of work now on hybrids, the sort of technology that talks to sustainability whilst keeping capability." Still, "design is fundamental to creating emotional connection. Luxury products are things you don't need, you have to want them."

While Range Rover's grounding is in that DNA, the appreciation of luxury in Gerry's case is informed by his love of design, hard work and plain talking. The youngest of four boys born to Irish parents living in Coventry, his mother worked in a jam factory, and his Dad was a baker. "We never ran out of bread and jam," he laughs. "Dad lived to be 90, never drove a car in his life," Gerry smiles. His mother nurtured his appreciation for design: "she was very aesthetically aware."

Returning to his design team, Gerry observes: "Victoria came from a normal background like me, and she doesn't pretend to come from privilege. She's got three kids, she's very easy to talk to. She's focused, serious and dedicated. She doesn't have to work, but she's carved her own career. It'll be interesting to see how it develops. But ultimately I'm the boss, it's my design integrity at stake."

Moving away from its 'to the manor born' past as his Lordship's Chelsea tractor, the Evoque completes a shift towards Range Rover breaking free of its Landed roots. With the design ethos comes the unapologetically accomplished feeling of defining yourself in the present. The basis of modernism, now a grand tradition itself.

„Wir können stolz auf unser reiches Erbe sein. Als ich hier anfing, stellte ich ein Design-Handbuch zusammen, in dem ich die Schlüsselwörter und Merkmale, die Philosophie der Marke sammelte. Aber ich möchte eine Zukunftsperspektive schaffen, nach der wir uns richten können. Wir müssen uns weiterentwickeln, dürfen dabei aber nicht unser Wesen verraten. Die Technologie eröffnet uns neue Möglichkeiten: Dies ist der leichteste Range Rover aller Zeiten. Er enthält nachhaltige Materialien, Poly-Verbundstoffe, wiederverwerteten Kunststoff. Wir arbeiten an der Entwicklung von Hybriden, die nachhaltig und trotzdem leistungsfähig sind", legt McGovern dar. Aber immer noch „ist Design zur Schaffung einer emotionalen Bindung unverzichtbar. Luxusprodukte brauchen wir nicht, wir begehren sie."
Während Range Rover für diese Einstellung steht, beruht Luxus für McGovern auf der Liebe zum Design, auf harter Arbeit und auf einem ehrlichen Austausch über das Thema. McGovern wuchs als jüngster von vier Brüdern in einer irischen Familie in Coventry auf. Seine Mutter arbeitete in einer Marmeladenfabrik, sein Vater war Bäcker. „Wir hatten immer Brot und Marmelade im Überfluss. Mein Vater wurde 90 Jahre alt und hat nie ein Auto gefahren." Seine Mutter weckte in ihm das Bewusstsein für Design: „Ästhetik war ihr wichtig."

McGovern kommt noch einmal auf sein Design-Team zurück: „Victoria stammt wie ich aus einer normalen Familie, und sie steht dazu. Sie hat vier Kinder und ist eine klasse Gesprächspartnerin, konzentriert, ernsthaft und aufmerksam. Sie muss nicht arbeiten, hat sich aber ihre eigene Karriere aufgebaut. Mal sehen, wie sich das Ganze entwickelt. Aber am Ende bin ich immer noch der Chef und trage die Verantwortung." Mit dem Evoque lässt Range Rover endgültig die Herrenhäuser des Landadels hinter sich und streift das Image als Hersteller dekadenter Allradantriebe für reiche Städter, spöttisch auch „Chelsea Tractors" genannt, ab. Das Design-Ethos legt den Grundstein für eine selbstbewusste Rolle in der Gegenwart. Das war auch Ausgangspunkt des Modernismus, der mittlerweile selbst zu einer großen Tradition geworden ist.

hybrides pour explorer la durabilité tout en conservant les performances. » Il n'en reste pas moins que « le design est fondamental pour créer un lien émotionnel. Vous n'avez pas besoin des produits de luxe, il faut que vous les désiriez. »

Dans le cas de Gerry, l'appréciation du luxe est informée par son amour du design, du travail et de l'échange. Il est le plus jeune des quatre enfants que ses parents irlandais ont élevés à Coventry. Sa mère travaillait dans une usine de confiture, et son père était boulanger. « Nous n'étions jamais à court de tartines », plaisante-t-il. « Mon père a vécu jusqu'à l'âge de 90 ans, et n'a jamais conduit de sa vie », confie-t-il en souriant. Sa mère a nourri sa sensibilité pour le design : « elle avait une conscience aigüe de l'esthétique. »

Revenant à son équipe de design, Gerry remarque : « Victoria ne fait pas semblant d'être née dans un milieu privilégié. Elle a quatre enfants, et elle est d'un abord très facile. Elle est sérieuse et déterminée. Elle n'a pas besoin de travailler, mais s'est forgé sa propre carrière. Ce sera intéressant de voir comment elle évoluera. Mais en fin de compte c'est moi le patron, c'est l'intégrité de mon design qui est en jeu. »

S'éloignant de son passé aristocratique, l'Evoque opère un revirement qui libère Range Rover de ses racines terriennes. La philosophie du design s'accompagne du sentiment mérité et hautement satisfaisant de se définir soi-même dans le présent. C'est la base du modernisme, une nouvelle grande tradition.

LEXUS

FOUNDED: **1989**
HEADQUARTERS: **TOYOTA, JAPAN**
2010 PRODUCTION: **410,100**

LOGO HISTORY:

Born in 1989, Toyota's upmarket brand is a relative newcomer in luxury car terms, but it has quickly established itself through a great reputation for build quality and customer satisfaction – witness endless victories in JD Power surveys – if not originality. Early models referenced a mixture of German luxury motoring marques (hello Mercedes) but recently the brand's design vagueness has been offset by developing a name for itself as a hybrid specialist across a range which now starts with the CT200h, through various coupes and SUVs and up to a $375,000 gas-guzzling supercar. Design is the card we'd love to see this brand play.

Die 1989 gegründete Oberklassenmarke von Toyota ist ein Neuling unter den Luxusautos, hat sich aber durch hohe Qualität und zufriedene Kunden schnell einen guten Ruf gesichert – und kann sich als Gewinner von zahllosen J.D.Power-Kundenzufriedenheitsstudien brüsten. Die frühen Modelle erinnerten stark an deutsche Luxusmarken (Mercedes), aber in jüngster Zeit hat die Marke ihre Zurückhaltung in Sachen Design abgelegt und sich einen eigenen Namen gemacht, und zwar als Hybrid-Spezialist mit einem Sortiment, das mit dem CT200h startet, ein paar Coupés und SUVs enthält und schließlich mit einem sportlichen, 375.000 USD (260.000 EUR) teuren Benzinschleuder gekrönt wird. Wir freuen uns aber auf noch mehr gestalterische Finesse.

Née en 1989, la marque haut de gamme de Toyota est une relative nouvelle venue chez les voitures de luxe, mais elle a vite trouvé sa place grâce à une réputation bâtie sur la qualité de la construction et sur la satisfaction des clients (en sont preuve les innombrables victoires de la marque dans les sondages de JD Power), même si l'originalité n'est pas au rendez-vous. Les premiers modèles s'inspiraient de plusieurs marques de luxe allemandes (bonjour Mercedes), mais récemment Lexus a compensé l'indécision de son design en se forgeant un nom en tant que spécialiste des véhicules hybrides. Sa gamme commence aujourd'hui avec la CT200h, passe par plusieurs coupés et SUV, et culmine avec une supercar à 375 000 $ (env. 260 000 EUR) qui engloutit les litres d'essence. Nous aimerions beaucoup voir cette marque jouer la carte du design.

CT200H Rival: Audi A3		World's first premium compact hybrid. Erster Luxuskompakter mit Hybridtechnik. Première compacte hybride haut de gamme.
IS Rival: BMW 3		Ageing sedan & coupe/cabrio, avoid. Als Limousine, Coupé und Cabrio. Berline et coupé/cabriolet vieillissant.
IS-F Rival: BMW M3		V8 with design tweaks altogether better. Sportliches Design und V8-Motor. V8 avec un design amélioré.
ES Rival: BMW 5-series		Toyota Camry-related uninspiring sedan. Fade Limousine mit Toyota Camry-Geschmack. Berline terne, parente de la Toyota Camry.
GS Rival: Jaguar XF		Old swaggering big coupe now with hybrid. Großes Angeber-Coupé, auch als Hybrid. Vieux coupé frimeur, option hybride.
RX Rival: Infiniti FX		World's first hybrid luxury SUV. Erster Luxus-SUV mit Hybridtechnik. Le premier SUV hybride de luxe au monde.
GX460 Rival: Merc ML-Class		Ungainly 7-seat US-only large SUV. Plumper, riesiger SUV mit 7 Sitzen. SUV à 7 places vendu aux États-Unis.
LX570 Rival: Merc GL-Class		Even bigger 8-seat US-only SUV. Noch größerer 8-Sitzer, nur USA. SUV à 8 places vendu aux États-Unis.
LS Rival: Merc S-Class		Super reliable limo, hybrid option. Zuverlässige Limousine, auch als Hybrid. Limousine super fiable, option hybride.
SC430 Rival: Merc SL		Wannabe Merc sporstcar now US-only. Möchtegern-Mercedes, nur USA. Sportive qui voudrait être une Mercedes.
LFA Rival: Merc SLS		Limited edition 200mph supercar. Limitierter 325 km/h-Sportler. Supercar en édition limitée, 325 km/h.

LEXUS LFA

This long awaited supercar from Lexus is an odd Japanese mix of V10 power and gaming interaction through its multi-layer instrument display. The result is extraordinary, both in its performance and looks. But we're baffled that it isn't a hybrid, the obvious gap for the brand to fill. And after 10 years in development its arrival can't help but be something of an anticlimax. Hopefully its influence will filter down the range a little faster in future.

Dieser lange erwartete Supersportwagen von Lexus ist ein verrückter japanischer Mix aus V10-Power und verspielt-futuristischem Cockpit. Das Ergebnis kann sich in Sachen Look und Leistung sehen lassen. Dennoch wundern wir uns, dass es kein Hybrid-Modell geworden ist, denn diese Lücke muss die Marke noch schließen. Nach zehn Jahren Entwicklung ist das dann doch eine kleine Enttäuschung. Wir hoffen trotzdem, dass das Modell einen positiven Einfluss auf die künftige Produktpalette von Lexus hat.

Cette supercar longtemps attendue de Lexus est un drôle de mélange nippon entre la puissance du V10 et le mode d'interaction d'un jeu vidéo, avec l'affichage multi-strate des instruments. Le résultat est extraordinaire, que ce soit en termes de performances ou d'esthétique. Mais nous ne comprenons pas pourquoi elle n'est pas hybride, c'était un manque à combler évident pour la marque. Et après dix ans de développement, son arrivée n'est pas vraiment à la hauteur de l'attente. Nous espérons que son influence se fera sentir sur le reste de la gamme plus rapidement.

SECRET DETAIL

Lexus claims weight savings by adding a flat-bottomed steering wheel –
only to add a weight at the bottom to 'aid self-centring'.

U. a. durch ein abgeflachtes Lenkrad schafft der Lexus eine
Gewichtsreduzierung, die mit Maßnahmen zur Erhöhung der
Fahrstabilität wieder zunichtegemacht wird.

Lexus prétend économiser du poids en équipant la voiture d'un volant
tronqué – mais ajoute un poids dans le bas pour « faciliter le centrage
automatique ».

LINCOLN

(USA)

FOUNDED: **1917**
HEADQUARTERS: **MICHIGAN**, USA
2010 PRODUCTION: **96,367**

LOGO HISTORY:

Started by ex-Cadillac founder Henry M Leland in 1917, it gained its name from one of Leland's heroes - US president Abraham Lincoln. Under Ford ownership since 1922 it rose to become one of the top US luxury brands providing presidential transport to a succession of American leaders from Roosevelt to Reagan – but most famously and fatefully – to John F Kennedy assassinated in a 1961 Continental Convertible. Its signature long and square look lost its way in the 90s before a new wave of more curvaceous product in the late 00s. Still not back to its mid-20th century heyday but showing new promise.

Nachdem Henry M. Leland sein ehemaliges Unternehmen Cadillac verlassen hatte, gründete er 1917 eine neue Firma, die er nach einem seiner größten Helden Abraham Lincoln benannte. Lincoln wurde 1922 von Ford aufgekauft und machte sich als eine der besten US-amerikanischen Luxusmarken einen Namen: Roosevelt bis Reagan nutzten den Lincoln als Präsidentenauto. Traurige Berühmtheit erlangte die Marke, als John F. Kennedy in einem Continental Convertible von 1961 ermordet wurde. Seine charakteristisch lange und eckige Form ging in den 90er Jahren langsam verloren und wich in den Nullerjahren einer kurvigeren Silhouette. Lincoln hat zwar nicht mehr den alten Ruhm erreicht, zeigt aber eine viel versprechende Entwicklung.

La marque Lincoln a été créée en 1917 par l'ex-fondateur de Cadillac, Henry M. Leland, et tient son nom de l'un des héros de Leland, le président américain Abraham Lincoln. Sous la direction de Ford depuis 1922, elle est devenue l'une des plus grandes marques de luxe des États-Unis et a fourni des véhicules présidentiels à toute une série de dirigeants américains, de Roosevelt à Reagan, et c'est dans une Continental Convertible 1961 que John F. Kennedy a été assassiné. La ligne caractéristique de Lincoln, allongée et carrée, s'est perdue dans les années 1990 avant de laisser place à une nouvelle vague de modèles aux courbes plus prononcées à la fin des années 2000. La marque a vécu son âge d'or au milieu du XXe siècle, mais l'avenir est rempli de nouvelles promesses.

MKS Rival: Cadillac CTS		Large luxury sedan with hybrid option. Luxus-Limousine mit Hybrid-Option. Berline luxueuse avec une option hybride.
MKT Rival: Merc R-Class		Large 6-seat high-roofed crossover. Crossover mit 6 Sitzen und hohem Dach. Crossover à 6 places haut sous plafond.
MKX Rival: Acura MDX		Lux version of Ford Edge mid-sized SUV. Luxus-Version des SUV Ford Edge. Version luxe du SUV Edge de Ford.
MKZ Rival: Lexus ES		Mid-size entry-level lux sedan, hybrid option. Einsteiger-Luxus-Limousine, Hybrid-Option. Berline de luxe, option hybride.
NAVIGATOR Rival: Cadillac Escalade		8-seat SUV beloved of R Kelly. SUV mit 8 Sitzen, größter Fan ist R. Kelly. SUV à 8 places qui a les faveurs de R. Kelly.
TOWN CAR Rival: Cadillac DTS		Old school large 4dr V8 on run-out. 4-Türer mit V8-Motor, Auslaufmodell. 4-portes classique, V8, en fin de parcours.

LOCAL MOTORS

FOUNDED: **2009**
HEADQUARTERS: **WAREHAM, USA**

LOGO HISTORY:

The world's first open-source car company is a genuine USP in an industry used to ruthlessly guarding its intellectual property. Local Motors works by attracting an online community to submit designs, democratically votes on the best one, and then collaborates to make it, getting paid by the part. Cars use off-the-shelf components, with patches filling in the gaps then the final kit is shipped to a local workshop to build. Everything is open source, from CAD drawings to instruction manual. The first model – Rally Fighter – a stripped-out off-road coupe, has already become a stunning reality (at $50,000) and more designs are in the pipeline.

Das erste Open Source-Auto der Welt ist in einer Branche, die normalerweise sehr darauf bedacht ist, ihr geistiges Eigentum zu schützen, eine einmalige Neuheit. Local Motors lässt über die von seiner Online-Community eingereichten Designs demokratisch abstimmen und anschließend das beste Modell dezentral auf Bestellung produzieren. Die Autos werden zum Teil aus serienmäßig hergestellten, zum Teil aus speziell für das jeweilige Modell gefertigten Bauteilen zusammengestellt. Der fertige Bausatz wird anschließend zum Zusammenbauen an eine lokale Werkstatt geschickt. Von den CAD-Zeichnungen bis hin zum Handbuch unterliegt hier alles dem Open Source-Prinzip. Das erste Modell – der Rally Fighter – sieht aus wie ein minimalistisches Offroad-Coupé und kann für 50.000 USD (35.000 EUR) bereits bestellt werden. Weitere Modelle sind in Vorbereitung.

La première compagnie automobile en source libre du monde incarne une proposition unique et originale dans un secteur habitué à protéger farouchement sa propriété intellectuelle. Local Motors fonctionne en demandant à la communauté des internautes d'envoyer des projets de voiture et d'élire démocratiquement le meilleur projet, puis participe à sa fabrication et se fait payer à l'unité. Les voitures sont composées de pièces qui existent déjà dans le commerce, avec des patchs pour combler les manques, puis le kit final est envoyé à un atelier local pour passer à la construction. Tout est en source libre, depuis les dessins CAD jusqu'au manuel d'instructions. Le Rally Fighter, un superbe coupé tout-terrain à l'intérieur minimaliste, est déjà devenu réalité (à 50 000 $), et d'autres modèles sont prévus pour bientôt.

RALLY FIGHTER
Rival: No-one and everyone

Open-source serious off-roader.
Offroader nach dem Open Source-Prinzip.
Tout-terrain en source libre qui ne plaisante pas.

Local Motors founder Jay Rogers

LOCAL MOTORS RALLY FIGHTER

The Rally Fighter – the world's first open source car – was designed by Art Center graduate Sangho Kim after positive feedback from the Local Motors online community demanding it get made. Only a maximum of 2000 will get made and more models are planned from city car EVs to 2+2 roadsters.

Der Rally Fighter wurde als erstes Open Source-Auto der Welt vom Art Center-Absolventen Sangho Kim designt, nachdem die Online-Community von Local Motors für ihn gestimmt hatte. Höchstens 2.000 Exemplare werden hergestellt. Die innovative Start-up-Firma plant weitere Modelle, z. B. einen Elektro-Kleinwagen und einen 2+2-Roadster.

Le Rally Fighter, la première voiture en source libre du monde, a été conçue par Sangho Kim, diplômé de l'Art Center, suite aux votes que les visiteurs du site web de Local Motors. La production ne pourra pas dépasser 2 000 unités, mais cette jeune entreprise innovante a prévu d'autres modèles, notamment des citadines électriques et des roadsters 2+2.

Rally Fighter

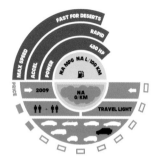

SECRET DETAIL

All cars come vinyl-wrapped – unless you specify them bare – as vinyl is lighter and less expensive and harmful to apply than paint, plus easier to customize, like this special edition by Brixton-based print specialists Eley Kishimoto.

Sämtliche Modelle sind Vinyl-verkleidet, da dieses Material leichter, einfacher aufzutragen, preisgünstiger und einfacher individualisierbar ist als eine Farblackierung – so wie dieses Sondermodell des Designunternehmens Eley Kishimoto aus Brixton.

Toutes les voitures sont habillées de vinyle (à moins que vous ne préfériez la vôtre sans rien) parce que ce matériau est plus léger et moins cher que la peinture, et son application est moins nocive. De plus il est plus facile à personnaliser, comme sur cette édition spéciale réalisée par les graphistes d'Eley Kishimoto à Brixton.

LONDON TAXI

GB

FOUNDED: **1984**

HEADQUARTERS: **COVENTRY, ENGLAND**

2010 PRODUCTION: **1,816**

LOGO HISTORY:

Producers of arguably the world's most iconic vehicle – the black taxi cab – that's become as much a part of UK's street furniture as red telephone boxes and mail boxes. Unlike these, the so-called Hackney Carriage is as much in demand now as it was when bespoke taxis first appeared on London's streets over 70 years ago and not just by cabbies – Britain's Prince Phillip and actor Stephen Fry also own versions for private use. Parent company Manganese Bronze Holdings' partnership with Chinese carmaker Geely sees knockdown kits now produced in China and shipped to the UK for assembly and sales worldwide.

Die Hersteller des möglicherweise legendärsten Fahrzeugs der Welt – des schwarzen London-Taxis – ist wie die roten Telefonzellen und Briefkästen ein unverzichtbarer Teil von London. Anders als diese jedoch wird der sogenannte Hackney Carriage noch so stark nachgefragt wie in seinen ersten Jahren auf Londons Straßen vor über 70 Jahren – und das nicht nur von Taxifahrern: Prinz Phillip und der Schauspieler Stephen Fry besitzen Modelle für den privaten Gebrauch. Das chinesische Partnerunternehmen des Mutterkonzerns Manganese Bronze Holding – Geely – stellt Billigbausätze in China her, verschifft diese ins Vereinigte Königreich und verkauft die Billigmodelle weltweit.

Les producteurs de ce qui est le véhicule le plus emblématique du monde, le taxi noir qui peuple le paysage urbain britannique au même titre que les cabines téléphoniques et les boîtes aux lettres rouges. Contrairement à ces dernières, le « Hackney Carriage » est toujours aussi demandé aujourd'hui que lorsque ces véhicules spécialisés ont fait leur première apparition dans les rues de Londres il y a plus de 70 ans, et pas seulement par les conducteurs de taxi : le prince Philippe et l'acteur Stephen Fry en possèdent chacun un exemplaire pour leur usage privé. Le partenariat de la société mère Manganese Bronze Holding avec le constructeur automobile chinois Geely a donné lieu à des kits bon marché qui sont maintenant produits en Chine et envoyés au Royaume-Uni pour être assemblés et vendus dans le monde entier.

TX4
Rival: Routemaster Bus

Classic icon of a city.
Klassische Stadtlegende.
Icône classique d'une ville.

Wide-wheeled TX4 concept at Beijing
Auto Show 2008

LOTUS

FOUNDED: **1952**

HEADQUARTERS: **NORFOLK, ENGLAND**

2010 PRODUCTION: **2,611**

LOGO HISTORY:

Lotus has stayed true to founder Colin Chapman's 'speed through lightness' mantra to this day. Having won seven F1 championships and given more input to other manufacturers' cars for ride and handling than it can legally admit to, Lotus may be small but it's mighty. The F1-winning team disappeared many years ago, but it's back now, although it's unlikely ever to attract the Clark, Hills and Sennas of its glory days. The road cars remain brilliant examples of lightweight engineering and design. Ambitious plans for an expanded range, backed by parent company Proton, will place a make-or-break bet on thousands more drivers embracing the brand in the near future.

Lotus ist dem Motto des Gründers Colin Chapman „Geschwindigkeit durch Leichtigkeit" bis heute treu geblieben. Nach dem Sieg auf sieben Formel-1-Meisterschaften und der (teilweise grenzwertigen) technischen Kooperation mit anderen Herstellern, ist Lotus zwar eine kleine, aber dennoch mächtige Marke. Das vor vielen Jahren verschwundene Formel-1-Erfolgsteam ist zwar 2010 als Lotus Racing zurückgekehrt, hat aber den Ruhm der Clarks, Hills und Sennas nicht mehr erreichen können. Die Straßenautos sind brillante Beispiele für eine leichtgewichtige Kombination aus Technik und Design. Die ambitionierten und mutigen Pläne für ein erweitertes Sortiment werden vom Mutterunternehmen Proton unterstützt. Es wird sich noch zeigen, ob die angekündigten Modelle angenommen werden oder zum Scheitern verurteilt sind.

À ce jour, Lotus est restée fidèle à la philosophie de son fondateur Colin Chapman : « la vitesse grâce à la légèreté ». La marque a remporté sept championnats de F1 et a donné aux autres constructeurs automobiles plus de conseils en matière de conduite et de maniement qu'elle ne peut l'admettre légalement. Petite, mais costaude. L'équipe de F1 a disparu il y a déjà longtemps, mais s'est maintenant reformée, bien qu'elle aura sans doute du mal à attirer les Clark, Hill et Senna de son heure de gloire. Les routières de Lotus sont toujours de brillants exemples de mécanique et design poids plume. La marque compte attirer bientôt des milliers de clients supplémentaires avec d'ambitieux projets d'élargissement de la gamme, soutenus par la société mère Proton. C'est un pari audacieux.

ELISE
Rival: Mazda MX-5

Simple, light, quick, nimble.
Schlicht, leicht, schnell, wendig.
Simple, légère, rapide, maniable.

EXIGE
Rival: KTM X-Bow

As above, but faster. Even better.
Wie oben, aber schneller – und besser.
Idem, en plus rapide. Encore meilleure.

EVORA
Rival: Porsche Cayman

Astonishing dynamics, but quality bettered.
Pure Dynamik, verbesserte Qualität.
Dynamique étonnante, qualité améliorée.

2-ELEVEN
Rival: Radical

Open, light, racecar for road. Sensational.
Sensationelles Rennauto für die Straße.
Excellent modèle de course pour la route.

LOTUS EXIGE S

Fix a roof to the Elise, dial up the power and tweak the suspension and you've got an Exige. There's probably a bit more to it than that, but the driving experience is phenomenal. It steers, stops and goes like little else.

Nimm einen Elise, verpasse ihm ein Dach, schraube die Leistung hoch und optimiere die Aufhängung: Was herauskommt, ist ein Exige. Na ja, ein bisschen mehr muss man wahrscheinlich noch machen – aber das Fahrerlebnis ist wirklich beeindruckend. Steuerung, Bremsen und Antrieb sind unvergleichlich!

Posez un toit sur l'Elise, augmentez la puissance et arrangez la suspension, et vous obtenez une Exige. C'est sans doute un peu plus compliqué que ça, mais la conduire est une expérience phénoménale. La maniabilité, le freinage et l'accélération sont pratiquement sans pareil.

Exige S

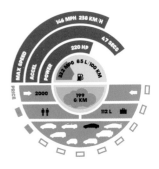

SECRET DETAIL

Famously lightweight (935kg) the Exige's specification gets by fine without niceties like standard air-conditioning – just open the windows and drive fast.

Der nur 935 kg leichte Exige kommt ohne Schnickschnack daher und hat nicht mal eine Klimaanlage: Einfach die Fenster öffnen und schnell fahren.

L'Exige est célèbre pour son poids plume (935 kg), et se débrouille très bien sans certains raffinements tels que l'air conditionné en série. Ouvrez les fenêtres et roulez vite.

LUMENEO

FOUNDED: **2006**
HEADQUARTERS: **PARIS, FRANCE**
2010 PRODUCTION: **30**

Lumeneo offer an enticing new personal mobility concept. Designed to deal with ever-increasing urban congestion without sacrificing safety and comfort its first product, the SMERA, mixes the stability, all-weather protection and safety of a car with the narrowness and manoeuvrability of a motorcycle. With major manufacturers like Renault launching similar products, it's an area that's expected to rapidly grow in the near future. Sophisticated design, lithium-ion electric power and a complex tilting mechanism add to the SMERA's appeal. Heavy investment from French rail company SNCF suggests a future role in a wider, integrated mobility network too. Something truly new.

Lumeneo bietet ein verführerisches neues, personalisiertes Mobilitätskonzept an. Der superschmale Zweisitzer SMERA schlängelt sich durch jeden Stau und gewährleistet trotzdem Sicherheit und Komfort: Das erste Lumeneo-Produkt vereint die Stabilität, Wettertauglichkeit und Sicherheit eines Autos mit der Wendigkeit eines Motorrads. Da auch große Hersteller wie Renault nach und nach ähnliche Produkte auf den Markt bringen, wird dieses Segment in nächster Zukunft sicherlich weiter wachsen. Ein edles Design, Lithium-Ionen-Batterien und die raffinierte Neigetechnik machen die Attraktivität des SMERA aus. Hohe Investitionen vom französischen Bahnunternehmen SNCF versprechen zudem ein breites, gut verteiltes Mobilitätsnetzwerk. Ein wirklich neuartiges Konzept.

Lumeneo propose un tout nouveau concept fort séduisant de transport personnel. Conçue pour répondre aux problèmes de circulation urbaine qui ne cessent d'empirer, sans pour autant sacrifier la sécurité et le confort, la SMERA, premier produit de la marque, allie la stabilité, la protection contre les intempéries et la sécurité d'une voiture à l'étroitesse et la maniabilité d'une moto. De grands constructeurs tels que Renault sont en train de lancer des produits similaires, et l'on peut s'attendre à ce que ce segment connaisse une croissance rapide dans un avenir très proche. Un design raffiné, un pack de batteries lithium-ion et un mécanisme d'inclinaison complexe ajoutent encore au charme de la SMERA. L'important investissement de la SNCF suggère également un futur rôle à jouer au sein d'un réseau de transport intégré plus large. Une vraie nouveauté.

SMERA
Rival: Renault Twizy

Future city mobility pioneers?
Die Zukunft des Stadtautos?
Pionnière de la mobilité urbaine ?

Father Daniel and son Thierry Moulène,
Lumeneo President and Technology Director

MAHINDRA

FOUNDED: **1947**

HEADQUARTERS: **MUMBAI, INDIA**

LOGO HISTORY:

An Indian industrial conglomerate with a car division, Mahindra Automotive has been producing utility vehicles since 1947. And it still does today, but with a wide range of passenger and commercial vehicles suited to the tough life they'll experience both in India and in worldwide emerging markets. Basic and rugged, which is no complaint given the roads most Mahindras must travel on, the firm also has real ambition too, buying a majority stake in Reva in 2010 to add an electric city car to its line-up (known as the G-Wiz in the west). For the most part though, Mahindras are more blacksmith metal, which suits their intended use perfectly.

Der Industriekonzern Mahindra Automotive ist seit 1947 mit einem eigenen Geschäftsbereich im Nutzfahrzeugsektor tätig. Heute wartet der Hersteller mit einer umfangreichen Palette an Personen- und Nutzfahrzeugen auf, die für die harten Einsatzbedingungen in Indien und anderen Schwellenländern gerüstet sind. Mahindras können als einfach und robust beschrieben werden, was angesichts der Straßen, über die sie rollen müssen, eher als Vorteil anzusehen ist. Die Inder haben aber auch höhere Ansprüche und erwarben 2010 eine Mehrheitsbeteiligung bei Reva, um ihre Fahrzeugflotte um ein Elektroauto zu erweitern, das im Westen als G-Wiz bekannt ist. Doch wie oben erwähnt bauen sie hauptsächlich schwere Kasten, die ihrem vorgesehenen Zweck entsprechen.

Mahindra Automotive est un conglomérat industriel indien qui possède une division automobile, et produit des véhicules utilitaires depuis 1947. C'est toujours le cas aujourd'hui, mais avec en plus une large gamme de véhicules personnels et commerciaux adaptés à la dure vie qu'ils connaîtront en Inde et sur les marchés émergents du monde entier. Les voitures de Mahindra sont rudimentaires et solides, et tant mieux, si l'on considère les routes sur lesquelles la plupart doivent rouler. Mais l'entreprise a également de grandes ambitions : elle est actionnaire majoritaire de Reva depuis 2010 afin d'ajouter une citadine électrique à sa gamme (connue sous le nom de G-Wiz en Occident). Cependant la plupart des Mahindra sont plutôt du genre métal forgé, ce qui convient parfaitement à l'utilisation qui leur est réservée.

BOLERO
Rival: Santana Anibal

Boxy, slow, but rugged and useful.
Kastig-langsam, aber robust und praktisch.
Carrée, lente, mais solide et utile.

LOGAN
Rival: VW Golf

Renault/Dacia small sedan.
Renault/Dacia, kleine Limousine.
Petite berline Renault/Dacia.

REVA ELECTRIC
Rival: G-Wiz

Ugly city EV for early-adopting greens.
Unschönes Elektroauto für Umweltbewusste.
Citadine électrique et laide.

SCORPIO
Rival: Ssangyong Rexton

Sold in EU as the Goa.
In der EU als Goa verkauft. Nicht kaufen!
Vendue sous le nom de Goa en Europe.

THAR
Rival: Jeep Wrangler

A WWII Jeep, without the olive paint.
Wie aus dem 2. Weltkrieg, ohne Olivgrün.
Une Jeep de la Deuxième Guerre mondiale.

XYLO
Rival: A horse and cart

Utility people carrier, basic.
Einfacher Minivan.
Monospace utilitaire de base.

MARUSSIA

(RUS)

FOUNDED: **2007**
HEADQUARTERS: **MOSCOW, RUSSIA**

LOGO HISTORY:

No prizes for guessing the nationality of this new supercar builder that arrived in 2007 (Ma-Russia). The B1 introduced the brand, the convincingly styled supercar soon followed by its B2 sister. Powered by Cosworth V6s – either turbocharged or naturally aspirated – Marussia has created two credible cars very quickly. Aiming high the company is also involved in F1 through Virgin Racing. A new player, but if its progress remains as quick as it's been so far Marussia will be a company to watch with interest.

In diesem Fall ist die Nationalität dieses 2007 gebauten Supersportwagens nicht sonderlich schwierig zu erraten. Eingeführt wurde die Marke mit dem überzeugenden B1, dem kurze Zeit später der B2 folgte. Mit den beiden Modellen – die Cosworth-Antriebe gibt es als Turbolader oder Saugmotor – sind Marussia zwei Volltreffer gelungen. Dass die russische Firma hochgesteckte Ziele hat, verrät ihre Zusammenarbeit mit dem Formel-1-Rennstall Virgin Racing. Der Moskauer Wagenhersteller ist zwar noch relativ neu im Geschäft, seine rasante Progression sollte jedoch aufmerksam beobachtet werden.

Pas de médaille pour ceux qui ont deviné la nationalité de ce nouveau constructeur de supercars arrivé en 2007 (Ma-Russia). La marque a fait ses débuts avec la B1, une supercar au style convaincant qui a bientôt été suivie par la B2. Avec des moteurs V6 de Cosworth (turbocompressés ou atmosphériques), Marussia a créé deux voitures crédibles très rapidement. Ambitieuse, l'entreprise s'intéresse également à la F1 à travers Virgin Racing. C'est une nouvelle venue, mais si elle continue sur sa lancée, Marussia devrait se révéler très intéressante.

B1
Rival: Audi R8

Prettier of Marussia's duo and its first.
Hübscheres Modell des Marussia-Duos.
La plus belle des deux Marussia.

B2
Rival: Audi R8

B1 in more aggressive dress.
Der draufgängerische Bruder des B1.
Comme la B1, mais en plus agressive.

MASERATI

FOUNDED: **1914**
HEADQUARTERS: **MODENA**, **ITALY**

LOGO HISTORY:

Wearing the trident symbol of the company's Bologna birthplace Maserati was set up by the Maserati brothers to build racing cars. Since then the firm has changed hands many times, currently partnered with Fiat's Alfa Romeo brand. Beautiful but often flawed, Maserati has been resurgent over the past decade on road and track. Its Quattroporte and GranTurismo are highly regarded, while the Ferrari Enzo-derived MC12 is an unstoppable force in GT racing. With its basket case past seemingly now behind it Maserati could do with some new models soon, as the constant updating of the aging, if beautiful existing range can only go on so long.

Die Firma mit dem Dreizack-Emblem ihrer Geburtsstadt Bologna wurde von den Maserati-Brüdern gegründet, um Rennautos zu bauen. Seitdem hat die Firma zahlreiche Eigentümer gehabt. Zurzeit besteht eine enge Zusammenarbeit mit Alfa Romeo unter Fiats Führung. Die bildschönen, aber mitunter mangelhaften Maserati haben in den letzten zehn Jahren auf Straße und Rennstrecke ein Comeback erlebt. Die Modelle Quattroporte und GranTurismo sind hoch geschätzt, und der auf dem Ferrari Enzo basierende MC12 erweist sich bei den GT-Rennserien als unhaltbar. Der einstige Sanierungsfall Maserati sollte aber bald neue Designs auf den Markt bringen, denn das ständige Aktualisieren der alten Modelle ist – trotz ihrer Schönheit – keine zukunftsträchtige Strategie.

Le trident qui figure sur le logo de Maserati est le symbole de son lieu de naissance, Bologne. Les frères Maserati ont créé cette entreprise pour construire des voitures de course. Depuis, de nombreux propriétaires se sont succédé, et c'est aujourd'hui un partenariat avec la marque Alfa Romeo de Fiat. Belles mais souvent imparfaites, les Maserati ont connu un nouvel essor sur la route et sur les circuits cette dernière décennie. La Quattroporte et la Gran Turismo jouissent d'un grand respect, et la MC12 dérivée de la Ferrari Enzo est une force irrésistible dans les courses de voitures grand tourisme. Ses mésaventures passées étant apparemment oubliées, Maserati devrait se dépêcher de lancer de nouveaux modèles, car l'actualisation constante de la gamme vieillissante, même si elle a de beaux restes, ne peut pas continuer indéfiniment.

QUATTROPORTE
Rival: Porsche
Panamera

Elegant large sedan.
Elegante Großlimousine.
Grande berline élégante.

GRANTURISMO
Rival: Aston Martin
DB9

Gorgeous grand tourer.
Ein Sportwagen zum Verlieben.
Superbe grand tourisme.

GRANCABRIO
Rival: Aston DB9
Volante

Wobbly but beautiful.
Etwas wacklig, aber wunderschön.
Bancale mais magnifique.

Maserati's Modena showroom features a loop sculpture by Ron Arad

MASERATI GRANTURISMO MC STRADALE

Based on the Granturismo MC Trofeo race car – itself an adaptation of the Granturismo S road car – the GranTurismo MC Stradale aims to become the best of both worlds. Lower, longer and an impressive 110kg lighter than the S it's most easily recognized by the lack of rear seats and its 'volume within a volume' floating grille.

Der Granturismo MC Stradale basiert auf dem Rennwagen Granturismo MC Trofeo – der wiederum vom Straßenauto Granturismo S abstammt – und soll beide Modelle bei Weitem übertreffen. Er ist niedriger, länger und beeindruckende 110 kg leichter als der S, und zeichnet sich durch fehlende Rücksitze und einen neuartigen Kühlergrill aus.

Basée sur la voiture de course GranTurismo MC Trofeo (qui est elle-même une adaptation de la routière GranTurismo S), la GranTurismo MC Stradale veut incarner le meilleur de ces deux mondes. Plus basse, plus longue et d'une légèreté impressionnante, avec 110 kg de moins que la S, elle est surtout caractérisée par l'absence de sièges arrière et par sa calandre flottante.

Granturismo MC Stradale

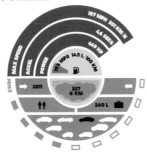

SECRET DETAIL

A racing kit with customized Sparco gloves, racing suit and racing helmet with handmade Maserati graphics is available for drivers wanting the full track-day experience. Who want to look like tools.

Für Fahrer, die sich ein Rundum-Fahrerlebnis wünschen, wird ein Renn-Set aus individuellen Sparco-Handschuhen, Anzug und Helm mit handgefertigten Maserati-Designs angeboten. Aber wer will schon aussehen wie ein Spielzeug?

Un kit de course comprenant des gants Sparco, une combinaison et un casque personnalisés à la main aux couleurs de Maserati est disponible pour les conducteurs qui veulent vivre l'expérience des circuits, et qui n'ont pas peur d'avoir l'air d'imbéciles.

MASTRETTA

FOUNDED: **1987**

HEADQUARTERS: **MEXICO CITY, MEXICO**

LOGO HISTORY:

Former kit-car producer Mastretta is promising to put its MXT sports car into production this year. It's a good-looking potential rival to the Lotus Elise, with an emphasis on lightweight construction and entertaining handling. Power comes from a turbocharged 2.0-liter Ford engine that allows the MXT to reach 62mph in 4.9 seconds and a 148mph top speed. Few would have heard about it if it wasn't for *Top Gear's* on-air ribbing about its Mexican origins, which created a minor diplomatic incident, but if it lives up to its on-paper promise the MXT could have the last laugh.

Der ehemalige Kit-Car-Hersteller Mastretta hat angekündigt, dieses Jahr mit der Produktion des Sportwagen MXT zu beginnen. Dabei handelt es sich um einen würdigen Konkurrenten des Lotus Elise, der sich durch Leichtigkeit und Fahrspaß hervorhebt. Angetrieben wird er von einem 2,0-Liter-Turbolader von Ford, der aus dem Stand auf 100 km/h in 4,9 Sekunden beschleunigen und eine Höchstgeschwindigkeit von 240 km/h erreichen kann. Möglicherweise wären nur wenige auf den Wagen aufmerksam geworden, wenn er nicht in einer BBC-Sendung unter Anspielungen auf seine mexikanische Herkunft niedergemacht worden wäre – was einen kleinen diplomatischen Eklat verursachte. Doch wenn der MXT erfüllt, was er verspricht, könnte er noch recht behalten.

L'ancien fabricant de kit-cars Mastretta promet de commencer la production de sa voiture de sport MXT l'année prochaine. C'est une rivale potentiellement sérieuse pour la Lotus Elise, avec un accent sur la légèreté de la construction et une conduite qui privilégie les sensations. Sa puissance lui vient d'un moteur Ford turbocompressé de 2,0 litres qui lui permet d'atteindre les 100 km/h en 4,9 secondes, et une vitesse maximale de 238 km/h. Peu de gens en auraient entendu parler si l'émission de télévision britannique Top Gear ne s'était pas moquée de son origine mexicaine, ce qui a créé un petit incident diplomatique. Mais si elle tient ses promesses, la MXT pourrait bien avoir le dernier mot dans cette histoire.

MXT
Rival: Lotus Elise

As yet unknown quantity, with promise.
Ein vielversprechendes Fragezeichen.
C'est encore un mystère, mais elle semble avoir du potentiel.

Mastretta took a subtle approach when launching its car in Novermber 2010

MAYBACH

FOUNDED: **1909**

HEADQUARTERS: **STUTTGART**, **GERMANY**

2010 PRODUCTION: **157**

LOGO HISTORY:

Long-forgotten super-luxury German marque revived by Mercedes to rival Rolls-Royce. One sedan is offered in two lengths, 5.7m or 6.2m, and badged 57 or 62 accordingly. Launched on the QE2 in 2002 Maybach promised a unique ownership experience replete with a concierge service for every buyer, but sales have been disappointing due to the questionable associations of the original Maybach brand, an overly conservative design, and two models with little to differentiate them from each other or set them sufficiently far apart from the excellent Mercedes S Class. New models have been limited to tweaks of existing cars, and include the S, Zeppelin and the bizarre, partially open-topped Landaulet. Despite talk of a collaboration with Aston Martin, Maybach's future remains unknown, particularly in the current economic climate but it still has its fans: P. Diddy recently bought his son a second one for his 17th birthday.

Die in Vergessenheit geratene Luxus-Marke aus Deutschland wurde von Mercedes als Rolls-Royce-Konkurrent wiederbelebt. Die Modellbezeichnungen 57 und 62 weisen auf die verfügbaren Längen der Limousinen hin. Seine Weltpremiere an Bord der Queen Elisabeth 2 im Jahre 2002 sollte die Exklusivität der Marke betonen, die Verkaufszahlen bleiben jedoch hinter den Erwartungen zurück. Grund dafür sind die zweifelhafte Vergangenheit der Marke, das konservative Design und zwei Modelle, die einander zu sehr ähneln und kaum Unterschiede zur hervorragenden S-Klasse von Mercedes aufweisen. Die neuen Fahrzeuge – lediglich Optimierungen bestehender Modelle – umfassen den S, den Zeppelin und den exzentrischen, halboffenen Landaulet. Über eine Zusammenarbeit mit Aston Martin wurde zwar spekuliert, die Zukunft von Maybach ist jedoch angesichts der wirtschaftlichen Lage ungewiss. Aber Anhänger hat die Marke noch: Der US-amerikanischer Rapper P. Diddy kaufte neulich seinem Sohn zum 17. Geburtstag einen zweiten Maybach.

Cette marque allemande de super luxe oubliée depuis longtemps a été ressuscitée par Mercedes pour concurrencer Rolls-Royce. Sa berline est proposée en deux longueurs, 5,7 ou 6,2 mètres, badgées respectivement 57 et 62. Son lancement a eu lieu sur le paquebot Queen Elizabeth 2. Maybach a promis un niveau de service exceptionnel et ultra-personnalisé, mais les chiffres de vente ont été décevants. Les associations douteuses de la marque Maybach d'origine sont en partie responsables, ainsi que le manque d'originalité du design. De plus, les deux versions se ressemblent trop, et font aussi beaucoup penser à l'excellente Mercedes Classe S. Les nouveaux modèles ne sont que des dérivés de voitures existantes, ce sont les variantes S, Zeppelin, et l'étrange carrosserie Landaulet, partiellement décapotable. Malgré la possibilité d'une collaboration avec Aston Martin, l'avenir de Maybach reste flou, surtout dans le climat économique actuel. Cependant la marque a toujours des fans : P. Diddy a récemment acheté à son fils une deuxième Maybach pour son 17e anniversaire.

57 | 62

Rival: Rolls-Royce Phantom

Super-long and luxe Merc S-Class.
Mercedes S-Klasse, nur länger und luxuriöser.
Mercedes Classe S de luxe super longue.

The bullet-riddled and painted Maybach art car by Julian Schnabel (pictured)

MAZDA

FOUNDED: **1920**
HEADQUARTERS: **HIROSHIMA, JAPAN**
2010 PRODUCTION: **921,763**

LOGO HISTORY:

Mazda is emerging from its years reliant on Ford's investment as a powerful manufacturer once again in its own right. Offering mainstream cars with added 'zoom zoom', the MX-5/Miata and RX-8 have long delivered on the creed. But the brand's somewhat comical marketing catchphrase and non-committal design, combined with a range focused on conventional family categories keep it just off the radar for most drivers looking for something distinctive. With the MX-5/Miata long established, and the RX-8's rotary engine technology looking anachronistic while its novel 'suicide doors' have now been adopted by models as varied as the Mini Clubman and Rolls-Royce Phantom, Mazda needs something new. Its former design director created a novel form language called 'Nagare', Japanese for 'Flow'. But aside from a few wavy lines on an MPV, nothing materialized. Now his successor Ikuo Maeda tells us 'Kodo', meaning 'soul of motion', will reshape the range. The imminent CX-5 will be the test.

Mazda nabelt sich langsam von Ford ab. Die Marke des „Zoom Zoom" hatte mit dem MX-5/Miata und dem RX-8 Erfolg. Doch das zurückhaltende Design und eine konventionelle Fahrzeugflotte haben potenzielle Käufer abgeschreckt. Der MX-5/Miata ist längst bekannt, der RX-8-Wankelmotor überholt und seine „Selbstmördertüren" nicht mehr exklusiv – Mazda muss sich etwas Neues einfallen lassen. Der ehemalige Designchef erfand die neue Formsprache „Nagare" (Fluss). Bis auf die Wellenformen eines Minivans brachte das Konzept nicht viel. Ikuo Maeda will jetzt mit „Kodo" (Seele der Bewegung) eine neue Designsprache einführen. Warten wir die Vorstellung des CX-5 ab.

Mazda propose des voitures enrichies en « zoom zoom ». Mais le slogan comique de la marque et son design évasif, combinés à une gamme familiale et conventionnelle, la rendent invisible. La MX-5/Miata date déjà, le moteur rotatif de la RX-8 semble anachronique, et ses portes suicide ne sont plus aussi originales. Mazda a besoin de nouveauté. Son ancien directeur du design avait créé un langage des formes baptisé « Nagare » (« flux » en japonais). Mais à part quelques ondulations sur un monospace, rien de concret. Aujourd'hui, son successeur Ikuo Maeda déclare que le « Kodo », ou « âme du mouvement » va tout changer. L'imminente CX-5 en sera le test.

MAZDA2|DEMIO
Rival: Ford Fiesta

Brilliant car with Fiesta DNA.
Tolles Auto mit Fiesta-Reminiszenzen.
Excellente voiture avec un ADN de Fiesta.

VERISA
Rival: Ford Fiesta

Upmarket supermini for Japan.
Gehobener Supermini für Japan.
Polyvalente haut de gamme pour le Japon.

MAZDA3
Rival: Ford Focus

Credible Ford Focus rival.
Ernster Rivale für den Ford Focus.
Rivale crédible pour la Ford Focus.

MAZDA5
Rival: Toyota Corolla Verso

MPV with wavy "flow" lines.
Minivan mit „Flusslinien".
Monospace qui suit le « flux ».

MAZDA6|ATENZA
Rival: Toyota Avensis

Impressive family saloon.
Beeindruckende Familienlimousine.
Berline familiale impressionnante.

MX-5|MIATA
Rival: MG TF

Genre-reviving roadster, still brilliant.
Die Renaissance des Roadster – genial.
Roadster qui a réinventé son genre.

CX-7
Rival: Nissan Murano

SUV that's great on the road.
Ein Geländewagen, der sich gut anfühlt.
SUV brillant sur la route.

CX-9
Rival: Nissan Qashqai+2

Same as CX-7, with 2 more seats.
Wie der CX-7, nur mit 2 weiteren Sitzen.
Idem, avec deux places de plus.

RX-8
Rival: Nissan 370Z

Rotary, fast, thirsty, cool suicide doors.
Wankelmotor, schnell, durstig, Fondtüren.
Moteur rotatif, rapide et gourmand.

MPV
Rival: Citroen C8

Go on, guess what it is, can you? (7st).
Na raten Sie mal, was ist das? (7-Sitzer).
Monospace à 7 places.

ALSO AVAILABLE

Carol, ScruM, Tribute.

MAZDA MX-5

MX-5 2.0 Sport

Best-selling sports car ever and for good reason – it's been mixing the same blend of practicality, affordability and good old-fashioned motoring joy since way back in 1989. Others may scoff butt they've probably never had the pleasure.

Der aus gutem Grund bestverkaufte Sportwagen aller Zeiten: seit 1989 die optimale Mischung aus Zweckmäßigkeit, erschwinglichem Preis und altmodisch-zuverlässigem Fahrerlebnis. Es gibt Leute, die darüber spotten, aber die hatten wahrscheinlich noch nicht das Vergnügen.

C'est la voiture de sport qui s'est le mieux vendue de l'histoire, et pour cause : depuis 1989, c'est toujours le même mélange de sens pratique, prix raisonnable et pur plaisir de la conduite. Ceux qui ricanent n'ont probablement jamais eu l'occasion de l'essayer.

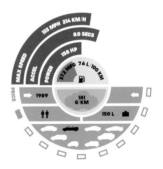

SECRET DETAIL

Mazda's under-the-radar Design Chronograph made by German watchmaker Sinn is one of the best car/watch brand collaborations we've seen – and was actually designed by a car (not watch) designer, Mazda's Hasip Girgin.

Die Einkerbung in der Motorhaube dient als visueller Ausgleich zu der extrem weit hinten liegenden Position des Motors, durch die eine perfekte Balance erreicht wird.

La marque en forme de losange sur le capot est une allusion visuelle à la position du moteur, très en arrière, qui donne à la voiture son équilibre parfait.

MAZDA RX-8

Unlike anything else on the streets – suicide doors offer kerbside theatre and the unique Wankel rotary engine emits an X-Wing Starfighter scream. Practical enough to seat Luke, Han, Chewie and Leia in its sports coupe cabin with space enough for R2-D2 in the trunk. Catch it while you can, as the model is expiring.

Die absolute Ausnahme auf der Straße: Die gegenläufig öffnenden Türen sind spektakulär, und der speziell entwickelte Wankelmotor hört sich an wie ein X-Wing Starfighter aus Star Wars. Sein geräumiges Inneres bietet locker Platz für Luke, Han, Chewie und Leia – und R2-D2 kann es sich im Kofferraum bequem machen. Bei Interesse am besten schnell kaufen, denn das Modell läuft aus.

Cette voiture ne ressemble à aucune autre. Ses portes suicide attirent les regards des passants, et son moteur rotatif Wankel unique émet le rugissement d'un chasseur stellaire X-Wing. L'habitacle de ce coupé sportif pourra accueillir Luke, Han, Chewbacca et Leia, et le coffre accommodera R2-D2 sans peine. Ne traînez pas pour mettre la main dessus, le modèle arrive à expiration.

RX-8 R3

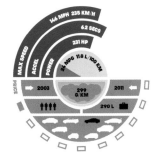

SECRET DETAIL

The recurring triangular design motif is inspired by the shape of the engine's twin rotors, which can spin smoothly to over 9,000rpm.

Das dreieckige Design-Motiv ist von den zwei Rotoren abgeleitet, die es spielend bis auf 9.000 Upm schaffen.

Le motif triangulaire récurrent est inspiré par la forme des deux rotors du moteur, qui peuvent dépasser les 9 000 tours/mn.

MCLAREN

GB

FOUNDED: **1989**
HEADQUARTERS: **WOKING, ENGLAND**

LOGO HISTORY:

Producer of what many still regard as the ultimate supercar – the F1 – McLaren has just launched its new, less catchily named MP4-12C. Unlike the money-is-no-object 241mph F1 from 1992, the MP4-12C will be produced in relatively large volumes, and priced to take on Ferrari's 458 Italia. Fastidious attention to detail, considerable engineering expertise and Formula 1 technology combine in the 12C, which delivers staggering performance for a car in its category. There's more to come too, with a hypercar planned to sit above the 12C, its performance promising to be truly extraordinary. A new, small, but hugely significant player, Ferrari should be very worried.

Der Hersteller des in den Augen zahlreicher Fans ultimativen Supersportwagens – des F1 – hat gerade sein neues Modell mit dem etwas sperrigen Namen MP4-12C vorgestellt. Im Unterschied zum knapp 390 km/h schnellen, extrem teuren F1 von 1992 soll der MP4-12C in großen Stückzahlen produziert und in der Preiskategorie des Ferrari 458 Italia angesiedelt werden. Der 12C zeichnet sich durch eine geradezu obsessive Liebe zum Detail, technisches Können und Formel-1-Technologie aus und liefert eine für die Kategorie atemberaubende Leistung. Und das ist noch nicht alles: Ein weiteres „Hypercar" soll die Leistung des 12C noch übertreffen. Ferrari sollte den Aufstieg des noch kleinen Neulings genauer verfolgen.

McLaren est la marque qui a produit ce que beaucoup considèrent toujours comme la supercar suprême (la F1) et vient juste de lancer un nouveau modèle au nom moins accrocheur : MP4-12C. Contrairement à la F1 de 1992, capable de monter jusqu'à 388 km/h et dégagée de toute considération budgétaire, la MP4-12C sera produite à une échelle relativement grande, et son prix sera aligné sur celui de la Ferrari 458 Italia. Sens du détail exacerbé, considérable expertise mécanique et technologie de Formule 1 s'allient dans la 12C, dont la performance est stupéfiante pour une voiture de sa catégorie. Et ce n'est pas tout, une hypercar que l'on promet vraiment extraordinaire viendra se placer au-dessus de la 12C dans la gamme McLaren. C'est un nouvel acteur petit mais très costaud, Ferrari a du mouron à se faire.

MP4-12C
Rival: Ferrari 458

Establishment busting supercar.
Eine Herausforderung in Form eines Supersportwagens.
Supercar qui lance un pavé dans la mare.

MCLAREN MP4–12C

McLaren's second supercar once again tears up convention to produce a spectacular driving experience. An F1 expertise-derived technical tour-de-force the MP4-12C might not look as dramatic as its Italian rivals, but it's mightily effective against them on road and track.

Der zweite Supersportwagen von McLaren soll wieder ein aufregendes Fahrgefühl bieten. Der MP4-12C, eine aus der Formel-1-Erfahrung resultierende technische Glanzleistung, sieht vielleicht nicht ganz so spektakulär aus wie seine italienischen Konkurrenten. Er ist aber auf Straße und Rennstrecke um einiges leistungsstärker!

La deuxième supercar de McLaren se joue encore une fois de toutes les conventions pour proposer une expérience de conduite spectaculaire. La MP4-12C est un tour de force technique issu de l'expertise de la F1. De l'extérieur, elle n'est peut-être pas aussi impressionnante que ses rivales italiennes, mais elle est considérablement efficace à côté d'elles sur les routes et sur les circuits.

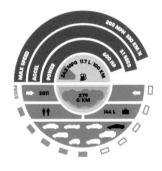

SECRET DETAIL

So many. Carbon 'MonoCell' weighs just 75kg, clever non-roll
bar suspension, active airbrake, even the MP4-12C's factory is
groundbreaking.

Da gibt es viel. Zum Beispiel: Ein 75 kg leichtes Kohlefaser-Monocoque
(„MonoCell"), eine clevere neuartige Aufhängung, die aktive Luftbremse –
sogar das Werk, in dem der MP4-12C hergestellt wird, ist innovativ!

Il y en a tant. La monocoque en carbone ne pèse que 75 kg. Citons aussi
la suspension intelligente à barre anti-roulis et l'aérofrein actif. Même
l'usine de la MP4-12C est en avance sur son temps.

MERCEDES-BENZ

FOUNDED: **1886**
HEADQUARTERS: **STUTTGART, GERMANY**
2010 PRODUCTION: **1,167,700**

LOGO HISTORY:

Celebrating 125 years in 2011 Mercedes-Benz can lay claim to inventing the car. It's continued inventing since, offering one of the widest ranges of any manufacturer anywhere. Along with that range – virtually every model series offers numerous variants like coupes, cabriolets and wagons – Mercedes has also been truly innovative in developing car technology for safety, performance, economy and more. The brand remains mighty and all cars drive well with the skunkworks AMG division creating some extraordinary performance cars, but its laurels can't be rested on with German prestige rivals Audi and BMW both coming up on its inside with smart and relevant product appealing to younger drivers. In recent years, drained by its ownership of Chrysler, the star seemed to lose some of its shine, with stodgy entry-level offerings and executive mainstays looking increasingly generic amid a growing field of imitators from brands like Hyundai. But the banana-shaped CLS reminded fans why Mercedes came to define automotive luxury and style, and to hammer home the point the SLS revived the iconic gull-wing.

Mercedes-Benz ist die Marke, die heute vor 125 Jahren das Auto erfand. Der Erfindergeist der Stuttgarter ist seitdem nicht erloschen und hat eine der umfassendsten Fahrzeugflotten weltweit hervorgebracht. Die deutsche Traditionsmarke hat aber nicht nur ein breites Angebot – praktisch jedes Modell gibt es als Coupé, Cabrio oder Kombi –, sie hat außerdem zahlreiche technologische Innovationen vorzuweisen, die zu mehr Sicherheit, Leistung und Sparsamkeit geführt haben. Mercedes-Benz ist heute noch eine mächtige Marke, die zuverlässige Autos baut und in AMG einen Hersteller von Hochleistungs-Sportfahrzeugen hat. Sie darf sich aber nicht auf ihren Lorbeeren ausruhen, wenn sie verhindern möchte, dass ihr die im Aufstieg begriffenen Rivalen Audi und BMW mit ihren beim jungen Publikum beliebten Modellen den Rang ablaufen. Nach dem erfolglosen Chrysler-Abenteuer scheint der Mercedes-Stern etwas von seinem einstigen Glanz verloren zu haben. Dazu beigetragen haben auch die etwas schwerfälligen Einsteigermodelle sowie die angesichts der wachsenden Konkurrenz von Nachahmern wie Hyundai immer mutloser wirkenden Leistungsträger der Mercedes-Flotte. Allerdings hat der bananenförmige CLS alle Fans noch einmal daran erinnert, warum Mercedes als Synonym für mobilen Luxus und Eleganz gilt. Und wer noch nicht überzeugt ist, sollte sich die Flügeltüren des SLS genauer ansehen.

Mercedes-Benz fête ses 125 ans en 2011 et peut se vanter d'avoir inventé la voiture. La marque n'a jamais cessé d'inventer et propose l'une des gammes les plus variées du monde. Outre cette gamme (pratiquement chaque série est déclinée en de nombreuses variantes, coupés, cabriolets, breaks, etc.), Mercedes a également fait preuve d'un véritable esprit novateur dans le développement technologique en matières de sécurité, performance et économie, entre autres. La marque a su conserver sa puissance, toutes ses voitures ont une excellente conduite et l'équipe de choc de la division AMG crée des machines aux performances extraordinaires. Mais ses prestigieux rivaux allemands Audi et BMW ne laissent pas Mercedes se reposer sur ses lauriers, car ils attaquent la marque par le flanc avec des produits intelligents qui font mouche et séduisent les jeunes conducteurs. Ces dernières années, épuisée par Chrysler, l'étoile avait perdu de son éclat. Ses produits d'entrée de gamme étaient indigestes et ses modèles phares devenaient de plus en plus génériques au milieu d'une masse grandissante d'imitations venues de marques telles que Hyundai. Mais la CLS en forme de banane a rappelé à ses fans pourquoi Mercedes est synonyme de luxe et de style dans l'automobile, et pour enfoncer le clou, la SLS a ressuscité la légendaire porte papillon.

Mercedes Museum, Stuttgart – 2001 F400 'Carving' concept (silver, foreground) late 60s/early 70s C111 (orange, background)

A-CLASS
Rival: BMW 1 Series

Merc for practical and old. Replaced 2012.
Für den täglichen Gebrauch. Ersatz ab 2012.
Une Mercedes économique.

C-CLASS
Rival: BMW 3 Series

Premium small sedan, wagon & coupe.
Premium-Limousine, -Kombi und -Coupé.
Break, coupé et berline haut de gamme.

E-CLASS
Rival: BMW 5 Series

Exec class saloon, estate & cabrio.
Obere Mittelklasse in allen Versionen.
Grand coupé, break, cabriolet et berline.

R-CLASS
Rival: Renault Espace

Weird and vast 6- to 7-seat MPV.
6- und 7-Sitzer, eigenartig und riesengroß.
Monospace étrange de 6 à 7 places.

S-CLASS
Rival: BMW 7

Arguably the world's greatest sedan.
Wohl die weltweit größte Limousine.
Sans doute la meilleure berline du monde.

CLS
Rival: Porsche Panamera

Aggression trumps elegance in new version.
Mehr Aggressivität als Eleganz.
Nouvelle version du coupé 4 portes.

SL
Rival: Porsche 911 Cabriolet

Hugely desirable GT/Roadster.
Ein GT/Roadster, den sich jeder wünscht.
Grand tourisme/roadster très séduisant.

SLK
Rival: BMW Z4

Junior SL looks, for the lighter of pocket.
Die kleine, preiswertere Version des SL.
SL junior, plus économique.

SLS
Rival: Porsche 911 Turbo S

The gull-wing is back, it's good.
Die Flügeltüren sind wieder da – gut so.
La porte papillon est de retour, tant mieux.

M-CLASS
Rival: BMW X5

SUV for the roads, around 90210.
SUV für die Straße – und 90210.
SUV pour les routes de Beverly Hills.

G-WAGEN
Rival: Tonka Toys

Ancient but brilliant boxyt 4x4.
Uralter Allradantrieb, immer noch fein.
4x4 carré antique mais excellent.

ALSO AVAILABLE
B-Class, CL, GL.

CARCHITECHTURE MERCEDES MUSEUM

A gold-wheeled G-Wagen Popemobile, a wonderfully aerodynamic racing car carrier and some of the first ever cars made are among 160 of the historically important vehicles featured in Mercedes' nine-level museum in Stuttgart – designed by Ben van Berkel of UN Studio and opened in 2006. So much more than a bunch of cars in a big room, the ambition and execution is in keeping with the brand that invented the automobile, from the space-age metal elevators that glide up the walls of the atrium to deposit visitors at the start of the exhibition to the gently flowing, right-angle-devoid, 16,500 sq m exhibition space that spirals back down to the museum's reception.

Ein Papamobil mit goldenen Radkappen, ein unglaublich aerodynamischer Rennwagen und einige der ersten Autos der Welt befinden sich unter den 160 historisch wichtigen Fahrzeugen in dem neunstöckigen Museum in Stuttgart, das von Ben van Berkel (UN Studio) entworfen und im Jahr 2006 eröffnet wurde. Das Museum ist jedoch mehr als ein paar Autos in einem riesigen spiralförmigen Ausstellungsgebäude. Auf 16.500 Quadratmetern mit futuristischen Aufzügen und einem sanft fließenden, ecken- und kantenlosen Design ist der Erfindergeist des Unternehmens zu spüren, in dem das erste Auto der Welt gefertigt wurde.

Parmi les 160 véhicules historiques du musée de Mercedes à Stuttgart, on trouve une papamobile Classe G à roues dorées, un transporteur de voiture de course merveilleusement aérodynamique et quelques-unes des toutes premières voitures de l'histoire. Ce bâtiment de neuf étages conçu par Ben van Berkel, d'UN Studio, a ouvert ses portes en 2006. C'est infiniment plus qu'une collection de voitures : l'ambition et l'exécution de l'ensemble sont à la hauteur de la marque qui a inventé l'automobile, depuis les ascenseurs métalliques dignes d'un vaisseau spatial, glissant le long de l'atrium pour déposer les visiteurs au point de départ de l'exposition, jusqu'à l'espace d'exposition de 16 500 m² dénué de tout angle droit, qui décrit une spirale en pente douce pour revenir à la réception du musée.

Can you spot the G-Wagen Popemobile?

MERCEDES-BENZ C63 AMG

C63 AMG

Compact business sedan gains a 6.2-liter V8 under the hood and AMG wizardry elsewhere to produce a credible M3 rival. Sounds glorious, is indecently quick and surprisingly usable. Let your favored executives sneak this one by the fleet manager.

Eine kompakte Business-Limousine mit 6,2-Liter-V8-Motor und AMG-Zauberkraft, die dem M3 Paroli bieten soll. Das klingt nicht nur beeindruckend, sondern ist auch noch unglaublich schnell und überraschend brauchbar. Gönnen Sie Ihrem besten Manager dieses fahrende Wunder als Firmenwagen.

Cette berline compacte gagne un V8 6,2 litres sous le capot et la magie d'AMG partout ailleurs pour se convertir en rivale crédible de la M3. Elle a un rugissement somptueux, elle est capable d'une vitesse indécente, et est étonnamment maniable. Laissez vos managers préférés la faire passer sous le nez du responsable de la flotte.

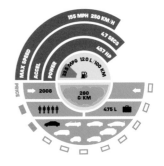

SECRET DETAIL

The badge says 6.3 but the C63's engine is actually 6.2 liters. Why? Historical significance or some other doublespeak.

Auf dem Schild steht 6,3, aber der Motor des C63 verbraucht tatsächlich 6,2 Liter. Warum? Historische Bedeutung oder Doppelzüngigkeit?

Le badge dit 6,3 mais le moteur C63 ne fait que 6,2 litres. Pourquoi ? La cohérence historique, ou quelque chose comme ça.

MERCEDES-BENZ G-WAGEN

The Geländewagen has morphed from a utilitarian military tool into a super-luxury gin palace despite its basic design remaining resolutely unchanged for over 30 years. Hand built AMG versions pack supercar power even its brutal aerodynamics can't resist.

Aus einem praktischen Militärfahrzeug wurde ein luxuriöser Geländewagen. Das schlichte Design bleibt seit über 30 Jahren unangetastet. Die handgefertigten AMG-Versionen sind so leistungsstark wie ein Supersportwagen und schlagen sogar die plumpe Aerodynamik.

Le Geländewagen (tout-terrain en allemand) est passé d'outil militaire à emblème du luxe bien que son design rudimentaire n'ait pas changé d'un iota depuis plus de trente ans. Les versions AMG construites à la main ont la puissance d'une supercar et rien ne leur résiste, pas même cette aérodynamique mal dégrossie.

G55 AMG

DESIGNER Q+ A

Gordon Wagener
Head of design, Mercedes

On duty:
Suit: Boss Selection
Shoes: Lloyd (tailored)
Watch: Mercedes custom gold chrono

Off-duty:
Clothes: Abercrombie, deck shoes and shorts!

What does your brand stand for?
Past: "Heritage, clean, distinctive, Teutonic."
Present: "Dawn of a new age – the SLS and CLS."
Future: "The avantgarde of aesthetics and style – perfect for a luxury brand."

MERCEDES–BENZ UNIMOG

Utility doesn't cover it, the Unimog being the ultimate all-round vehicle. It'll go absolutely anywhere with no fuss and is tougher than anything else on or off the road. When nuclear apocalypse strikes only scorpions and Unimogs will survive. Fact.

Mehr als nur nützlich – das absolute Allround-Fahrzeug. Der Unimog ist stärker als alles andere auf der Straße und kann absolut überall gefahren werden. Bei einer Atomkatastrophe überleben die Skorpione – und die Unimogs.

Utilitaire n'est pas le terme qui convient, car l'Unimog est le plus complet des véhicules. Il ira absolument n'importe où sans faire d'histoires, et est plus coriace que tout ce que vous pourrez rencontrer sur la route ou ailleurs. Lorsque l'apocalypse nucléaire nous frappera, les seuls survivants seront les scorpions et les Unimog. C'est scientifiquement prouvé.

Unimog U4000

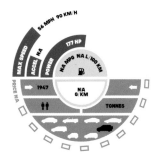

SECRET DETAIL

Ever wish you could move your steering wheel to the other side of the cabin (for foreign driving with toll booths on the wrong side etc)? Buy a Unimog with the Vario Pilot system and wish no longer.

Sie haben sich immer schon gewünscht, Ihr Lenkrad auch auf der Beifahrerseite nutzen zu können (im Ausland, bei Mautstationen auf der falschen Seite usw.)? Kaufen Sie sich einen Unimog mit Vario Pilot-System!

Avez-vous déjà rêvé pouvoir mettre le volant de l'autre côté de l'habitacle (pour conduire à l'étranger, pour les cabines de péage situées du mauvais côté, etc.) ? Achetez un Unimog doté du système Vario Pilot, et votre rêve deviendra réalité.

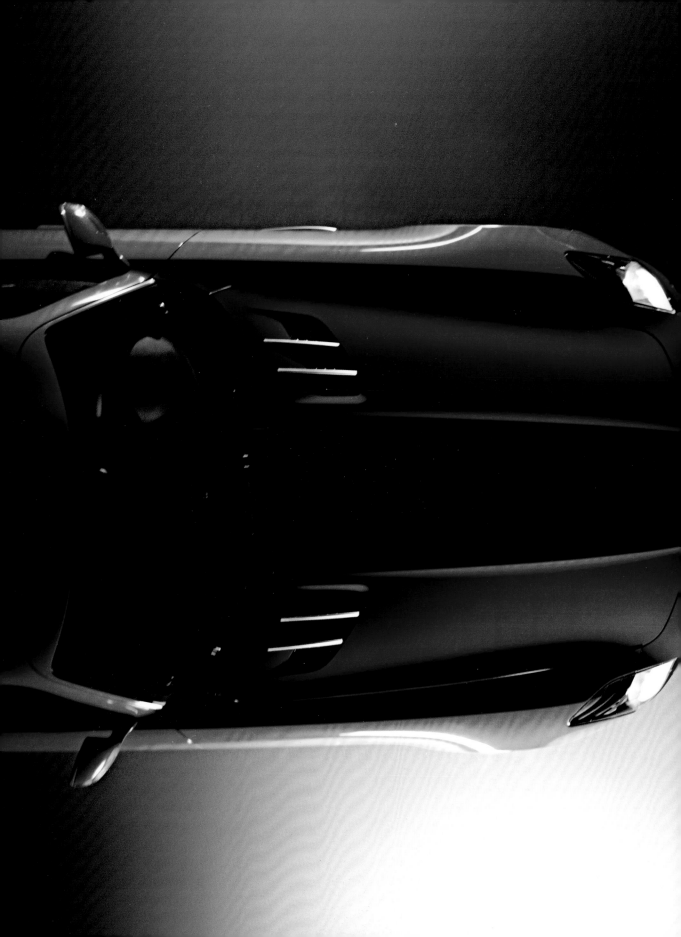

MERCEDES-BENZ SLS AMG

300 SL-inspired gull-wing retro ride that's AMG's first wholly developed car. It's quite a car too, combining proper grand touring ability with supercar pace and poise. The doors are pure theatre, yet so surprisingly light they seem almost practical.

Der vom 300 SL inspirierte Retro mit Flügeltüren ist das erste, von AMG eigenständig entwickelte Auto. Eine beeindruckende Kombination aus Gran Turismo und Supersportwagen. Die Türen sind der absolute Traum und so leicht, dass man sie fast als praktisch bezeichnen könnte.

Ce bolide à portes papillon inspiré de la 300 SL est la première voiture entièrement développée par AMG. Et quelle voiture ! Elle allie les compétences d'une vraie grand tourisme avec la vitesse et l'allure d'une supercar. Les portes ne sont que pure mise en scène, mais elles sont tellement légères qu'elles semblent presque pratiques.

SLS AMG

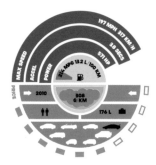

SECRET DETAIL

If you're careless enough to roll your gull-wing-doored SLS you can still get out thanks to explosive door hinges.

Wenn Sie unvorsichtig genug sind, mit Ihrem SLS zu fahren, können Sie sich im Notfall aus den superschnell öffnenden Flügeltüren retten.

Si vous avez la négligence de coucher votre SLS à portes papillon sur le flanc, vous pourrez quand même en sortir grâce à des charnières explosives.

MERCURY

(USA)

FOUNDED: **1939** DIED: **2011**
HEADQUARTERS: **DEARBORN**, USA
2010 PRODUCTION: **82,534**

LOGO HISTORY:

  MERCURY

A victim of Ford's brand slashing, Mercury no longer produces cars. There's some stock around, with its re-badged Fords likely to be available for a while yet – with sizeable discounts. Mercury was conceived in 1939 as a brand bridge between Ford's blue-collar Blue Oval cars and its upmarket Lincolns, although in 2011 it'll cease to exist. Will any mourn its passing? Doubtful, with Mercury never really rising above the status of a thinly veiled, unimaginative badge-engineered brand it's been on a downward decline for decades. High points include introducing the European Capri to the USA but really, that's about it.

Mercury gehört zu den Opfern der Schlankheitskur von Ford. Auf den Straßen werden die Autos der Amerikaner (u. a. die umgetauften Ford-Modelle) noch eine Weile zu sehen – und zu saftigen Rabatten zu kaufen – sein. Gegründet wurde Mercury 1939 als Brücke zwischen den Ford-Modellen für die Arbeiterklasse und den gehobeneren Lincolns. 2011 jedoch soll die Produktion eingestellt werden. Wird jemand der Marke eine Träne nachweinen? Kaum, denn der Autohersteller aus Dearborn galt allgemein als uninspirierter Ableger, der schon seit Jahrzehnten im Abwärtstrend war. Zu den Höhepunkten gehört die Einführung des europäischen Capri in den USA – weitere Heldentaten gab es nicht.

Mercury a été sacrifiée par Ford, et ne produit donc plus de voitures. Il y a encore du stock, et ses Ford rebadgées seront sans doute encore disponibles pendant un temps, avec des remises substantielles. La marque Mercury a été créée en 1939 pour occuper un segment intermédiaire entre les voitures grand public de Ford et ses Lincoln haut de gamme, mais a disparu en 2011. Sa disparition sera-t-elle pleurée ? On peut en douter, car Mercury n'a jamais vraiment été autre chose qu'une marque sans originalité proposant des véhicules rebadgés avec peu de discrétion, et a été sur le déclin pendant des décennies. L'un de ses moments forts à été l'introduction de la Capri européenne aux États-Unis, mais c'est à peu près tout.

MILAN
Rival: Ford Fusion

A Ford Fusion with a Mercury grille.
Ford Fusion mit Kühlergrill von Mercury.
Ford Fusion avec une calandre Mercury.

GRAND MARQUIS
Rival: Ford Crown Victoria

Crown Vic with a...
Ein Ford Crown Victoria mit ...
Crown Victoria avec une...

MARINER
Rival: Ford Escape

Ford Escape, you get the idea.
Ein Ford Escape ... Sie wissen schon.
Ford Escape avec vous savez quoi.

MOUNTAINEER
Rival: Ford Explorer

See why it's died?
Kein Wunder, dass die Marke pleite ist.
Vous voyez pourquoi ça n'a pas marché ?

Main image: 1967 Cougar
Inset: 1957 Monterey

MG

FOUNDED: **1924**
HEADQUARTERS: **LONGBRIDGE, ENGLAND**
2010 PRODUCTION: **160,397 [INC. ROEWE]**

LOGO HISTORY:

MG got its name from Morris Garages, a dealer of Morris cars who customized Morris cars in the early 1920s. Beyond a break due to WWII, production continued until 1980 as the brand became synonymous with fun and affordable two-seater sportscars like the MGB (as well as sedans and the odd coupe). More changes of ownership and a period as merely go-faster versions of Austin and then Rover models led to its demise in 2005 before Chinese powerhouse SAIC brought it back to life. Back on sale with a reasonable range, mainly shared with sister brand start-up Roewe, MG is now making a tentative recovery.

MG steht für Morris Garages, ein Morris-Händler, der in den 1920er Jahren Morris-Autos individuell herrichtete. Nach einer Produktionspause während des Zweiten Weltkrieges wurde die Fertigung bis 1980 fortgesetzt. In dieser Zeit wurde die Marke zum Synonym für preisgünstige Spaßwagen, siehe den MGB (oder auch Limousinen und Coupés). Mehrere Eigentümerwechsel und eine Periode, in der lediglich schnellere Versionen von Austin- und später Rover-Modellen entwickelt wurden, führte 2005 zur Insolvenzanmeldung. Erst der chinesische Konzern SAIC konnte die Engländer wiederbeleben. Zurzeit hat der Hersteller aus Longbridge eine relativ umfassende Palette, die er sich mit dem Schwesterunternehmen Roewe teilt. Die Erholung ist im Gange.

MG tient son nom de Morris Garages, un concessionnaire de voitures Morris qui produisait des versions modifiées de ces voitures au début des années 1920. À part une pause due à la Deuxième Guerre mondiale, la production a continué jusqu'à 1980 et la marque est devenue célèbre pour ses voitures de sport à deux places fun et abordables comme la MGB (ainsi que pour ses berlines, et quelques coupés). Plusieurs changements de propriétaire et une période durant laquelle la marque s'est limitée à booster des modèles d'Austin, puis de Rover, ont mené à sa chute en 2005 avant que le puissant groupe chinois SAIC ne la ressuscite. MG tente aujourd'hui de se récupérer avec une gamme raisonnable, partagée en grande partie avec Roewe, nouvelle marque du même groupe.

TF
Rival: Mazda MX-5

Ancient, but still fun, two-seat roadster.
Uralter 2-Sitzer, macht aber noch Spaß.
Roadster à 2 places antique mais plaisant.

3
Rival: Ford Fiesta

Okay supermini, but others do it better.
Passabel, aber die Konkurrenz ist besser.
Citadine polyvalente honnête.

6
Rival: Ford Focus

Okay compact hatchback and sedan.
Als Fließheck und Limousine, auch OK.
Nouvelle compacte et berline, passable.

MIA ELECTRIC

LOGO HISTORY:

Imagine a tiny electric-powered VW Camper van for the city and you pretty much have the idea behind Mia Electric's new car trio. Born out of the ashes of French vehicle developer Heuliez's electric car division, German-based start-up Mia Electric took it over and developed the three-seat Mia, four-seat Mia L and one-seat commercial vehicle Mia Box Van. Design credibility comes via Murat Gunak and David Wilkie (ex-design bosses at VW and Bertone respectively) and all feature smartly stripped-out interiors, sliding doors and slim footprints for the city. Launching in France and Germany in 2011, other countries should follow pending local government grants. One to watch.

Denken Sie an einen elektrisch betriebenen VW-Bus für die Stadt und Sie haben den Kerngedanken hinter dem Dreigestirn von mia electric begriffen. Das deutsche Start-up-Unternehmen mia electric entstand auf den Trümmern der Elektroautosparte des französischen Fahrzeugentwicklers Heuliez. Entwickelt wurden bisher die dreisitzige mia, die viersitzige mia L sowie der einsitzige mia Kastenwagen. Für das Design sind Murat Gunak und David Wilkie verantwortlich (ehemalige Designchefs jeweils bei VW und Bertone). Kennzeichnend dabei sind die minimalistisch gehaltenen Interieurs, die Schiebetüren sowie reduzierte Maße für die Stadt. 2011 werden die Modelle in Frankreich und Deutschland eingeführt, in anderen Ländern laufen noch die Genehmigungsverfahren. Nicht aus den Augen verlieren.

Imaginez un tout petit van Camper Volkswagen électrique pour la ville, et vous aurez compris l'essence du concept du nouveau trio de voitures de Mia Electric. Née des cendres de la division des véhicules électriques du développeur français Heuliez, la jeune entreprise Mia Electric a créé la Mia à trois places, la Mia L à quatre places et le véhicule commercial à une place Mia Box Van. Murat Gunak et David Wilkie (respectivement anciens directeurs du design chez VW et Bertone) donnent au design sa crédibilité, et tous ces modèles sont dotés d'intérieurs élégamment dépouillés, de portes coulissantes, et d'une empreinte carbone réduite pour la ville. Ils seront disponibles en France et en Allemagne en 2011, et d'autres pays suivront en fonction des subventions accordées par les gouvernements concernés. À suivre.

MIA
Rival: Aixam-Mega City

One central seat plus two behind.
Fahrersitz in der Mitte und zwei Rücksitze.
Un siège central plus deux à l'arrière.

MIA L
Rival: Aixam-Mega Crossline

One central seat plus three behind.
Fahrersitz in der Mitte und drei Rücksitze.
Un siège central plus trois autres à l'arrière.

MIA BOX VAN
Rival: Citroen Berlingo EV

One central seat plus load bay.
Fahrersitz in der Mitte und Laderaum.
Un siège central plus une plateforme.

MINI

FOUNDED: **1994**

HEADQUARTERS: **OXFORD, ENGLAND**

2010 PRODUCTION: **234,175**

LOGO HISTORY:

The Mini as a model has been around since 1959, but it's only been a brand in its own right since 2001 when BMW relaunched it, and began a dramatic expansion of the concept, literally and figuratively. The original 'small outside, useful inside' mantra has been updated or compromised, depending on who you ask. But the new MINI has been an unarguable success. In Britain, drivers embraced the reborn icon for its fun styling and bargain-BMW engineering. It helped that it arrived at a time when the political talk of a 'classless society' melded with the reality of wealthy kids trading up from economy compacts, while struggling parents found a face-saving way to downsize from executive sedans. In the US, the MINI made a convincing case for small cars long before fuel prices tipped the scales in their favor. And globally, its pop image and cleverly diversified range, has found fans who never knew the original. The question today, however, is has the brand's one-line joke worn thin?

Als Modell gibt es den Mini seit 1959, als eigenständige Marke jedoch erst seit 2001, als BMW sie wiedereinführte und das zugrundeliegende Konzept weiterentwickelte – in wörtlichem und übertragenem Sinne. Die ursprüngliche Formel „small outside, useful inside" wurde je nach Standpunkt aktualisiert oder verraten, da scheiden sich die Geister. Den Erfolg des neuen MINI kann aber keiner übersehen. In Großbritannien wurde der Kultwagen wegen des originellen Designs und seiner BMW-Technologie zu einem wahren Renner. Der günstige Startzeitpunkt schadete auch nicht: Vor dem Hintergrund einer politischen Grundstimmung, in der die klassenlose Gesellschaft zum Ziel erklärt wurde, war der Mini der goldene Mittelweg sowohl für gut gestellte Sprösslinge, die ihre Kleinwagen ablegen wollten, als auch für ihre Eltern, die ihre protzigen Limousinen ersetzen und dabei das Gesicht wahren konnten. In den USA fand der MINI als Kleinwagen bereits vor dem Anstieg der Spritpreise großen Anklang. Auch in anderen Ländern haben das stylische Design und die breit gefächerte Palette zahlreiche Anhänger, die das Original nicht gekannt haben. Die Frage lautet indes: Wie lange wird das riskante Konzept noch funktionieren?

La Mini en tant que modèle existe depuis 1959, mais n'est une vraie marque que depuis 2001, lorsque BMW l'a relancée et a procédé à un élargissement spectaculaire du concept, au sens littéral et figuré. La philosophie d'origine (« petite à l'extérieur, utile à l'intérieur ») a été mise au goût du jour, ou dénaturée, les opinions divergent. Mais la nouvelle MINI a été un indéniable succès. Les conducteurs britanniques apprécient cette icône ressuscitée pour son style sympathique et sa mécanique BMW à un prix allégé. Elle est arrivée à un moment favorable, où les politiciens parlaient de disparition des classes sociales, et où les jeunes aisés troquaient leurs compactes économiques contre des modèles supérieurs, tandis que les parents qui rencontraient des difficultés financières y ont trouvé le moyen de sauver la face lorsqu'ils ont été obligés d'abandonner leurs grandes berlines. Aux États-Unis, la MINI a joué en faveur des petites voitures bien avant que le prix des carburants ne fasse pencher la balance dans cette direction. Et dans le monde entier, son image pop et la diversification intelligente de la gamme ont trouvé des amateurs qui n'ont jamais connu le modèle d'origine. Aujourd'hui, la question est cependant de savoir si le concept de la marque est toujours d'actualité.

HATCHBACK Rival: Audi A1		Retro looks, great drive, little space. Retro-Look, tolles Fahrgefühl, wenig Platz. Style rétro, excellente conduite, petit espace.
CONVERTIBLE Rival: Fiat 500 C		As above with a stroller roof. Wie oben, nur mit Dachluke. Comme ci-dessus, avec un toit décapotable.
CLUBMAN Rival: Skoda Fabia Estate		Wagon with odd doors. Ein Wagen mit auffälligen Türen. Break avec de drôles de portes.
COUNTRYMAN Rival: Skoda Yeti		Fat Mini with 4x4. Fetter Mini-Geländewagen. Grosse Mini 4x4.

MINI COUPE CONCEPT

While the Countryman takes Mini bigger than purists say is reasonable, the new Coupe at least keeps things fairly compact. Strictly a two-seater only offered with high-powered engines, it has a lower and faster rear roofline and threatens to be the best-handling Mini yet. No rear seats means more rear luggage space accessed by a large hatchback for flexibility too.

Während Puristen den Countryman für viel zu groß halten, bleibt das neue Coupé eindeutig im Rahmen eines Minis. Der Zweisitzer, der nur mit leistungsstarkem Motor angeboten wird, wartet mit einer niedrigeren und somit schnelleren Dachlinie auf und fährt sich besser als alle Vorgänger-Minis. Keine Rücksitze plus Fließheck bedeutet mehr Platz im Kofferraum und mehr Flexibilität.

La Countryman est une Mini que les puristes jugent déraisonnablement grande, mais le nouveau coupé reste dans les limites du compact. C'est une stricte deux places, avec un moteur puissant, et une ligne de toit plus basse à l'arrière taillée pour la vitesse. Elle menace d'être la Mini la plus maniable à ce jour. L'absence de sièges arrière signifie qu'il y a plus d'espace dans le coffre, et son grand hayon ajoute encore plus de flexibilité.

SECRET DETAIL

Another concept (main picture) that's made production virtually unscathed. Here's the production version for evidence…

Ein weiteres Konzeptmodell (Hauptbild), das nahezu unverändert umgesetzt wurde. Zum Beweis ein Bild des Serienmodells …

Encore un concept (image principale) qui est arrivé indemne jusqu'à la phase de production. Et pour preuve, voici la version de production…

MITSUBISHI

J

FOUNDED: **1917**

HEADQUARTERS: **TOKYO, JAPAN**

2010 PRODUCTION: **1,019,142**

LOGO HISTORY:

MITSUBISHI
MOTORS

MMC officially arrived in the 1970s, formalizing the automotive division within Mitsubishi Heavy Industries that had been producing cars as far back as 1917. Its history is littered with alliances, allowing it to penetrate the US market early, with many links to carmakers still existing – including the French PSA group. The line-up contains some real stars, with the Shogun 4x4 and L200 pick-up well respected and the Lancer Evo having a glittering rallying record and cult following. Its mainstream models are average, although its iMiEV is a new electric high point, if expensive, in an oddly disparate model range.

Die Mitsubishi Motors Corporation wurde offiziell erst 1970 gegründet, der Mitsubishi-Konzern hatte aber bereits seit 1917 unter dem Dach einer Tochtergesellschaft Fahrzeuge hergestellt. Die Firmengeschichte ist mit Allianzen übersät, die den Japanern einen frühen Einstieg in den amerikanischen Markt ermöglichten. Noch heute unterhält Mitsubishi Verbindungen zu zahlreichen Autobauern, so z. B. zur französischen PSA-Gruppe. Ein paar Volltreffer haben die Tokioter gelandet, siehe z. B. den Geländewagen Pajero und den Pick-up L200 sowie die im Motorsport erfolgreichen Lancer Evo-Modelle. Mitsubishis Mainstream-Modelle sind zwar durchschnittlich, der Elektro-Kleinstwagen i-MiEV ist jedoch ein würdiger – wenngleich teurer – Höhepunkt mit langer Modellhistorie.

MMC est officiellement née dans les années 1970 pour donner un nom à la division automobile de Mitsubishi Heavy Industries, qui produisait des voitures depuis 1917. Son histoire est remplie d'alliances qui lui ont permis de pénétrer très tôt le marché américain, et elle conserve de nombreux liens avec d'autres fabricants automobiles, notamment le groupe français PSA. Sa gamme de véhicules comprend de véritables vedettes, comme le 4x4 Shogun et le pick-up L200, très respectables, et le Lancer Evo dont les résultats dans les rallyes lui valent des adeptes dévoués. Les modèles grand public sont moyens, bien que l'iMiEV représente un nouveau sommet électrique (à prix fort) dans une gamme curieusement hétérogène.

I-MIEV
Rival: Nissan Leaf

Plug it in and drive – but not very far.
Aufladen und los … aber nicht so weit.
Branchez et conduisez, mais pas trop loin.

COLT
Rival: Renault Twingo

Average sub-supermini.
Durchschnittlicher Kompaktwagen.
Sous-compacte polyvalente moyenne.

LANCER
Rival: Ford Focus

Lacklustre sedan or hatchback.
Als Limousine oder Fließheck, glanzlos.
Berline ou compacte terne.

EVO X
Rival: Subaru
WRX STI

Giant killing, rally-bred weapon.
Motorsport-Kind mit großen Ambitionen.
Une arme contre les géants des rallyes.

GALANT
Rival: Toyota Camry

Big, capable but forgettable sedan.
Groß und leistungsfähig, aber langweilig.
Berline capable mais peu mémorable.

ECLIPSE
Rival: Audi TT

Respected coupe, not for Europe.
Beliebtes Coupé, nicht für den EU-Markt.
Coupé respecté, non disponible en Europe.

OUTLANDER
Rival: Nissan
Qashqai+2

Neat 7-seat crossover SUV.
Nettes, 7-sitziges Crossover-SUV.
Bon SUV crossover à 7 places.

ASX
Rival: Nissan Qashqai

Sportier Outlander with 2 less seats.
Sportlicher Outlander mit 2 Sitzen weniger.
Outlander sportif avec 2 places de moins.

PAJERO MINI
Rival: Daihatsu Terios

Tiny 4x4 for your city farm.
Winziger 4x4 für Stadt-Bauernhöfe.
Tout petit 4x4 pour votre ferme urbaine.

SHOGUN
Rival: Toyota Land Cruiser

Mighty off-roader.
Mächtiger Geländewagen.
Puissant tout-terrain.

L200
Rival: Nissan Navara

Builders' and lifestyle pick-up favourite.
Pick-up für Bauarbeiter und Städter.
Pick-up de choix pour les entrepreneurs.

ALSO AVAILABLE

Pajero Sport, Delica D:5.

MITSUBISHI IMIEV

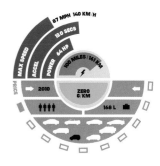

iMiEV

This diminutive, high-roofed city car fits four six-foot adults inside with ease (plus weekend bags). First a tiny 0.6-litre petrol engine powered the i version, now the iMiEV replaces that unit with full-electric power. The iMiEV's expensive for a small car, but it's still a superb package and a genuine EV trailblazer.

In diesen Kleinstwagen mit hohem Dach passen locker vier Erwachsene plus Wochenend-Gepäck. Die i-Version wurde noch von einem 0,6-Liter-Motor betrieben. Dieser wurde im iMiEV durch einen Elektromotor ersetzt. Trotz hohem Preis überzeugt dieser Miniflitzer, der zudem ein klasse Elektroauto-Pionier ist.

Cette citadine minuscule au toit surélevé peut accueillir quatre adultes d'1,80 m sans problème (avec leurs bagages pour un week-end). Un tout petit moteur conventionnel de 0,6 litre faisait avancer la version i, et maintenant la iMiEV le remplace par une propulsion entièrement électrique. L'iMiEV est chère pour une petite voiture, mais son concept est convaincant, et c'est une vraie pionnière de l'électrique.

SECRET DETAIL

If you spot a Citroen C-Zero or Peugeot iOn in almost identical clothes remember they're basically Mitsubishis in disguise.

Wenn Sie einen Citroën C-Zero oder einen Peugeot iOn haben wollten, denken Sie daran: Das sind auch nur verkleidete Mitsubishis …

Si vous repérez une Citroën C-Zero ou une Peugeot iOn portant une robe presque identique, n'oubliez pas que ce ne sont que des Mitsubishi déguisées.

MITSUOKA

(J)

FOUNDED: **1979**

HEADQUARTERS: **TOYAMA CITY, JAPAN**

LOGO HISTORY:

MITSUOKA

Perhaps better considered as a re-manufacturer, Mitsuoka takes existing Japanese cars and creates fantastical models from them. Whether you're looking for a Nissan Micra that looks like a shrunken MkII Jaguar, or a MX-5 that's been turned into a swooping roadster, Mitsuoka builds it. It's a big deal in its home market, Mitsuoka's designs helping persuade the larger Japanese firms there's a place, and demand for, retro-designed vehicles. Few are exported outside its native Japan, and cars like the Orochi should perhaps have remained as mythical as its eight-headed serpent namesake. An odd firm perhaps, but a little bit magical too.

Mitsuoka ist weniger ein Auto- als ein Replika-Bauer, der sich bestehende japanische Modelle vornimmt und daraus fantastische Fahrzeuge zaubert. Suchen Sie einen Nissan Micra mit dem Aussehen eines Jaguar MkII oder einen MX-5, der sich schwuppdiwupp in einen Roadster verwandelt hat? Dann rufen Sie bei Mitsuoka an. Auf dem japanischen Markt ist der Veredeler aus Toyama eine große Nummer und konnte auch größere Hersteller davon überzeugen, dass es doch eine Nachfrage nach Fahrzeugen in Retro-Stil gibt. Außerhalb Japans werden nur wenige Exemplare abgesetzt und sind kaum bekannt. So umgeben sich Modelle wie der Orochi mit der mythischen Aura der gleichnamigen achtköpfigen Schlange. Eigenartig ist Mitsuoka schon, aber auch irgendwie bezaubernd.

Mitsuoka est peut-être mieux connue pour ses activités de transformation : l'entreprise prend des voitures japonaises existantes et en fait de nouveaux modèles fantastiques. Que vous vouliez une Nissan Micra qui ressemble à une Jaguar deuxième génération en format réduit, ou une MX-5 transformée en roadster avec de nouvelles courbes, Mitsuoka s'en charge. Cette marque a son importance sur son marché local, car ses voitures font réaliser aux grandes marques japonaises qu'il y a de la place, et une demande, pour les véhicules de style rétro. Peu d'unités sont exportées en-dehors de leur Japon natal, et des voitures telles que l'Orochi auraient peut-être dû rester aussi fictives que le serpent à huit têtes dont elle a pris le nom. C'est une marque un peu étrange, mais elle a aussi une certaine magie.

LIKE
Rival: Mitsubishi iMiEV

Mitsubishi iMiEV with a new face.
Mitsubishi iMiEV mit neuem Gesicht.
Mitsubishi iMiEV avec un nouveau visage.

VIEWT
Rival: Nissan Micra

Old Jag looks, Nissan Micra underneath.
Nissan Micra in ehrwürdigem Kostüm.
Une Jaguar qui cache une Nissan Micra.

GALUE-III
Rival: Nissan Fuga

As Viewt, but larger. Based on Fuga.
Wie der Viewt, nur größer. Auf Fuga-Basis.
Idem, en plus grande. Basée sur la Fuga.

GALUE 204
Rival: Mazda MX-5

As above, but Toyota-flavoured.
Wie oben, aber mit Toyota-Geschmack.
Idem, mais basée sur une Toyota.

HIMIKO
Rival: Mazda MX-5

MX-5 based classic roadster.
Klassischer Roadster mit MX-5-Fundament.
Roadster classique basé sur une MX-5.

OROCHI
Rival: A monkfish

Weird bottom-feeding sports car.
Science-Fiction-Sportwagen.
Sportive qui ressemble à un poisson.

MORGAN

GB

FOUNDED: **1909**

HEADQUARTERS: **MALVERN, ENGLAND**

LOGO HISTORY:

Family-run car firm that's got one foot in the past and one stepping to the future. It offers stunning hand-built cars with styling from a bygone era but with modern performance. The Aero SuperSports gets a BMW powertrain, the German giant loving the tiny UK firm so much it's got a couple of Morgan-dedicated engineers in Germany. The Roadster can trace its roots back many decades, with the more modern 'Aero' based cars like the SuperSports blending classic lines with serious performance. Undoubtedly quirky, but quite brilliant, Morgan is re-introducing a three-wheeler, while the EvaGT and experimental green LIFECar remain ongoing projects.

Bei Morgan handelt es sich um ein Familienunternehmen, das mit einem Auge in lang vergangene Zeiten und mit dem anderen in die Zukunft schaut. So sehen die Morgan-Fahrzeuge wie Autos aus vergangenen Epochen aus, ihre Leistung aber ist hochmodern. Der Aero SuperSports ist mit einem Antriebsstrang von BMW ausgestattet. Die Bayern haben sich übrigens so sehr in Morgan verliebt, dass sie ein paar Ingenieure zur Unterstützung des kleinen englischen Herstellers abkommandiert haben. Die Roadster sind schon einige Jahrzehnte alt und die Aero-Modelle – siehe den SuperSports – vereinen klassische Linien mit atemberaubender Leistung. Trotz einer gewissen Tendenz zur Verschnörkelung ist die Modellpalette ausgezeichnet. Zurzeit werden dreirädrige Fahrzeuge wieder eingeführt, der EvaGT und das Lifecar sind noch in der Entwurfsphase.

Compagnie automobile familiale qui a un pied dans le passé et l'autre tourné vers l'avenir. Elle propose de superbes voitures construites à la main dans le style d'un temps jadis mais avec des performances tout à fait modernes. L'Aero SuperSports est dotée d'un groupe motopropulseur BMW. Le géant allemand aime tellement cette minuscule marque britannique qu'il a deux ingénieurs entièrement consacrés à Morgan en Allemagne. Les racines du Roadster traversent de nombreuses décennies, et les voitures plus modernes basées sur l'« Aero », comme la SuperSports, allient lignes classiques et performances sérieuses. Morgan est une marque indubitablement excentrique, mais assez brillante. Elle relance une voiture à trois roues, tandis que l'EvaGT et la LIFECar verte expérimentale restent des projets en cours de réalisation.

ROADSTER
Rival: BMW Z4

Simple classic Morgan.
Einfacher, klassischer Morgan.
Morgan classique et simple.

PLUS 4
Rival: BMW Z4

More of the same.
Dasselbe in Grün.
Idem.

FOUR SEATER
Rival: Merc E-Class Cab

More seats, awkward styling.
Mehr Sitze, ungeschickte Gestaltung.
Plus de sièges, mais design maladroit.

AERO SUPERSPORTS
Rival: Merc SL

Sensational looks/performance.
Sensationelles Design, tolle Leistung.
Style et performance sensationnels.

3-WHEELER
Rival: Grinnall Scorpion

As its name suggests.
Der Name ist Programm.
Comme son nom le suggère, à trois roues.

MORGAN 3-WHEELER

In reference to a blast from Morgan's past, a modern 3-Wheeler was shown at Geneva in 2011 and interest was high enough to start production. Yes, it's a little impractical, but it's still a really fun machine and highly suited to Morgan's eccentrically British range.

Auf dem Genfer Automobilsalon 2011 erinnerte Morgan mit der Präsentation seines modernen 3-Wheeler an seine Vergangenheit. Das Interesse war so groß, dass man sich für die Serienproduktion entschied. Er ist zugegebener-maßen ein bisschen unpraktisch, bietet aber dennoch viel Fahrspaß und passt hervorragend zum exzentrischen Angebot des britischen Autoherstellers.

En référence à un succès passé de Morgan, une 3-Wheeler moderne a été présentée à Genève en 2011 et a généré suffisamment d'intérêt pour que la production soit mise en route. Bien sûr, elle n'est pas très pratique, mais c'est tout de même une machine très amusante, et elle a parfaitement sa place dans la gamme de Morgan, pleine d'excentricité britannique.

3-Wheeler

* Estimated CO2 emissions

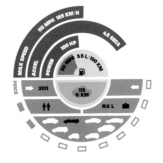

SECRET DETAIL

WWII aero graphics are an official option and you can also have bullets, numbers, shark's teeth and even a pin-up girl.

Es stehen Flugzeugmotive aus dem Zweiten Weltkrieg, Kugeln, Zahlen, Haifischzähne und sogar ein Pin-up-Girl zur Auswahl!

La décoration « armée de l'air » de la Deuxième Guerre mondiale est une option officielle. Vous pouvez demander des balles, des chiffres, des dents de requin, et même une pin-up.

MORGAN AERO MAX

Aeromax (automatic)

Swiss banker-envisioned, handcrafted deco-future coolness with BMW power and styled by a student that amazingly made it into production. Its limited run means you'll need to pry the keys off an existing owner. But if you can, you definitely should.

Der mit Liebe zum Detail handgefertigte Traum eines jeden Schweizer Bankiers strahlt futuristische Coolness aus und beeindruckt mit purer BMW-Power. Den Entwurf hat sein Designer noch als Student zu Papier gebracht. Da der Wagen nur in limitierter Auflage hergestellt wird, müssen Sie die Schlüssel einem Besitzer entreißen. Wenn Sie die Gelegenheit dazu haben, nutzen Sie sie!

Petite merveille rêvée par un banquier suisse, faite à la main dans un style Art déco futuriste, propulsée par un moteur BMW et dessinée par un étudiant, on s'étonne que cette rareté soit arrivée jusqu'à la phase de production. Sa série étant très limitée, vous devrez trouver l'un de ses propriétaires et lui arracher les clés des mains. Si vous en avez l'occasion, n'hésitez pas.

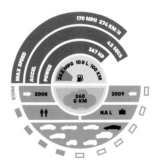

SECRET DETAIL

The rear lights on that gloriously sculpted body are borrowed from Lancia's little known, and otherwise forgettable Thesis sedan.

Die Rücklichter dieser Schönheit basieren auf dem recht unbekannten und fast vergessenen Thesis.

Les feux arrière de cette caisse merveilleusement sculptée sont empruntés à la berline Thesis de Lancia, peu connue et par ailleurs peu mémorable.

MOSLER

FOUNDED: **1988**
HEADQUARTERS: **FLORIDA, USA**
2010 PRODUCTION: **10**

LOGO HISTORY:

Mosler has been killing giants on the track since 1988. Naturally there are always a few customers who want to take their racers on the road and Mosler is happy to oblige. The MT900 is its current road car, although that's a loose term, as it looks like it's just done 24 hours at Le Mans. It could, competitively, thanks to lightweight carbon composite construction and huge GM-sourced V8 engines. Even the 'slowest' MT900S is bonkers fast, while the MT900SGT is completely unhinged. Not for everyone sure, but if you like your performance big then Mosler delivers in spades.

Seit 1988 ist Mosler der Schreck der großen Fische auf der Rennstrecke. Nun ist es aber so, dass sich manche Kunden eine Straßenversion ihrer Flitzer wünschen – und Mosler tut ihnen den Gefallen. Der MT900 ist sein aktueller Straßenwagen, wobei der Begriff „Straßenwagen" hier stark gedehnt wurde – das Auto sieht nämlich so aus, als käme es gerade vom 24-Stunden-Rennen von Le Mans. Und in der Tat würde der MT900 dabei eine gute Figur machen – dafür sorgen eine leichte Karosserie aus kohlenstofffaserverstärktem Kunststoff sowie ein GM-V8-Motor. Selbst der „langsamste" MT900 S ist wahnsinnig schnell, der MT900 GT hat dabei noch mehr zu bieten. Nicht jedermanns Sache, aber auf jeden Fall für Liebhaber von extrem hohen Leistungen.

Mosler terrasse des géants sur les circuits depuis 1988. Naturellement, il y a toujours quelques clients qui veulent emmener leur voiture de course sur la route, et Mosler se fait un plaisir de rendre service. La MT900 est sa routière actuelle, bien que ce terme soit utilisé dans un sens très large, car elle a l'air tout juste débarquée des 24 Heures du Mans. Elle pourrait d'ailleurs y faire bonne figure, grâce à son châssis léger en composite de carbone et à son énorme V8 de GM. Même la MT900S censée être « la plus lente » est follement rapide, tandis que la MT900SGT est complètement démente. Ce n'est pas pour tout le monde, mais si vous aimez les performances superlatives, Mosler ne vous décevra pas.

MT900
Rival: Ultima GTR

Racecar with a licence plate.
Rennwagen mit Nummernschild.
Voiture de sport avec une plaque d'immatriculation.

NISSAN

FOUNDED: **1933**
HEADQUARTERS: **YOKOHAMA, JAPAN**
2010 PRODUCTION: **4,080,588**

LOGO HISTORY:

Nissan gained its name as an abbreviation of Nippon Sangyo back in the 1930s and made trucks and planes for the Japanese military. Post WWII collaboration with UK brand Austin accelerated know-how with its Datsun brand, but it wasn't until the stylish and reliable 1968 Datsun 240Z – that sold 500,000-plus units and won two grueling African rallies – that the world really took notice. Unfortunately the 'style' part remained elusive from its mainstream cars until an alliance with Renault in 1999 led to better management, trailblazing new designs and clever niche filling. Today it is one of Japan's big three carmakers, with a knack for teasing out niches no-one else thought existed, rather than simply churning out metal to tried-and-tested formulas. Pioneering electric Leaf marks the start of a major push towards popularizing sustainable motoring, and with star CEO Carlos Ghosn at the wheel, turning a decent profit for its efforts.

Der Name Nissan wurde in den 1930er Jahren als Abkürzung von Nippon Sangyo geprägt. Zunächst wurden LKWs und Flugzeuge für das japanische Militär gebaut. Nach dem 2. Weltkrieg ging bei der Kooperation mit Austin viel Know-how von Großbritannien nach Japan zur Marke Datsun über. Weltweite Aufmerksamkeit erlangten die Japaner erst mit dem eleganten Datsun 240Z von 1968 (über 500.000-mal verkauft) und in Afrika zwei Rallyes gewann. Diese Eleganz ging bei den Mainstream-Modellen verloren. Erst die Allianz mit Renault 1999 brachte bahnbrechende Designs und kluge Strategien. Heute zählt Nissan zu den Top 3 in Japan. Verantwortlich dafür ist ein feines Gespür für Nischen, die sonst niemand wahrnimmt. Einfach Metall nach altbewährten Formeln zu verarbeiten will der Hersteller aus Yokohama nicht. Mit dem Elektroauto Leaf wurde ein erster Schritt in Richtung Nachhaltigkeit gemacht. Geführt wird Nissan von Carlos Ghosn, der bisher gute Arbeit geleistet hat.

Nippon Sangyo fabriquait des camions et des avions pour l'armée japonaise, et le nom s'est abrégé en Nissan dans les années 1930. Après la Deuxième Guerre mondiale, Nissan a travaillé avec Austin, ce qui a bénéficié à son savoir-faire avec sa marque Datsun, mais ce n'est qu'en 1968, avec la Datsun 240Z (500 000 unités vendues, deux rallyes africains remportés) que le monde s'est aperçu de sa présence. Le style de ses voitures grand public est resté un problème jusqu'à ce qu'une alliance avec Renault en 1999 conduise à un renouvellement du design et à l'occupation intelligente des niches du marché. Nissan est l'un des trois grands fabricants automobiles du Japon, et a le don de découvrir des niches insoupçonnées. La Leaf est une pionnière de l'électrique, et marque le début d'un gros effort dans l'automobile durable. Avec une star comme le PDG Carlos Ghosn au volant, ces efforts se révéleront très rentables.

ROOX
Rival: Suzuki Palette

Japan-only tallboy Kei car slim box cool.
Cooler Kei-Car-Microvan für Japan.
Keijidosha pratique vendue au Japon.

MICRA | MARCH
Rival: Ford Ka

Massive-selling bit dull global city car.
Ein großer Hit, nicht mehr so langweilig.
Citadine qui se vend très bien.

CUBE
Rival: Kia Soul

Asymmetric boxcar design genius.
Asymmetrische Kiste mit tollem Design.
Voiture carrée au design génial.

LEAF
Rival: Mitsubishi iMiEV

Mass-production bespoke hatch EV.
Elektro-Steilheck für die Massen.
Compacte électrique grand public.

JUKE
Rival: Mini Countryman

Bold jacked-up supermini/SUV/coupe.
Supermini/SUV/Coupé mit Mut.
Polyvalente/SUV/coupé surélevé.

ROGUE | QASHQAI | DUALIS
Rival: Skoda Yeti

Huge hit compact crossover.
Crossover mit sensationellem Erfolg.
Crossover compact, énorme succès.

ALTIMA
Rival: Honda Accord

US best selling sedan, hybrid variant.
Bestseller in den USA, mit Hybrid-Option.
Gros succès aux États-Unis, option hybride.

MURANO
Rival: Audi Q5

Formerly curvy now dull SUV plus quirky cabrio.
Glanzlos, das Cabrio ist besser.
SUV tout en courbes, nouveau cabriolet.

ELGRAND
Rival: Honda Elysion

Big chrome-grilled 8-st majestic MPV.
Van mit Chrom-Kühlergrill und 8 Sitzen.
Monospace 8 places, calandre chromée.

370Z
Rival: BMW Z4

Brawny and able V6 coupe and roadster.
Sportcoupé und Roadster mit V6-Motor.
Coupé et roadster musclé doté d'un V6.

GT-R
Rival: Porsche Cayman R

Porsche-beating bargain supercar.
Porsche-Bezwinger mit günstigem Preis.
Bat les Porsche, et meilleur marché.

ALSO AVAILABLE

Otti, Moco, Clipper Rio, Pixo, Note, X-Trail, Pathfinder, Patrol, Livina, Tiida/Versa/Latio, Wingroad, Bluebird Sylphy, Lafesta, Serena, Teana, Fuga, Kix, Sentra, Maxima, Quest, Rogue, X-Terra, Armada

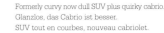

NISSAN CUBE

The perfect antidote to endless go-faster clichés, Francois Bancon, Nissan's head of advance planning, describes the Cube as designed "to look still even when it is moving". Its product design aesthetic results in a simple but beautiful cube on wheels that acts as a spacious mobile lounge. And the asymmetric rear window shows Nissan thinks inside the box.

Das perfekte Gegenmittel gegen den ständigen Geschwindig-keitswettbewerb … François Bancon, Head of Advance Planning bei Nissan, erklärt, das Design des Cube sei so angelegt, dass er „sogar in Bewegung gut aussieht". Seine Ästhetik besteht darin, ein einfacher, aber wunderschöner Würfel auf Rädern zu sein, der zudem noch als geräumige mobile Lounge dient. Und mit dem asymmetrischen Rückfenster setzt Nissan in Sachen Designbewusstsein noch eins drauf.

La Cube est le parfait antidote aux interminables clichés sur la vitesse. François Bancon, directeur de la planification avancée chez Nissan, dit qu'elle a été conçue « pour avoir l'air d'être à l'arrêt même quand elle roule ». C'est un cube sur roues simple mais beau, un grand salon mobile. Et la fenêtre arrière asymétrique montre que Nissan a des idées plein ses cartons.

Cube 1.6 manual Kaizen

SECRET DETAIL

Although still uniquely brilliant, we prefer the purity of the older and boxier second-gen model, preferably the Conran limited edition.

Auch die aktuellste Ausführung ist wie erwartet brillant. Wir ziehen aber die Klarheit der älteren, kastigeren Modelle der zweiten Generation vor, darunter vor allem den Conran der limitierten Ausgabe.

Bien que la version actuelle soit toujours unique et géniale, nous préférons la pureté plus carrée de la deuxième génération, qui l'a précédée, surtout l'édition limitée Conran.

NISSAN JUKE

There's no danger of confusing the Juke for any other car. A mash-up of SUV bottom half and Coupe top sitting on a supermini-sized chassis with multiple rally-style headlights, the Juke is another perfect Nissan example of how to avoid me-too products. Not to everyone's taste – and that's the point – we like it a lot.

Der Juke ist unverwechselbar. Eine Mischung aus SUV-Unterteil und Coupé-Oberteil, die Karosserie in Miniaturgröße, Scheinwerfer im Rallye-Stil: ein weiterer Beweis des Originalitätsstrebens von Nissan. Nicht jedermanns Geschmack, und genau das mögen wir.

Aucun danger de confondre la Juke avec une autre voiture. Le bas d'un SUV et le haut d'un coupé se rejoignent sur un châssis de citadine polyvalente, avec une abondance de phares style rallye. Avec la Juke, Nissan donne encore une leçon magistrale d'originalité. Ce n'est pas du goût de tout le monde (et c'est fait exprès). Nous aimons beaucoup.

Juke 1.6 Tekna 5-speed manual

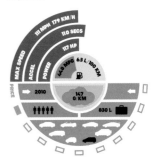

2009 Qazana concept (white, left)
2010 production Juke

SECRET DETAIL

The interior has a central transmission tunnel that apes the look of a motorbike's fuel tank. Specify in red to stand out.

Der Getriebetunnel im Innenraum sieht aus wie ein Motorradtank.

L'intérieur est doté d'un tunnel de transmission central qui imite le look d'un réservoir à essence de moto.

NISSAN GT-R

Japanese Gundam robots were the inspiration for the aggressively angular exterior treatment of the GT-R. This brutal cladding hides technical wizardry that delivers even faster rocket-like performance with its 2011 facelift. But all you really need to know is that Porsche 911 Turbo owners have never felt less smug. Perfect.

Japanische Gundam-Roboter waren die Inspirationsgrundlage des kantigen GT-R. In der aggressiven Hülle verbirgt sich ein technologisches Wunder, das nach dem Facelift von 2011 raketengleiche Leistung bringt. Kurz gesagt: Der Porsche 911 Turbo ist dagegen ein alter Spießer. Einfach perfekt.

Ce sont les robots Gundam japonais qui ont inspiré l'extérieur angulaire et agressif de la GT-R. Cette carrosserie brutale cache une mécanique magique qui donne des performances dignes d'une fusée spatiale, encore plus depuis le lifting de 2011. Mais il suffit de savoir que les propriétaires de Porsche 911 Turbo ont perdu leur air arrogant. Parfait.

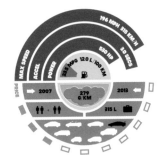

DESIGNER Q+A

Shiro Nakamura
Senior VP Design and
Chief Creative Officer, Nissan

On duty:
Suit: Boglioli
Shoes: Crockett & Jones
Watch: Jaeger-LeCoultre
Reverso (dual-time zone flip)
– "I've got them set to UK and
Japan time at the moment. It's
very useful."

Off-duty:
Clothes: Shirts and sweaters,
Boss and Louis Vuitton sneakers

**What does your brand stand
for?**
Past: "Technology."
Present: "Bold."
Future: "Innovative."

NISSAN 370Z

Muscle car, Japanese style. Classic long hood, short tail sports car remixed with a GT-R supercar sample. Tighter and more agile than a US sports car, more powerful than its European rivals. A choice of coupe or roadster bodies, we suspect the next generation will look a little more interesting.

Muscle Car im japanischen Stil. Sportwagen mit klassischer langer Haube und kurzem Heck sowie unverkennbaren Einflüssen vom Supersportwagen GT-R. Schmaler und agiler als ein US-Sportwagen und leistungsstärker als seine europäischen Konkurrenten. Als Coupé oder Roadster erhältlich. Wir vermuten, dass die nächste Generation etwas interessanter aussehen wird.

Muscle car à la japonaise, voiture de sport à long capot classique et arrière-train court, fusionnée avec une supercar GT-R. Plus affûtée et agile qu'une sportive américaine, plus puissante que ses rivales européennes. Avec un choix de carrosseries coupé ou roadster, nous pensons que la prochaine génération sera un peu plus intéressante du point de vue esthétique.

370Z GT Coupe

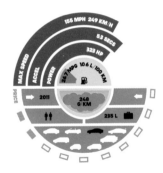

SECRET DETAIL

SynchroRev makes you look like a heal-and-toe legend by automatically revving the engine when changing to a lower gear.

Mit der Synchro Rev Control für das manuelle Getriebe wird die Drehzahl beim Hoch- oder Herunterschalten automatisch angepasst – einfach klasse!

Le système SynchroRev vous fait passer pour un as du pointe-talon en adaptant le régime moteur automatiquement lorsque vous passez à une vitesse inférieure.

NISSAN MURANO CROSSCABRIOLET

Audi showed a 4x4 cabrio concept a few years back but currently Nissan's the only manufacturer to actually make one. There might be a good reason for that, but we still admire Nissan's bravery in thinking beyond the mainstream. It makes up for the blunted face of the regular Murano, a step back from the model it replaced.

Audi hat vor ein paar Jahren ein 4x4 Cabrio-Konzept vorgestellt, Nissan ist jedoch derzeit die einzige Marke, die eins herstellt. Möglicherweise gibt es gute Gründe dafür, wir bewundern allerdings den Mut von Nissan, stets abseits des Mainstream zu denken. Das Cabrio hat ein frischeres Gesicht als der reguläre Murano und distanziert sich von seinem Vorgängermodell.

Audi a révélé un concept de 4x4 cabriolet il y a quelques années, mais Nissan est le seul fabricant à en proposer un actuellement. Il y a peut-être une bonne raison à cela, mais nous admirons quand même le courage de Nissan, qui sort des sentiers battus. Cela compense le visage écrasé de la Murano de base, qui représente un pas en arrière par rapport au modèle qu'elle a remplacé.

Murano Crosscabriolet 3.5 V6
* MPG based on US gallon

SECRET DETAIL

Nissan design boss Shiro Nakamura says one of the best ways to understand the car's appeal is to get onboard and look outwards. Although an open-top, the high belt line means it's far less overlooked than most other convertibles.

Design-Chef von Nissan Shiro Nakamura ist der Meinung, man könne dieses Auto nur verstehen, wenn man drinsitzt und hinausschaut. Denn es ist zwar ein Cabrio, liegt aber aufgrund der hohen Gürtellinie viel höher als die meisten anderen seiner Klasse.

Pour bien comprendre l'attrait de cette voiture, le patron du design chez Nissan, Shiro Nakamura, conseille de monter dedans et de regarder vers l'extérieur. La hauteur de sa ceinture de caisse lui donne un point de vue beaucoup plus élevé que la plupart des autres décapotables.

NOBLE

GB

FOUNDED: **2001**

HEADQUARTERS: **BARWELL, ENGLAND**

LOGO HISTORY:

Set up by respected car engineer Lee Noble in 2001, Noble Automotive's first car, the M10, gained serious critical acclaim for its performance and handling, although styling wasn't a strong point. The M10's short production run was followed by the M12 GTO model; a car that also wowed with its ability and evolved into the highly regarded M400. Businessman Peter Dyson bought the company in 2006 and Lee left in 2009 to set up Fenix Automotive. From the stillborn M14/M15 cars the M600 has now been created – a 650hp supercar that retains Noble's giant-killing reputation.

Das erste Modell der 2001 vom angesehenen Automobilingenieur Lee Noble gegründeten Manufaktur, der M10, wurde von der Kritik mit Beifall aufgenommen. Leistung und Fahrverhalten wurden gelobt, das Design dagegen fand weniger Anhänger. Nach der kurzen Produktionsphase des M10 wurde der M12 GTO vorgestellt. Auch dieses Modell entpuppte sich als hochleistungsfähig und wurde schließlich mit dem M400 weiter perfektioniert. Die Firma wurde 2006 vom Geschäftsmann Peter Dyson erworben. Noble verließ 2009 das Unternehmen, um bei Fenix Automotive einzusteigen. Aus den tot geborenen Modellen M14/M15 ist der M600 entstanden – ein 650 PS starker Supersportwagen nach allen Regeln der Kunst.

Créée par le prestigieux ingénieur automobile Lee Noble en 2001, la première voiture de Noble Automotive, la M10, a été saluée par la critique pour ses performances et sa conduite, même si l'esthétique n'était pas son point fort. Elle a été fabriquée pendant une courte période, puis a été remplacée par la M12 GTO, une voiture qui a également su séduire par ses capacités, et dont l'évolution a donné la M400, qui jouit d'une grande considération. L'homme d'affaires Peter Dyson a acheté l'entreprise en 2006 et Lee en est parti en 2009 pour créer Fenix Automotive. Les M14/M15 mort-nées ont laissé la place à la M600, une supercar de 650 chevaux qui fait honneur à la réputation de Noble d'être capable de terrasser les plus grands.

M600

Rival: Fenix

650hp supercar retains Noble's giant-killing rep.
Supersportwagen mit satten 650 PS – einfach ausgezeichnet.
Supercar de 650 chevaux, sublime malgré le départ du fondateur.

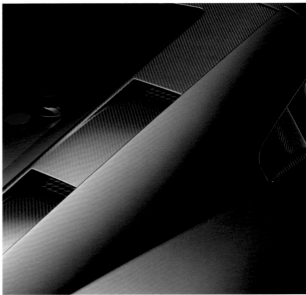

OPEL | VAUXHALL

FOUNDED: **1862 | 1903**

HEADQUARTERS: **RÜSSELSHEIM, GERMANY | LUTON, ENGLAND**

2010 PRODUCTION: **1,206,620**

LOGO HISTORY:

GM's European subsidiary is one of its most important units today. Opel – and UK-based Vauxhall – are key to GM's global strategy thanks to its range of high-quality, fuel-efficient and compact cars: perfect for bailing out the US parent following the recent financial crisis. Buick in particular is taking advantage of the hardware available from its cousins across the pond, while the recently discontinued Saturn brand consisted almost entirely of European-based compacts. Chief designer Mark Adams takes full credit for refreshing the thoroughly underwhelming range. One of the most impressive turnarounds in the industry. That said, it's difficult to identify a model we'd want to own.

Das Tochterunternehmen von GM in Europa ist heute eine der wichtigsten Geschäftseinheiten des amerikanischen Giganten. Opel – und die britische Marke Vauxhall – sind dank ihrer zuverlässigen, sparsamen Kompaktmodelle für die globale Strategie von GM unverzichtbar. Die beiden Marken sollen dem wegen der Finanzkrise notleidenden Mutterkonzern aus der Patsche helfen. Insbesondere Buick profitiert gerade von den Schwesterunternehmen auf der anderen Seite des Atlantiks. Auch die inzwischen eingestellte Marke Saturn war stark von Europa abhängig. GM-Chefdesigner Mark Adams hat für die Rüsselsheimer ganze Arbeit geleistet. Opels Auferstehung ist einer der größten Heldentaten der Automobilindustrie. Dennoch: Zum Verlieben finden wir Opel nicht gerade.

La filiale européenne de GM est l'une de ses divisions les plus importantes à l'heure actuelle. Opel (et Vauxhall pour la Grande-Bretagne) joue un rôle essentiel dans la stratégie mondiale de GM avec sa gamme de voitures compactes de grande qualité et économes en carburant : parfaite pour renflouer la maison-mère américaine après la récente crise financière. Buick profite particulièrement du matériel que sa cousine d'outre-Atlantique lui met à disposition, tandis que Saturn, marque récemment abandonnée, se composait presque exclusivement de compactes européennes. C'est le directeur du design, Mark Adams, qu'il faut remercier pour le rafraîchissement de la gamme, qui était vraiment décevante. C'est l'un des redressements les plus spectaculaires du secteur. Ceci dit, il est difficile d'identifier un modèle que l'on aurait vraiment envie d'acheter.

AGILA
Rival: Fiat Panda

Bug-eyed compact city car.
Mikrovan für die Stadt.
Citadine compacte au regard d'insecte.

CORSA
Rival: Renault Clio

Hugely popular, spacious supermini.
Sehr beliebter, geräumiger Kleinwagen.
Polyvalente spacieuse très populaire.

MERIVA
Rival: Citroën C3 Picasso

Mini-MPV rocking suicide doors.
Minivan mit Portaltüren.
Mini-monospace doté de portes suicide.

ASTRA
Rival: Ford Focus

Handsome compact hatchback.
Hübscher Kompaktwagen.
Belle compacte.

INSIGNIA
Rival: VW Passat

Classy mid-sized family wheels.
Mittelklasse-Familienauto.
Familiale élégante de taille moyenne.

ZAFIRA
Rival: Renault Grand Scenic

Clever seven-seat MPV.
Praktischer Kompaktvan mit 7 Sitzen.
Monospace malin à 7 places.

ANTARA
Rival: Toyota RAV4

Decent small SUV.
Kleines SUV, gar nicht übel.
Petit SUV honnête.

PAGANI

LOGO HISTORY:

Argentinian Horacio Pagani has achieved what every wannabe supercar creator dreams of: credibility. Pagani Automobili has the clout to take on and beat its Ferrari and Lamborghini neighbors. The Zonda C12 started it all, with the former Lamborghini composites expert applying all his carbon-weave mastery – Bugatti approached Horacio to provide carbon for the Veyron but he said he was too busy building his own, AMG V12-powered machine. The Zonda has developed since, with ever increasing outputs and more special edition one-offs than is perhaps sensible. Its replacement, the Huayra isn't pretty, but it'll be fast, stupidly so.

Der Argentinier Horacio Pagani hat erreicht, was jeder Sportautohersteller anstrebt – Glaubwürdigkeit. Pagani Automobili hat auch die notwendige Schlagkraft, um mit seinen Landsleuten bei Ferrari und Lamborghini zu konkurrieren. Alles begann mit dem Zonda C12, in den der ehemalige Experte für Verbundwerkstoffe von Lamborghini sein ganzes Können steckte. Butatti versuchte, ihn für den Bau der Kohlefaser-Karosserie des Veyron zu gewinnen, doch er lehnte ab: Die Arbeit an seiner mit AMG-V12-Motoren betriebenen Maschine lasse ihn keine Zeit. Seitdem wurde der Zonda weiterentwickelt und immer leistungsfähiger. Außerdem wurden einige maßgeschneiderte Versionen gebaut, vielleicht sogar mehr als ratsam. Das Nachfolgemodell ist der Huayara, der zwar nicht schön aussieht, dafür aber verboten schnell ist.

L'Argentin Horacio Pagani a obtenu ce à quoi tout créateur de supercar aspire : la crédibilité. Pagani Automobili a assez de poids pour se mesurer à ses voisins Ferrari et Lamborghini, et pour les battre. C'est avec la Zonda C12 que tout a commencé. L'ancien expert des composites chez Lamborghini y a concentré toute sa maîtrise de l'art du carbone. Bugatti avait demandé à Horacio de se charger du carbone pour la Veyron, mais il a répondu qu'il était trop occupé à construire sa propre machine équipée d'un V12 AMG. La Zonda a depuis poursuivi son développement, avec une production en constante hausse et beaucoup de modèles uniques en édition spéciale, voire trop. La Huayra qui la remplacera n'est pas belle, mais elle sera absurdement rapide.

ZONDA
Rival: Bugatti Veyron

Establishment-shaking masterpiece.
Die großen Namen ziehen sich warm an.
Chef-d'œuvre qui secoue l'ordre établi.

HUAYRA
Rival: Ditto

Zonda replacement, expect fireworks.
Spektakuläres Nachfolgemodell des Zonda.
Remplaçante de la Zonda, explosive.

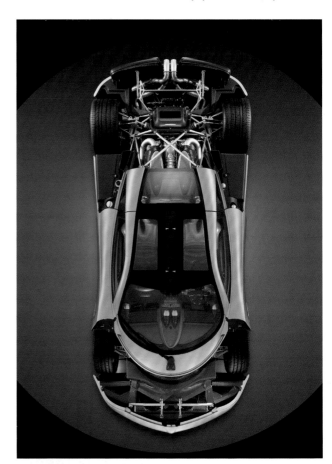

PAGANI HUAYRA

More awkward-looking than its Zonda predecessor, the Huayra still promises to turn heads like no Ferrari ever could. The intricacy of the detailing inside and out is incredible and with rarity, V12 power and huge cost it's a modern supercar with few equals.

Der Huayra sieht zwar etwas plumper aus als sein Vorgänger Zonda, sorgt aber auf der Straße immer noch für mehr Aufsehen als ein Ferrari. Die optische Verbindung zwischen der Innen- und Außenseite ist etwas ganz Besonderes. Mit V12-Power und einem enormen Preis ein moderner Supersportwagen mit nur wenig Konkurrenz.

Avec un look plus maladroit que celui de la Zonda, qu'elle remplace, la Huayra promet néanmoins de faire tourner les têtes encore mieux qu'une Ferrari. À l'intérieur comme à l'extérieur, c'est une débauche incroyable de détails finement travaillés, auxquels s'ajoutent la puissance rare du V12 et un coût astronomique, qui en font une supercar moderne pratiquement sans égale.

Huayra
* Estimated CO2 emissions and MPG

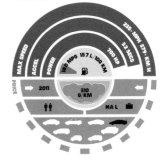

SECRET DETAIL

Each customer of the previous model got a pair of hand-made shoes lovingly crafted by the Pope's own cobbler no less.

Jeder Kunde des Vorgängermodells erhielt ein Paar handgefertigte Schuhe, das von niemand Geringerem als dem persönlichen Schumacher des Papstes hergestellt wurde.

Chaque acheteur du modèle précédent a eu droit à une paire de chaussures faites à la main avec amour par le cordonnier du Pape, s'il vous plaît.

PANOZ

FOUNDED: **1989**
HEADQUARTERS: **HOSCHTON, USA**

LOGO HISTORY:

A racecar team with Le Mans pedigree, Panoz was established by Dan Panoz, who usefully has a dad called Don who made a fortune developing pharmaceuticals. Panoz makes its own road cars in order to allow it to compete in GT racing. The Roadster was its first, the Esperante having been its mainstay since 2000. It's produced in handfuls for patriotic US drivers wanting a sports car that's not a Corvette or Viper. As ever, there's a new car planned, called Abruzzi 'Spirit of Le Mans', although the 'spirit' here might refer to the stuff you'd need to consume to like its looks…

Der Rennstall mit Le Mans-Erfahrung wurde von Dan Panoz gegründet, dessen Vater Don Panoz in der Pharmabranche zum Milliardär wurde – ein durchaus nützlicher Umstand. Panoz baut eigene Rennautos für GT-Rennserien. Erstes Modell war der Roadster, wobei der Esperante die Hauptstütze der Firma seit 2000 darstellt. Der Hersteller hat zahlreiche Fahrzeuge für patriotische US-Rennfahrer gebaut, die weder in eine Corvette noch in eine Viper steigen wollten. Zurzeit wird das neue Modell entwickelt, das auf den Namen Abruzzi „Spirit of Le Mans" hört. Möglich, dass „Spirit" auf die Menge Spirituosen anspielt, die man trinken muss, um das Auto hübsch zu finden.

Panoz est un constructeur de voitures de course, entre autres pour Le Mans. L'entreprise a été créée par Dan Panoz, dont le père Don a eu la bonne idée de faire fortune dans le développement de médicaments. Panoz fabrique ses propres routières afin de participer aux courses GT. La Roadster a été la première, et l'Esperante est son pilier depuis 2000. Elle est produite en petit nombre pour les conducteurs américains patriotiques qui veulent une voiture de sport, mais ni une Corvette ni une Viper. Comme toujours, une nouvelle voiture est prévue. Elle est baptisée Abruzzi « Spirit of Le Mans », bien que « spirit » fasse sans doute allusion aux spiritueux qu'il vous faudra ingurgiter avant de la trouver belle…

ESPERANTE
Rival: Dodge Viper

24hr racer looks like it's been up all night.
Für das 24-Stunden-Rennen von Le Mans.
Voiture de course pour les 24 Heures.

ABRUZZI
Rival: Corvette and change

Swoopy and no doubt loopy.
Das neue Batmobil?
Tout en courbes et complètement barge.

Dan Panoz, CEO of Panoz Auto Development.

PERODUA

FOUNDED: **1993**
HEADQUARTERS: **SERENDAH, MALAYSIA**

LOGO HISTORY:

Malaysia's second-largest carmaker has built a solid customer base among those looking for affordable, simple and dependable transport. Of course these customers couldn't care less that its products are hand-me-down designs from the likes of Daihatsu. Perodua has never designed or developed its own vehicles and its line-of-least-resistance approach to car manufacture suits it just fine. Tried and trusted technology and plentiful spare parts are higher up the priority list than having the latest exterior designs or infotainment system. Perodua's staple markets are spread around the Middle- and Far East although its brand of bargain-basement city cars has also enjoyed some success in the UK.

Der zweitgrößter Autohersteller Malaysias hat sich mit seinem Angebot an erschwinglichen, einfachen und zuverlässigen Fahrzeugen einen breiten und treuen Kundenstamm aufgebaut. Dass die Wagen des 1993 gegründeten Unternehmens Lizenzbauten von Daihatsu-Modellen sind, kümmert die Kunden wenig. Eigene Designs kann Perodua, der sich für den Weg des geringsten Widerstands entschieden hat, nicht vorweisen. Bewährte Technologie und hohe Verfügbarkeit von Ersatzteilen werden ausgefallenen Designs und Infotainmentsystemen vorgezogen. Abgesetzt werden Peroduas Fahrzeuge vor allem in Nah- und Fernost, ihre preisgünstigen Stadtautos sind aber auch in Großbritannien relativ erfolgreich.

Le second plus grand fabricant automobile de Malaisie s'est forgé une solide clientèle auprès de ceux qui cherchent un moyen de transport abordable, simple et fiable. Bien sûr, ces client se fichent pas mal de savoir que ses produits sont des modèles hérités de Daihatsu, entre autres. Perodua n'a jamais conçu ou développé ses propres véhicules, et son approche de la fabrication automobile, qui consiste à choisir la facilité, lui convient très bien. La fiabilité de la technologie et l'abondance des pièces détachées priment sur la modernité du style ou les systèmes de divertissement à bord. Les principaux marchés de Perodua recouvrent le Moyen et l'Extrême-Orient, bien que ses citadines bon marché aient également rencontré un certain succès au Royaume-Uni.

VIVA
Rival: Nissan Pixo

Back-to-basics urban runabout.
Einfacher Stadtflitzer.
Petite citadine qui retourne à la simplicité.

MYVI
Rival: Chevrolet Spark

Chunky, roomy city car.
Bulliges, geräumiges Stadtauto.
Citadine trapue et spacieuse.

ALZA
Rival: Honda Jazz

Neatly packaged mini-MPV.
Gut gebauter, hübscher Minivan.
Mini-monospace bien fait.

PEUGEOT

(F)
FOUNDED: **1882**
HEADQUARTERS: **PARIS, FRANCE**
2010 PRODUCTION: **1,937,114**

LOGO HISTORY:

From inauspicious beginnings as a pepper mill manufacturer, Peugeot has become one of Europe's biggest automotive players. Now the breadth of its product portfolio is unrivalled in Europe – from bicycles to vans and everything in between – something that will be increasingly relevant as we move into a new age of personal mobility. Its cars' design language took a turn for the worse after decades of classic, understatement from Pininfarina's pen. New design head, Gilles Vidal, looks set to restore order and banish its gaping mouth grille to the history books. Oh and its pepper mills are still some of the world's finest.

Nach bescheidenen Anfängen als Hersteller von Pfeffermühlen hat sich Peugeot zu einem der größten Automobilhersteller in Europa emporgekämpft. Auf dem alten Kontinent gibt es heute kein Unternehmen mit einem breiteren Angebot – von Fahrrädern bis Vans bauen die Franzosen so ziemlich alles –, was angesichts der sich schnell wandelnden Mobilitätsgewohnheiten einen Wettbewerbsvorteil darstellen. Nach mehreren Jahrzehnten, in denen Pininfarinas klassische Formen und ein Hang zum Understatement dominierten, wurde die Designsprache geändert – mit mäßigen Ergebnissen. Mit dem neuen Designchef Gilles Vidal werden die alte Ordnung wiederhergestellt und der gähnende Kühlergrill endgültig abgeschafft. Übrigens: Die Peugeot-Pfeffermühlen gehören noch zu den besten der Welt.

Depuis des débuts improbables dans la fabrication de moulins à poivre, Peugeot est devenu l'un des plus grands de l'automobile en Europe. Son portefeuille de produits est aujourd'hui le plus diversifié d'Europe (des vélos aux camions en passant par tout le reste), ce qui aura de plus en plus d'importance avec le passage à une nouvelle ère de la mobilité personnelle. Le style de ses voitures s'est gâté après des décennies d'élégance discrète et classique sous le crayon de Pininfarina. Le nouveau directeur du design, Gilles Vidal, semble déterminé à ramener l'ordre et à reléguer la calandre à large bouche dans les livres d'histoire. Ah, et les moulins à poivre de Peugeot sont toujours parmi les meilleurs du monde.

107
Rival: Suzuki Alto

Chic, back-to-basics city car.
Schickes, einfaches Stadtauto.
Citadine chic et basique.

1007
Rival: Vauxhall Meriva

Misguided heavyweight, sliding doors.
Misslungener Brummer mit Schiebetüren.
Portes coulissantes, poids lourd, dommage.

207
Rival: Steven Tyler

Big-mouthed supermini.
Kleinwagen mit großem Maul.
Citadine polyvalente à grande bouche.

308
Rival: Ford Focus

Decent hatchback with great interior.
Fließheck mit erstaunlichem Innenleben.
Compacte honnête avec un bel intérieur.

3008
Rival: Nissan Qashqai

Ungainly but talented crossover.
Plumper, aber talentierter Crossover.
Crossover disgracieux mais talentueux.

408
Rival: BYD F3

Chinese-market compact sedan.
Kompaktlimousine für China.
Berline compacte pour le marché chinois.

508
Rival: VW Passat

New, understated family sedan and wagon.
Mittelklasse-Familienlimousine und -kombi.
Berline familiale sobre, aussi en break.

5008
Rival: Renault Grand Scenic

Handsome 7-seat MPV.
Hübscher Minivan mit 7 Sitzen.
Beau monospace à 7 places.

RCZ
Rival: Audi TT

Brand-building coupe doesn't quite convince.
Dem Flaggschiff-Sportcoupé fehlt etwas.
Coupé censé valoriser la marque.

ION
Rival: Citroën C-zero

Rebadged Mitsubishi electric car.
Wiederbelebtes Mitsubishi-Elektroauto.
Mitsubishi électrique rebadgée.

HOGGAR
Rival: Fiat Strada

Small Brazilian pick-up.
Kleiner Pick-up für Brasilien.
Petit pick-up brésilien.

ALSO AVAILABLE
206, 407 Coupe, 4007, 607, 807.

PEUGEOT RCZ

Peugeot has a fantastic heritage in racing and design but hasn't made a decent-looking, great-driving car for more than a generation The RCZ is supposed to be the antidote. The curvy double bubble rear glass window roof is something more often seen on supercars while the 200hp 1.6 turbocharged petrol unit will put a smile on your face.

Peugeot glänzt mit einer sagenhaften Tradition im Bereich Rennwagen und Design, hat jedoch seit über einer Generation kein ansehnliches, gut fahrbares Auto mehr auf den Markt gebracht. Der RCZ soll das jetzt endlich gutmachen. Die kurvige Heckscheibe erinnert an einen Supersportwagen, und der 1,6-Liter-Motor mit 200 PS zaubert ein Lächeln auf das Gesicht eines jeden Autofans.

Peugeot peut se vanter d'une trajectoire fantastique dans la course et le design, mais n'a pas fait une seule voiture raisonnablement belle et agréable à conduire depuis plus d'une génération. La RCZ est censée redresser la situation. Son toit rond en verre formant une double bulle est souvent vu sur les supercars, tandis que le moteur à essence turbocompressé 1,6 l de 200 chevaux vous mettra le sourire aux lèvres.

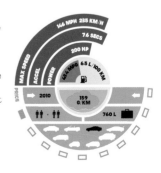

DESIGNER Q+A

Gilles Vidal
Director of style, Peugeot

On duty:
Suit: Kooples
Boots: Unknown (Italian)
Watch: Tag Heuer Carrera
Automatic
Off-duty:
Clothes: Mostly black and white
Kooples, Prada Sport – "I like
one sharp piece mixed with
basic stuff."

What does your brand stand for?
Past/Present/Future:
"The true past of Peugeot
is the same as the future.
It's about beauty. We want
elegance. Cars that are instantly
understandable but innovative
too. Reflecting excellence in
proportion and charisma in
the front end in particular. The
'present' is transition."

PONTIAC

FOUNDED: **1926** DIED: **2010**
HEADQUARTERS: **DETROIT**, USA
2010 PRODUCTION: **1,182**

LOGO HISTORY:

Pontiac is perhaps the most mourned casualty of the recent Carpocalypse. Founded as a sister brand to GM's Oakland subsidiary, it built a reputation for producing affordable, solid and vaguely sporting Chevy-based cars but things really took off under John DeLorean's stewardship in the 1960s. His plan was to drop a 6.3-liter V8 under the hood of the comely Tempest coupe and tack the letters G, T and O to the grille. The muscle car was born. The 1960s and 70s were Pontiac's heyday but, with a few exceptions, by the time its doors shut for good in 2010, it's model range was a shadow of its former self. The bizarre Aztek may have been a turning point that it couldn't recover from, although the svelte Solstice might have helped Pontiac turn a corner if it drove as good as it looked – it didn't.

Pontiac ist möglicherweise der traurigste Todesfall, den die „Autokalypse" der letzten Jahre verursacht hat. Dem Schwesterunternehmen einer GM-Tochterfirma in Oakland eilte bald der Ruf voraus, erschwingliche, robuste, Chevrolet-basierte Fahrzeuge mit einem Anflug von Sportlichkeit zu bauen. Die großen Zeiten begannen aber erst in den 1960er Jahren unter John DeLorean. Der berühmte Sportwagenbauer ließ einen 6,3-Liter-V8-Motor unter die Haube des anmutigen Tempest Coupé einbauen und die Buchstaben G, T und O an den Kühlergrill heften. Das Muscle-Car war geboren. In den 60ern und 70ern hatte Pontiac seine Glanzzeit. Bei Produktionseinstellung 2010 war aber das Angebot der Amerikaner nur noch ein Schatten seiner selbst. Der seltsame Aztek markierte einen Wendepunkt, ab dem es nur noch abwärts ging. Nur der ansprechende Solstice hätte das Zeug gehabt, Pontiac aus dem Loch zu ziehen – doch dafür hätte sein Fahrverhalten mindestens so gut wie sein Aussehen sein müssen.

Pontiac est peut-être la victime la plus regrettée de la récente apocalypse de l'automobile. Créée comme sous-marque de la filiale de GM à Oakland, elle s'est forgé la réputation de produire des voitures abordables, solides et vaguement sportives basées sur des Chevrolet, mais a vraiment décollé sous la direction de John DeLorean dans les années 1960. Son idée était de glisser un V8 de 6,3 litres sous le capot de l'avenant coupé Tempest et de coller les lettres G, T et O sur la calandre. La « muscle car » était née. Les années 1960 et 1970 ont été l'âge d'or de Pontiac mais, sauf quelques exceptions, lorsqu'elle a disparu en 2010, sa gamme de modèles n'était plus que l'ombre de ce qu'elle avait été. L'étrange Aztek a peut-être marqué un tournant en même temps qu'un point de non retour, quoique la svelte Solstice aurait pu aider Pontiac à avancer si son ramage avait été aussi beau que son plumage. Ce qui n'a pas été le cas.

STAR CHIEF 1956		First truly sporting model, powerful V8. Erster wahrer Sportler, mit V8-Motor. La première vraie sportive, avec un V8.
BONNEVILLE 1959		Outrageous quad tail finned land shark. Ungeheuerlicher Landhai mit Heckflossen. Extravagant requin de terre.
GTO 1964		Started America's Muscle Car obsession. Begründer der Muscle-Car-Mode. L'origine du culte des muscle cars.
CATALINA 2+2 1965		GTO's even bigger brother. Der (sogar) größere Bruder des GTO. La grande sœur de la GTO.
FIREBIRD 1967		Chevy Camaro's pony car twin. Pony Car auf Grundlage des Chevy Camaro. Pony car jumelle de la Chevrolet Camaro.
TRANS AM 1978		Long hood, big eagle graphics, Burt Reynolds. Lange Haube, großer Adler, Knight Rider. Long capot décoré d'un aigle énorme.
FIERO 1984		Mid-engined sports car deserved more success. Mittelmotor-Sportler, besser als sein Ruf. Sportive à moteur central très méritante.
AZTEK 2001		Unforgettable ugliness. Legendäre Hässlichkeit. Inoubliable laideur.
SOLSTICE 2006		Euro-style, lightweight sports car. Leichter Sportwagen europäischen Stils. Sportive légère de style européen.
G8 GXP 2008		Aussie sedan briefly re-lit muscle car fire. Kurzes Comeback des Muscle Car. Berline australienne.

MICHIGAN
19M909
MANUFACTURER
PLATE

1978 Pontiac Trans Am Firebird

PORSCHE

FOUNDED: **1931**
HEADQUARTERS: **STUTTGART**, **GERMANY**
2010 PRODUCTION: **97,267**

LOGO HISTORY:

Automotive brand royalty, wildly profitable and universally admired, with unrivalled racing success and serious engineering to underpin its product range. The 911 is to many the archetypal sportscar, able to trace its roots way back to Volkswagen's Beetle – designed by Ferdinand Porsche. The VW link has always been in the background, although after some recent financial shenanigans VW gained control when a fit of takeover hubris by the far smaller company backfired. Sports cars like the 911, Boxster and Cayman remain at the company's core, although models like the Cayenne SUV and new, more sympathetically proportioned Panamera help keep the money flowing in. It might be entrenched design-wise, but its sportscars are always the very best in their respective classes. The (grudging?) introduction of hybrid options shows willingness to change dramatically with the times under the skin, but with arguably the perfect sportscar shape, this is one brand where change is more a cause for concern than excitement.

Die weltweit beliebte Edelschmiede aus Stuttgart gehört zur Elite der Automobilbranche, ist hochprofitabel, im Rennsport erfolgreich und stützt ihre Produktpalette auf solide Ingenieurskunst. Der Porsche 911, dessen Wurzeln bis zum VW-Käfer reichen, ist für viele der Sportwagen schlechthin – und wurde von Ferdinand Porsche höchstpersönlich entworfen. Porsche und Volkswagen haben übrigens eine lange gemeinsame Geschichte, deren vorläufiger Höhepunkt die Übernahme des Sportwagenherstellers durch VW ist. Zuvor hatte der kleine David aus Zuffenhausen versucht, den Wolfsburger Goliath zu schlucken – und sich dabei übernommen. Verkaufsschlager sind nach wie vor der 911, der Boxster und der Cayman, doch auch andere Kreationen wie der Cayenne und der wohlgeformte Panamera haben die Kassen gefüllt. Auf Designebene mag Porsche zwar etwas festgefahren sein, ihre Fahrzeuge gehören aber zu den Besten ihrer jeweiligen Wagenklassen. Mit der (widerwilligen?) Einführung von Hybridversionen stellt Porsche außerdem eine außerordentliche Wandlungsfähigkeit unter Beweis. Bei einer Marke, die in Besitz der wohl perfekten Sportwagenform ist, verursachen Veränderungen eher Sorgen als Freude.

Tête couronnée des marques automobiles, extrêmement rentable et universellement admirée, avec un succès sans pareil sur les circuits et une mécanique qui ne plaisante pas sous le capot de chacun des modèles de la gamme. La 911 est pour beaucoup l'archétype de la voiture de sport. Ses racines remontent très haut, jusqu'à la Coccinelle de Volkswagen, conçue par Ferdinand Porsche. Ce lien avec VW est toujours resté à l'arrière-plan, bien qu'après quelques manigances financières VW ait récemment pris le contrôle lorsque les velléités de prise de pouvoir de Porsche se sont retournées contre elle. Les voitures de sport telles que la 911, la Boxster et la Cayman sont toujours les fanions de l'entreprise, bien que des modèles comme le SUV Cayenne et une nouvelle Panamera aux proportions plus agréables contribuent à faire pleuvoir les recettes. Porsche est peut-être figée en termes de design, mais ses voitures de sport sont toujours les meilleures dans leurs catégories respectives. L'introduction (à contrecœur ?) d'options hybrides montre la volonté de changer radicalement et en profondeur pour coller à l'époque, mais étant donné que Porsche a sans doute trouvé la forme parfaite pour une voiture de sport, tout changement est un sujet d'inquiétude plutôt que de réjouissance.

BOXSTER
Rival: BMW Z4

Brilliant roadster, Spyder offers striking looks.
Toller Roadster, der Spyder ist genial.
Excellent roadster, la Spyder est superbe.

CAYMAN R
Rival: BMW M3

Boxster brilliance, with a roof. R better still.
Ein Boxster mit Dach. Der R ist noch besser.
Idem, avec un toit en plus.

911
Rival: Very little

Iconic, useable, rapid and unrivalled.
Inbegriff der Marke, ohne Konkurrenz.
Mythique, maniable, rapide, sans pareille.

911 TURBO
Rival: Nissan GT-R

More power, no compromises.
Mehr Leistung, keine Kompromisse.
Plus de puissance, zéro compromis.

911 GT3 RS
Rival: Lotus Exige S

Lighter, fitter purist 911.
Leichterer 911 für Puristen.
911 plus légère et plus athlétique.

911 GT2 RS
Rival: A grenade

Unhinged GT3 RS/Turbo mash-up.
GT3 RS/Turbo mit mehr Leistung.
Mélange démentiel de GT3 RS/Turbo.

CAYENNE
Rival: BMW X5

SUV with sports car moves, still not pretty.
SUV mit Sportlergeschmack, nicht schön.
SUV qui réagit comme une sportive.

PANAMERA
Rival: Merc CLS

Incredible sedan, incredulous looks.
Luxuslimousine mit überraschendem Look.
Berline incroyable, style invraisemblable.

PORSCHE PANAMERA HYBRID

Not pretty, but effective. From the Turbo S downward all Panameras drive with exceptional agility. The S Hybrid won't make sense in all markets, but it ably demonstrates Porsche's impressive quest for economy and can drive up to 52mph on electricity alone.

Nicht so schön wie ein Aston Martin Rapide, aber um einiges effektiver. Vom Turbo S abwärts sind sämtliche Panameras außergewöhnlich wendig. Der S Hybrid wird zwar nicht jede Zielgruppe ansprechen, stellt aber Porsches Bemühungen um sparsame Antriebe unter Beweis. Und er schafft es bis auf 84 km/h, bis sich der V6 meldet.

Pas aussi jolie que l'Aston Martin Rapide, mais sans doute plus efficace. De la Turbo S jusqu'au bas de la gamme, toutes les Panamera sont d'une agilité exceptionnelle. La S Hybrid ne trouvera pas sa place sur tous les marchés, mais c'est une belle preuve de la quête impressionnante que Porsche a entreprise dans l'économie de carburant, et elle peut monter à 84 km/h sur sa seule propulsion électrique.

Panamera S Hybrid
* CO2 emissions and MPG figured based on low rolling resistance tyres

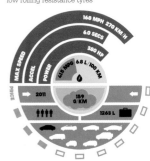

DESIGNER Q+A

Michael Mauer
Head of style, Porsche

On duty:
Suit: Frantina
Shoes: Tod's
Watch: IWC Portuguese
Rattraponte

Off-duty:
Clothes: Jeans, T-shirts – "And
sport-related clothing – surfing

and cycling but mainly Salomon
for skiing."

**What does your brand stand
for?**
Past/Present/Future
"Emotion and reliability, the
combination is unique. You
don't have to suffer when
driving a Porsche. 30 years
ago if you wanted a reliable
sports car there weren't many
options."

PORSCHE BOXSTER SPYDER

With a stylish 'double-bubble' rear profile and cool retro-leaning exterior graphics the Spyder looks fantastic. There's substance too. 80kg lighter than its Boxster S sibling model – by slinging out the radio, big interior door handles and more – it becomes the lightest car in the current Porsche range, the lower weight benefiting agility, performance, fuel economy and emissions.

Mit den markanten Auswölbungen am Heck und dem eleganten Retro-Design ist der Spyder eine Augenweide. Aber er hat auch innere Werte. Er wiegt 80 kg weniger als sein Bruder Boxster S: Unnötige Teile wie Radio, große Türinnengriffe usw. wurden einfach weggelassen. Somit ist der Boxster Spyder der leichteste Porsche und überzeugt durch hohe Wendigkeit, gute Leistung, Sparsamkeit und niedrige Emissionen.

Avec un arrière élégant à « double bulle » et un extérieur rétro, la Spyder est très belle. Mais pas seulement. Elle pèse 80 kg de moins que la Boxster S (la radio, les grandes poignées de porte intérieures et quelque autres détails sont passés par la fenêtre) et devient la plus légère de la gamme Porsche actuelle. Cela profite à son agilité, sa performance, sa consommation et ses émissions de carbone.

Boxster 3.4 Spyder manual

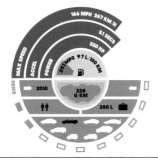

SECRET DETAIL

If you're good at putting up old-school tents you might find the manual rather than electric roof system – in the name of weight-saving – acceptable, or even fun. As we aren't, we don't. It took us 12 minutes, including reading the ten pages of the manual devoted to the subject. Lucky it wasn't raining.

Wenn Sie schon bei den Pfadfindern gerne Zelte aufgebaut haben, wird Ihnen das manuelle – und somit gewichtssparende – Verdeck gefallen. Wir mögen es allerdings nicht: Wir haben 12 Minuten gebraucht und mussten die Bedienungsanleitung studieren, um es zu schließen. Zum Glück hat es nicht geregnet.

Si vous savez monter les tentes à l'ancienne, il se peut que vous préfériez le système de toit manuel au système électrique pour économiser du poids, voire pour vous amuser. Mais pas nous. Il nous a fallu 12 minutes pour réaliser l'opération, en comptant la lecture du manuel consacré à ce sujet. Heureusement qu'il ne pleuvait pas.

PORSCHE 911 GT3 RS

911 GT3 RS

The lightest, fastest naturally aspirated 911 owes its existence to racing, being built to adhere to homologation rules. That might mean nothing to a lot of people, but no matter, it creates one of the most intense, involving and thrilling cars money can buy. Brilliant.

Der leichteste, schnellste 911 mit Saugmotor geht auf den Rennsport zurück, wurde aber entsprechend den Zulassungsvorschriften gebaut. Vielen mag das egal sein, aber wir wissen es zu würdigen: Dies ist eines der stärksten und aufregendsten Autos aller Zeiten – Chapeau!

La 911 la plus légère, avec l'aspiration naturelle la plus rapide, doit son existence à la course, car elle a été construite pour adhérer aux règles de l'homologation. Cela ne veut peut-être pas dire grand-chose pour certains, mais le résultat est l'une des voitures les plus intenses, les plus passionnantes et électrisantes que l'argent puisse acheter. Géniale.

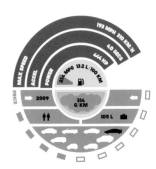

SECRET DETAIL

Porsche's obsession with weight-saving goes as far as the door handles inside. Straps here, as they're lighter.

Porsche ist so besessen von der Gewichtsreduktion, dass sogar die Türgriffe fehlen! Sie wurden durch leichtere Riemen ersetzt.

L'obsession de Porsche pour l'élimination du moindre gramme superflu va assez loin pour remplacer les poignées de porte par des courroies à l'intérieur.

CARCHITECTURE: PORSCHE MUSEUM

Porsche was so impressed with Mercedes' museum it employed the same exhibition organisers and curator. The results include Damien Hirst-style dissections of 911s split into multiple glass boxes and a beautiful folded metal sculpture of a Rothmans-sponsored 956 by French artist Arman, to add substance to exhibition director Markus Betz's claim "not to be an automotive Disney World, but more similar to an art museum". The 100m-euro, 25,800 sq m project – designed by Viennese architects Delugan Meissl and opened in 2009 – features a rolling selection of 400 exhibits, a 'transparent' workshop where customers can view their classic cars being restored plus a roof terrace overlooking its Zuffenhausen locale.

Bei Porsche war man so beeindruckt vom Mercedes-Museum, dass man bei Ausstellungsorganisatoren und Kurator die gleiche Wahl traf. Damien Hirst steuerte einen auf mehrere Glaswürfel verteilten 911 bei, und der französische Künstler Arman schuf eine wunderschöne Metallskulptur aus einem Rothmans-Porsche 956. Ausstellungsdirektor Markus Betz erläutert hierzu, man wolle „kein Disney-World für Autos, sondern ein Kunstmuseum" sein. Das vom Wiener Architekt Delugan Meissl kreierte 100-Millionen-Euro-Projekt erstreckt sich über 25.800 Quadratmeter und wurde 2009 eröffnet. In dem ‚Rollenden Museum', für das insgesamt 400 Fahrzeuge zum Einsatz kommen, können Besucher restaurierte Klassiker bewundern und dabei von der Dachterrasse den Ausblick auf Zuffenhausen genießen.

Le musée de Mercedes a tellement plu à Porsche que l'entreprise a embauché les mêmes organisateurs pour l'exposition, et le même commissaire. Le résultat comprend notamment des dissections de 911 dans le style de Damien Hirst, avec des voitures réparties sur plusieurs cubes de verre, et une magnifique sculpture en métal plié d'une 956 parrainée par Rothman, œuvre de l'artiste français Arman. Tout ceci pour confirmer les paroles du directeur de l'exposition Markus Betz : « ne pas être un Disney World de l'automobile, mais plutôt quelque chose de similaire à un musée d'art ». Ce bâtiment de 25 800 m² a coûté 100 millions d'euros et a été dessiné par les architectes viennois Delugan Meissl. Ses portes se sont ouvertes en 2009 sur une sélection changeante de 400 pièces, un atelier « transparent » où les clients peuvent suivre la restauration de leurs voitures classiques, et une terrasse de toit qui surplombe le quartier de Zuffenhausen.

PROTON

LOGO HISTORY:

Founded in 1983 as a 'national car' company for Malaysia, partially state-owned Proton has enjoyed a dominant market share in its home market until archrival Perodua appeared a decade later. Initially offering warmed-over Mitsubishis, the Proton brand soon built itself a reputation for offering good quality, reliable, if uninspiring, cars. The purchase of British sports car manufacturer, Lotus, in 1996 has not only added to its cache, but also allowed in-house development of its own range of cars, which, while still not the last word in sophistication, are respectable.

Die 1983 gegründete „nationale Automobilgesellschaft" mit dem malaysischen Staat als Hauptaktionär hatte bis zur Ankunft des Erzrivalen Perodua den heimischen Markt klar beherrscht. Proton bot zunächst lediglich „aufgewärmte" Mitsubishis. Bald jedoch wurde die Firma für die Qualität seiner zuverlässigen Autos bekannt, die allerdings etwas uninspiriert anmuten. Der Kauf des britischen Sportwagenherstellers Lotus im Jahre 1996 hob das Ansehen der Malaysier und ermöglichte die Entwicklung eigener Fahrzeuge, die zwar keinen Höhepunkt des Automobildesigns darstellen, aber sich den Respekt der Fachwelt verdient haben.

Proton est une société automobile partiellement nationalisée créée en 1983 pour produire la « voiture de la nation ». Elle a dominé son marché national jusqu'à l'arrivée de son ennemie jurée Perodua dix ans plus tard. La marque Proton a initialement proposé des Mitsubishi réchauffées, mais s'est vite construit une réputation de faire des voitures fiables et de bonne qualité, bien que peu enthousiasmantes. Le rachat du fabricant britannique de voitures de sport Lotus en 1996 lui a non seulement donné du prestige, mais lui a également permis de développer sa propre gamme de voitures en interne. Sans être le nec plus ultra de la sophistication, le résultat est tout à fait respectable.

SAVVY
Rival: Hyundai i10

Characterful if unsophisticated city car.
Stadtauto mit Charakter, etwas bieder.
Citadine pleine de personnalité.

SAGA FL
Rival: Mazda2

Neatly designed mini-sedan.
Kompaktwagen mit niedlichem Design.
Mini berline bien conçue.

SATRIA NEO
Rival: Kia Rio

Average supermini, rally car offshoot.
Matter Sprößling eines Rallyewagens.
Polyvalente honnête issue des rallyes.

GEN-2
Rival: Ford Focus

Below-par compact hatchback.
Unterdurchschnittliches Schrägheck.
Compacte médiocre.

PERSONA
Rival: XXXX

As above with sedan body.
Wie oben, aber als Limousine.
Idem, avec une carrosserie de berline.

EXORA
Rival: Kia Carens

Malaysia's first MPV. Excited?
Erster Minivan Malaysias. Aufgeregt?
Le premier monospace malaisien.

INSPIRA
Rival: Kia Forte

See Mitsubishi Lancer.
Siehe Mitsubishi Lancer.
Voir Mitsubishi Lancer.

WAJA
Rival: Nissan Latio

First ever Malaysian-design car.
Allererstes in Malaysia entworfenes Auto.
Toute première voiture conçue en Malaisie.

RADICAL

GB

FOUNDED: **1997**
HEADQUARTERS: **PETERBOROUGH, ENGLAND**
2010 PRODUCTION: **220**

LOGO HISTORY:

Small companies in small premises making specialist cars in small numbers – that's the UK-owned car industry now. Except nobody told Radical, that builds a range of specialist racing/road cars in decent numbers – 220 in 2010 – including the SR3/4 that rivals the Lotus 2-eleven. There are no compromises to performance here, with every Radical having the ability to thrill like little else on road or track. They're all fast, in fact so fast, Radical regularly takes a car to the Nurburgring to smash the production car record. It's also embracing the electric revolution, with the battery-powered Radical SRZero undertaking grueling public tests. The name may just be deserved.

Kleine Unternehmen mit kleinen Fertigungsstätten, die Spezialautos in kleinen Stückzahlen bauen – so lässt sich heute die britische Automobilindustrie beschreiben. Radical aber will sich nicht in dieses Korsett hineinzwängen lassen. Die Firma fertigt spezielle Renn- und Straßenautos in anständigen Stückzahlen – 220 im Jahre 2010 –, darunter den SR3/4, das Konkurrenzmodell des Lotus 2-Eleven. In Sachen Leistung werden keine Kompromisse eingegangen, auf der Rennstrecke oder auf der Straße gibt es kaum Aufregenderes als ein Radical. Alle Modelle sind schnell – so schnell, dass sie auf dem Nürburgring den Serienwagen-Rekord regelmäßig brechen. Die elektrische Revolution wollen die Briten auch nicht verpassen und sind gerade dabei, den von einem Elektromotor betriebenen SRZero den härtesten Prüfungen zu unterziehen. Sie machen ihrem Namen alle Ehre.

De petites sociétés logées dans de petits locaux pour fabriquer des voitures spécialisées en petit nombre. C'est ainsi que fonctionne l'industrie automobile britannique de nos jours. Mais personne n'en a informé Radical, qui construit une gamme de voitures de course/route en nombre relativement élevé (220 en 2010), notamment la SR3/4 qui fait concurrence à la Lotus 2-eleven. La performance ne fait ici aucun compromis, chaque Radical est capable de donner des frissons exceptionnels sur la route ou sur les circuits. Elles sont toutes rapides, et même tellement rapides que Radical emmène régulièrement l'un de ses modèles sur le Nürburgring pour pulvériser le record dans la catégorie des voitures de série. La marque a décidé de rejoindre la révolution électrique, et son modèle Radical SRZero à batteries est actuellement soumis à des tests publics draconiens. Son nom pourrait bien être mérité.

SR3/4
Rival: Lotus 2-eleven

Prototype racer looks, epic drive.
Sieht aus wie ein Rennauto-Prototyp, tolles Fahrgefühl.
Un look de prototype de course, une conduite épique.

RENAULT

FOUNDED: **1899**
HEADQUARTERS: **BOULOGNE-BILLIANCOURT, FRANCE**
2010 PRODUCTION: **1,806,013**

LOGO HISTORY:

Renault has, at various times in its illustrious history, been the undisputed champion of avant-garde design. The 90s Scenic and Twingo marked La Régie out as a true innovator again, while a range of ever more extravagant concept cars – as well as the infamous Avantime MPV/coupe crossover – displayed its conviction in boundary-pushing during the following decade. After an uncharacteristic quiet spell, new design chief, Laurens van den Acker has made it his mission to "make people fall in love with Renault again". With ingenious marvels such as the four-wheeled electric scooter/car Twizy arriving, better times could be ahead.

Im Laufe seiner glorreichen Geschichte war Renault mehrmals unangefochtene Nummer Eins des avantgardistischen Designs. In den 90er Jahren setzte die französische Traditionsmarke mit dem Scenic und dem Twingo erneut Maßstäbe, um gleich nach der Jahrtausendwende erneut die Grenzen zu testen mit noch ausgefalleneren Konzeptautos – und dem berühmt-berüchtigten Minivan Avantime. Nach einer ungewöhnlich ruhigen Phase hat sich der neue Designchef Laurens van den Acker vorgenommen, Fahrzeuge zu bauen, „in die man sich wieder verlieben kann". Geniale Einfälle wie der Elektro-Roller auf vier Rädern namens Twizy kündigen spannende Zeiten an.

Au cours de son illustre histoire, Renault a été plusieurs fois le champion incontesté du design avant-gardiste. Dans les années 1990, la Scénic et la Twingo ont rappelé que la Régie savait innover, tandis qu'un éventail de concepts tous plus extravagants les uns que les autres (notamment le terrible monospace/crossover coupé Avantime) signalaient sa détermination à repousser les limites au cours de la décennie suivante. Après une période de calme inaccoutumée, le nouveau directeur du design, Laurens van den Acker, a entrepris de « faire en sorte que le public retombe amoureux de Renault. » Avec des prodiges tels que la Twizy, une voiture/scooter à quatre roues électrique, des jours meilleurs pourraient bientôt arriver.

TWIZY
Rival: Public transport

Mobility device of the decade or joke butt?
Genialer Einfall oder genial daneben?
Le véhicule qui marquera la décennie ?

TWINGO
Rival: Fiat 500

Disappointing city car sequel.
Enttäuschender Nachfolger des Stadtautos.
Citadine qui devient décevante.

WIND
Rival: Mazda MX-5

Breezy two-seat roadster.
Luftiger, 2-sitziger Roadster.
Pétulant roadster à 2 places.

CLIO
Rival: VW Polo

Gracefully ageing supermini.
In Würde gealterter Kleinwagen.
Citadine polyvalente qui vieillit bien.

MODUS
Rival: Lancia Musa

Characterful mini-MPV.
Minivan mit Charakter.
Mini-monospace plein de caractère.

MEGANE
Rival: Citroën C4

Confident hatch, wagon and cabrio.
Als Limousine, Kombi, Cabrio und Van.
Compacte, break et cabriolet déterminé.

FLUENCE
Rival: Nissan LEAF

Compact sedan, optional electric power.
Kompaktlimousine, auch mit Elektroantrieb.
Berline compacte, électrique en option.

SCENIC
Rival: Ford C-Max

Third-generation of small-MPV pioneer.
Dritte Generation des Minivan-Pioniers.
Pionnier des petits monospaces.

LAGUNA
Rival: Mazda6

Dull hatch and wagon, beautiful coupe.
Coupé hui, Schrägheck und Kombi pfui.
Compacte et break insipide, superbe coupé.

ESPACE
Rival: Ford Galaxy

The Range Rover of MPVs.
Der Range Rover der Minivans.
La Range Rover des monospaces.

LATITUDE
Rival: Skoda Superb

Bland large sedan of Samsung origin.
Fade Limousine auf Samsung-Basis.
Grande berline terne issue de Samsung.

ALSO AVAILABLE
Kangoo, Symbol/Thalia, Koleos, Safrane.

RENAULT MEGANE RENAULTSPORT

Megane Renaultsport 250

With its purposeful and squat stance, a 2.0-litre turbocharged engine with 250hp the Megane Renaultsport 250 and its even more hardcore Cup sibling are rightfully acclaimed as the best hot hatches you can buy. Normal Meganes don't bear comparison.

Mit seiner gedrungenen Statur und einem 2,0-Liter/250 PS-Turbomotor wird der treffend benannte Megane Renaultsport 250 – ebenso wie sein Hardcore-Bruder Cup – als einer der besten Kompaktsportwagen auf dem Markt angesehen. Ein normaler Megane kann da nicht mithalten.

Avec son allure déterminée, sa posture surbaissée et un moteur 2,0 l de 250 chevaux, la Mégane Renaultsport 250 porte bien son nom. Elle et sa cousine encore plus enragée, la Cup, sont encensées avec raison, ce sont les compactes les plus survoltées du marché. Les Mégane normales ne soutiennent pas la comparaison.

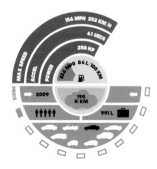

DESIGNER Q+A

Laurens van der Acker
Senior VP, Corp. design, Renault

On duty:
Suit: Zara
Shoes: Mi Adidas Superstar
– "They've been customized
to match the color of the 2011
Renault Captur concept car
we're launching."
Watch: Prototype Mazda design
watch "I'm always late so
maybe it's not working so well."

Off-duty:
Clothes: Y-3, Porsche Design
– "And Japanese brands, but
they're hard to find in my size,
I'm 1.94m (6ft 3)."

**What does your brand stand
for?**
Past: "French, the Alpine
Monaco."
Present: "Breakthrough, rupture,
transition."
Future: "Bright, color, life."

RENAULT TWIZY

Arguably the most important vehicle of the decade could change the urban landscape forever with its scooter-like convenience, car-rivalling safety and electric zero-emissions credentials. Brilliantly simple design is sure to become an icon of the new mobility age. Welcome to the future.

Das wahrscheinlich wichtigste Fahrzeug des Jahrzehnts könnte die städtische Landschaft für immer verändern: Roller-ähnliche Erscheinung, autogleiche Sicherheit und null Emissionen dank Elektroantrieb. Das hervorragend einfache Design hat das Zeug, zum Symbol eines neuen Mobilitätszeitalters zu werden. Willkommen in der Zukunft!

C'est sans doute le véhicule le plus important de la décennie, il pourrait changer le paysage urbain pour toujours. Aussi pratique qu'un scooter, aussi sûr qu'une voiture et zéro émissions. Son design est superbement simple et deviendra à coup sûr l'emblème de la nouvelle ère du transport. Bienvenue dans le futur.

Twizy Urban

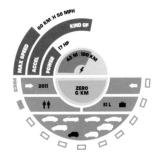

CONCEPT LINE

TWIZY Z.E CONCEPT
Frankfurt 2009

Renault shocked the world once with this one-plus-one tandem seater, four-wheel EV concept package, then shocked it again by announcing its imminent production.

Renault hat schon einmal die Welt mit diesem „Elektro-Tandem" auf vier Rädern in Staunen versetzt. Die Ankündigung des Produktionsstarts war nicht minder staunenswert.

Renault a choqué une première fois avec son concept de voiture électrique 1+1 à quatre roues, puis une deuxième fois en annonçant sa production imminente.

TWIZY [FINAL PRODUCTION]
Paris 2010

The Flintstones-style crazy concept wheel covers are gone in this final production vehicle as is the honeycomb front detailing, replaced by Renault's new front face.

Die Radkappen im Stil der Familie Feuerstein und die Wabenstruktur der Frontpartie sind im endgültigen Produktionsdesign weggefallen.

Les roues façon *Famille Pierrafeu* ont disparu dans ce modèle de production, tout comme les motifs hexagonaux, remplacés par le nouvel avant de Renault.

ROEWE

CN

FOUNDED: **2006**

HEADQUARTERS: **SHANGHAI, CHINA**

2010 PRODUCTION: **160,397 [INC. MG]**

LOGO HISTORY:

Once the pride of Britain, the classic Rover brand was sold to the Chinese carmaker SAIC in 2006, where its name and Viking longboat emblem were subtly updated (SAIC didn't have the right to the Rover name or badge so had to choose something close to them). The same is true of Roewe's first car – the 750, effectively a reworked and stretched version of the Rover 75, itself originally engineered under the expert eye of BMW. Subsequent models have been co-developed by teams in both the UK and China and are regarded by many to be the best offerings from the Chinese domestic market. Expected to become a significant multi-national player in the not-too-distant future.

Die Traditionsmarke Rover, einst der Stolz Großbritanniens, wurde 2006 an den chinesischen Autobauer SAIC veräußert, der den Namen und das Wikinger-Drachenschiff des Logos subtil anpasste (da SAIC weder die Namens- noch die Emblemrechte besaß, mussten sich die Chinesen etwas Ähnliches einfallen lassen). Dasselbe gilt für das erste Roewe-Modell, den 750, an sich eine überarbeitete, längere Version des Rover 75, der seinerzeit mit technischer BMW-Hilfe entstand. Darauf folgende Modelle wurden von zusammenarbeitenden Teams aus Großbritannien und China entworfen und gehören nach allgemeiner Meinung zum Besten, was der chinesischen Markt zu bieten hat. Der Hersteller wird voraussichtlich zum Global Player in einer nicht allzu fernen Zukunft.

La marque classique Rover a jadis été la fierté de la Grande-Bretagne, mais a été vendue au fabricant automobile chinois SAIC en 2006. Le nom de la marque et le drakkar viking de son logo ont été subtilement mis à jour (SAIC n'avait pas le droit d'utiliser le nom de Rover, ni son badge, et a donc dû choisir quelque chose d'approchant). C'est également ce qui est arrivé à la première voiture de Roewe, la 750, qui est en fait une version retravaillée et allongée de la Rover 75, elle-même conçue à l'origine sous le regard expert de BMW. Les modèles suivants ont été développés en collaboration entre la Grande-Bretagne et la Chine, et nombreux sont ceux qui les considèrent comme ce que le marché chinois a de mieux à offrir. Cette marque deviendra bientôt un acteur multinational important sur le marché mondial.

350
Rival: BYD F3

Understated, refined compact sedan.
Feine, dezente Kompaktklasse-Limousine.
Berline compacte sobre et raffinée.

550
Rival: Peugeot 408

Resurrected Rover project, hi-tech interior.
Rover-Projekt mit Hichtech-Innenleben.
Rover ressuscitée, intérieur high-tech.

750
Rival: VW Passat

Luxurious, classy executive sedan.
Luxus-Limousine der oberen Mittelklasse.
Grande berline élégante et luxueuse.

ROLLS-ROYCE

GB

FOUNDED: **1906**

HEADQUARTERS: **GOODWOOD, ENGLAND**

2010 PRODUCTION: **2,711**

LOGO HISTORY:

Founded at a time when motoring was the reserve of the wealthy and often eccentric, Rolls-Royce soon established a reputation for building the finest motorcars in the world, starting with the iconic 1907 Silver Ghost. It wasn't always so, however, with the company falling on hard times during the 80s and 90s when more sophisticated, refined and affordable luxury cars from Germany and Japan stole the sales of its traditional heads-of-the-board customers. All this changed when new owners BMW unveiled the Phantom flagship in 2003 – a luxury car unrivalled on every measurable and emotional level. Smaller Ghost model brings relative affordability, while teak-effect drop-top and starlight-ceiling coupe versions of the Phantom add style to ceremony.

Gegründet in einer Zeit, als das Autofahren ein Privileg der Reichen und Exzentriker war, erwarb sich Rolls-Royce bald den Ruf des weltweit besten Herstellers von motorisierten Wagen. Entscheidend dabei war das erste Rolls-Royce-Modell – der „Silver Ghost" aus dem Jahr 1907. Die Geschichte des britischen Autobauers hat aber auch Schattenseiten, so z. B. die 80er und 90er Jahre, als deutsche und japanische Luxusmarken der Edelschmiede aus Goodwood die Kunden abspenstig machten. Alles änderte sich jedoch, als 2003 BMW als neuer Eigentümer das Flaggschiff-Modell enthüllte – ein Luxuswagen der Extraklasse in technischer und emotionaler Hinsicht. Das kleinere Ghost-Modell ist etwas „günstiger" zu haben, und die Coupé-Versionen des Phantom mit Teakholz-Abdeckung und Sternenhimmel vereinen Eleganz und Feierlichkeit.

Fondée à une époque où l'automobile était réservée aux riches et aux excentriques, Rolls-Royce n'a pas tardé à se forger la réputation de construire les meilleures voitures au monde, à commencer par la légendaire Silver Ghost de 1907. Mais cette réputation n'est pas restée immuable : la société a connu des difficultés dans les années 1980 et 1990 lorsque des voitures plus sophistiquées, plus raffinées et meilleur marché sont arrivées de l'Allemagne et du Japon et ont volé à la marque ses clients habituels, généralement présidents d'un quelconque conseil d'administration. Tout cela a changé lorsque le nouveau propriétaire BMW a dévoilé la Phantom en 2003, une voiture de luxe inégalée sur tous les plans quantifiables ou affectifs. La Ghost plus petite est plus abordable, tandis que les versions décapotable à toit façon teck et coupé à plafond étoilé de la Phantom ajoutent le style à la cérémonie.

GHOST
Rival: Bentley Flying Spur

Exclusive large luxury sedan.
Exklusive Luxuslimousine der Oberklasse.
Grande berline de luxe exclusive.

PHANTOM
Rival: Maybach 62

The Don.
Ehrwürde auf Rädern.
La patronne.

PHANTOM COUPE
Rival: Bentley Brooklands

Enormous two-door ship.
2-sitziger Riesenschiff.
Énorme bateau deux portes.

DROPHEAD COUPE
Rival: Wally yacht

World's finest convertible.
Das feinste Cabrio der Welt.
La meilleure décapotable du monde.

ROLLS-ROYCE GHOST

Calling it a baby Rolls-Royce is like saying Windsor Castle is a shrunken sized Buckingham Palace. But while the bigger Phantom is trussed up for a royal dinner party, the Ghost's softer tailoring is perfect for an afternoon at the polo. We're waiting for one of the less business-like model variants that are to follow the four door sedan, ideally one that employs the recently previewed electric-motored concept.

Dieses Modell einen Baby-Rolls-Royce zu nennen ist in etwa so, als würde man das Windsor Castle als geschrumpften Buckingham Palace bezeichnen. Während der größere Phantom eher für ein königliches Abendessen ausgelegt ist, eignet sich der etwas sanfter geformte Ghost perfekt für einen Nachmittag beim Polo. Wir warten auf weniger businessorientierte Modelle als Nachfolger der viertürigen Limousine, idealerweise mit der kürzlich vorgestellten Elektromotorstudie.

La qualifier de « bébé » Rolls-Royce reviendrait à dire que le château de Windsor est un modèle réduit de Buckingham Palace. Mais alors que la grande Phantom est habillée pour un dîner avec la famille royale, le costume plus sobre de la Ghost est parfait pour un après-midi au club de polo. Nous sommes impatients de voir une version moins cérémonieuse parmi celles qui suivront la berline quatre portes, dans l'idéal avec le concept à moteur électrique récemment dévoilé.

Ghost

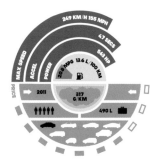

SECRET DETAIL

Most owners will never bother lifting the bonnet, which is a shame because it reveals a beautiful art-deco V12 engine room.

Die wenigsten Besitzer kommen auf die Idee, unter die Motorhaube zu schauen, was schade ist, denn hier verbirgt sich ein wunderschöner V-12-Motorraum im Art-déco-Stil.

La plupart des propriétaires ne prendront jamais la peine de soulever le capot, ce qui est bien dommage car il cache un superbe V12 art déco.

ROLLS-ROYCE PHANTOM COUPE

You can't drive a Rolls-Royce without a sense of humor about yourself. The Phantom Coupe is the model in the line-up that is in on the joke. With an optional starlight ceiling of pin-prick lights, this car is best test driven while wearing a costume chauffeur's cap, with an attractive young female friend in short shorts riding shotgun, to a resort island within a gas tank of Manhattan. In such circumstances as arriving at a busy fashionable restaurant and being told by a towering security guard who has just turned away a Ferrari and a Bentley that the car park is full, one is compelled to point out, without blinking, that it's ok as you intend to park directly in front of the entrance, waiting a beat, and being told "I'm gonna allow you to go on and do that."

Wer einen Rolls-Royce fährt, muss eine gute Portion Selbstironie mitbringen. Bei dem Phantom Coupé verhält es sich nicht anders. Eine Testfahrt in diesem Schmuckstück (optional mit Sternenhimmel aus LED-Lichtern erhältlich) unternehmen Sie am besten mit Chauffeursmütze und einer attraktiven Freundin auf dem Beifahrersitz. Wenn Sie dann vor dem Fünfsterne-Restaurant die Mitteilung erhalten, dass der Privatparkplatz voll ist, da man zuletzt einen Ferrari und einen Bentley eingeparkt hat, antworten Sie ganz cool, dass das kein Problem sei, da Sie sowieso vorhatten, direkt vor dem Eingang zu parken. Man wird Ihnen diese kleine Frechheit gerne verzeihen.

Vous ne pouvez pas conduire une Rolls-Royce sans avoir le sens de l'autodérision. Le coupé Phantom est parfait pour l'exercer. L'une des options proposées est un plafond étoilé de trous d'épingle lumineux. Pour tester cette voiture, il faut porter une casquette de chauffeur, demander à une amie court-vêtue de vous accompagner, et partir vers une station balnéaire extrêmement exclusive. En arrivant devant un restaurant à la mode, le vigile (qui vient de refuser une Ferrari et une Bentley) vous informe que le parking est complet. Précisez nonchalamment que cela ne fait rien, puisque vous aviez l'intention de vous garer devant l'entrée. Un ange passe, et il répond « Mais bien sûr, je vous en prie. »

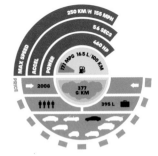

SECRET DETAIL

The starlight roof is so absurd, and so needlessly expensive an option, that it would be churlish not to order it.

Der Sternenhimmel im Dach ist so überflüssig und so teuer, dass es kleinlich wirkt, ihn nicht dazuzubestellen.

Le plafond étoilé est une option si absurde et si inutilement chère qu'il serait vraiment déplacé de ne pas la commander.

RUF

FOUNDED: **1939**
HEADQUARTERS: **PFAFFENHAUSEN, GERMANY**

LOGO HISTORY:

With a history stretching back to 1939 RUF has long been linked to the Porsche brand. It was in the 1970s that its association turned to complete models, with RUF taking production Porsches and creating its own vehicles from them. The most famous, and the star of Nurburgring video legend "Fascination", is the CTR, nicknamed Yellowbird. It's produced various iterations since, each successively faster. Its latest CTR 3 is RUF's most advanced yet, with a mid-engined layout and a 234mph potential top speed. Dabbling in electric models and ever-faster versions of Porsche's familiar models RUF wears its 70-plus years very well indeed.

Der oberschwäbische Hersteller RUF, dessen Geschichte bis 1939 zurückreicht, ist seit Langem mit Porsche verbunden. Seit den 1970er Jahren widmet sich die Firma der Veredelung von Porsche-Fahrzeugen und baut eigene Wagen auf Basis von Porsche-Karosserien. Der berühmteste unter ihnen ist der Star des Videos „Faszination auf dem Nürburgring" – der legendäre CTR, auch bekannt unter dem Spitznamen „Yellow Bird". Seitdem wurden weitere Nachfolgemodelle auf den Markt gebracht, das eine schneller als das andere. Das neueste, der CTR 3, ist die bisher modernste Entwicklung, ein Mittelmotorfahrzeug mit 420 km/h Höchstgeschwindigkeit. Mit einem ersten Elektrofahrzeug und schnelleren Versionen der bekannten Porsche-Modelle sieht RUF für seine über 70 Jahre eigentlich ziemlich jung aus.

L'histoire de RUF remonte à 1939, et a longtemps été liée à Porsche. C'est dans les années 1970 que cette association a produit ses premiers vrais modèles : RUF a commencé à prendre des Porsche de série comme base pour créer ses propres voitures. La plus célèbre, star de la vidéo légendaire sur Nürburgring « Fascination », est la CTR, qui a reçu le sobriquet de Yellow Bird. Elle s'est depuis déclinée en plusieurs itérations, chacune plus rapide que la précédente. La dernière, la CTR 3, est le modèle le plus avancé de RUF à ce jour, avec un moteur en position centrale et une vitesse maximale potentielle de 376 km/h. RUF s'essaie aux modèles électriques et travaille à construire des versions toujours plus rapides des modèles de Porsche. La marque porte très bien ses 70 ans passés.

CT3
Rival: Lamborghini Aventador

Mid-engined car Porsche won't build.
Mittelmotorwagen, den Porsche nicht baut.
Une Porsche à moteur central.

DAKARA
Rival: Porsche Cayenne

Cayenne with 911 headlamps.
Cayenne mit 911 Scheinwerfern.
Cayenne avec les phares avant de la 911.

RT 12 S
Rival: Porsche 911 Turbo with NOX

Turbo mayhem.
Turbo-Supersportler.
Pandémonium turbo.

RGT-8
Rival: Lamborghini Gallardo

An 8-cylinder 911.
Ein Achtzylinder-911.
Une 911 8 cylindres.

ROADSTER
Rival: 911 Targa + change

Targa-topped oddity.
Merkwürdige Targa-Veredelung.
Bizzarerie à toit Targa.

SAAB

FOUNDED: **1937**
HEADQUARTERS: **TROLLHATTAN, SWEDEN**
2010 PRODUCTION: **31,696**

LOGO HISTORY:

As an airplane maker turned car producer, Saab has always majored on aerodynamics, from the curvaceous purity of the original late-40s Ursaab prototype to the more brutal 99 and 900 Turbo of the 1970s and 80s. Equally known for rally success, green tech and pioneering safety, Saab used to be synonymous with leftfield middle-class customers working within the creative industries. However, GM's poor stewardship of the brand between 1989 and 2010 led to Saab being left for dead until tiny Dutch supercar maker Spyker came to the rescue. After more financial wobbles in 2011 additional cash from Chinese partner Pang Da has seen Saab back making cars again. Fingers crossed.

Wegen der Erfahrungen im Flugzeugbau hat Saab schon immer großen Wert auf die Aerodynamik gelegt, sichtbar sowohl in der kurvenreichen Reinheit des Ursaab vom Ende der 1940er als auch in den kantigeren Modellen 99 und 900 Turbo der 1970er und 80er Jahre. Saab wurde bekannt durch Erfolge im Rallye-Sport sowie umweltfreundliche und sicherheitstechnische Innovationen und war früher die Hausmarke von Mittelschichtkunden aus den kreativen Berufen, die offen für neue Ideen waren. Unter der erfolglosen Führung von GM zwischen 1989 und 2010 geriet Saab an den Rand der Insolvenz und wurde schließlich vom kleinen niederländischen Sportwagenhersteller Spyker aufgekauft. Nach weiteren finanziellen Schwierigkeiten wurde 2011 der chinesische Automobilvertriebskonzern Pang Da als Investor mit ins Boot geholt. Seitdem konzentriert sich Saab wieder aufs Autobauen. Drücken wir ihnen die Daumen.

Fabricant d'avions devenu fabricant de voitures, Saab a toujours eu du flair pour l'aérodynamique, depuis la pureté sinueuse du prototype de l'Ursaab à la fin des années 1940 jusqu'aux 99 et 900 Turbo plus brutales des années 1970 et 1980. Saab est également connue pour ses succès dans les rallyes, sa technologie verte et son avant-gardisme en matière de sécurité, et a longtemps été la chouchoute d'une clientèle de créatifs de la classe moyenne innovante. Mais GM a mal géré la marque entre 1989 et 2010, et Saab a été laissée pour morte jusqu'à ce que le tout petit fabricant de supercars néerlandais Spyker vienne à la rescousse. Son partenaire chinois Pang Da a injecté de l'argent en 2011 pour résoudre des problèmes financiers supplémentaires, ce qui a permis à Saab de se remettre à la fabrication. On croise les doigts.

9-3
Rival: BMW 3

Ageing sedan, wagon & cabrio. Replaced 2012.
Limousine, Kombi & Cabrio, Ersatz 2012.
Berline, break et cabriolet sur le retour.

9-5
Rival: BMW 5

Decent sedan kick-started rebirth in 2010.
Stufenheck der oberen Mittelklasse.
Grande berline honnête relancée en 2010.

9-5 SPORTWAGON
Rival: Audi A6 Avant

All-new leftfield large estate.
Komplett neuer Premium-Kombi.
Un tout nouveau grand break inattendu.

9-4X
Rival: Audi A6
Allroad

Smartly jacked-up AWD crossover.
Ein Allrad-SUV, bullig und elegant zugleich.
Crossover à transmission intégrale.

SAMSUNG

FOUNDED: **1994**
HEADQUARTERS: **SEOUL, SOUTH KOREA**
2010 PRODUCTION: **161,917**

LOGO HISTORY:

A name more associated with televisions and cell phones, Samsung Motors was conceived in 1994. It wasn't until 1998 when Renault got involved with an 80.1% stake that Renault Samsung began producing cars. Unsurprisingly its cars are largely based around Renault models – and those of its alliance partner Nissan. Ranked fourth in its home market, Samsung is focusing now on potential for growth in emerging markets. Five models are currently produced at its Busan production facility, although with its 300,000 production capacity Samsung has plenty of room for its expected growth.

Unter dem Markennamen Samsung, der eher mit Fernsehern und Mobiltelefonen in Verbindung gebracht wird, werden seit 1994 Fahrzeuge hergestellt. Mit der eigentlichen Fertigung konnte aber erst 1998 begonnen werden, als Renault 80,1 % der Firmenanteile erwarb. Wenig überraschend basieren die Fahrzeuge von Renault Samsung Motors hauptsächlich auf Modellen der Franzosen sowie des Partnerunternehmens Nissan. Die Nummer vier auf dem südkoreanischen Markt ist auf der Suche nach Wachstumsmöglichkeiten in Schwellenländern. Fünf Modelle werden zurzeit in der Produktionsstätte in Busan gefertigt. Die dortige Produktionskapazität von 300.000 Einheiten soll dabei die Grundlage des ersehnten Wachstums sein.

Avec un nom plutôt associé aux télévisions et aux téléphones mobiles, Samsung Motors a été créé en 1994. Mais ce n'est qu'en 1998, lorsque Renault a acheté 80,1 % des parts, que Renault Samsung a commencé à produire des voitures. Sans surprise, elles rappellent beaucoup les modèles de Renault, ainsi que ceux de son partenaire Nissan. En quatrième place sur son marché national, Samsung cherche maintenant à exploiter son potentiel de croissance sur les marchés émergents. Cinq modèles sont actuellement produits à son usine de Busan, mais avec une capacité de production de 300 000 unités, Samsung a largement de quoi grandir.

SM3 CE Rival: Skoda Octavia		Nissan-based, not so sunny. Auf Nissan-Basis, nicht so heiter. Basée sur Nissan, mais moins enjouée.
SM5 Rival: Neat, mid-sized vans		Neat, mid-sized sedan. Schöne Limousine der oberen Mittelklasse. Berline de taille moyenne bien faite.
SM7 Rival: Audi A4		Neat, luxury sedan. Hübsche Luxus-Limousine. Berline de luxe bien faite.
QM5 Rival: Renault Koleos		Renault Koleos with a new grille. Renault Koleos mit neuem Kühlergrill. Renault Koleos avec une nouvelle calandre.

SCION

FOUNDED: **2002**
HEADQUARTERS: **CALIFORNIA, USA**
2010 PRODUCTION: **45,678**

LOGO HISTORY:

Born of a secret project by parent company Toyota to target the Generation Y youth market back in 1999, Scion started selling cars in 2003, first in California, then across the US. The brand's initial success can be put down to innovative marketing that pushed the car industry into areas previously not noticed – its extravagant patronage of youth culture famously prompted an underground hit, asking for some of that "Scion money". Tailoring its message to these overlooked 'young' customers (the typical Scion owner is 39, still the youngest average in the industry), the brand's good basic prices and customization options proved a successful approach, much copied since. Scion's star has fallen from its heady 173,000 sales peak in 2006, prompting some to wonder if the concept of a youth automotive brand had much substance. Ironically today the Scion model we're most excited about is simply a rebadged Toyota, sold as the iQ elsewhere. But perhaps like Saturn in its prime, Scion can position itself away from forced, corporate cool towards simply a progressive, approachable and intelligent brand choice with natural appeal to younger drivers – a proposition the iQ exemplifies perfectly.

Ursprünglich 1999 als Geheimprojekt des Mutterkonzerns Toyota geboren, um die Generation Y zu bedienen, begann Scion 2003 mit dem Verkauf von Fahrzeugen, zuerst in Kalifornien und dann in den gesamten USA. Der Anfangserfolg der Marke kann auf innovative und bis dahin in der Autoindustrie unbekannte Marketingstrategien zurückgeführt werden. Bald wurde die Marke unter der extravaganten Kundschaft aus jungen Städtern zu einem Hit. Die gezielte Ansprache dieser von anderen Herstellern übersehenen „jungen" Zielgruppe (der durchschnittliche Scion-Besitzer ist 39, und damit der jüngste Kunde in der Branche), die erschwinglichen Grundpreise und die vielfältigen Anpassungsmöglichkeiten erwiesen sich als erfolgreicher Ansatz und wurden seitdem häufig nachgeahmt. Seit der Umsatzspitze von 173.000 Fahrzeugen im Jahre 2003 sind die Verkaufszahlen rückläufig, was Spekulationen über die Tragfähigkeit des Konzepts ausgelöst hat. Ironischerweise ist das zurzeit aufregendste Scion-Modell ein Toyota, der für den amerikanischen Markt in Scion iQ umbenannt wurde. Doch wie Saturn vor ihnen könnten die Kalifornier die etwas künstlich wirkende Coolnes ablegen und sich ein neues Image als fortschrittliche Marke für smarte junge Kunden verpassen – ein Weg, den der iQ problemlos ebnen könnte.

Née d'un projet secret de la maison mère Toyota pour cibler le marché jeune en 1999, Scion a commencé à vendre des voitures en 2003, tout d'abord en Californie, puis dans tous les États-Unis. Le succès initial de la marque peut s'attribuer à une stratégie de marketing innovante qui a emmené l'industrie automobile sur des terrains inexplorés. L'extravagance de son mécénat culturel a même inspiré un succès musical underground, qui réclamait « de l'argent de Scion ». Avec un message taillé sur mesure pour ces « jeunes » clients négligés (le propriétaire de Scion a en moyenne 39 ans, c'est le chiffre le plus bas du secteur), les bons prix de la marque et ses options personnalisées ont eu du succès, et ont beaucoup été copiées. Scion a atteint un pic de 173 000 unités vendues en 2006 et est retombée beaucoup plus bas depuis, ce qui a incité certains à se demander si le concept de marque automobile pour les jeunes avait vraiment une raison d'être. Ironie du sort, aujourd'hui le modèle de Scion que nous trouvons le plus intéressant n'est qu'une Toyota rebadgée, vendue sous le nom d'iQ sur les autres marchés. Mais peut-être que, comme Saturn à sa meilleure époque, Scion peut contrer l'attitude artificiellement branchée des grandes marques et représenter un choix progressiste, abordable et intelligent qui séduira naturellement les jeunes conducteurs.

IQ
Rival: Fiat 500

Re-skin of Toyota's super city car of same name.
US-Ableger des Toyota-Modells.
Reprise de la super citadine de Toyota.

TC
Rival: Honda Civic

Basic two-door coupe designed to customize.
Individualisierbares Coupé mit 2 Sitzen.
Coupé 2 portes de base à personnaliser.

XB
Rival: Nissan Cube

Boxy, compact wagon is icon of the brand.
Kastiger Kompaktklasse-Kombi.
Break carré et compact emblème de Scion.

XD
Rival: Kia Soul

Duller, softer-shaped Toyota Yaris-based 5dr.
Fader 5-Türer auf Toyota Yaris-Basis.
5 portes basée sur la Toyota Yaris.

SEAT

FOUNDED: **1950**

HEADQUARTERS: **MARTORELL, SPAIN**

2010 PRODUCTION: **339,500**

LOGO HISTORY:

For a brand with 60-plus years of history, Seat has a remarkable lack of iconic vehicles. The reason? It's always been in bed with other stronger brands – first with Fiat until 1981 and then VW from 1986 – borrowing expertise, designs and technology from both. One exception was the 1975 1200 Sport 'Bocanegra'. Although it had Fiat 127 underpinnings and a body bought from NSU it is credited with being Seat's first self-developed car. Since VW's takeover, Seat has grown into a credible lower-cost but sporty Euro-centric brand with significant sales, some World Rally Championship success and good bespoke designs. But after all these years it's still in search of its own identity.

Für eine Marke mit einer über 60-jährigen Geschichte hat Seat erstaunlich wenig bedeutende Modelle hergestellt. Der Grund dafür? Die Spanier waren immer mit stärkeren Marken liiert – zunächst mit Fiat bis 1981 und dann mit VW ab 1986 –, aus denen sie Know-how, Designs und Technologie bezogen. Die Ausnahme zu dieser Regel bildet der 1200 Sport „Bocanegra" von 1975. Obwohl der Fiat 127 seine Grundlage bildet und die Karosserie von NSU ausgeliehen wird, gilt das Modell als erste Eigenentwicklung von Seat. Seit der Übernahme durch VW haben sich die Spanier zu einem zuverlässigen Hersteller von erschwinglichen und trotzdem sportlichen Fahrzeugen für den europäischen Markt entwickelt, der beeindruckende Absatzzahlen, einige Erfolge in Rallye-Meisterschaften und vielfältige Konfigurationsmöglichkeiten vorzuweisen hat. Aber eine eigene Identität haben die Iberer bis heute nicht gefunden.

Pour une marque qui a plus de 60 ans d'histoire, Seat manque singulièrement de modèles marquants. La raison ? Elle a toujours créé des alliances avec d'autres marques plus fortes (tout d'abord avec Fiat jusqu'en 1981, puis VW à partir de 1986) et leur a emprunté leur expertise, leurs concepts et leur technologie. Le modèle 1200 Sport « Bocanegra » de 1975 est une exception à cette règle. Il était basé sur la Fiat 127 et son corps avait été acheté à NSU, mais il est tout de même considéré comme la première voiture que Seat ait développée. Depuis son rachat par VW, Seat est devenue une euro-marque crédible qui fait des voitures économiques mais plutôt sportives, rencontre des succès satisfaisants dans les ventes et aussi parfois au championnat du monde des rallyes, et propose de bons concepts personnalisés. Mais après toutes ces années, elle est toujours à la recherche de sa propre identité.

IBIZA
Rival: Peugeot 207

Smartly styled lower-cost VW Polo.
Eleganter VW Polo zum niedrigen Preis.
VW Polo économique et stylée.

LEON
Rival: Ford Focus

Smartly styled lower-cost VW Golf.
Eleganter VW Golf zum niedrigen Preis.
VW Golf économique et stylée.

ALTEA
Rival: Renault Scenic

Mini-MPV with long and high options.
Kompaktvan in unterschiedlichen Größen.
Monospace proposé en plusieurs versions.

EXEO
Rival: Ford Mondeo

Sedan & wagon based on old Audi A6.
Limousine und Kombi auf Audi A6-Basis.
Berline et break avec une base d'Audi A6.

ALHAMBRA
Rival: Ford Galaxy

7-seat large MPV VW Sharan sibling.
7-sitzige Großraumlimousine.
Monospace 7 pl. proche du VW Sharan.

Black mouths: The 1975 1200 Sport 'Bocanegra' (green) and 2009 Seat Ibiza Bocanegra (red)

SKODA

FOUNDED: **1895**

HEADQUARTERS: **MLADĀ BOLESLAV, CZECH REPUBLIC**

2010 PRODUCTION: **762,600**

LOGO HISTORY:

Skoda's roots can be traced back to bicycle makers Laurin & Klement in Austria-Hungary before they branched out into motorcycles and cars. Acquired by arms maker Skoda Works in 1924, the cars were sold under the Skoda name, which was well-regarded in its day. Post-WWII communist control lost the brand vital engineering support from Western countries, and it started making good value vehicles with increasingly archaic technology, so much so that the brand became a standing joke for poor quality, especially in the UK. The fall of Communism led to the eventual takeover by the VW Group in 2000 and its range hasn't looked back, adding new reliability to its previous good value.

Die Wurzeln von Skoda können bis auf die Fahrradbauer Laurin & Klement zurückverfolgt werden, die zur Zeit der Donaumonarchie auch Autos und Motorräder herstellten. Nach dem Verkauf 1924 an die Rüstungsschmiede Skoda-Werke wurden die Fahrzeuge unter dem Namen Skoda vertrieben, seinerzeit eine angesehene Marke. Mit dem Ende des Zweiten Weltkrieges geriet der Hersteller in die Hände der kommunistischen Führung, die die wertvolle technische Unterstützung der westlichen Länder verlor. Fortan wurden preiswerte Autos mit zunehmend veralteter Technik gebaut, die allmählich zum Inbegriff von schlechter Qualität wurden. Nach der Wende wurde die Marke 2000 von der VW-Gruppe übernommen und hat seitdem den gewohnt preiswerten Modellen technische Zuverlässigkeit verliehen.

Les racines de Skoda remontent aux fabricants de cycles austro-hongrois Laurin & Klement, avant qu'ils n'étendent leurs activités aux motos et aux voitures. L'entreprise a été rachetée par le fabricant d'armes Skoda Works en 1924, et les voitures étaient vendues sous le nom de Skoda, qui était très bien considéré à l'époque. Après la Deuxième Guerre mondiale, le communisme a coûté à la marque le soutien technique vital des pays occidentaux. Elle a commencé à faire des véhicules bon marché basés sur une technologie de plus en plus archaïque, tant et si bien que Skoda est devenue synonyme de mauvaise qualité, particulièrement au Royaume-Uni. La chute du communisme a finalement abouti à un rachat par le groupe VW en 2000, et la gamme de Skoda est allée de l'avant en ajoutant la fiabilité à ses modèles bon marché.

FABIA
Rival: Ford Fiesta

Top value supermini hatch and wagon.
Als Steilheck, Kombi und Stufenheck.
Citadine compacte et break bon marché.

OCTAVIA
Rival: Ford Focus

Dependable mid-sized sedan and wagon.
In den Versionen Limousine und Kombi.
Berline et break fiable de taille moyenne.

SUPERB
Rival: Audi A6

For the price. Big, clever sedan/hatch + wagon.
Als Stufenheck und Kombi, toller Preis.
Berline/compacte + break à très bon prix.

ROOMSTER
Rival: Renault Kangoo

Clever concept, but ugly reality.
Cleveres Konzept, unschön umgesetzt.
Concept malin, réalisation hideuse.

YETI
Rival: Nissan Qashqai

Inspired name, good small crossover.
Geländewagen mit originellem Namen.
Bon petit crossover au nom inspiré.

SMART

LOGO HISTORY:

Born of a collaboration with Swiss watch brand Swatch, the microcar brand eventually launched under Mercedes-Benz parent Daimler as a well-received two-seater, sporting a tiny 0.6-liter gasoline engine. Its party piece was the ability to park nose-on to the sidewalk rather than side-on. The range expanded in the 00s to include a wonderful coupe and roadster but also a dismal four-door supermini, effectively a goofily re-skinned Mitsubishi, which severed any links to the brand's initial concept, and squandered its credibility. Smart has since dwindled back to just the two-seater fortwo model, which has been restyled slightly over the years, with mediocre results. After a spell during which is existence was in doubt, Daimler re-upped its commitment. With environmental and congestion pressures rising, the brand is expanding again with an all-electric fortwo in 2012, an electric bike and scooter in 2013 and a new four-seater by 2014.

Der aus der Zusammenarbeit mit der Schweizer Uhrenmarke Swatch entstandene Hersteller von Kleinstfahrzeugen wurde als Daimler-Benz-Tochter aus der Taufe gehoben und bald als Zweisitzer mit einem winzigen 0,6-Liter-Motor bekannt und geschätzt. Charakteristisch für den Zwerg ist, dass er quer zum Bürgersteig geparkt werden kann. In den Nullerjahren kamen ein ausgezeichnetes Coupé und ein Roadster dazu, aber auch ein viertüriges Kleinwagenmodell, das wie eine alberne Mitsubishi-Kopie wirkte und gegen das ursprüngliche Firmenkonzept verstieß, was der Glaubwürdigkeit der Marke nicht gerade zuträglich war. Später kehrten die Böblinger zu den zweisitzigen Wurzeln des Fortwo zurück, dessen Design leicht verändert wurde – mit mittelmäßigem Ergebnis. Nach einer kurzen Periode voller Existenzängste sprach Daimler der Marke sein Vertrauen erneut aus. Das steigende Umweltbewusstsein und die immer lästigeren Staus haben die Marke auf den Wachstumspfad gebracht. 2012 soll eine Elektroversion auf den Markt gebracht werden, 2013 ein Elektroroller und 2014 ein neuer Viersitzer.

Née d'une collaboration avec la marque horlogère suisse Swatch, cette marque de microvoitures a lancé sous l'égide de la maison mère de Mercedes-Benz, Daimler, un modèle à deux places équipé d'un minuscule moteur 0,6 litre qui a été très bien accueilli. Son grand avantage est de pouvoir se garer face au trottoir, et non de côté. Dans les années 2000 la gamme s'est agrandie avec un magnifique coupé et roadster, mais aussi une lamentable citadine polyvalente qui n'était qu'une Mitsubishi maladroitement restylée. Elle allait contre le concept initial de la marque et sapait sa crédibilité. Smart a depuis éliminé les autres modèles et est revenue à son modèle deux places, la Fortwo, dont le look a évolué au cours des années avec des résultats plutôt médiocres. L'existence de la marque a été en péril pendant un moment, jusqu'à ce que Daimler décide d'intensifier son investissement. Avec l'aggravation des problèmes liés à l'environnement et à l'encombrement dans les villes, Smart reprend son expansion et se dotera d'une Fortwo électrique en 2012, d'un vélo/scooter électrique en 2013, et d'une nouvelle quatre places pour 2014.

FORTWO
Rival: Toyota IQ

Two-seat-only trailblazing microcar.
Innovativer Kleinstwagen mit 2 Sitzen.
Microvoiture pionnière à 2 places.

FORTWO ED
Rival: Mitsubishi iMiEV

Electric version of the above.
Elektroversion des oberen Modells.
Version électrique.

Smart is big on accessories. We like this 2007 collection digital watch

SMART FORTWO ED

The Smart's original design brief was for an electric car to carry two students and a crate of beer to a party on the other side of town. Now it all makes sense as the ED brings electric drive and a car-sharing scheme. All it needs is a redesign to match.

Der Originalentwurf des Smart war darauf ausgelegt, zwei Studenten und eine Kiste Bier zum anderen Ende der Stadt zu transportieren. Mittlerweile ist er als Elektroauto erhältlich und Teil eines Car-Sharing-Konzepts. Er bräuchte nur mal ein kleines Facelifting.

Les instructions initiales pour le design de la Smart étaient de pouvoir transporter deux étudiants et une caisse de bière pour aller à une fête à l'autre bout de la ville. Cela prend aujourd'hui tout son sens avec la propulsion électrique de l'ED et son programme de sharing. Il ne lui manque plus qu'un relookage à l'avenant.

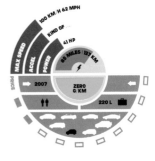

SECRET DETAIL

Push the accelerator pedal past its stop for a secret burst of overboost power, bringing the fight to pesky scooters.

Wenn Sie das Gaspedal ganz durchdrücken, können Sie sich mit dem nächsten vorbeituckernden Moped ein Rennen liefern.

Appuyez sur l'accélérateur de façon à dépasser la butée de la pédale, et vous obtiendrez une bouffée de puissance supplémentaire qui laissera les scooters importuns sur le carreau.

SPYKER

(NL)

FOUNDED: **1999**

HEADQUARTERS: **ZEEWOLDE, HOLLAND**

2010 PRODUCTION: < **25**

LOGO HISTORY:

The Spyker brand dates back to the early 20th century, before disappearing in 1929. Businessman Victor Muller resurrected the Dutch nameplate 70 years later and set about launching a range of ultra-exclusive supercars. Gaining some cache with celebrity owners including US rapper Busta Rhymes, the mainstay of the range has been the scissor-doored C8 two-seater, offered in Spyder soft-top or Laviolette removable glass canopy guise. Recently most famous for saving the far bigger Saab brand from extinction against all odds, Spkyer sold its car business to UK coachbuilder CPP in 2011 so chairman Muller can concentrate on Saab's revival.

Die Marke Spyker kann bis ins frühe 20. Jahrhundert zurückverfolgt werden. 1929 wurde das Unternehmen aufgelöst – und 70 Jahre später vom niederländischen Geschäftsmann Victor Muller wieder belebt, um exklusive Supersportwagen herzustellen. Prominente Käufer wie der US-Rapper Busta Rhymes verliehen der Marke Bekanntheit. Hauptstütze der Firma ist jedoch der zweisitzige Flügeltürer C8, der mit Softtop (Spyder) oder entfernbarem Glasdach (Laviolette) zu haben ist. Für Schlagzeilen sorgte zuletzt die niederländische Manufaktur, als sie den um einiges größeren Hersteller Saab vor dem sicheren Tod rettete. 2011 verkaufte Spyker das Automobilgeschäft an den britischen Zulieferer CPP, damit Muller sich der Wiederbelebung von Saab widmen kann.

La marque Spyker est née au début du XXᵉ siècle, et a disparu en 1929. L'homme d'affaires Victor Muller a ressuscité ce nom néerlandais 70 ans plus tard et a entrepris de lancer une gamme de supercars ultra exclusives. Quelques clients célèbres, notamment le rappeur américain Busta Rhymes, ont donné du prestige au vaisseau amiral de la gamme, la C8 à deux places et portes en ciseaux. Elle est proposée en versions décapotable Spyder ou Laviolette avec un toit amovible en verre. Spyker s'est récemment fait remarquer en sauvant la marque Saab, bien plus grande et très mal partie, et a vendu son activité au carrossier britannique CPP en 2011 pour que son président Muller puisse se consacrer à la renaissance de Saab.

C8 AILERON
Rival: Pagani Zonda

Extrovert scissor-doored Dutch supercar.
Der fliegende Holländer.
Supercar néerlandaise extravertie à portes en ciseaux.

SPYKER C8 AILERON

Stunning detailing, lightweight aluminum construction and plenty of performance the C8 is Spyker's current supercar offering. There's a roadster too. If you like your supercars exclusive then Spyker is worth seeking out, and the C8's not that expensive either (relatively).

Der C8 bietet als Spykers aktuellster Supersportwagen sorgfältig ausgearbeitete Details, eine leichte Aluminiumkarosserie und viel Leistung! Es gibt auch einen Roadster. Wenn Sie einen wirklich exklusiven Supersportwagen haben möchten, empfehlen wir Ihnen Spyker, und der C8 ist – relativ gesehen – gar nicht mal so teuer.

Des détails superbes, une construction légère en aluminium et des performances superlatives, voici ce que propose Spyker avec sa supercar actuelle, la C8. Elle existe aussi en roadster. Si vous aimez que vos supercars soient exclusives, alors cela vaut la peine d'envisager Spyker, et la C8 n'est pas si chère que ça (par rapport à d'autres).

C8 Aileron

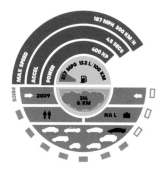

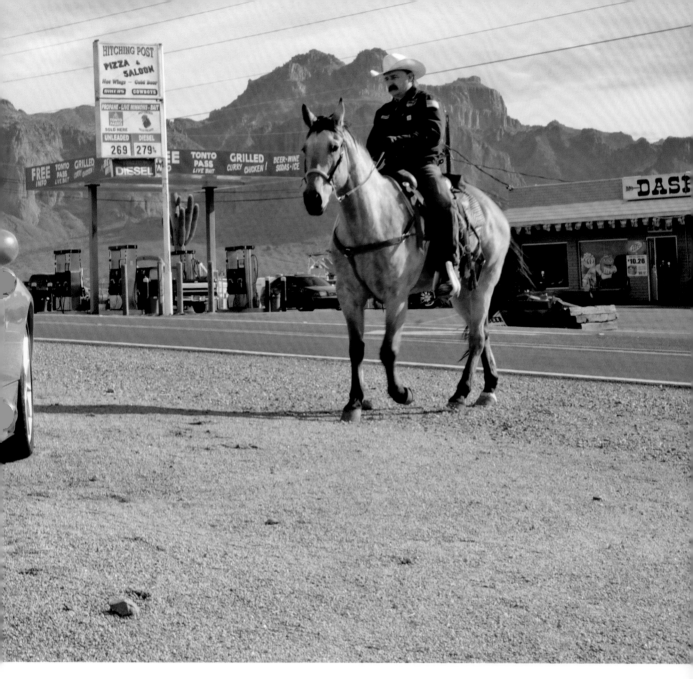

SECRET DETAIL

Spyker is proud of its aeronautical past so there are references to it everywhere, aptly including the air vents.

Spyker ist stolz auf seine Luftfahrt-Vergangenheit. Daher finden sich überall Hinweise darauf, sogar bei den Lüftungsschlitzen.

La marque Spyker est fière de son passé dans l'aéronautique, on retrouve donc des références partout, y compris, bien sûr, dans les bouches d'aération.

SSANGYONG

FOUNDED: **1954**
HEADQUARTERS: **SEOUL, SOUTH KOREA**
2010 PRODUCTION: **85,000**

LOGO HISTORY:

Ssangyong – meaning 'double dragons' – has a long but chequered history making jeeps, trucks and buses. The company didn't get the Ssangyong name until 1986 when the Ssangyong Business Group took over. It started getting noticed after a 1991 liaison with Daimler to use old Mercedes engines and technology, but the value 4x4 brand still lacked a clear identity and a succession of owners Daewoo (1997-2000) and SAIC (2004-2009) failed to help it succeed. Put into receivership by SAIC, the brand was formally resurrected by Indian owners Mahindra & Mahindra in 2011. Time will tell whether they can do what others couldn't with it. Our advice – first step, change the name.

Ssangyong – zu Deutsch: „Zwillingsdrache" – darf auf eine lange und bewegte Geschichte als Hersteller von Jeeps, LKWs und Bussen zurückblicken. Den Namen Ssangyong erhielt der Hersteller erst 1986, als die gleichnamige Unternehmensgruppe die Führung übernahm. Internationale Bekanntheit erlangten die Südkoreaner 1991, als sie mit Daimler eine Technologie-Transfer-Partnerschaft vereinbarten. Der Marke mit den günstigen Geländewagen fehlte aber noch eine klar definierte Identität, und weder Daewoo (1997-2000) noch SAIC (2004-2009) gelang es, der Firma zum Erfolg zu verhelfen. Unter der Führung von SAIC musste Gläubigerschutz beantragt werden, 2011 übernahm die indische Mahindra & Mahindra den angeschlagenen Autobauer. Die Zukunft wird zeigen, ob die Inder Erfolg haben werden, wo andere gescheitert sind. Als erste Maßnahme wäre vielleicht ein Namenswechsel empfehlenswert.

Ssangyong (ce qui signifie « double dragon ») a une histoire longue et mouvementée dans la fabrication de jeeps, camions et bus. La société n'a pris le nom de Ssangyong qu'en 1986, lorsque le groupe Ssangyong Business l'a rachetée. Elle a commencé à se faire remarquer après avoir formé un partenariat avec Daimler en 1991 pour exploiter les moteurs et la technologie dont Mercedes ne se servait plus. Mais la marque de 4x4 bon marché ne s'était toujours pas trouvé une identité bien à elle, et ses propriétaires suivants (Daewoo de 1997 à 2000 et SAIC de 2004 à 2009) n'ont pas résolu ce problème. Placée en redressement judiciaire par SAIC, la marque a été ressuscitée par ses nouveaux propriétaires indiens Mahindra & Mahindra en 2011. Voyons s'ils feront mieux que leurs prédécesseurs. Notre conseil : qu'ils commencent par changer le nom.

KORANDO
Rival: Kia Sportage

Decent new Giugiaro-designed crossover.
Anständiges Giugiaro-Design.
Nouveau crossover honnête par Giugiaro.

RODIUS
Rival: The bus

Hideous but huge old up-to-11-seat MPV.
Hässlicher Minivan mit bis zu 11 Sitzen.
Monospace hideux de jusqu'à 11 places.

KYRON
Rival: Nissan X-Trail

Compact SUV lacking any distinction.
Mittelgroßes SUV ohne jegliches Flair.
SUV compact sans aucune distinction.

REXTON
Rival: Tractor

Bigger SUV lacking distinction.
Größeres SUV ohne jegliches Flair.
SUV plus grand, sans distinction.

CHAIRMAN
Rival: Hyundai Equus

Big sedan for aspiring chairmen.
Großlimousine für angehende Chefs.
Grande berline pour les aspirants PDG.

SUBARU

LOGO HISTORY:

The first Subaru car was the 1500 or P-1 in 1954. Born out of Fuji Heavy Industries (FHI), Subaru developed a name for boxer engines, turbo-charging and all-wheel drive, which helped breed World Rally success in the late 1990s with Colin McRae at the wheel and an iconic gold-wheeled Impreza WRX road car. Since that success, newer Imprezas have got successively uglier and duller (although still great to drive) and Subaru has failed to find another icon. Now FHI is part owned by Toyota, some new Subarus – like the Trezia – will share Toyota product underpinnings. In summary: A brand in need of a major makeover.

Das erste Subaru-Auto ist der 1500 oder P-1 aus dem Jahr 1954. Die Automobilmarke des Konzerns Fuji Heavy Industries (FHI) ist bekannt für ihre Boxermotoren, Turbolader und Allradantriebe, die in den späten 1990ern ihren Beitrag zum Erfolg in der Rallye-Weltmeisterschaft mit Colin McRae und seinem Impreza WRX mit den goldenen Felgen leisteten. Seitdem sind die Impreza-Nachfolgemodelle immer hässlicher und langweiliger geworden (das ausgezeichnete Fahrgefühl ist jedoch erhalten geblieben), und einen weiteren Volltreffer haben die Japaner nicht zustande gebracht. Heute hält Toyota eine Beteiligung an FHI, weshalb einige Subaru-Modelle wie der Trezia auf Toyota-Fertigungslinien gebaut werden. Alles in allem: Die Marke müsste von Grund auf erneuert werden.

La première Subaru a été la 1500, ou P-1, en 1954. Mise au monde par Fuji Heavy Industries (FHI), Subaru s'est bâti un nom à coups de moteurs boxer, de turbocompresseurs et de transmissions intégrales. C'est ainsi que la marque a remporté de beaux succès au championnat du monde des rallyes à la fin des années 1990 avec Colin McRae au volant et une voiture de course aux roues dorées légendaire, l'Impreza WRX. Depuis ce succès, les nouvelles Impreza sont devenues tour à tour plus laides et plus ternes (mais ont conservé une excellente conduite) et Subaru n'a pas réussi à trouver un autre vaisseau amiral. Aujourd'hui, Toyota a racheté une partie de FHI, et certaines nouvelles Subaru seront basées sur sa gamme (comme la Trezia). Pour résumer : cette marque a besoin d'une révision en profondeur.

PLEO | LUCRA
Rival: Daihatsu Mira

Dull tall-boy four-door microcar.
Hochgewachsener, 4-türiger Kleinwagen.
Microvoiture verticale terne à 4 portes.

DEX
Rival: Nissan Roox

Cool Kei car five-seat box.
Cooles Kei-Car mit 5 Sitzen.
Belle Keijidosha carrée à 5 places.

JUSTY
Rival: Daihatsu Sirion

Re-badged Sirion softer tall-boy car.
Sanfte Version des Sirion.
Sirion rebadgée, aux lignes plus douces.

TREZIA
Rival: Nissan Note

Toyota Verso-S supermini MPV in drag.
Zum Toyota Verso-S baugleicher Mikrovan.
Monospace, Toyota Verso-S en plus lent.

IMPREZA
Rival: Ford Focus

Dull as ditchwater basic 4x4 hatch.
Stinklangweiliger Geländewagen.
Compacte 4x4 de base soporifique.

IMPREZA STI
Rival: Mitsubishi
Lancer Evo

Balls-out rally car for the road.
Straßenversion des Rallye-Wagens.
Puissante voiture de rallye pour la route.

LEGACY
Rival: Audi A4 Avant

Anonymous, uninspiring sedan/wagon.
Als Limousine und Kombi, uninspiriert.
Berline/break anonyme et sans intérêt.

OUTBACK
Rival: Audi A4
Allroad

Jacked up version of Legacy.
Höhergelegte Version des Legacy.
Version surélevée de la Legacy.

FORESTER
Rival: Ford Kuga

Chunky 5dr 4x4 jacked-up wagon.
Bulliger Allradantrieb mit 5 Türen.
Break 4x4 trapu et surélevé à 5 portes.

TRIBECA
Rival: Infiniti FX

Large 7st 4x4 crossover, now less ugly.
7-sitziges SUV, nicht mehr so hässlich.
Crossover 4x4 à 7 pl., moins laid qu'avant.

EXIGA
Rival: Honda Oddysey

7st Far East-only MPV/wagon.
7-sitziger Großraumkombi für Japan.
Monospace/break 7 places pour le Japon.

SUZUKI

(J)
FOUNDED: **1909**
HEADQUARTERS: **SHIZUOKA, JAPAN**
2010 PRODUCTION: **1,940,000**

LOGO HISTORY:

Bit of dark horse, Suzuki, making nearly two million vehicles in 2010 as well as motorcycles, all-terrain vehicles, boat engines and wheelchairs. It started, unusually for a future carmaker, in weaving loom-manufacture more than 100 years ago and didn't make its first proper car until the 1955 Suzulight. Since then collaboration with other carmakers including GM, Fiat, Nissan, Daewoo and Mitsubishi has diluted its brand's uniqueness but a few stars stand out, notably the small and boxy late 1980s Vitara 4x4 and the 00s Swift Sport hot hatch. Now has a major subsidiary in the key Indian market in Maruti Suzuki while VW Group has taken a stake in the overall business.

Mit knapp zwei Millionen gebauten Fahrzeugen im Jahre 2010 ist der Hersteller von Motorrädern, Geländewagen, Außenbordmotoren und motorisierten Rollstühlen irgendwie noch ein unbeschriebenes Blatt. Für einen Autobauer ungewöhnlich, begann Suzuki vor über 100 Jahren als Hersteller von Webstühlen und fertigte keinen Wagen bis 1955. Durch die Zusammenarbeit mit anderen Automobilherstellern wie GM, Fiat, Nissan, Daewoo und Mitsubishi wurde die Einzigartigkeit der Marke etwas verwässert. Dennoch – ein paar unverwechselbare Modelle hat Suzuki doch hingekriegt, insbesondere den kastigen Geländewagen Vitara aus den späten 1980ern sowie den kompakten Swift Sport aus den Nullerjahren des laufenden Jahrhunderts. Auf dem wichtigen indischen Markt sind die Japaner mit Maruti Suzuki präsent. 2010 stieg die VW-Gruppe bei Suzuki ein.

Suzuki a vendu près de deux millions de voitures en 2010, ainsi que des motos, des véhicules tout terrain, des moteurs de bateau et des fauteuils roulants. Cette entreprise a connu un démarrage inhabituel pour un futur fabricant de voitures. Il y a plus d'un siècle, c'était une usine textile. Sa première vraie voiture, la Suzulight, n'est sortie qu'en 1955. Depuis, la marque a collaboré avec d'autres fabricants automobiles, notamment GM, Fiat, Nissan, Daewoo et Mitsubishi, et y a perdu un peu de son caractère. Mais elle a tout de même quelques modèles remarquables, comme la petite Vitara 4x4 carrée de la fin des années 1980, et la compacte rapide Swift Sport des années 2000. Avec sa filiale Maruti Suzuki elle s'est très bien placée sur le marché indien, de grande importance stratégique, tandis que le groupe VW s'est intéressé à son activité globale.

ALTO
Rival: Peugeot 107

Indian-built smart city car.
Smartes Stadtauto indischer Herstellung.
Citadine chic construite en Inde.

SPLASH
Rival: Opel Agila

Good-looking tall and roomy city car.
Gut aussehendes Stadtauto mit viel Raum.
Belle citadine haute et spacieuse.

SWIFT
Rival: Ford Focus

Superb supermini, especially Sport model.
Toller Mikrovan, vor allem das Sport-Modell.
Superbe polyvalente, surtout la Sport.

JIMNY
Rival: Daihatsu Fourtrak

Old-school tiny 4x4 with real ability.
Altmodischer, leichter Geländewagen.
Minuscule 4x4 classique très doué.

SX4
Rival: Fiat Sedici

Hatchback/SUV thingy with limo version.
Steilheck/SUV ohne Limousine-Version.
Compacte/SUV avec version limousine.

GRAND VITARA
Rival: Toyota RAV4

Trailblazing small SUV, now less distinctive.
Bahnbrechendes SUV kleinerer Ausmaße.
Petit SUV pionnier, devenu passe-partout.

KIZASHI
Rival: Skoda Octavia

Fair stab at a medium sedan.
Mittelklasse-Limousine.
Tentative de berline de taille moyenne.

LAPIN
Rival: Mazda Spiano

Shrunken Nissan Cube mkII look-alike.
Geschrumpfter Nissan Cube.
Sosie de la Nissan Cube en plus petit.

MR WAGON
Rival: Nissan Moco

Japan-only lower-roof city MPV.
Niedriger Stadt-Minivan für Japan.
Monospace citadin, pour le Japon.

PALETTE
Rival: Nissan Roox

Japan-only tall-roof, boxy city MPV.
Hochdach-Kleinstkombi für Japan.
Monospace citadin, pour le Japon.

SOLIO
Rival: Mitsubishi Delica D:2

Long & wider sliding-doored MPV.
Kleinwagen mit Schiebetüren.
Monospace à portes coulissantes.

TATA

(IND)

FOUNDED: **1945**

HEADQUARTERS: **MUMBAI, INDIA**

2010 PRODUCTION: **230,715**

LOGO HISTORY:

This ex-locomotive maker turned commercial transport manufacturer only started making passenger vehicles in the 1990s – and even then only commercial vehicles and 4x4s with more seats and creature comforts. The first out-and-out passenger car was the 1998 Indica supermini that was a big success in India, and was briefly badged as a Rover CityRover in UK where it was less so. The world started to take notice of Tata Motors when it acquired Jaguar Land Rover from Ford in 2008 and then went on to develop the world's cheapest car – the controversial no frills Nano. The 2011 Pixel EV concept shows greater design ambition that could soon bear fruit.

Der ursprünglich auf den Bau von Lokomotiven spezialisierte Nutzfahrzeughersteller begann erst in den 1990ern mit der Fertigung von Kraftfahrzeugen. Zur Palette gehörten aber auch ausschließlich Nutzfahrzeuge und Geländewagen mit mehr Sitzen und Annehmlichkeiten. Einen „echten" Personenkraftwagen baute Tata Motors erst 1998 mit dem Kleinwagen Indica, ein Riesenerfolg in Indien. Als City Rover wurde das Auto mit nur mäßigem Erfolg nach Großbritannien exportiert. Weltweite Aufmerksamkeit erlang der Autobauer aus Mumbai erst 2008 mit der Übernahme von Jaguar und Land Rover und der Entwicklung des günstigsten Fahrzeugs der Welt – das umstrittene Billiggefährt Nano. Das 2011 präsentierte Konzept Pixel EV ist von der Gestaltung her ambitionierter und könnte bald Früchte tragen.

Cet ancien fabricant de locomotives devenu fabricant de véhicules commerciaux n'a commencé à faire des véhicules personnels que dans les années 1990, et encore, seulement des 4x4 avec plus de sièges et de confort que les camionnettes. Sa première vraie voiture a été la citadine polyvalente Indica en 1998. Elle a remporté un grand succès en Inde, et a été brièvement badgée CityRover au Royaume-Uni, où elle a reçu un accueil plus mitigé. Le monde a commencé à remarquer l'existence de Tata Motors lorsque l'entreprise a racheté Jaguar Land Rover à Ford en 2008, puis s'est mise à développer la voiture la moins chère du monde : la Nano, modeste et controversée. Le concept de la Pixel EV sorti en 2011 affiche un design plus ambitieux qui pourrait bientôt porter ses fruits.

NANO
Rival: Maruti 800

Cheapest car in the world (circa $3000).
Billigstes Auto der Welt (ca. 3.000 USD, 2000 EUR).
La moins chère du monde (env. 2 000 EUR).

INDICA V2
Rival: Maruti A-Star

Value supermini.
Kleinwagen mit Mehrwert.
Citadine polyvalente bon marché.

INDICA VISTA
Rival: Mitsubishi i-MiEV

Bigger, modern Indica with EV aims.
Größerer Indica mit Elektroantrieb.
Indica avec des vues sur l'électrique.

INDIGO CS
Rival: Ford Ikon

CS= compact sedan. Still humdrum.
CS = compact sedan (Kompaktlimousine).
Berline compacte sans grand intérêt.

MANZA
Rival: Maruti Swift Dzire

New compact sedan.
Neue kompakte Limousine.
Nouvelle berline compacte.

ARIA
Rival: Mahindra Xylo

New, modern-looking 7st crossover SUV.
Neues Crossover-SUV mit 7 Sitzen.
Nouvel SUV crossover moderne à 7 places.

SAFARI
Rival: Mahindra Scorpio

Low-price old school 4x4.
Altmodischer Allradantrieb zum Billigtarif.
4x4 vieille école à bas prix.

SUMO GRANDE
Rival: Mahindra Scorpio

Big and more curvy 7st 4x4.
Kurvenreicher Geländewagen mit 7 Sitzen.
Grand 4x4 à 7 places avec plus de courbes.

TATA NANO

The 'one-lakh' (100,000 Rupee) car is the cheapest in the world. Beyond the headlines its aim is to get Indian families off their motorbikes and into safer, more comfortable cars. The environmental compromises of upscaling millions from two wheels to four need to be mitigated somehow, but few can deny it's a marvel of industrial design sure to save and improve many lives.

Das „One Lakh Car" (100.000 Rupien) ist das billigste Auto der Welt. Sein eigentlicher Sinn ist es, indische Familien herunter vom Moped und hinein in sichere, komfortablere Autos zu holen. Was es für die Umwelt bedeutet, wenn Millionen Fahrer von zwei auf vier Räder umsteigen, kann man sich vorstellen. Ein kleines Wunderwerk des Industriedesigns ist der Wagen trotzdem – das zudem noch Leben rettet.

Cette voiture à un lakh (100 000 roupies) est la moins chère du monde. Son objectif est de faire descendre les familles indiennes de leurs motos et de les faire monter dans des voitures, plus sûres et plus confortables. Le coût environnemental de ce changement appliqué à des millions de personnes devra être compensé d'une façon ou d'une autre, mais il faut bien admettre que c'est une merveille de la conception industrielle qui sauvera et améliorera de nombreuses vies.

Nano

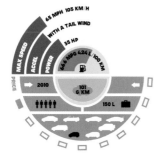

SECRET DETAIL

To save cost, weight and complication, the tailgate doesn't open, meaning the only way to access luggage is from the inside.

Kosten, Gewicht und Aufwand lassen sich dadurch reduzieren, dass die Heckklappe nicht geöffnet werden kann, d. h. man kommt nur von innen an den Kofferraum.

Pour économiser sur les coûts, le poids et les complications, le panneau arrière ne s'ouvre pas. Ce qui veut dire que la seule façon d'accéder aux bagages est de passer par l'intérieur.

TESLA

USA

FOUNDED: **2003**
HEADQUARTERS: **CALIFORNIA, USA**

LOGO HISTORY:

TESLA MOTORS

Taking more than its name from electrical engineer Nikola Tesla, the inventor's 1982 AC motor design inspired the one used in the electric car company's debut model, the Roadster. Elon Musk took control of Tesla after making an initial investment hot off the success of his internet payment venture, Paypal. A few years on, however, the business and its backer were taken to the brink, due to delays, cost overruns and a crashing economy. But in a remarkable turnaround, the company emerged as one of the biggest winners from the recession. Heavily supported by US government loans, bolstered by investments by Daimler and Toyota – both keen to tap its ahead-of-the-battery-pack technology – and with production streamlined, the high profile startup now has a serious chance of becoming a major player in the automotive industry. With 1500-plus Roadsters already delivered for around $109,000 a pop, enough heads have been turned on streets to prime the market for step two in the brand's plan of introducing ever-cheaper models as the technology advances. The Model S has to be the most anticipated car of 2012. At half the price of the Roadster, Tesla is betting the farm on it proving a major hit.

Vom Erfinder und Elektroingenieur Nikola Tesla liehen sich die Kalifornier nicht nur den Namen, sondern auch die Inspiration für den Elektromotor ihres Erstlings – der Roadster. Geleitet wird die Firma von Elon Musk, der nach dem Erfolg seines Online-Bezahlsystems Paypal in den Fahrzeughersteller als Investor einstieg. Nach einigen Jahren gerieten Unternehmen und Anleger aufgrund von Verzögerungen, Kostenexplosion und Wirtschaftskrise in eine finanzielle Schieflage. Doch völlig unerwartet schaffte Tesla den Umschwung und stieg als einer der größten Gewinner der Rezession auf. Die Darlehen der US-Regierung, die Investitionen von Daimler und Toyota – die auf die Akkutechnologie der Amerikaner schielen – und die Rationalisierung von Produktionsverfahren erhöhen die Chancen von Tesla, in Zukunft eine herausragende Rolle in der Automobilindustrie zu spielen. Nach über 1.500 verkauften Roadstern zum Preis von ca. 109.000 USD (75.000 EUR) pro Stück sind einige Beobachter auf eine Marke aufmerksam geworden, die die technologischen Fortschritte nutzen möchten, um günstigere Modelle auf den Markt zu bringen. Das Tesla Model S ist das am sehnlichsten erwartete Auto des Jahres 2012. Halb so teuer wie der Roadster, könnte der Wagen ein richtiger Schlager werden.

Cette marque ne se contente pas d'emprunter son nom à l'ingénieur électricien Nikola Tesla : le moteur électrique que l'inventeur avait imaginé en 1882 a inspiré celui du premier modèle de l'entreprise, la Roadster. Elon Musk a pris les commandes de Tesla après un investissement initial réalisé grâce au succès de son site de paiement par Internet, Paypal. Quelques années plus tard, l'entreprise et son financeur ont connu de graves difficultés dues à des retards, à des dépassements de coûts et à une économie en crise. Mais dans un retournement de situation remarquable, l'entreprise est en fait devenue l'une des grandes gagnantes de la récession. Elle a reçu un soutien énorme de la part du gouvernement américain et de Daimler et Toyota, très intéressés par sa technologie électrique avant-gardiste. Maintenant que sa production est rationalisée, cette jeune entreprise a des chances sérieuses de devenir un acteur majeur dans l'industrie automobile. Plus de 1 500 Roadster ont déjà été livrés à environ 109 000 $ (75 000 EUR) l'unité et se sont suffisamment fait remarquer dans les rues pour préparer le marché à la deuxième étape du plan de la marque : lancer des modèles de moins en moins chers au fur et à mesure que la technologie progresse. La Model S est sans doute la voiture la plus attendue de 2012. Elle coûte moitié moins cher que la Roadster, et Tesla parie gros sur son succès.

ROADSTER
Rival: Lotus Elise

Fast, sharp and environmentally friendly.
Schnell, scharf und umweltfreundlich.
Rapide, affûtée, et écologique.

MODEL S
Rival: Fisker Karma

All-electric 7-seat sporty sedan due in 2012.
7-sitzige Elektrolimousine, ab 2012.
Berline sportive électrique à 7 places.

TESLA MODEL S

A svelte sedan from Silicon Valley (in spirit, as its HQ is a few hundred miles south), the S mashes Jaguar-esque looks with full electric power. The perfect upgrade for grown-up .com boomers with its seven seats, two of them hiding in the trunk. Tesla promises the longest range and fastest recharge of any electric car – well worth a test drive.

Eine schlanke Limousine aus dem Silicon Valley (zumindest im Geiste, denn der Firmensitz liegt ein paar Hundert Kilometer weiter südlich): Der S ist eine gewagte Mischung aus Jaguar-Look und Elektroantrieb. Ein perfektes Upgrade für erwachsen gewordene Dotcom-Aufsteiger. Mit sieben Sitzen, von denen sich zwei im Kofferraum verbergen. Tesla verspricht die höchste Reichweite und den schnellsten Aufladevorgang unter allen Elektroautos – das ist eine Testfahrt wert!

Svelte berline de la Silicon Valley (en esprit, car le siège est en fait à quelques centaines de miles plus au sud), la S allie le look d'une Jaguar avec une propulsion entièrement électrique. Avec ses sept sièges, dont deux cachés dans le coffre, c'est le modèle haut de gamme parfait pour les boomers de la .com. Tesla promet l'autonomie la plus grande et la recharge la plus rapide de toutes les voitures électriques.

Model S Signature
* Estimated luggage space

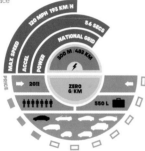

SECRET DETAIL

World's biggest in-car touch screen with full internet connectivity. Just don't mention that touch screens can be a bad safety idea in cars…

Der größte Touchscreen der Welt, mit Internetzugang. Da hat man wohl übersehen, dass ein Touchscreen im Auto nicht gerade für Verkehrssicherheit sorgt …

Le plus grand écran tactile embarqué, avec connexion à Internet. Mais ne parlons pas du fait que les écrans tactiles peuvent être une mauvaise idée du point de vue de la sécurité automobile…

TESLA ROADSTER

A re-bodied Lotus Elise may have been the starting point for the Tesla Roadster but the end point – a fully-electric sportscar with a seamless sub-four-second 0-60mph time – is a very different and quite astounding accomplishment that has to be experienced first hand to fully comprehend. Expensive to be sure, but the Model S sedan promises economies of scale and cheaper prices in 2012.

Ein neu aufgelegter Lotus Elise war der Ausgangspunkt für den Tesla Roadster. Aber das Ergebnis – ein komplett elektrisch betriebener Supersportwagen, der es in knapp vier Sekunden auf 100 km/h schafft – ist eine erstaunliche Leistung, die man am eigenen Leib erleben sollte. Ein teures Vergnügen … die Produktion des für 2012 geplanten Tesla Sedan S soll jedoch optimiert werden, was den Preis wohl senken wird.

Le point de départ de la Tesla Roadster était peut-être une Lotus Elise modifiée, mais le résultat (une voiture de sport entièrement électrique avec une accélération continue de 0 à 100 en moins de 4 secondes) est une réussite très différente et assez étonnante, qu'il faut vivre directement pour la comprendre pleinement. Elle est chère, c'est sûr, mais la berline Model S promet des économies d'échelle et des prix allégés en 2012.

Roadster

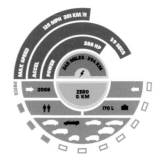

SECRET DETAIL

The deep carbon fire bonnet vents are literally groovy but have function too – helping to vent air from the fans that keep the electric motor cool.

Die tiefen Lüftungsschlitze aus Kohlefaser sehen nicht nur schick aus, sondern haben sogar eine Funktion: Sie leiten Luft zum Motor und halten ihn somit kühl.

Les profondes prises d'air sur le capot en fibre de carbone ont beaucoup de style, mais ont aussi une fonction : aider à refroidir le moteur.

Tesla founder Elon Musk

THINK

FOUNDED: **1991**

HEADQUARTERS: **FORNEBU, NORWAY**

2010 PRODUCTION: **1043**

LOGO HISTORY:

Th!nk can trace its roots back to a 1991 prototype but it didn't put its all-electric City car into small-run production until 1999 supported by Ford. Despite a $150m investment from the Detroit giant Th!nk failed to make a real impact and Ford sold the brand in 2003. In 2006 Norwegian investors bought the business and have since brought heavyweight automotive management on board and re-started production in both Finland through specialist manufacturing facility Valmet – who make the Boxster and Cayman for Porsche – as well as a new US factory in Indiana. But at circa $36,000 before incentives it's still a very pricey small car. and at the time of going to press the firm had again filed for bankruptcy due to a failure to secure long-term investment and is seeking new potential suitors to resurrect it.

Die Wurzeln von Th!nk reichen bis zum Prototyp von 1991 zurück, eine Kleinserienfertigung des Elektroautos begann jedoch erst 1999 mit Unterstützung von Ford. Trotz der 150 Millionen starken Investition durch den Giganten aus Detroit blieb der erwartete Erfolg aus, und Ford stieß 2003 die Marke ab. 2006 erwarben norwegische Investoren das Unternehmen und gaben der Firmenpolitik eine neue Ausrichtung. Gebaut wird in Finnland in der Fertigungsanlage von Valmet – der für Porsche den Boxster und den Cayman baut – sowie in einem neuen Werk im US-Bundesstaat Indiana. Der Verkaufspreis von 36.000 USD (25.000 EUR), ohne Vergünstigungen, ist jedoch noch ziemlich hoch für einen Kleinwagen.

Les racines de Th!nk remontent à un prototype de 1991, mais ce n'est qu'en 1999 que la marque a mis en route une petite série de sa citadine entièrement électrique, la City, avec l'aide de Ford. Bien que le géant de Detroit ait investi 150 millions de dollars, Th!nk n'a pas réussi à se faire une vraie place et Ford a vendu la marque en 2003. Des investisseurs norvégiens ont racheté l'activité en 2006 et ont depuis installé une équipe de gestion ultraperformante. Ils ont relancé la production en Finlande, chez Valmet, une usine spécialisée qui produit également la Boxster et la Cayman de Porsche, ainsi que dans une nouvelle usine américaine dans l'Indiana. Mais à environ 36 000 $ (25 000 EUR) hors subventions, cette petite voiture reste très chère.

CITY

Rival: Nissan Leaf

Expensive but credible EV city car.
Teueres, jedoch überzeugendes Elektroauto.
Citadine électrique chère mais crédible.

TOYOTA

(J)

FOUNDED: **1937**
HEADQUARTERS: **TOYOTA CITY, JAPAN**
2010 PRODUCTION: **7,117,900**

LOGO HISTORY:

The world's biggest vehicle maker started off making weaving equipment before turning to cars in the mid-1930s under the family name 'Toyoda'. Changed to 'Toyota' in 1937 partly because it was easier to write in Japanese, its first key car was the home-produced 1955 Crown. In 1966 the massive-selling Corolla sedan arrived and by the 70s Toyota was number three in world sales behind GM and Ford and renowned for making well-equipped and reliable cars. Alongside its other brands acquired (Hino and Daihatsu) or invented (Lexus and Scion), Toyota has consistently won customer satisfaction surveys while in the 00s blazed a new trail for more eco-focused hybrid petrol/electric cars. As rivals absorbed and perfected its high quality manufacturing processes, Toyota itself seemed to slip – its recall problems badly hit its reputation and profits. With a vast portfolio of products, very few stand out from the competent range of affordable automotive appliances. But when they do, they truly pop. The iQ and FJ Cruiser carry the flag for Toyota's design, in the way the Prius established its environmental leadership. Next up, the forthcoming FT-86 sports car should inject a bit of excitement in the often bland, but occasionally brilliant brand.

Der weltgrößte Automobilhersteller baute ursprünglich Spinnmaschinen, bevor er Mitte der 1930er Jahre unter dem Familiennamen „Toyoda" mit der Fertigung von Automodellen begann. 1937 wurde der Name zu „Toyota" geändert, u. a. wegen der auf Japanisch einfacheren Schreibweise. Ihren ersten „Hit" landeten die Japaner 1955 mit dem Crown. 1966 folgte der Verkaufsschlager Corolla. In den 1970ern war Toyota bereits zum drittgrößten Autobauer hinter GM und Ford aufgestiegen und für zuverlässige Fahrzeuge mit hochwertiger Ausstattung bekannt. Zusammen mit aufgekauften Unternehmen (Hino und Daihatsu) oder selbst eingeführten Marken (Lexus und Scion) ist es Toyota immer wieder gelungen, höchste Kundenzufriedenheitswerte zu erreichen. In den Nullerjahren kam das Interesse an umweltfreundlichen Hybridantrieben hinzu. Während seine Rivalen die effektiven Fertigungsprozesse der Japaner nachahmen und sogar verbessern konnten, blieb Toyota auf diesem Gebiet stecken. Die Rückrufaktionen der letzten Jahre haben sich verhängnisvoll auf Ansehen und Verkaufszahlen ausgewirkt. Aus dem breiten Angebot aus glaubwürdigen, erschwinglichen Fahrzeugen ragen nur wenige heraus. Die wenigen überragenden Modelle sind aber wahre Lichtgestalten. Der iQ und der FJ Cruiser stehen für Toyotas Designphilosophie, so wie der Prius Toyotas umwelttechnische Vorherrschaft symbolisiert. Bald soll der Sportwagen FT-86 der häufig faden, mitunter jedoch genialen Marke etwas mehr Leidenschaft verleihen.

Le plus grand constructeur de voitures au monde a commencé par construire des machines à tisser avant de se mettre aux voitures au milieu des années 1930 sous le nom de famille « Toyoda ». Ce nom est devenu « Toyota » en 1937, en partie parce qu'il était plus facile à écrire en japonais. Le premier modèle important de la marque a été la Crown de 1955, produite au Japon. La berline Corolla est arrivée en 1966, et a remporté un énorme succès de ventes. Dans les années 1970 Toyota a pris la troisième place dans les classements de ventes derrière GM et Ford, et était renommée pour fabriquer des voitures bien équipées et fiables. Toyota et les autres marques qu'elle a acquises (Hino et Daihatsu) ou créées (Lexus et Scion) ont pris l'habitude de remporter des scores très positifs lors des enquêtes sur la satisfaction des clients, tout en ouvrant une nouvelle voie dans les années 2000 pour des voitures hybrides essence/électrique plus écologiques. Au fur et à mesure que ses concurrents ont copié et raffiné ses processus de fabrication de grande qualité, Toyota a semblé sombrer. Plusieurs rappels de produits ont porté un grand préjudice à sa renommée et à ses profits. Dans son vaste portefeuille de produits abordables et compétents, rares sont les modèles qui se démarquent vraiment du reste. Mais lorsque c'est le cas, c'est un vrai feu d'artifice. L'iQ et la FJ Cruiser sont les porte-drapeaux du design de Toyota, et la Prius a fait de la marque un leader de l'environnementalisme automobile. La sportive FT-86 prévue pour bientôt devrait créer un peu d'animation autour de cette marque souvent fade mais parfois géniale.

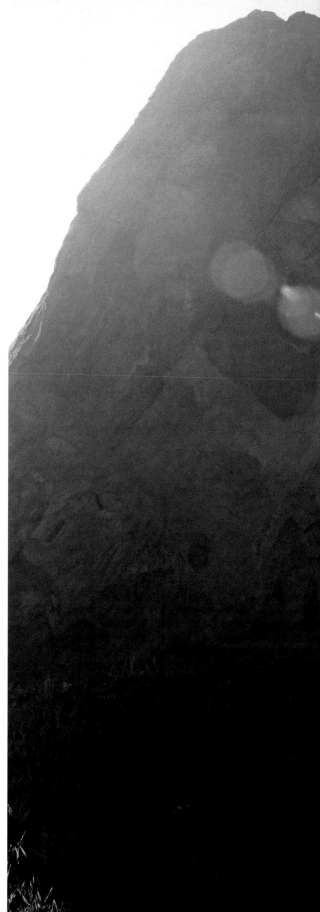

IQ
Rival: Smart ForTwo

Truly innovative tiny 4-seat city car.
Innovativer Kleinwagen mit 4 Sitzen.
Minuscule citadine à 4 places innovante.

AYGO
Rival: Peugeot 107

Great basic good value city car.
Tolles Stadtauto für Einsteiger.
Excellente citadine de base, bon marché.

YARIS | FITZ
Rival: Ford Fiesta

Decent supermini.
Anständiger Kleinwagen.
Citadine polyvalente honnête.

COROLLA
Rival: Ford Focus

World's best-selling car.
Das weltweit meistverkaufte Auto.
La voiture la plus vendue au monde.

COROLLA RUMION | RUKUS
Rival: Nissan Cube

Cool box (Scion xB US).
Cooler Kasten (in den USA: Scion xB).
Carrée, stylée (Scion xB aux États-Unis).

CAMRY
Rival: Chevy Malibu

Big sedan, big US seller, elsewhere less so.
Großlimousine, nur in den USA erfolgreich.
Berline, gros succès aux États-Unis.

CENTURY
Rival: (Used) Nissan President

Wing-mirrors-on-wings old-school limo.
Rückspiegel auf den vorderen Kotflügeln.
Limousine vieille école.

PRIUS
Rival: Honda Insight

Trailblazing hybrid soon to spawn a family.
Bahnbrechende Hybridauto-Familie.
Hybride pionnière qui va faire des petits.

RAV 4
Rival: Nissan Qashqai

The original small soft-roader.
Der kleine Original-Softroader.
Le petit 4x4 urbain original.

FJ CRUISER
Rival: Land Rover Defender

Superb retro design 4x4.
Exzellenter Allradantrieb mit Retro-Look.
4x4 au superbe design rétro.

LAND CRUISER
Rival: Jeep Grand Cherokee

4x4 legend, but bloated.
4x4-Legende, jedoch etwas aufgeblasen.
4x4 légendaire mais ballonné.

ALSO AVAILABLE

4Runner, Allion, Alphard, Auris, Avalon, Avanza, Avensis, Belta/Vios, Blade, Crown Athlete/Hybrid/Majesta/Royal, Estima/Previa, Fortuner, Harrier, Hiace, Highlander, Hilux, Isis, Innova, Liteace, Mark X/Reiz, Matrix, Noah, Passo, Porte, Premio, Probox, Ractis/Verso-S, Raum, Rush, SAI, Sequoia, Sienna, Sienta, Succeed, Tacoma, Townace, Tundra, Urban Cruiser, Vanguard, Vellfire, Venza, Voxy, WISH

TOYOTA FJ CRUISER

Retro-futuristic off-roader started life as a concept car homage to the 1960s original. Although its role has changed from schlepping across Africa to cruising Californian boulevards don't listen to the Barbie car jibes – this one's for GI Joe.

Ein retro-futuristischer Geländewagen, dessen Studie eine Hommage an das Original von 1960 war. Auch wenn er seinen Arbeitsplatz von den Steppen Afrikas auf die Glamour-Boulevards von Kalifornien verlegt hat, ist und bleibt er *das* Auto für G. I. Joe.

Ce tout-terrain rétro-futuriste a commencé sa vie en tant que concept car créé pour rendre hommage au modèle original des années 1960. Son rôle n'est plus de transbahuter ses passagers à travers l'Afrique, mais de descendre les boulevards californiens… Attention, cette voiture n'est cependant pas pour Barbie, mais plutôt pour G.I. Joe.

FJ Cruiser 4x4 MT
*MPG based on US Gallon

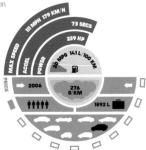

SECRET DETAIL

The FJ is part of an exclusive club of cars – including the Jaguar E-Type – that have three windscreen wipers.

Der FJ gehört – wie auch der Jaguar E-Type – zu dem exklusiven Club der Autos mit drei Scheibenwischern.

La FJ fait partie du club très fermé (auquel appartient également la Jaguar Type E) des voitures qui ont trois balais essuie-glace à l'avant.

TOYOTA IQ

The iQ is an incredible piece of design engineering. Half a meter shorter than the new Fiat 500 the iQ offers four seats, an upmarket interior and sub-100g/km CO2 emissions. Aston Martin liked the car so much it used the iQ as the base for its Cygnet super city car.

Der iQ ist eine außerordentliche Kombination aus Technik und Design. Er ist einen halben Meter kürzer als der neue Fiat 500, hat vier Sitze, ein hochwertiges Innenleben, und der CO$_2$-Ausstoß liegt unter 100 g pro km. Bei Aston Martin war man von dem iQ so begeistert, dass man ihn als Grundlage für den Kleinstwagen Cygnet verwendete.

L'iQ est un incroyable exemplaire de design technique. Elle fait 50 cm de moins en longueur que la nouvelle Fiat 500, et propose quatre places, un intérieur haut de gamme, et des émissions de CO$_2$ inférieures à 100 g/km. Aston Martin a tellement aimé cette voiture que la marque a utilisé l'iQ comme base pour sa super citadine, la Cygnet.

iQ 1.0 VVT-I

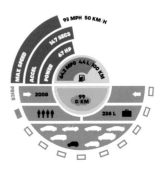

SECRET DETAIL

Key to the iQ's innovation is its '3+1' seating – with room for three adults and a child – made possible by an asymmetric dashboard, pushed further forward on the passenger side. Clever stuff.

Der Schlüssel zur Neuartigkeit des iQ sind seine 3+1 Sitze, die Platz für drei Erwachsene und ein Kind bieten. Hierfür wurde das asymmetrische Armaturenbrett auf der Beifahrerseite einfach weiter nach vorne verlagert. Gute Idee.

Les sièges « 3+1 » (trois adultes et un enfant) de l'iQ sont un élément essentiel de son caractère innovant. Cette configuration est possible grâce au tableau de bord asymétrique, qui s'avance plus du côté du passager. Malin.

TOYOTA FT-86

Sure to become the drifters' coupe de jour like the 1980s AE-86, star of cult Japanese movie *Initial D*, Toyota's long-awaited return to the sportscar market matches a classic rear-drive chassis with a boxer engine for perfect balance.

Der AE-86 von 1980 wurde zum Star des japanischen Manga-Films „Initial D". Auch vom FT-86 verspricht man sich viel. Mit der lange erwarteten Rückkehr auf den Supersportwagenmarkt liefert Toyota eine klassische Karosserie mit Hinterachsantrieb und Boxermotor in perfekter Balance.

Ce nouveau coupé de jour pour drifters se situe dans la lignée de l'AE-86 des années 1980, vedette du film japonais culte *Initial D*. C'est le retour longtemps attendu de Toyota sur le marché de la voiture de sport, et elle allie un châssis typique des véhicules à roues arrière motrices avec un moteur boxer pour un équilibre parfait.

CONCEPT LINE

FT-86 Tokyo 2009

The first unveil of the FT-86 sportscar, although it shared many styling cues from the earlier white 2007 Detroit FT-HS hybrid concept.

Die erste Präsentation des Supersport wagens FT-86 – die allerdings einige Gemeinsamkeiten mit der FT-HS Hybrid-Studie von der Detroit Auto Show 2007 aufwies.

C'est la première apparition de la sportive FT-86, bien qu'elle partage de nombreuses caractéristiques stylistiques avec le concept hybride blanc FT-HS montré à Detroit en 2007.

FT-86 G SPORT CONCEPT
Tokyo Auto Salon 2010

Modded white version for Japanese custom show with a newly vented black carbon fibre hood, large rear spoiler and new wheels.

Eine weiße Version für die japanische Kundenmesse mit Motorhaube aus Kohlefaser und überarbeiteter Belüftung, großem Rückspoiler und neuen Reifen.

Version blanche modifiée pour un custom show japonais avec un capot en fibre de carbone ventilé, un grand spoiler à l'arrière et de nouvelles roues.

FT-86 II Geneva 2011

All-black version of 'Future Toyota' is closest glimpse yet of the - Celica? - production car due late in 2011.

Die schwarze Version des „Future Toyota" lässt schon erahnen, wie das neueste, für Ende 2011 angekündigte Modell – der Celica? – aussehen wird.

La version toute noire de la « future Toyota » est l'aperçu le plus proche à ce jour de… la Celica ? Le modèle de production est prévu pour fin 2011.

VENTURI

FOUNDED: **1984**

HEADQUARTERS: **MONACO**, FRANCE

LOGO HISTORY:

Previously known for GT, Le Mans and F1 racing, Venturi changed tack in 2000 when Gildo Pallanca Pastor – grandson of the largest real estate owner in Monaco – bought the company and made it electric-only. Since then it's launched concept and production vehicles with independent product designer Sacha Lakic including the 2004 Fetish – beating Tesla to be the world's first electric two-seater sports car – the 2006 Eclectic, a golf buggy with Eames lounger-style seats, the Astrolab electro-solar hybrid sports car and the 2010 America dune buggy. Also helps pay the bills by making electric versions of Citroen Berlingo vans for the French post office. While Venturi may not be leading the charge on fossil fuel on a scale to make the Saudis scared, we love the Antarctica, an electric vehicle tailored to the demands of the frozen continent. First and foremost – leave it how you found it.

Die früher für ihre Teilnahme an GT, Le Mans und Formel 1 bekannte Marke Venturi änderte 2000 ihre Strategie, als der Milliardär Pallanca Pastor die Sportwagenmanufaktur erwarb und mit dem Bau von Elektroautos begann. Seitdem hat Venturi mit dem Produktdesigner Sacha Lakic mehrere Konzept- und Serienautos kreiert, z. B. den Fetish (womit Venturi noch vor Tesla den ersten elektrischen Zweisitzer-Sportwagen herstellte), den Eclectic (mit Sitzen im Stil der Eames Lounge Chairs), das Solar-Hybrid-Fahrzeug Astrolab und den Hightech-Buggy America. Zudem stellen die Monegassen Elektroversionen des Citroën Berlingo für die französische Post her. Die Elektroautoschmiede mag noch keine ernstzunehmende Gefahr für die ölreichen Saudis darstellen, mit dem Venturi Antarctica hat sie aber ein wundervolles Fahrzeug für die Erkundung des gefrorenen Kontinents gezaubert. Dazu haben wir nur einen Kommentar: Wenn ihr dort seid, bitte alles so lassen, wie es ist.

Anciennement connue pour la course GT, F1 et au Mans, Venturi a changé de tactique en 2000 lorsque Gildo Pallanca Pastor (le petit-fils du plus grand propriétaire immobilier de Monaco) l'a rachetée et l'a consacrée à l'électrique. La société a depuis lancé des modèles avec le concepteur indépendant Sacha Lakic, notamment la Fetish en 2004 (qui a coiffé Tesla au poteau et est devenue la première sportive électrique à deux places du monde), l'Eclectic en 2006, un buggy de golf dont les sièges rappellent les fauteuils Eames, l'Astrolab, une sportive hybride électro-solaire , et en 2010 l'America, un buggy du désert. Elle arrondit les fins de mois en fabriquant des versions électriques de la Berlingo de Citroën pour la Poste française. Venturi n'est peut-être pas assez puissante pour faire trembler les rois du pétrole, mais nous adorons l'Antartica, un véhicule électrique fait pour rouler sur le continent glacé, et pour le respecter

FETISH
Rival: Tesla S

Limited run 300,000 Euro EV sportscar.
300.000 Euro teurer Elektrosportwagen.
Voiture de sport électrique en série limitée.

ASTROLAB
Rival: Honda solar car

Solar-paneled sportscar prototype.
Sportwagenprototyp mit Solarzellendeck.
Prototype de sportive à panneaux solaires.

ECLECTIC
Rival: Golf cart

Bug-eyed designer golf cart prototype.
Golfmobil mit Wind- und Sonnenantrieb.
Prototype de voiturette de golf design.

ANTARCTICA
Rival: Snowmobile

Go-anywhere EV tractor prototype.
Für polare Forschungseinrichtungen.
Prototype électrique pour l'exploration.

AMERICA
Rival: Mini
Beachcomber concept

No-doored, fresh air, EV beach buggy.
Elektroauto ohne Türen für den Strand.
Buggy de plage électrique sans portes.

VOLAGE
Rival: Various Audi
E-Tron sports concepts

Classic Delage-inspired two-seater coupe GT.
2-sitziges Coupé mit Delage-Geschmack.
Coupé GT 2 places inspiré d'une Delage.

Venturi CEO Gildo Pallanca Pastor on board his Astrolab prototype

VOLKSWAGEN

FOUNDED: **1937**
HEADQUARTERS: **WOLFSBURG, GERMANY**
2010 PRODUCTION: **4,500,000**

LOGO HISTORY:

The humble original Beetle may still be VW's most famous model but its parent Volkswagen Group has now become the third biggest carmaker in the world in charge of eight of the globe's biggest brands – VW, Audi, Bugatti, Bentley, Lamborghini, Seat, Skoda and soon Porsche. Under the VW brand (Volkswagen = "people's car" in German) it has created some of the truly iconic late 20th everyman cars including the Beetle, Type 2 'Camper van', Polo, Golf and Scirocco. Since the 90s it has moved more upmarket (going a step too far with the Phaeton) and is now widely seen as the benchmark for well-built and high quality mainstream cars. The new Up! range is set to innovate once more for the brand, plus a recent teaser concept looks set to revive the Camper. Meanwhile a more masculine and sporty version of the Beetle brings the original icon up to date again.

Noch heute ist der bescheiden daherkommende Käfer das weltweit bekannteste Modell der Volkswagen-Gruppe. Die Wolfsburger sind inzwischen drittgrößter Fahrzeughersteller der Welt und als Eigentümer von acht der größten Automarken – VW, Audi, Bugatti, Bentley, Lamborghini, Seat, Skoda und bald Porsche – nicht gerade eine bescheiden daherkommende Firma. Auf die Marke „Volkswagen" gehen einige der legendärsten Modelle des 20. Jahrhunderts zurück, so z. B. der Käfer, der VW Bus, der Polo, der Golf und der Scirocco. Seit den 1990ern versucht die Marke, höhere Marktsegmente zu erobern (mit dem Phaeton haben sie sich jedoch etwas übernommen). Heute gilt VW als weltweiter Referenzhersteller für zuverlässigen und hochwertigen Mainstream-Autos. Das neue Serienmodell Up! soll die Innovationskraft von VW wieder einmal unter Beweis stellen, und auch der legendäre Bulli soll bald neu aufgelegt werden. Mit einer maskulineren, sportlicheren Version wird auch der VW Beetle aktualisiert.

L'humble Coccinelle d'origine est peut-être toujours le modèle le plus célèbre de VW, mais la maison mère Volkswagen AG est maintenant devenue le troisième constructeur de voitures dans le monde, et possède huit des plus grandes marques de la planète : VW, Audi, Bugatti, Bentley, Lamborghini, Seat, Skoda et bientôt Porsche. La marque VW (Volkswagen = « voiture du peuple » en allemand) a créé quelques-unes des voitures grand public les plus emblématiques du XXᵉ siècle, notamment la Coccinelle, le Combi Type 2, la Polo, la Golf et la Scirocco. Depuis les années 1990, elle s'est orientée vers le haut de gamme, et c'est maintenant la référence des voitures grand public bien construites et de qualité. La nouvelle gamme Up! devrait être une grande innovation de plus pour la marque, et un concept récemment dévoilé semble indiquer que le Combi va être ressuscité. En attendant, une version plus masculine et sportive de la Beetle remet encore une fois la légendaire Coccinelle au goût du jour.

UP!
Rival: Ford B-Max

New range of city cars set to delight.
Neue, vielversprechende Stadtauto-Reihe.
Nouvelle gamme de citadines séduisantes.

POLO
Rival: Ford Fiesta

Perfect 'less-is-more' supermini design.
Es ist erwiesen: „Weniger ist mehr."
Polyvalente minimaliste et parfaite.

GOLF
Rival: Ford Focus

Iconic hatchback six generations deep.
Schrägheck-Legende seit 6 Generationen.
Légendaire compacte, 6ᵉ génération.

NEW BEETLE
Rival: Fiat 500

Nostalgic hit, replacement on its way.
Nostalgie pur, Ersatz wird bald eingeführt.
Succès nostalgique, une nouvelle arrive.

JETTA
Rival: Ford Focus

Golf-sized sedan with many global variants.
Limousine in Golf-Größe mit Varianten.
Berline aux dimensions d'une Golf.

SCIROCCO
Rival: Peugeot RCZ

Super stylish small 2+2 coupe.
Stylisches Sportcoupé als 2+2-Sitzer.
Petit coupé 2+2 avec beaucoup de style.

PASSAT
Rival: Ford Mondeo

Quality but dull family sedan + estate.
Familienlimousine und -kombi.
Berline + break de qualité mais insipide.

TOURAN
Rival: Renault Grand Scenic

Well-built, dull compact MPV.
Hochwertiger, langweiliger Kompaktvan.
Monospace compact insipide mais bien fait.

SHARAN
Rival: Renault Espace

Well-built, dull large MPV.
Hochwertiger, langweiliger Großminivan.
Grand monospace insipide mais bien fait.

TOUAREG
Rival: Lexus RX

Smart, large SUV, hybrid option.
Großes, praktisches SUV mit Hybrid-Option.
Grand SUV élégant avec option hybride.

TIGUAN
Rival: Ford Kuga

Competent, compact SUV. Still a bit dull.
Kompakt-SUV hoher Qualität. Etwas reizlos.
SUV compact et compétent.

ALSO AVAILABLE

Fox, Golf Plus, Gol, Parati, Sagitar, Passat CC, Lavida, Santana, Phaeton, Sharan, Eos.

VOLKSWAGEN UP!

More than a new model, the Up! signals a new range of small vehicles from a tiny sub-Fox-sized city car to a super compact camper van. All will maximize interior space. As the cars only start arriving in early 2012, details at the time of going to press are scarce but the string of concepts shown since 2007 reveal the various potential directions – including this London Taxi concept from 2010.

Mehr als nur ein neues Modell: Der Up! ist der Startschuss für eine neue Reihe von Kleinfahrzeugen. Diese reicht von einem winzigen Kleinstwagen (kleiner als der Fox) bis hin zu einem superkompakten Wohnmobil und soll viel Platz im Innenraum bieten. Da die Autos erst Anfang 2012 auf den Markt kommen sollen, sind die Presseinfos derzeit dürftig, aber die seit 2007 gezeigten Studien – einschließlich die vom London Taxi aus dem Jahr 2010 – lassen etwas von dem Potenzial erahnen, das dahinter steckt.

Up! propose bien plus que quelques nouveaux modèles. C'est une nouvelle gamme de petits véhicules, depuis une citadine minuscule, encore plus petite que la Fox, jusqu'à un van combi super compact. Tous les modèles maximiseront leur espace intérieur. Comme ils n'arriveront que début 2012, au moment où nous écrivons ces lignes les détails concrets sont rares, mais les concepts montrés depuis 2007 indiquent plusieurs directions possibles, comme ce concept de taxi londonien de 2010.

CONCEPT LINE

UP! Frankfurt 2007

Rear-engined car. VW had a major re-think since.

Mit Heckmotor. Wurde noch mal überdacht.

Voiture à roues motrices arrière. VW a complètement changé d'avis depuis.

SPACE UP! Tokyo 2007

Bigger suicide-doored concept with camper van vibe.

Größere Studie mit Flügeltüren und Wohnmobil-Ambitionen.

Concept plus grand doté de portes suicide et d'un air de combi.

SPACE UP! BLUE LA 2007

More camper van overtones with Samba-style roof windows.

Mehr Wohnmobil-Elemente und Dachfenster, die an den Samba erinnern.

Encore un air de combi, et des fenêtres de toit de Samba.

E-UP! Frankfurt 2009

Electric 3+1 seater prefaces production EV for 2013.

Elektrisch angetriebener 3+1-Sitzer, der voraussichtlich 2013 auf den Markt kommt.

Une 3+1 places électrique qui préface la production de l'EV pour 2013.

UP! LITE LA 2009

Hybrid with close-able front grille to improve aerodynamics.

Hybrid mit automatisch schließbarem Kühlergrill zur Erhöhung der Aerodynamik.

Hybride avec une calandre qui se ferme à l'avant pour améliorer l'aérodynamique.

VOLKSWAGEN SCIROCCO

More fun, better looking and yet cheaper than the Golf GTI with which it shares much of its guts. Be sure to smile smugly at badge-obsessed hot hatchers because as far as all-rounders go, the Scirocco's a knockout. Guaranteed future classic.

Mehr Fahrspaß, besseres Aussehen und günstigerer Preis als der Golf GTI, mit dem es allerdings einige Gemeinsamkeiten gibt. Vergessen Sie nicht, den markengeilen Kompaktwagenfahrern beim Einsteigen ein arrogantes Lächeln zuzuwerfen, denn der Scirocco ist die absolute Wucht. Ein Klassiker mit Zukunft.

Plus amusante à conduire, plus belle et pourtant moins chère que la Golf GTI, avec laquelle elle partage une grande partie de ses entrailles. Prenez soin d'adresser un sourire arrogant aux propriétaires de compactes sportives obsédés par les logos, car la Scirocco est douée en tout, et pulvérise toutes les autres. Ce sera à coup sûr un grand classique.

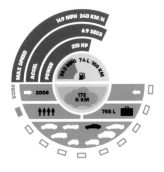

SECRET DETAIL

Its designers created a roofline so low that the boot hinges have to protrude in a pair of discreet humps.

Die Dachlinie ist so niedrig, dass die Heckklappenscharniere als zwei kleine Wölbungen herausragen.

Ses créateurs ont dessiné une ligne de toit tellement basse que les charnières du coffre sont obligées de dépasser et de former deux petites bosses.

VOLKSWAGEN BEETLE

One of the world's most iconic cars – 21.5m sales and counting – gets a new look for 2011. The easiest way to see the difference is to look at the profiles. In a bid to reference the original 1938 Beetle better the 2011 model is made up of two simple curved lines with a longer hood while the former 1998 'New Beetle' almost has a third curve at the rear.

Der VW Käfer ist mit über 21,5 Millionen verkauften Exemplaren eine der größten Autolegenden aller Zeiten. 2011 tritt er mit einem neuen Look auf. Am einfachsten erkennt man den Unterschied im Profil: Das 2011er-Modell erinnert ein bisschen an den Original-Käfer von 1938. Zwei schlichte Kurven und eine längere Motorhaube unterscheiden ihn vom 1998er „New Beetle", der eine dritte Kurve am Heck hatte.

C'est l'une des voitures les plus emblématiques au monde (21,5 millions d'unités vendues à ce jour). Elle s'offre un relookage pour 2011. Pour voir la différence, le plus facile est de regarder le profil. Pour mieux faire allusion à la Coccinelle originale de 1938, le modèle 2011 se compose de deux courbes simples avec un capot plus long, tandis que l'ancienne « New Beetle » de 1998 amorce une troisième courbe à l'arrière.

Beetle 1.6 Bluemotion manual
* Estimated max speed and acceleration

SECRET DETAIL

A criticism of the 1998 model was its overly cartoon-ish character. The 2011 model aims to address that with a longer, wider and lower stance and a more masculine interior. No flower vase then.

Einer der wichtigsten Kritikpunkte des Modells von 1998 war sein Comic-ähnliches Aussehen. Das Modell von 2011 gleicht dies mit einer längeren, breiteren und niedrigeren Statur sowie mit einem maskulineren Inneren aus. Keine Blumenvase diesmal …

Le modèle de 1998 était critiqué parce qu'il faisait trop dessin animé. Le modèle de 2011 cherche à rectifier cela avec une posture plus longue, plus large et plus basse, et un intérieur plus masculin. Oubliez les petites fleurs.

VOLVO

FOUNDED: **1927**

HEADQUARTERS: **GOTHENBURG, SWEDEN**

2010 PRODUCTION: **373,525**

LOGO HISTORY:

With roots as a subsidiary of ball-bearing maker SKF, Volvo (Latin for "I roll") grew to become the biggest Swedish car brand in the world in the latter half of the 20th century. Safety has always been one of its key selling points. It invented the modern three-point seatbelt, standard on all Volvo cars since 1959, and introduced laminated glass (1944), padded dashboards (1956) and more recently fully self-braking cars (City Safety 2009). Stylistically, its boxy shape signified solid, earthy Scandinavian quality. Under Ford's ownership, Volvo maintained its independent point of view, insisting on maintaining the same safety and environmental standards as its cars, leading to the progressive and attractive XC90 hit model. Sold by Ford in 2010 to China-based Geely, it is slowly trying to outgrow its image as safe middle-class family transport and create more design-conscious models for younger drivers. The electric C30 is a step in that direction, as is a recent luxurious but restrained concept sedan. But we question why Volvo would ever want to escape its image – it's the most human car brand there is.

Der ursprünglich als Tochtergesellschaft des Kugellagerfabrikants SKF gegründete Automobilhersteller Volvo (lateinisch für „ich rolle") wurde in der zweiten Hälfte des 20. Jahrhunderts zur größten schwedischen Automarke. Dabei war schon immer die Sicherheit eines der wichtigsten Verkaufsargumente von Volvo. Die Schweden erfanden den Dreipunktgurt, der seit 1959 zur Standardausstattung aller Modelle gehört, und führten Windschutzscheiben aus Verbundglas (1944), gepolsterte Armaturenbretter (1956) und erst neulich das Notbremssystem City Safety (2009) ein. Aus stilistischer Sicht stehen die kastigen Volvo-Formen für solide, skandinavische Qualitätsautos. Nach der Übernahme durch Ford behielt Volvo seine unabhängige Sicht und konzentrierte sich weiterhin auf sicherheits- und umwelttechnische Aspekte, wie der fortschrittliche und attraktive XC90 beweist. 2010 verkaufte Ford seine Volvo-Anteile an den chinesischen Hersteller Geely. Seitdem versucht der Autobauer aus Göteborg das Image des sicheren Mittelklasse-Familienwagens abzustreifen und sucht nach neuen Designs, die ein jüngeres Publikum ansprechen sollen. Einen ersten Schritt in diese Richtung stellt der Elektro-C30 dar, ein zwar luxuriöses, jedoch zurückhaltendes Limousinenkonzept. Doch es stellt sich die Frage, ob ein neues Image überhaupt notwendig ist – Volvo ist doch die menschlichste Marke der Welt.

Volvo (« Je roule » en latin) a commencé en tant que filiale du fabricant de roulements à bille SKF, et est devenue la plus grande marque automobile suédoise dans la deuxième moitié du XXᵉ siècle. La sécurité a toujours été l'un de ses plus grands arguments de vente. Elle a inventé la ceinture de sécurité à trois points moderne, en série sur toutes les Volvo depuis 1959, et a lancé le verre feuilleté (1944), les tableaux de bord rembourrés (1956) et plus récemment des voitures qui freinent seules (City Safety 2009). Du point de vue du style, la forme carrée signifiait solidité et qualité scandinave pragmatique. Volvo a conservé son point de vue indépendant lorsque Ford l'a rachetée, et a insisté pour conserver ses qualités en matière de sécurité et d'environnement, ce qui a conduit au succès du modèle XC90. Ford a vendu la marque à la chinoise Geely en 2010, et Volvo essaie de sortir des limites de son image de moyen de transport familial et sûr pour les classes moyennes en créant des modèles au style plus affûté pour les jeunes conducteurs. La C30 électrique est un pas dans cette direction, tout comme un récent concept de berline luxueuse mais sobre. Mais nous nous demandons bien pourquoi Volvo veut échapper à son image : c'est la marque automobile la plus humaine qui existe.

C30 Rival: Audi A3		Sporty 3dr coupe, electric version coming. 3-türiges Sportcoupé, bald auch elektrisch. Coupé sportif 3 portes, bientôt électrique.
C70 Rival: BMW 3 Series		Not so good metal-roofed coupe/cabrio. Coupé/Cabrio mit Stahlklappdach, naja ... Coupé/cabriolet pas très réussi.
S40|V50 Rival: Ford Focus		Compact sedan (S) and estate (V). Kompaktlimousine (S) und Kombi (V). Berline (S) et break (V) compacts.
S60|V60 Rival: BMW 3 Series		Alternative new family sedan (S) & estate (V). Renovierte Mittelklasse-Limousine. Nouvelle berline familiale (S) et break (V).

S80 Rival: Merc E-Class		Large, well-made but fairly dull sedan. Gut gebaute Limousine ohne Reiz. Grande berline bien faite mais insipide.
V70 Rival: Audi A6 Avant		Brand-defining, large, safe, family wagon. Groß und sicher ... der Volvo schlechthin. Grand break familial très sûr.
XC60 Rival: BMW X3		Compact SUV with curvy new design. Kompakt-SUV mit kurvenreichem Design. SUV compact qui a gagné des courbes.
XC90 Rival: BMW X5		Safe, 7st SUV driven mainly by mums. Groß, sicher, 7 Sitze: Alle Mütter lieben es. Grand monospace très sûr à 7 places.

VOLVO XC60

Another smoothed-out Volvo
with more curves and a world-first
City Safety system designed to
reduce low-speed but high-cost
rear end shunts by slamming on
the brakes if the driver forgets.
A very decent compact SUV
Crossover.

Ein weiterer geglätteter Volvo
mit mehr Kurven und dem ersten
City Safety-System der Welt, mit
dem Auffahrunfälle bei niedriger
Geschwindigkeit durch eine
automatische Notbremsung
vermieden werden sollen. Ein
wirklich ordentlicher kompakter
Crossover-SUV.

Encore une Volvo lissée, avec
plus de courbes et un système
City Safety de première classe
conçu pour réduire les coûteux
chocs arrière à faible vitesse en
écrasant les freins si le conducteur
oublie de le faire. Un SUV
crossover compact tout à fait
honnête.

**XC60 D3 DRIVe R-Design
manual**

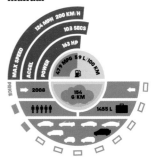

SECRET DETAIL

The XC60 was the first Volvo to get the new corporate front face – with its diagonal thin side lights that put 'quote marks' around the more 3D and bigger badged grille.

Der XC60 war der erste Wagen, der das neue Volvo-Gesicht erhielt: Die diagonalen schmalen Seitenlichter wirken wie Fragezeichen, die den nun plastischeren und größeren, mit Logo versehenen Grill umrahmen.

La XC60 a été la première Volvo à recevoir le nouvel avant de la marque, avec ses phares minces et en biais qui flanquent de leurs « apostrophes » la calandre plus grande et plus tridimensionnelle qui porte le logo.

VOLVO C30

Volvo has struggled with its identity ever since the 1970s when it became synonymous with safe and boxy family transport. The C30 coupe has gone some way to address that with a good-looking four-seater that harks back to both the 1980s 480 and 1960s P1800 coupe.

Volvo kämpft seit den 1970ern mit seiner Identität. Seit damals hat die Marke den Ruf, Hersteller für sichere, aber kastige Familienautos zu sein. Mit dem C30 Coupé versucht man, diesem Ruf entgegenzuwirken. Der gut aussehende Viersitzer erinnert ein wenig an den 480 von 1980 und den P1800 Coupé von 1960.

Volvo essaie de se réconcilier avec son identité depuis les années 1970, lorsque cette marque est devenue synonyme de transport familial carré et sûr. Le coupé C30 apporte un élément de réponse avec une belle quatre places qui évoque à la fois la 480 des années 1980 et le coupé P1800 des années 1960.

C30 DRIVe SE Start/Stop

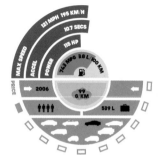

SECRET DETAIL

Volvo has recently started making full-electric versions of the C30 and is intending to lease them to customers from late 2011.

Volvo hat kürzlich damit begonnen, vollständig elektrisch betriebene Versionen des C30 herzustellen. Voraussichtlich ab Ende 2011 können diese geleast werden.

Vovlo s'est récemment mise à fabriquer des versions entièrement électriques de la C30 et a l'intention de les proposer en leasing à partir de fin 2011.

WESTFIELD

LOGO HISTORY:

Like all the best British car firms Westfield was born out of an enthusiast's garage before moving onto bigger premises. It's been building small, lightweight sports and racecars since 1983, in kit, or fully built form. Currently offering a light and fast on-road or track range to rival the Caterham 7 based around its SE model, with either GM or Ford engines, Westfield remains a well respected name in the sports car industry. However 2010 also saw Westfield enter a joint venture with a Malaysian vehicle manufacturer DRB-HICOM to develop and produce eco-friendly niche machines for a global audience. Big plans for a small and capable company.

Wie alle große Autofirmen aus Großbritannien wuchs Westfield aus dem Keim einer kleinen Garage, in der begeisterte Tüftler ihrer Leidenschaft nachgingen. Seit 1983 baut die Manufaktur leichte Sport- und Rennwagen, als Kit-Cars oder in der Großversion. Zurzeit werden leichte, schnelle Fahrzeuge der SE-Reihe mit GM- oder Ford-Motoren angeboten, die dem Carterham 7 das Leben schwer machen sollen und den guten Ruf der Marke Westfield festigen. Zu erwähnen ist außerdem das Joint Venture der Briten mit dem malaysischen Autobauer DRB-HICOM für die Entwicklung und Produktion umweltfreundlicher Fahrzeuge für eine weltweite Kundschaft. Große Pläne für eine kleine, jedoch sehr kompetente Firma.

Comme toutes les meilleures compagnies automobiles britanniques, Westfield est née dans le garage d'un enthousiaste avant de déménager dans des locaux plus spacieux. Depuis 1983, elle construit de petites voitures de sport et de course légères, en kit ou déjà assemblées. Avec sa gamme actuelle de véhicules rapides et légers pour la route ou les circuits, structurés autour du modèle SE et équipés de moteurs GM ou Ford qui concurrencent la Caterham 7, Westfield reste un nom respecté dans le secteur des voitures de course. En 2010 la marque a conclu une joint-venture avec un fabricant automobile malaisien, DRB-HICOM, pour développer et produire des engins écologiques de niche pour un public mondial. De grandes ambitions pour une petite société très compétente.

WESTFIELD SE

Rival: Caterham 7

Light and fast, on road or track.
Leicht und schnell auf Straße und Rennstrecke zugleich.
Légère et rapide, sur la route ou les circuits.

WIESMANN

FOUNDED: **1985**
HEADQUARTERS: **DÜLMEN, GERMANY**

LOGO HISTORY:

With a factory as individually styled as its retro-modern coupes and roadsters, Wiesmann has carved a niche for small volume, hand-built sports cars with BMW engines and transmissions. Set up by the Wiesmann brothers, the company produces hardtops for convertible cars alongside its own vehicles. Badged with a gecko, the factory is designed to ape the small lizard's shape. Odd. The product range currently consists of the Roadster and GT models, both selling reasonably well in Germany and throughout Europe. Individual styling nods to the past, with both Wiesmanns looking like something Dick Tracy might drive. Quickly.

Die Automanufaktur, dessen Firmengebäude so stylisch wie ihre Retro-Coupés und -Roadsters ist, hat sich eine Nische für kleine, handgefertigte Sportwagen mit BMW-Antriebstechnik geschaffen. Die von den Wiesmann-Brüdern gegründete Firma stellt Hardtops für Cabrios sowie eigene Fahrzeuge her. Das Firmenlogo – ein Gecko – ist in der Form des neuen Werksgebäudes präsent. Seltsam sieht es aus. Zurzeit umfasst die Produktpalette die Roadster- und GT-Modelle, die sowohl in Deutschland als auch im übrigen Europa zahlreiche Anhänger gefunden haben. Beim Anblick der im Retro-Design gehaltenen Wiesmann-Fahrzeuge glaubt man, in einen Film über das Chicago der 1930er Jahre eingetaucht zu sein.

L'usine et les coupés et roadsters rétro-modernes de Wiesmann ont tous un style très individuel. La marque s'est creusé une niche pour les petites voitures de sport construites à la main avec des moteurs et transmissions BMW. Créée par les frères Wiesmann, la société produit des toits rigides pour les voitures décapotables parallèlement à ses propres véhicules. Son logo est un gecko, et l'usine reproduit la forme de ce petit lézard. Insolite. La gamme de produits est actuellement composée des modèles Roadster et GT, qui se vendent raisonnablement bien en Allemagne et dans toute l'Europe. Leur design très personnel fait un clin d'œil au passé : elles auraient pu être conduites (à toute berzingue) par Dick Tracy.

ROADSTER
Rival: Morgan Aero 8

Old looks, modern performance.
Altmodisches Aussehen, moderne Leistung.
Style rétro, performances modernes.

GT
Rival: Morgan Aeromax

Like the roadster only less draughty.
Wie der Roadster, nur nicht so schnittig.
Idem, mais avec moins de courants d'air.

WIESMANN GT MF5

Lightweight, graphic novel retro looks and mighty BMW power combine in German brand Wiesmann's riposte to its countrymen's perceived lack of humour. With 555hp the performance should make you laugh like a child too.

Der leichtfüßige, an alte Graphic Novels erinnernde Look und die gewaltige BMW-Power sind die Antwort von Wiesmann auf den Vorwurf, die Deutschen hätten keinen Humor. Und die sagenhafte Leistung von 555 PS lässt uns ebenfalls erfreut auflachen.

La légèreté, un look rétro de roman graphique et la puissance du moteur BMW s'allient dans la riposte de Wiesmann au cliché selon lequel les Allemands manqueraient d'humour. Avec 555 chevaux, sa performance devrait vous faire rire aux anges.

GT MF5
* Estimated price

193 MPH 311 KM H · 3.9 SECS · 555 HP · 224 MPG 10.7 L /100 KM · 2008 · 281 G/KM · 260 L

PRICE · MAX SPEED · ACCEL. · POWER

SECRET DETAIL

Wiesmann's cars are all built in a factory that's shaped like the gecko which features in the company's badge.

Die Autos von Wiesmann werden in einem Werk geschaffen, das die Form des Geckos hat, aus dem das Logo der Marke besteht.

Les voitures de Wiesmann sont toutes fabriquées dans une usine qui a la forme du gecko qui trône sur le logo de la société.

WULING

CN

FOUNDED: **2002**

HEADQUARTERS: **GUANGXI, CHINA**

2010 PRODUCTION: **1,149,060**

LOGO HISTORY:

With its eye on the less populous, and historically poorer peoples of China's vast interior land mass, Wuling is a joint-venture between General Motors and domestic manufacturer, SAIC. Its target market is reflected in its humble, no-frills range of vehicles that focuses on simple, robust vans, minivans and pick-ups. Breaking the million-unit barrier underlines its huge success and market, while China's rural regions are expected to be the next big growth area as authorities begin to tighten up on the issuing of licenses in crowded cities.

Das Joint Venture zwischen General Motors und dem chinesischen Anbieter SAIC hat sich als Zielgebiet die dünner besiedelten und historisch weniger wohlhabenden binnenländischen Regionen Chinas vorgenommen. Passend dazu besteht die Fahrzeugflotte aus einfachen, schnörkellosen, robusten Vans, Minivans und Pick-ups. Mit über einer Million verkauften Fahrzeugen beweist Wuling, dass die Strategie zukunftsträchtig ist, zumal die ländlichen Gebiete große Wachstumschancen versprechen, nachdem die Regierung die Fahrzeugzulassungen in den überfüllten Städten einschränken will.

Wuling est une joint-venture entre General Motors et le fabricant chinois SAIC. Cette marque cible les populations moins nombreuses et historiquement plus pauvres des immenses territoires intérieurs du pays. Sa gamme de véhicules humbles et sans fioritures reflète cette stratégie avec des camionnettes, des monovolumes et des pick-ups simples et robustes. Elle a dépassé le seuil du million d'unités vendues, ce qui montre à quel point son succès et son marché sont énormes. De plus, les régions rurales de la Chine seront les prochaines grandes zones de croissance car le gouvernement commence à délivrer moins de licences dans les villes surpeuplées.

MINI CAR
Rival: Chery QQ3

Badge-engineered Chevrolet Matiz.
Version des Chevrolet Matiz.
Chevrolet Matiz rebadgée.

RONGGUANG
Rival: A small van

Great economy, folding-seat minivan.
Sparsamer Minivan mit Klappsitzen.
Excellent monovolume économique.

HONGGUANG
Rival: A big van

More refined business and leisure MPV.
Feiner Minivan für Geschäft und Freizeit.
Monospace plus raffiné.

XINGWANG
Rival: Dongfeng K07

Rudimentary van-based people carrier.
Rudimentärer Minivan.
Monospace-camionnette rudimentaire.

SUNSHINE
Rival: Shineray Mini Van

As above only bigger.
Wie oben, nur größer.
Comme ci-dessus, mais en plus grand.

CARS
NOW

INDEX

LIGHTSPEED

BAC MONO ①

Beautifully sculptured,
beautifully fast.

Vollendetes Design,
atemberaubende Schnelligkeit.

Magnifiquement sculptée,
magnifiquement rapide.

Mono
* Estimated CO2 emissions and MPG

KTM X-BOW ②

Superbike with four wheels.
Superbike auf vier Rädern.
Supermoto à quatre roues.

X-Bow Street

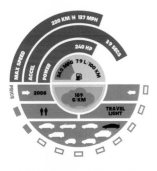

CATERHAM SUPERLIGHT CSR ③

Less weight, more speed.
Weniger Gewicht, mehr Geschwindigkeit.
Moins de poids, plus de vitesse.

CSR 260

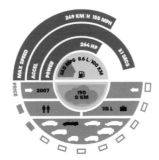

LOTUS EXIGE ④

Faster, more brilliant Elise with a fixed roof.
Schnellerer Elise mit festem Dach.
Elise plus rapide avec un toit fixe.

Exige S

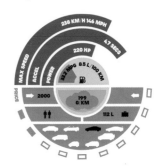

CITY CAR

FIAT 500 ②

Small, cute, hugely popular.
Klein, süß, unheimlich beliebt.
Petite, mignonne, extrêmement populaire.

500 1.4 16v Sport

MAX SPEED · ACCEL · POWER
113 MPH 182 KM/H
10.5 SECS
100 HP
42 MPG 6.3 L/100 KM
PRICE
2008
149 G/KM
550 L

SMART FORTWO ED ③

Electric version of the ForTwo.
Elektroversion des ForTwo.
Version électrique de la ForTwo.

ForTwo ED

MAX SPEED · ACCEL · POWER
100 KM/H 62 MPH
KIND OF ...
41 HP
85 MILES 137 KM
PRICE
2007
ZERO G/KM
220 L

MITSUBISHI IMIEV ④

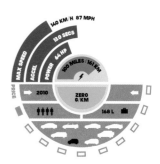

Plug it in and drive – but not very far.
Aufladen und los ... aber nicht so weit.
Branchez et conduisez, mais pas trop loin.

iMiEV

MAX SPEED · ACCEL · POWER
140 KM/H 87 MPH
13.0 SECS
64 HP
100 MILES 161 KM
PRICE
2010
ZERO G/KM
168 L

Truly innovative tiny city car package.

Wirklich innovatives Kleinstauto.

Minuscule citadine vraiment innovante.

iQ 1.0 VVT-I

RENAULT TWIZY ⑤

Chic, back-to-basics city car.
Schickes, einfaches Stadtauto.
Citadine chic qui retourne à l'essentiel.

Twizy Urban

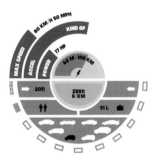

TATA NANO ⑥

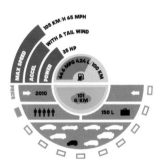

Cheapest car in the world (circa $3000).
Billigstes Auto der Welt (ca. 3.000 USD, 2000 EUR).
La moins chère du monde (env. 2 000 EUR).

Nano

ASTON MARTIN CYGNET ⑦

Designer suited Toyota iQ city car.
Kleinstwagen auf Toyota iQ-Basis.
La citadine Toyota iQ en habits de gala.

Cygnet

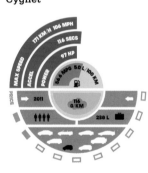

POCKET ROCKET

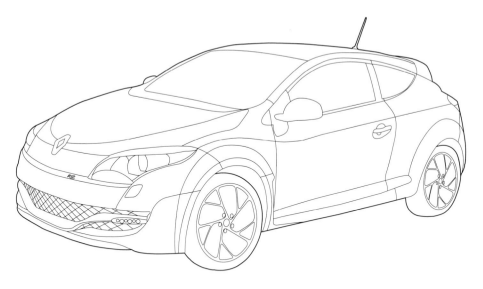

RENAULT MEGANE RENAULTSPORT ①

250hp version great, new 265hp better.

250 PS war gut, 265 PS ist besser.

Superbe en 250 ch., encore mieux en 265 ch.

Megane Renaultsport 250

252 KM/H 156 MPH
61 SECS
250 HP
33.6 MPG 8.4 L/100 KM
MAX SPEED · ACCEL · POWER
PRICE
2009
190 G/KM
991 L

BMW 1M COUPE ②

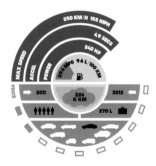

More muscle than Venice Beach's Gold's
Mehr Muskeln als im Fitnessstudio.
Plus de muscles qu'à Venice Beach.

1M Coupe

250 KM/H 155 MPH
4.9 SECS
340 HP
27.4 MPG 9.6 L/100 KM
MAX SPEED · ACCEL · POWER
PRICE
2011   2012
224 G/KM
370 L

CITROEN DS3 ③

Not fully-convincing posh C3 with add-ons.
C3-Upgrade mit Add-ons, kleine Schwächen.
C3 snob, pas vraiment convaincante.

DS3 1.6 THP DSport

214 KM/H 133 MPH
7.3 SECS
154 HP
42.2 MPG 6.7 L/100 KM
MAX SPEED · ACCEL · POWER
PRICE
2010
155 G/KM
285 L

ALFA ROMEO MITO CLOVERLEAF ④

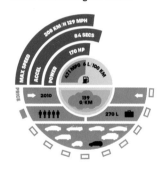

The car formerly known as Cloverleaf still gives great g
Das ehemalige „Kleeblatt" kann immer noch begeister
Ancienne Quadrifoglio, elle en a toujours sous le capot

MiTo Quadrifoglio Verde

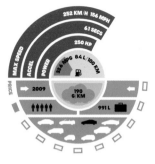

208 KM/H 129 MPH
8.4 SECS
170 HP
47.1 MPG 6 L/100 KM
MAX SPEED · ACCEL · POWER
PRICE
2010
139 G/KM
270 L

COMPACT COUPE

Self-declared 'world's-first hybrid sports car'.

„Erster Hybrid-Sportwagen der Welt."

« Première sportive hybride au monde. »

CR-Z Hybrid

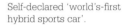

VOLKSWAGEN
SCIROCCO

Super stylish small 2+2 coupe.
Stylisches Sportcoupé als 2+2-Sitzer.
Petit coupé 2+2 avec beaucoup de style.

Scirocco 2.0 TSI GT

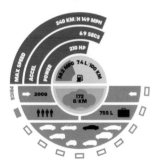

PEUGEOT
RCZ

Striking, brand-building coupe.
Schlüsselmodell der Marke.
Superbe coupé qui revalorise la marque.

RCZ 1.6 THP 200 GT manual

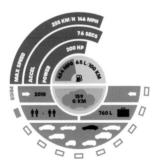

MINI
COUPE

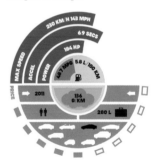

New go-faster, chopped two-seater.
2-Sitzer mit mehr Geschwindigkeit.
Nouvelle 2 places rapide et ciselée.

Cooper S Coupe

ALTERNATIVE

Asymmetric boxcar design
genius.

Asymmetrische Kiste mit tollem
Design.

Voiture carrée et asymétrique,
design génial.

Cube 1.6 manual Kaizen

KIA SOUL

Kia's take on cool boxy van-car vibe.
Cooles, kastiges Van-Auto.
La voiture carrée branchée selon Kia.

Soul 1.6 CRDi 2

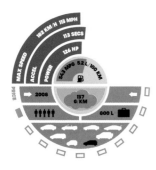

NISSAN MURANO CROSSCABRIOLET ③

Sawn-off SUV is in a league of its own.
Kurzer SUV – eine Größe für sich.
SUV à canon scié hors toutes catégories.

Murano Crosscabriolet 3.5 V6
* MPG based on US gallon

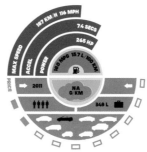

MORGAN 3-WHEELER ④

As its name suggests.
Der Name ist Programm.
Comme son nom le suggère, à trois roues.

3-Wheeler
* Estimated CO2 emissions

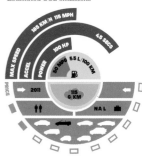

CABRIOLET

Less ferocious, still desirable.

Weniger wild, aber dennoch begehrenswert.

Moins féroce, mais toujours désirable.

California

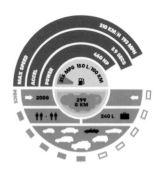

PORSCHE BOXSTER SPYDER ②

Brilliant roadster, lozenge looks.
Toller Roadster mit Rauten-Look.
Excellent roadster en losange.

Boxster 3.4 Spyder manual

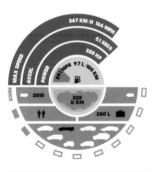

MAZDA MX-5 ③

Genre-reviving roadster, still brilliant.
Die Renaissance des Roadster – genial.
Roadster qui a réinventé son genre.

MX-5 2.0 Sport

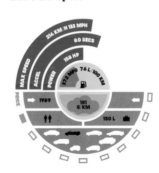

DAIHATSU COPEN ④

World's smallest sports car.
Das kleinste Sportauto der Welt.
La plus petite voiture de sport du monde.

Copen

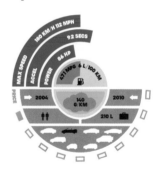

CROSSOVER

The modern face of Range Rover.

So sieht Range Rover heute aus.

Le visage moderne de Range Rover.

Evoque Coupe eD4 2WD
* Estimated CO2 emissions and MPG

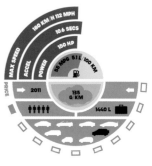

BMW X6

Huge SUV/coupe drives well but pointless.
SUV/Coupé, gutes Fahrgefühl, sonst nichts.
Gros SUV/coupé, roule bien, ne rime à rien

X6 xDrive50i

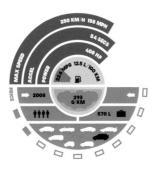

AUDI Q3

Q7 mini-me tails on Countryman rival.
Eine kleine Version des Q7.
Mini Q7 qui talonne la Countryman.

Q3 2.0TDI 2WD manual
* Estimated CO2 emissions

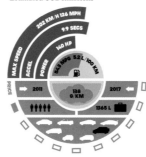

NISSAN JUKE ④

Bold jacked-up supermini/SUV/coupe.
Supermini/SUV/Coupé – ganz mutig.
Polyvalente/SUV/coupé surélevé.

Juke 1.6 Tekna 5-speed manual

UTILITY

Ancient but iconic.

Alt, aber legendär.

Antique mais légendaire.

Defender 90 Hard Top 3dr

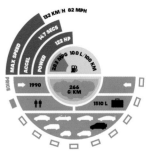

**MERCEDES-BENZ
G-WAGEN** ②

Ancient but brilliant boxyt 4x4.
Uralter Allradantrieb, immer noch fein.
4x4 carré antique mais excellent.

G55 AMG

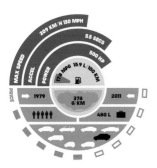

**LOCAL MOTORS
RALLY FIGHTER** ③

Open-source serious off-roader.
Offroader nach dem Open Source-Prinzip
Tout-terrain en source libre qui ne plaisante pas.

Rally Fighter

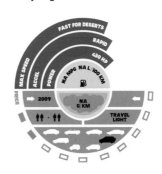

**TOYOTA
FJ CRUISER** ④

Superb retro design 4x4.
Exzellenter Allradantrieb mit Retro-Look.
4x4 au superbe design rétro.

FJ Cruiser 4x4 MT
*MPG based on US Gallon

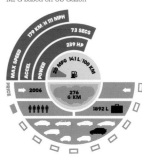

SPORTING COUPE

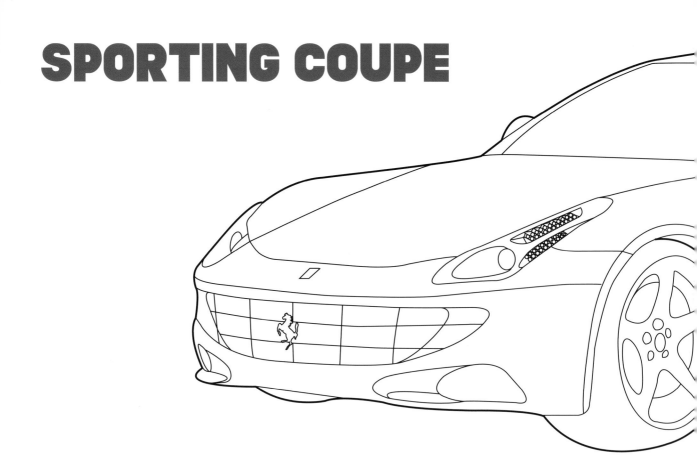

ROLLS-ROYCE PHANTOM COUPE

Enormous two-door ship.
2-sitziger Riesenschiff.
Énorme bateau deux portes.

Phantom Coupe

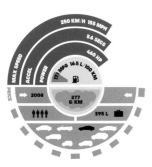

BENTLEY CONTINENTAL GT

Freshly-tailored new-money tourer.
Junger Sporttourer für Neureiche.
Nouveau tourisme pour fortunes récentes.

Continental GT

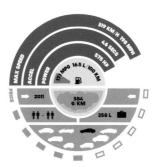

ASTON MARTIN RAPIDE

4-door, 4-seat successful stretch of DB9.
4-Türer, 4-Sitzer, Weiterentwicklung des DB9.
DB9 allongée, 4 portes, 4 places.

Rapide

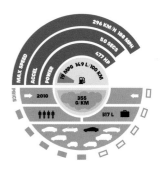

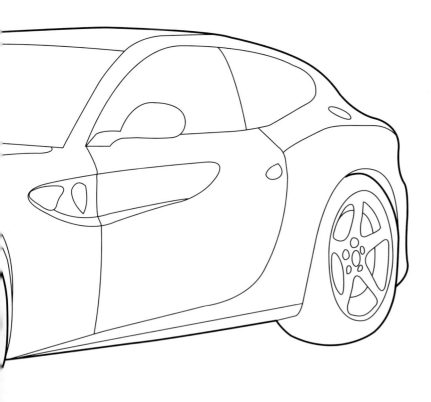

FERRARI
FF

4x4 hatchback, works well.

Gut laufender 4x4 mit Fließheck.

Break 4x4 qui roule bien.

FF

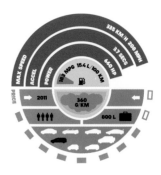

JAGUAR
XF

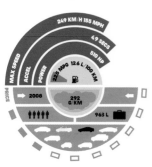

4-dr coupe, ace interior, go-fast V8 XFR.
4-türiges Coupé, Luxus-Interieur, V8-Motor.
Coupé 4 portes, bel intérieur et moteur V8.

XFR 5.0 V8 Supercharged

CADILLAC
CTS–V COUPE

Angular good looks, V8 power. Nice.
Eckig und dennoch attraktiv, V8-Power.
Beauté angulaire, puissance du V8. Pas mal.

CTS V-Coupe
* MPG based on US gallons

CHEVROLET
CAMARO

Great 21st century muscle car.
Klein, stark, legendär und zukunftstauglich.
Excellente muscle car du XXIᵉ siècle.

Camaro SS
* MPG based on US gallons

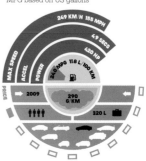

ECO LUXE

All-electric family sedan due in 2012.

Elektro-Familienlimousine, ab 2012.

Berline familiale électrique pour 2012.

Model S Signature
* Estimated luggage space

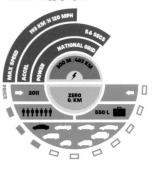

FISKER KARMA ②

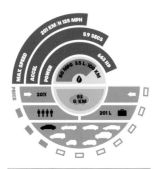

Beautiful conscience-salving sedan.
Wunderschöne Sportlimousine für ein gutes Umweltgewissen.
Superbe berline sportive qui soulage les consciences.

Karma

HONDA FCX CLARITY ③

Truly ground-breaking hydrogen fuel-cell.
Wasserstoffbetriebenes Brennstoffzellenauto.
Pile à hydrogène révolutionnaire.

FCX Clarity

TESLA ROADSTER ④

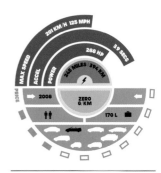

Electric and sporting dreams combine.
Elektrisch und sportlich zugleich.
L'électrique et le sport se rejoignent.

Roadster

LIMOUSINE

ROLLS-ROYCE GHOST

Exclusive large luxury sedan.

Exklusive Luxuslimousine der Oberklasse.

Grande berline de luxe exclusive.

Ghost

BENTLEY MULSANNE

184mph Blenheim Palace.
296 km/h schneller Blenheim Palace.
Un palais baroque qui roule à 296 km/h.

Mulsanne

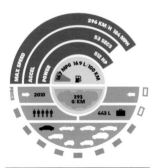

JAGUAR XJ

Dramatic flagship shaking up limo market.
Spektakuläre Spitzen-Limousine.
Spectaculaire vaisseau amiral.

XJ 3.0L V6 Diesel

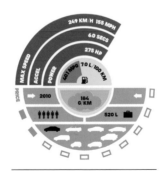

PORSCHE PANAMERA HYBRID

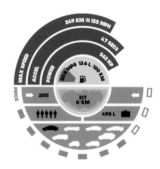

Not pretty, but effective and greener.
Nicht schön, aber effektiv und „grün".
Pas jolie, mais efficace et plus verte.

Panamera S Hybrid
* CO2 emissions and MPG figured based on low rolling resistance tyres

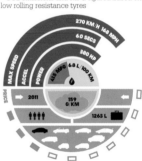

SUPERCAR

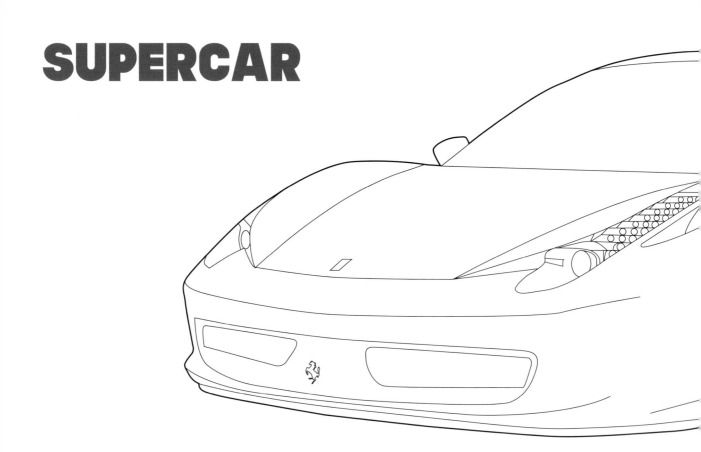

ASTON MARTIN ONE-77

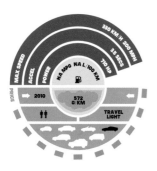

One of 77, carbon-fiber ultra-priced supercar.
1 von 77, teurer Kohlefaser-Supersportwagen.
77 unités, supercar ultra chère en carbone.

One-77

LAMBORGHINI AVENTADOR

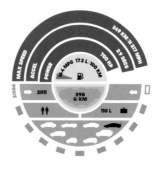

Big new 700hp V12 late 2011.
Groß, neu, 700 PS und V12-Motor, ab 2011.
Grande supercar, V12 de 700 ch. fin 2011.

Aventador LP700-4

MCLAREN MP4-12C

Establishment busting supercar.
Traumhafter Supersportwagen.
Supercar qui lance un pavé dans la mare.

MP4-12C

FERRARI
458 ITALIA

Sounds magnificent, goes like hell and looks incredible.

Klingt gut, fährt besser und sieht blendend aus.

Son divin, train d'enfer et belle à se damner.

458 Italia

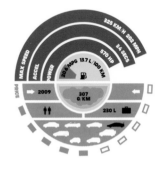

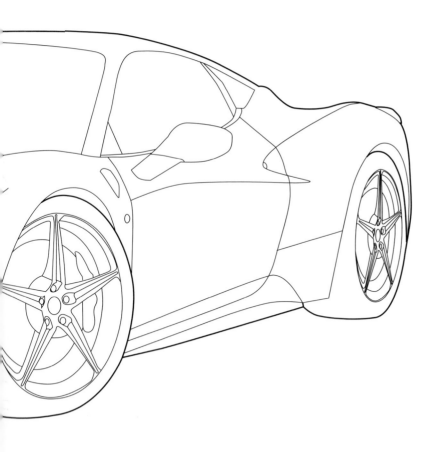

MERCEDES-BENZ
SLS

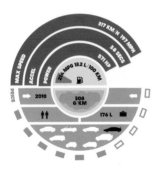

The gull-wing is back, it's good.
Die Flügeltüren sind wieder da – gut so.
La porte papillon est de retour, tant mieux.

SLS AMG

KOENIGSEGG
AGERA

New even faster, 910bhp ultra-ultra supercar.
Neu und mit 910 PS sogar schneller.
Ultra-ultracar encore plus rapide, 910 ch.

Agera R

AUDI
R8 V10

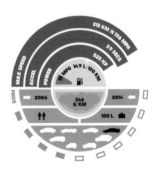

Audi's first supercar.
Audis erster Supersportwagen.
La première supercar d'Audi.

R8 V10 Spyder manual

MAN IN

INTER
SECTION

MOTION

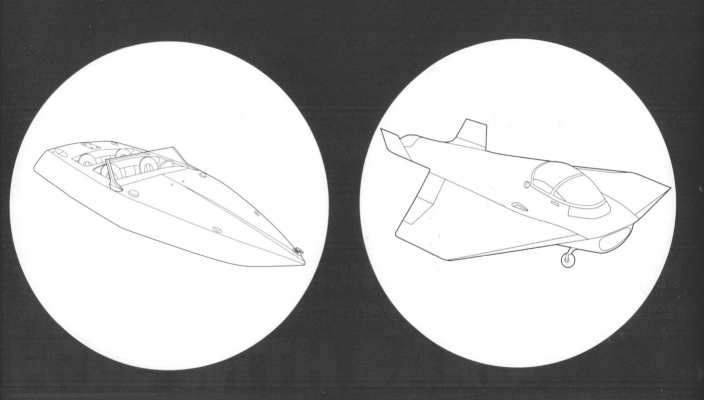

A–Z INDEX

CREDITS

IMAGES

Intersection Magazine and Taschen have no commercial relationship with any car brand featured. Unless credited below, all photography and use of logos are copyright of the respective brand. All drawings and graphics are copyright of Intersection Magazine unless otherwise noted.

The photographers/copyright owners:
© Bastien Lattanzio 5-9 / © Peka Devé 22 / © Julian Broad 23 (model Lapo Elkann) / © Amanda de Simone 26-29 / © David Barbour 32 / © Stanislas Wolff 33-35 (model Yulia @ Rush Models) / © Sasha Eisenman 36-37 / © Terry Obiora 38-41 / © Christophe Walz 45 / © Chris Leah 48-53 / © Maria Trofimova 50 (inset) / © Melanie Bordas Aubiès 55 (inset) / © Tinko Czetwertynski 56-57 / © Robert Wyatt 63-65 (model Grace Small at Storm) / © Manuel Hollenbach 66-67 / © Maria Trofimova 66 (inset) / © Björn Schütrumpf 68-69 / © Tone 70-71 / © Chris Leah 72-75 / © Peter Bohler 78 / © Björn Schütrumpf 79 / © David Shepherd 80-81 / © Björn Schütrumpf 84 / © Tone 85 / © Julian Broad 86-87 / © Jan Friese 88-89 / © Maria Trofimova 93 (inset) / © Jonathan Shapiro 106-107 / © Alan Clarke 117-119 / © Frank Liweizhe 123 / © Nikolaus Jung 125-127 / © Blake Sinclair 128-129 / © Scott Pommier 130-131 / © William Crozes 133 / © Stanislas Wolff 136-137 / © Romina Shama 138-139 / © Stanislas Wolff 141 / © Ruvan Wijesooriya 146-147 / © Hilary Walsh 149-153 (model Cintia Dicker @ Marilyn) / © Stephan van Leiden 154-155 / © Nikolaus Jung 159-161 / © Mirjam Wählen 162-163 / © Matteo Ferrari 164-165 / © Geoffroy de Boismenu 167-171 / © Maria Trofimova 170 (inset) / © Peter Bohler 174-175 / © Disco Meisch 178-179 / © Bohdan Cap 179 (inset) / © Alexandre Damasiewicz 195 / © Tinko Czetwertynski 196-197 / © Ewen Spencer 201 / © Gregoire Alexandre 203 / © Jonathan Shapiro 206 / © Peka Devé 207 / © David Barbour 211 / © Rémi Ferrante 214-215 / © Maria Trofimova 214 (inset) / © Peka Devé 217-221 / © Kristian Bengtsson 224-225 / © Matteo Ferrari 229-233 (model Zijun @ Major) / © David Ryle 236-239 / © Ludovic Parisot 243 / © David Barbour 244 / © Nick Clements 248-261 (models Felicity Jones shot for Intersection Magazine, Ollie @ Nevs) / © Melanie Bordas Aubiès 263 / © Mitsuo Okamoto 264-265 / © Spencer Lowell 269-275 / © Guy Bird 276 / © Richard Seymour 284 / © Liu Yiki 289 / © Lina Persson 290-291 / © Yogo Torpedo 295 / © Maurets Sillem 299 / © Nick Meek 302-303 / © Tone 308 / © Sasha Eisenman 316-317 / © Maria Trofimova 316 (inset) / © Alfred Jansen 318-319 / © Alex Straulino 320-323 (model Sarah Batt @ M4 Models) / © Melanie Bordas Aubiès 330-331 / © Julia Krüger 332-333 / © Justin Gardiner 335 / © Justin Gardiner 336-337 (models Sal @ Storm, Dan Sayer @ Select) / © Blinkk 344-345 / © Ben Rayner 349-351 (model Moses Manley @ D1) / © Nicholas Lawn 352 (model David Gant @ Models 1) / © Dan Martensen 354-355 / © Maria Trofimova 355 (inset) / © Elina Sirparanta 356-357 / © Robert Wunsch 363 / © Dimitri Coste 373-379 / © Maria Trofimova 379 (inset) / © Jan Friese 383 / © Hadley Hudson 384-385 / © Maria Trofimova 385 (inset) / © Hadley Hudson 386-389 (model Lars Burmeister @ Spin) / © Hollywood Porsche 390-391 / © Maria Trofimova 401 (inset) / © Rémi Ferrante 402-403 (model Coco shot for Intersection Magazine) / © Frank Liweizhe 405 / © Rankin 406 / © Dirk Seidenschwan 407 (models Santa Auzina @ Next, Hanna P @ Storm) / © Nicholas Lawn 408-413 (model Marc Goldfinger @ Models 1) / © Kristian Bengtsson 418 / © Kevin Gray 422 / © Peka Devé 424-425 / © Samuel Hicks 429 / © Mirjam Wählen 430-431 / © Peka Devé 424-425 / © Stephan van Leiden 432-433 / © Henry Lopez 439 / © Peka Devé 441 / © Mark Bramley 443-445 / © Mirjam Wählen 446 / © Bryan Sheffield 447-449 / © Jonathan Shapiro 450-451 / © Thomas Gerbeaux 455 / © Hilary Walsh 456-459 / © Cindy Dupont 464 / © Dimitri Coste 465-469 (model Pom Klementieff shot for Intersection Magazine) / © Mirjam Wählen 471 / © Tom Brown 474-475 / © Mirjam Wählen 476-477 / © Rebecca Moldenhauer 482-483 / © David Fischer 487

IMPRINT

To stay informed about upcoming TASCHEN titles, please request our magazine at www.taschen.com or write to TASCHEN, Hohenzollernring 53, D-50672 Cologne, Germany; contact@taschen.com; Fax: +49-221-254919.
We will be happy to send you a free copy of our Taschen magazine, which is filled with information about all of our books.

© 2011 TASCHEN GmbH Hohenzollernring 53, D–50672 Köln, Germany www.taschen.com

Editor: Dan Ross, London
Design: Peter Stadden, London and Yorgo Tloupas, Paris
Photography editor: Björn Schütrumpf, London
Managing editor: Guy Bird, London
Research consultant: Euan Sey, London
Editorial coordination: Florian Kobler, Cologne
Collaboration: Kathrin Murr and Inga Hallsson, Cologne
Production: Stefan Klatte, Cologne
Photo assistant: Rebecca Moldenhauer, London
Design assistants: Brigitta Anderson, Tom Gudgeon, Nick Robinson, Lewis Woolner
Writers: Guy Bird, Kyle Fortune, Owen Ready, Dan Ross, Euan Sey, Vivien Kotler
Translations and editing: Equipo de Edición, Barcelona
German translation: Katrin Kügler, Jesús Serrano
French translation: Aurélie Daniel
Special thanks to: Hendrik Lakeberg, Patrice Meignan, Götz Offegeld, Nelly di Pinto, Le Tone, André M. Wyst

Printed in Italy
ISBN 978–3–8365–1984–7